Anna Karenina

Anna Karenina

BY

LEO TOLSTOY

TRANSLATED FROM THE RUSSIAN BY

CONSTANCE GARNETT

WITH

AN INTRODUCTORY ESSAY BY THOMAS MANN

AND ILLUSTRATIONS BY PHILIP REISMAN

VOLUME ONE

RANDOM HOUSE · NEW YORK · 1939

Vengeance is mine;
I will repay, saith the Lord.

—ROMANS 12:19

Introductory Essay

BY

THOMAS MANN

HIGH tide today is at ten in the morning. Laden with bubbling foam and with jelly-fish—primitive offspring of the sea, whom the huge, raven-hearted mother will heedlessly leave behind on dry land, delivering them to death by evaporation—the waters press high on the shrunken shore, almost to the foot of my wicker shelter, forcing me every now and again, in flight before an unusually far-reaching wash, to jerk up my rug-wrapped legs. A little throb of excitement, tinged with respect, rises in me; my heart quivers with gayety over the mischievous prank played me by the mighty giant. A deep-welling, soul-expanding tenderness, a feeling of calm delight, comes over me, and in my emotion I quite forget the nuisance of it.

As yet the bathers have not appeared. They will wait until the noon-day sun has warmed the air, and then, closely watched by the cork-belted lifeguards, cautious sentinels sounding their horns in blasts of warning to amateurish folly, they will wade out into the ebbing sea, amidst a chorus of light, fluttering cries such as are involuntarily released by playful, timorously venturesome contacts with a monstrous creature.

My workshop, the finest I know, stands in a lonely spot. But, though it were livelier, I should still be insured against all disturbance by the isolating roar of the surf and the protecting sides of my beach basket, chair and room in one, a structure that has seemed to me ever since I can remember a peculiarly concealing and reassuring refuge. Cherished scene, incomparably soothing and harmonious, to which I return again and again, whenever the circumstances of life permit!

Beneath a sky in which gigantic, gently shifting cloud continents take outline from the blue depths below, rolls the sea, darkening to green against the clear horizon, surging onward in seven or eight whitely foaming rows of surf, spreading invisibly far in either direction. Yonder in the distance a magnificent piece of action is in play, where the sandbank repels the initial shock attack of the oncoming waves. The wall of water flashes bottle-green, metallic, as it rears up, hollows, arches forward, plunges flat, shattering into spume, the thunder of its ever-recurring crash playing deep bass to the higher hiss and murmur of the inshore breakers and the receding wash. . . . My eye is never sated with the drama, my ear never wearies of this music.

There could be no more appropriate setting for my task—the meditative recollection of that mighty book whose title I have penned above these lines. The scene itself embodies for me a long-held, almost, I might say, an innate, association of ideas—the soul's twin reactions to two elemental forces, one the image of the other: the sea and epic art. The element of epic art, with its rolling immensity, its breath of the primeval, of the very roots of life, its broadly sweeping rhythm, its engrossing monotony—how like it is to the sea, how like the sea to it! It is the Homeric element that I mean, continuously flowing narrative, half art, half nature, enveloped in a naïve grandeur, corporeality, objectivity, deathless health, deathless realism.

This was strong in Tolstoy, stronger than in any other epic writer of modern times; and it distinguishes his genius, in kind if not in degree, from the sickly greatness, the distorted and highly grotesque apocalyptic genius of Dostoyevsky. Tolstoy himself, speaking of his early work, *Childhood, Boyhood, Youth,* remarked: "All false modesty aside, it is something on the order of the *Iliad.*" That is unquestionably true, and it is only on external grounds that the statement applies even more closely to the gigantic work of his maturity, *War and Peace.* The purely narrative power in his writing is unequalled; his every contact with it, even after he no longer had any desire to employ art, reviling and rejecting it, making use of it solely from habit as a means to moral instruction, brought to his receptive talent—and, after all, there is no other kind—currents of strength and renewal, of creative impulse and of healthy vigor.

Rarely ever has art so completely given the effect of nature. Tolstoy's intensely self-reliant creativeness is merely another manifestation of Nature herself; and to re-read him, to feel the effect of the animal keenness of that glance, of the direct pressure in that formative grasp, to surrender to the greatness of his epic art, so unclouded by any faintest shadow of mysticism, so infallibly clear and true, is to take refuge from every least threat of artifice and sickly dexterity in originality and in health, in what is in ourselves healthy and original.

Turgenev once said: "We all of us have slipped out from under the mantle * of Gogol"— a diabolically clever pun, which incorporates the extraordinary uniformity, the tight mutuality, the traditionality of Russian literature. And indeed they do spring to light all at once, Russia's literary masters and geniuses, they reach out their hands to one another, their life circles intersect in wide arcs. Nikolai Gogol read chapters of his *Dead Souls* to the great Pushkin, and the poet of *Eugen Onegin* rocked with laughter—until sadness suddenly overcame him. Lermontov is a contemporary of both. Turgenev, as we are apt to forget, since his fame, like that of Dostoyevsky, Leskov and Tolstoy, belongs to the second half of the nineteenth century, was born only four years after Lermontov and ten years before Tolstoy—to whom, when he lay dying, he addressed a moving epistle of faith in the humanities and in art, exhorting him to "return to literature." What I call traditionality is illustrated in an anecdote which very significantly connects the most beautiful of Tolstoy's works, *Anna Karenina*, with Pushkin.

On an evening in the spring of 1873, Count Leo Tolstoy strolled into the room of his eldest son and found him reading aloud to his aged aunt from Pushkin's *Tales of Belkin*. The father picked up the volume and read the words: "The guests had gathered in the country house."

"That is the way to begin!" he said, and went into his study and wrote: "Confusion reigned in the house of the Oblonskys." That was the first sentence of *Anna Karenina*. The present beginning, the *aperçu* of happy and unhappy families, is a later arrangement.

It is a most charming little story. Tolstoy had by then made many a beginning, and carried through to many a triumphant ending. He had become famous, through his gigantic panorama, *War and Peace,* as the creator of the Russian national epic in

* "The Mantle," a short story by Nikolai Gogol.

modern novel form. And he was about to surpass, in artistic formalism, in style and in perfected harmony of balance, even this *tour-de-force* of his mid-thirties in the book now occupying his mind, which we may quite confidently call the greatest novel of society in the literature of the world. Yet there he was, wandering restlessly about the house, groping for guidance, not knowing how to begin. Pushkin taught him, tradition taught him; the classic master, from whose world his own, generally and particularly in the personal sense, had for some time stood so far removed, helped him past his stage fright by reminding him how to go straight to the point and with one swift, decisive thrust plunge the reader *in medias res*. The little historical incident represents the unity, the solidarity, of that amazing family of intelligences which we call Russian literature.

Mereschkovsky points out that, historically and from the premodern angle, Pushkin is the only one of these intelligences to give us pause. Pushkin, he says, inhabits a sphere of his own, a sphere shining with luminous, naïvely and joyously poetic thought. With Gogol, however, there was immediately ushered in the beginning of what Mereschkovsky calls "criticism," or the "transition from unconscious production to creative consciousness;" and although it signifies to him the end of poetry in the Pushkinian sense, at the same time it marks the beginning of something new and of the future. The observation is true and full of insight.

In much the same manner did Heine speak of Goethe's age, describing it as an aesthetic age, an epoch of art and of the objective and ironical outlook, represented and governed by the Olympian, and coming to an end with his death. The time then dawning was a time of decisions, of clashing convictions, of social cohesion, yes, of politics, and, in a word, of *morals*—morals that put the stamp of frivolity on every purely aesthetic approach to life.

Heine's demarcations, as well as Mereschkovsky's, confound the awareness of a timely change with that of a timeless and ever-existent contrast. Schiller, in an immortal essay, has reduced this contrast to the formula of the "naïve" and the "sentimental." What Mereschkovsky calls "criticism," or the "creative consciousness," and what seems to him, in comparison with the "unconscious production" of Pushkin, to be the modern and future mode in art, is precisely what Schiller means by the "sentimental" in contrast to the "naïve," though he also includes therein the timely, the evolutional, phase, and—*pro domo*, as we know—declares the "sentimental," that is, the consciously and critically directed creativeness, in short, the morally directed creativeness, to be the newer, modern stage in development.

We now have a double point to make: firstly, that by original conviction Tolstoy stood consistently on the side of the aesthetic, purely artistic, objectively formative, anti-moral principle; and secondly, that nevertheless, when that same historical change in the creative spirit noted by Mereschkovsky, that far transition from Pushkinian simplicity to critical responsibility and morality, occurred in Tolstoy, it took on such radical and tragic forms that—though he had first to go through most harrowing crises and much suffering, and, moreover, though he never completely succeeded in ridding himself of his mighty artistry—it carried him to a point where he denied art, rejecting it as an idle, voluptuous and immoral luxury, granting value only to moral precept designed for the benefit of mankind, though admitting that it might be disguised in the garb of art.

To come back to our "firstly." We are in possession of direct statements from Tolstoy himself to the effect that in his eyes a talent that was "purely artistic" stood higher than one that wore a social tinge. In 1859, when he was thirty-one, as a member of the Moscow Society of the Friends of Russian Literature, he delivered an address in which he so sharply emphasized the advantages of the purely artistic element in literature over all time-tendencies that the president of the Society, Chomakov, felt obliged to point out in his reply that a servant of pure art could very easily become an indicter of society without even knowing or desiring it. Contemporary critics saw in the author of *Anna Karenina* the successful champion of objectivity set free to function artistically, the representative of the psychological portrayal of man unaffected by any tendency or philosophy. This naturalism they held up as the characteristically new, giving warning that a public accustomed by others to the presence of "political and social ideas" in a work of art could come to appreciate it only by first ripening in its direction.

And indeed this was one aspect of the case. As an artist and a son of his time, namely, the nineteenth century, Tolstoy was a naturalist, and in this respect, insofar as any "trend" is concerned, he did represent the new. In spirit, however, he had passed —or was then making a determined, if tortured, effort to pass— beyond this new, in the direction of a goal that lay outside the confines of his, the naturalistic, epoch, toward a concept of art that brings it far closer to the intellect, to perception, to "criticism," than to Nature. And the commentators of 1875, in their enthusiasm over the first installments of *Anna Karenina,* which had been appearing in a magazine called the *Russian Messenger,* in their well-meant efforts to pave the way with the public for the naturalism of this work, never suspected that its author had already reached so extreme a stage in the development of his anti-art attitude that it was seriously hampering the writing of the masterpiece and actually endangering its completion.

This development was to lead far; nothing could curb the vehement drive of its logic—certainly no dread of running counter to culture, not even of impinging on the absurd and the ridiculous. Before long he was to express publicly his regret at having written *Childhood, Boyhood, Youth,* product of the freshest vigor of his young manhood—so bad, he said, so dishonest, so literary, so sinful, was this book; he was to dismiss, lock, stock and barrel, the twelve volumes of his works, as crammed "with a mass of artistic verbiage," to which "the people of our day had accorded an undeserved importance." It was the same undeserved importance that they accorded to art itself, to the plays of Shakespeare, for instance. He even went so far—let it be told in all respect, and without a smile, or at most with a very mild and cautious one— as to place the author of *Uncle Tom's Cabin,* Harriet Beecher Stowe, far above Shakespeare.

We must take pains to understand this rightly. Tolstoy's hatred of Shakespeare, which dates from far earlier than is commonly supposed, signifies a rebellion against a universal and all-condoning Nature; it signifies the envy of the morally tormented soul for the easy optimism and irony of the absolute creator; it signifies a straining away from Nature, from naïveté and from moral indifference, in the direction of the intelligence (using the word in its moral-critical sense), in the direction of ethical valuation

XIV

and of ameliorating precept. It was himself that Tolstoy hated in Shakespeare, his own vital and bearlike strength, originally of the same natural and artistically amoral calibre as that of Shakespeare. His mighty grappling for the good, the true and the right, for the meaning of life and for the healing principle, was but an ascetic form of expression of that strength, and it was through its violence that this same grappling took on the turn of titanic clumsiness that sometimes stirs us to a deferential smile. And yet it is this very helplessness, arising from the paradox of an ascetic application of a primitive force, that endows his work with its tremendous ethical weight, with the Atlas-like burdening and straining of moral sinew that makes us think of the world of figures wrought by the grieving hand of Michelangelo.

I have said that Tolstoy's hatred of Shakespeare dates from a much earlier day than is commonly supposed. But all those actions that later brought such sorrow to his friends and admirers—to Turgenev, for instance—his denial of art and culture, his radical moralism, the assumption of the rôle of prophet and exhorter-to-repentance of his later years, so admirable yet so questionable: all this may be traced to a much earlier origin. And we are entirely mistaken if we picture this emergence of soul as a climactic conversion, occurring suddenly in his declining years, or regard its beginning as at all coincidental with Tolstoy's old age. This is the same mistake that is repeated in the popular impression that Richard Wagner suddenly "became pious" in his *Parsifal;* whereas the truth of the matter is that it was a case of gradual development proceeding with superbly fatal consequence in a direction previously marked, clearly and plainly, in *The Flying Dutchman* and in *Tannhaeuser*. Thus the Frenchman, Vogué, showed great accuracy of judgment, when, on hearing a report that the Russian poet was "now as if paralyzed by a sort of mystical madness," he declared that he had long since foreseen it; that the seed of Tolstoy's thought development had long ago lain in his *Childhood, Boyhood, Youth* and that the psychology of Levin in *Anna Karenina* had indicated the direction of its further growth.

This is true. Levin, who is the real hero of the mighty novel, who rises as a triumphantly indestructible milestone on the poet's path of anguish, a monument to an elemental and bearlike creative strength, which by reason of an inner ferment of exaggerated conscience and fear of God is steadily subjected to a simultaneous process of increase and dissolution—this Levin is Tolstoy, almost completely the man himself, except that he is not an artist. Not only has Tolstoy allotted to this figure the decisive facts and dates of his own external life—his existence as landed proprietor, his love, his betrothal (told with exact autobiographical fidelity), the sacredly beautiful and terrifying experience of the birth of his first child and the equally unfathomably significant contrast thereto, the death of his brother—but he has also transmitted to it his own inward life, the craving of his conscience, his brooding search for the meaning of life and the mission of man, his ponderous grappling for the good and the right, which so utterly estranges him from the worldly activity of city society, his piercing doubts of culture itself, or of what that society calls culture, doubts that draw him closer and closer to the anachoretic and nihilistic outlook. . . The only thing lacking in Levin of Tolstoy is that he is not also a great artist.

But, in order to grasp the full value, human as well as artistic, of *Anna Karenina,* the reader should try to imagine that Konstantin Levin himself wrote the book; and, instead of my playing the part of the man with the pointer, who calls attention to the incomparable beauties contained in a broadly comprehensive painting, I should do better to speak of the extremely difficult and conflicting conditions under which the book came into being.

That is just the right word—it came into being. Yet it fell close to never coming into being at all. A work of this kind, so happy, so gripping, so completely in one mold, so perfect in every aspect, great and small, makes one feel that its author must have abandoned himself to it with every fibre of his impassioned being; that, divinely driven, he must have, so to speak, set it down on paper in a single stroke. That is an error—although, in fact, the writing of *Anna Karenina* fits into the happiest and most harmonious period of Tolstoy's life. The years in which he worked on it fall within the first decade and a half of his marriage to the woman whose fictionized portrait we see in Kitty Shtcherbatskaya, the woman who later suffered so greatly at the hands of her Levotschka, up to the time when the aged man, shortly before his death, deserted her and fled. In spite of recurring pregnancies, in spite of her manifold duties as mistress of a large estate, as mother and as housekeeper, she wrote out with her own hand seven successive copies of *War and Peace*—that first colossal fruit of genius to ripen in the period of comparative serenity granted to the melancholy doubter by the patriarchal animalism of marriage, fatherhood and life on the land. The time was to come when the poor Countess would look back to this interlude with despairing longing, after her "little Leo" had become "the Prophet of Yasnaya Polyana," after he had completed (though, to his torment, never, not even at the very end, *quite fully* completed) his scrutiny of human passions, instinctive and ideational—family, nation, state, church, love, the hunt, in fine, every remotest aspect of man's carnal being, and, most especially of all, art, which he held to be in essence a phase of sensuality and carnal being—reducing them all to atoms in the crucible of his reason and annihilating them within himself.

Those fifteen years, then, were a good, a happy time, even though later and higher standards show them to have been so only in the base, animal sense. Tolstoy's *War and Peace* had made of him "the great poet of the land of Russia," and as such he planned to write a new epic around a historic and national theme. The idea of a novel centered on the personality and period of Peter the Great haunted his mind, and for months he carried on extensive and conscientious research in the libraries and archives of Moscow in preparation therefor. "Levotschka reads and reads," say the letters of the Countess. Did he read too much? In so doing, did he learn too much, and did that dull his appetite? Strange! It developed that the figure of the Czar-reformer, the civilizer-by-force, was fundamentally unsympathetic to him. He had wished to continue in the merited rôle allotted him as epic poet to the Russian nation, to do once again what he had done in *War and Peace*. But he could make no headway; he met with an unexpected resistance. After endless preliminary pains, he threw the whole thing over, sacrificed his full investment of time and study, and turned to something of a totally different nature: to Anna Karenina's guilty passion, to the modern novel of high society in Petersburg and Moscow.

Thanks to Pushkin's help, the first attack came off with a flying start. Before long, however, a series of halts set in, which the ingenuous reader in the rush of his enjoyment never suspects. For weeks and for months the writing dragged on slowly, at times coming to a full stop. What was the matter? Domestic worries, illnesses among the children, fluctuations in his own health—oh, all that was nothing; a task like *Anna Karenina* was stronger than that sort of thing, or should be. What is really upsetting is to find ourselves faced with doubts of the importance and personal urgency of what we are doing. The question arises, for instance, whether it would not be wiser to take up the study of Greek, in order to get to the bottom of the New Testament; whether the schools for peasant children which we have founded haven't a greater claim on our time and attention; whether the whole business of *belles lettres* isn't all nonsense; and whether it may not be our duty, say, rather, is it not actually far more in accordance with our true need, to burrow deep into theologic-philosophic writings, so that once and for all we may ferret out the meaning of life. Contact with the enigma of death, brought him by the passing of his elder brother, had made a tremendous impression on Tolstoy's almost mystically intense vitality, and this experience clamored for intellectual interpretation, not through aesthetic channels, but through a confessional work after the pattern of Augustine and Rousseau. A book of this kind, honest as man could make it, to be entitled *My Faith,* occupied his thoughts, filling him with increasing distaste for the scribbling of novels. He would actually have stopped *Anna Karenina* short, and never completed it, had not the printing of the novel been prematurely begun in Katkov's *Rusky Vestnik* (*Russian Messenger*), thus placing the author under an obligation to both publisher and readers.

In January of 1875 and in the three following months, parts of the novel appeared in that magazine. Then the serial stopped, the author having nothing more to offer. The early months of the next year brought a few more fragments—then came a pause of seven months, and it was December before another installment appeared. We are enthralled by the book; we cannot imagine it as having been produced other than in the glow of a never-failing inspiration, yet Tolstoy groaned under it. "That wearisome, disgusting *Anna Karenina,*" he wrote from Samara, where he had gone to drink mare's milk. Sic! Literally! "I absolutely must come to an end with the novel," he remarks in March of 1876. "I am sick of it." Of course, this did not go on without frequent recurrences of zest, of enthusiasm, of inspiration. But those were the very times when progress was at its slowest, owing to an artistic insatiability that allowed no limits to filing, modeling and improving, insisting on a perfection of literary style that shines out through even the least adequate of translations. A strange sort of saint; the less he believed in art, the more scrupulously he devoted himself to it.

With interruption following interruption, publication of the novel dragged on as far as Book Eight. Then it came to a complete stop, for at this point politics crept in, and in the last part of his novel Russia's national epic poet had uttered such extreme heresies on the subject of Slavophilism, had shown such strong support of his Bulgarian, Serbian and Bosnian brethren in their fight for freedom against the Turks, had expressed such scorn of the buzz about volunteers and the babble about patriotism heard in Russian high society, that Katkov dared not print it. He demanded omissions and changes, which the author, insulted, refused. Tolstoy had the closing chapters of his novel published in the form of a pamphlet, which included a notice covering the points under dispute.

What I have unhesitatingly named the greatest novel of society in all literature is a novel *against* society—as is evident at the outset, from its Biblical motto: "Vengeance is mine, saith the Lord." The moral impulse for the book was a desire to scourge society for the cold, expelling cruelty with which it punishes illicit love in a woman who is fundamentally proud and noble-spirited, instead of entrusting the expiation of her sin to God—as it could all too confidently have done, since it is, after all, society and its immutable laws that God employs in enforcing expiation. This is proved by the sinister fatality and inevitability of Anna's destiny, as it progresses from her offense against the moral code step by step to its frightful conclusion. There is, therefore, a certain contradiction inherent in the author's originally moral theme, in the charge he raises against society; for one wonders what weapon of punishment God might use if society behaved other than it does. Morals and morality—how far do they differ, how far are they, in effect, one and the same, co-incident in the very breast of the socially bound human being? This question hangs suspended over the work of fiction before us—unanswered. But a work of fiction need not answer questions; it need only bring them within the range of feeling, only endow them with the full, harrowing intensity of their right to be asked, and it will have fulfilled its function—and in the present case this is achieved through our narrator's love for the heroine he has created, to whom he deals out sorrow upon sorrow with anguished but unrelenting hand.

Tolstoy loves Anna very dearly, as we are constantly aware. The book is named for her; it could be named for no other of its characters. Yet its hero is not Anna's lover, Count Vronsky, officer of the guard, compound of virility and propriety, of chivalry and banality; nor is he Anna's husband, Alexey Alexandrovitch, despite the artistry lavished on the modeling of that incomparable image of indignant yet prudent, comic yet pathetic, cuckoldry. He is quite another man, one who has practically nothing to do with Anna's destiny, whose introduction into the novel to a certain degree swerves it from its course, almost crowding its main motif into second place: he is Konstantin Levin, the melancholy brooder, the author's own counterpart. And it is primarily he, through his observations and reactions, through the singular force and insistence of his critical conscience and obstinacy, that converts the great novel of society into a work actually hostile to society.

What a strange fellow he is, this proxy of the poet in the novel! He plays the part in Tolstoy's drawing-room world of what the French in their problem plays called the *raisonneur,* but in how un-French a manner! In order to qualify as a critic of society, one would presumably have to be a part of it; yet this is the very weakest point in our tormented and extremely unusual *raisonneur,* for, though born into Russian high society, he is definitely not of it. Strong and timid, stubborn and doubt-ridden, possessing a lushness and helplessness of intelligence curiously anti-logical and natural in bent, Levin is of the firm conviction that decency, uprightness, sincerity and truthfulness are possible to a human being only in solitude, in silent self-communion, and that the slightest contact with society turns him into a chatterer, a liar and a fool. Let us observe him in Moscow, in some salon or at some cultural gathering, where he is expected to make conversation, to participate in the social game, to express his "views." How utterly silly people become when they mingle together, how red he blushes, and how often, at seeing himself among them, turning into a chatterer, a parrot and a fool! We are to learn that in the eyes of this Rousseau-ite the whole structure of city civilization, with all its intellectualism and prattle of culture, is nothing but a dungheap of sin, and that he considers the only existence worthy of man to be a life on the land—not, however, the life on the land that the city man in sentimental condescension finds so charming (as, for instance, is the case with Levin's cultivated brother, who is inclined to pride himself on being able to derive pleasure from so unintellectual an occupation as fishing)—but the actual, serious life on the land that requires physical labor, that practically and necessarily thrusts one up against Nature, whose "beauty" the visitor from civilization is sentimentally moved to admire.

Levin's morality and conscientiousness are of a strongly physical turn, related and bound to the body. "I must have physical exertion," he says to himself, "or my character will certainly suffer." And so he decides to go out and mow with the peasants, which brings him the fullest degree of combined moral and physical pleasure (a magnificent chapter, Tolstoy at his truest!). His scorn of the "intellectual," or, more properly, his disbelief in it, is unbounded. It has made of him, he feels, a creature of civilization, estranging him from his real self, plunging him into a welter of contradictions. It leads him, when he is called upon to speak, to paradoxes, to opinions unutterable in the company of civilized folk, as, for instance, on the subject of popular education, or, what is even worse, education in general. His attitude toward the peasantry is the same as his attitude toward Nature: " 'Those same peasants, whom, as you assert, you love . . .' 'I never made any such assertion,' thought Konstantin Levin. 'Why should I worry myself about schools to which I shall never send my children, to which even the peasants don't want to send their children, to which, moreover, I am not altogether convinced they ought to be sent?'—'The peasant who can read and write is of more use and value to you as a workman than one who cannot.' 'Oh, no!' replied Konstantin Levin with decision. 'You may ask anyone you please, a workman who has had schooling is considerably worse. . . .' 'Do you admit that education is a benefit for the people?' 'Yes, I admit it,' said Levin carelessly, and immediately became conscious that he had said what he did not 'really' think." An ugly business! Serious, and even dangerous! He admits the benefit of "education," because what he "really" thinks about it is unutterable in the nineteenth century, and therefore even actually unthinkable.

Of course, he follows the lines of thought of his century, which are definitely scientific. He "does not look upon man as something outside biological laws, but recognizes his dependence upon his environment, and in that dependence seeks to find the basic laws of his development." So, at least, his scientist friend quotes him as thinking, and it is plain, downright Taine that he here acknowledges, the good, great nineteenth century itself. There is, however, something in him that either lags behind the scientific approach of his day, or forges ahead of it, something immeasurably daring, inadmissible, conversationally impossible. "He lies on his back, gazing up at the high, cloudless sky. 'Do I not know,' he asks, 'that this is infinity of space, and not a round arch? But however tightly I screw up my eyes, however I strain my sight, I cannot see it as other than round and bounded, and in spite of my knowing about infinite space, I am *incontestably right* in telling myself that I see a solid, blue dome above me, and *am more right in doing so* than when I strain my eyes to see beyond it. . . . Can this be faith?' " *

But whether it be faith or the new realism, it is no longer the science of the nineteenth century. In a certain way it reminds us of Goethe. And a further reminder in this direction comes to us in Levin-Tolstoy's sceptically realistic and recalcitrant attitude toward patriotism, toward his Slavic brethren and the war volunteers. He declines to participate in the frenzy, he stands solitary in the midst of it, exactly as Goethe did at the time of the war for freedom in his day—although in both cases there was a new element, the democratic, allied to the national movement, and public will for the first time was determining the course of government action. This, too, is nineteenth century,

* The italics are Mann's, not Tolstoy's.—Ed.

and Levin, or "Levotschka," as the poor Countess used to call him, finds the comfortless verities of his time too scant for his needs. He is a step ahead of them, and I cannot help seeing as extremely perilous a step that, unless it be guided by profoundest love of truth and sympathy for mankind, may all too easily lead to obscurantism and barbarism.

We of today no longer consider it by any means a sign of solitary courage to toss overboard the scientific discipline of the nineteenth century and surrender oneself instead to "myth," to "faith," that is to say, to chaotic and culturally destructive vulgarity. This is taking place today in mass proportions, but it marks no forward step, rather a backward lapse of hundreds of miles. A step is progressive and beneficial to humanity only if it is immediately followed by a second step, one that leads away from the new realism of the "solid, blue dome," toward an idealism neither old nor new, but toward that idealism of truth, freedom and knowledge which is eternal in man. In our world of today there are insanely stupid notions afloat as to what constitutes the rear.

A digression — but one that insisted upon inclusion. Levin, then, finds the ideas of his time scant fare for his hunger; he cannot subsist on them. What I called his physical morality and conscientiousness is shaken to the core by his experience of the physically transcendent and transparent enigmas of birth and death; and what his time has to teach him of the organism and its disintegration, of the indestructibility of matter, of the law of the preservation of energy, of evolution, etc., seems to him not only sheer ignorance as far as the question of the meaning of life is concerned, but also a mode of thought that makes the discovery he craves impossible. That in the infinitude of time, of space, of matter, a tiny bubble, an organism, is formed, that this tiny bubble exists for a while, only to burst; and that this tiny bubble is himself — Levin — strikes him as the malicious jeer of some demon who cannot be conquered, yet must finally be routed through some other means than conquest, if one is not to be driven to suicide.

What here seems, to his deeper craving, to be deadly falsehood and a mode of thought utterly unemployable as a tool to the discovery of the real truth, is the naturalistic materialism of the

nineteenth century, descended from sober love of truth, yet none-
theless tainted with much unnecessary gloom and comfortless-
ness. A little brightness, a little spirituality, with no hurt to
honesty, would have sufficed for the appeasement of life and its
deeper demands.

There is a fine touch of humor in the fact that it is a plain
little peasant who shows the melancholy brooder the way out of
his despair. This little peasant teaches or recalls to Levin what
he has long since known: that, though it is the natural thing,
innate in us all and enjoined upon us, to live for our bodily
welfare and for the purpose of filling our bellies, it is nevertheless not the important and the right thing, but that we must live
"according to truth," "for the soul," "in God's way," "for the
good;" and that in some miraculous manner this need is just as
natural, just as innate and just as fully enjoined upon us as is
the need to fill our bellies. And it is, in truth, miraculous; for the
sure conviction, common to all men, that it is a shameful thing
to live only for the belly and that we must far rather live for God,
for truth and for the good, has nothing at all to do with reason.
It is, in fact, entirely contrary to reason; for reason much sooner
urges us to provide for our bodily welfare and, in the interest of
that welfare, to exploit our neighbor to the limit of our powers.
Perception of the good, declares Levin, does not lie in the realm
of reason; the good is outside the scientific chain of cause and
effect. The good is a miracle, because it eludes the understanding,
yet all men know what it is.

There is something beyond and above the sad science of the
nineteenth century, with its disclaimer of a meaning in life,
something that carries us further than science can, a spiritual
sense, an intuition: man's super-rational obligation to the good.
This discovery, so simple as to cause a smile, charms Konstantin
Levin and makes him blissfully happy. In his joy he forgets to
think back to the fact that the sad, materialistic science of the
nineteenth century was also a result of man's striving for the good,
and that it was idealism, strict and acrid love of truth, that led
science to deny a meaning to life. Science, too, lived for God—
even while denying God. Such is the simple fact, and Levin forgets it.

As for *art,* there is no occasion for his forgetting it; he knows, it would seem, absolutely nothing about it, but is obviously merely acquainted with it in the form of drawing-room prattle about the Luccas, Wagner, and this or that painting. That is the difference between him and Leo Tolstoy. The latter was well acquainted with art; he suffered frightfully because of it, under it, and for it; he contributed to it far more mightily than any of us can ever hope to contribute. And it is perhaps the very super-might of his artistry that is the explanation of his failure to see that the search for the good is the reverse of a reason for denying art. Art is the most beautiful, the most pungent, the most joyous and the most reverent of symbols for all man's super-rational striving toward the good, toward truth and toward perfection. And the breath of the surging sea of epic art would not so stirringly expand our breasts, did it not bring with it the pungent and invigorating roots of the spiritual and the divine.

THOMAS MANN

Noordwijk ann Zee
July, 1939

Part One

CHAPTER I

HAPPY families are all alike; every unhappy family is unhappy in its own way.

Everything was in confusion in the Oblonskys' house. The
wife had discovered that the husband was carrying on an intrigue with a French girl, who had been a governess in their
family, and she had announced to her husband that she could
not go on living in the same house with him. This position of
affairs had now lasted three days, and not only the husband and
wife themselves, but all the members of their family and household, were painfully conscious of it. Every person in the house
felt that there was no sense in their living together, and that the
stray people brought together by chance in any inn had more in
common with one another than they, the members of the family
and household of the Oblonskys. The wife did not leave her own
room, the husband had not been at home for three days. The
children ran wild all over the house; the English governess
quarreled with the housekeeper, and wrote to a friend asking

her to look out for a new situation for her; the man-cook had walked off the day before just at dinner-time; the kitchen-maid and the coachman had given warning.

Three days after the quarrel, Prince Stepan Arkadyevitch Oblonsky—Stiva, as he was called in the fashionable world— woke up at his usual hour, that is, at eight o'clock in the morning, not in his wife's bedroom, but on the leather-covered sofa in his study. He turned over his stout, well-cared-for person on the springy sofa, as though he would sink into a long sleep again; he vigorously embraced the pillow on the other side and buried his face in it; but all at once he jumped up, sat up on the sofa, and opened his eyes.

"Yes, yes, how was it now?" he thought, going over his dream. "Now, how was it? To be sure! Alabin was giving a dinner at Darmstadt; no, not Darmstadt, but something American. Yes, but then, Darmstadt was in America. Yes, Alabin was giving a dinner on glass tables, and the tables sang, *Il mio tesoro*—not *Il mio tesoro* though, but something better, and there were some sort of little decanters on the table, and they were women, too," he remembered.

Stepan Arkadyevitch's eyes twinkled gaily, and he pondered with a smile. "Yes, it was nice, very nice. There was a great deal more that was delightful, only there's no putting it into words, or even expressing it in one's thoughts awake." And noticing a gleam of light peeping in beside one of the serge curtains, he cheerfully dropped his feet over the edge of the sofa, and felt about with them for his slippers, a present on his last birthday, worked for him by his wife on gold-colored morocco. And, as he had done every day for the last nine years, he stretched out his hand, without getting up, towards the place where his dressing-gown always hung in his bedroom. And thereupon he suddenly remembered that he was not sleeping in his wife's room, but in his study, and why: the smile vanished from his face, he knitted his brows.

"Ah, ah, ah! Oo! . . ." he muttered, recalling everything that had happened. And again every detail of his quarrel with his wife was present to his imagination, all the hopelessness of his position, and worst of all, his own fault.

"Yes, she won't forgive me, and she can't forgive me. And the

4

most awful thing about it is that it's all my fault—all my fault, though I'm not to blame. That's the point of the whole situation," he reflected. "Oh, oh, oh!" he kept repeating in despair, as he remembered the acutely painful sensations caused him by this quarrel.

Most unpleasant of all was the first minute when, on coming, happy and good-humored, from the theater, with a huge pear in his hand for his wife, he had not found his wife in the drawing-room, to his surprise had not found her in the study either, and saw her at last in her bedroom with the unlucky letter that revealed everything in her hand.

She, his Dolly, forever fussing and worrying over household details, and limited in her ideas, as he considered, was sitting perfectly still with the letter in her hand, looking at him with an expression of horror, despair, and indignation.

"What's this? this?" she asked, pointing to the letter.

And at this recollection, Stepan Arkadyevitch, as is so often the case, was not so much annoyed at the fact itself as at the way in which he had met his wife's words.

There happened to him at that instant what does happen to people when they are unexpectedly caught in something very disgraceful. He did not succeed in adapting his face to the position in which he was placed towards his wife by the discovery of his fault. Instead of being hurt, denying, defending himself, begging forgiveness, instead of remaining indifferent even—anything would have been better than what he did do—his face utterly involuntarily (reflex spinal action, reflected Stepan Arkadyevitch, who was fond of physiology)—utterly involuntarily assumed its habitual, good-humored, and therefore idiotic smile.

This idiotic smile he could not forgive himself. Catching sight of that smile, Dolly shuddered as though at physical pain, broke out with her characteristic heat into a flood of cruel words, and rushed out of the room. Since then she had refused to see her husband.

"It's that idiotic smile that's to blame for it all," thought Stepan Arkadyevitch.

"But what's to be done? What's to be done?" he said to himself in despair, and found no answer.

5

STEPAN ARKADYEVITCH was a truthful man in his relations with himself. He was incapable of deceiving himself and persuading himself that he repented of his conduct. He could not at this date repent of the fact that he, a handsome, susceptible man of thirty-four, was not in love with his wife, the mother of five living and two dead children, and only a year younger than himself. All he repented of was that he had not succeeded better in hiding it from his wife. But he felt all the difficulty of his position and was sorry for his wife, his children, and himself. Possibly he might have managed to conceal his sins better from his wife if he had anticipated that the knowledge of them would have had such an effect on her. He had never clearly thought out the subject, but he had vaguely conceived that his wife must long ago have suspected him of being unfaithful to her, and shut her eyes to the fact. He had even supposed that she, a worn-out woman no longer young or good-looking, and in no way remarkable or interesting, merely a good mother, ought from a sense of fairness to take an indulgent view. It had turned out quite the other way.

"Oh, it's awful! oh dear, oh dear! awful!" Stepan Arkadyevitch kept repeating to himself, and he could think of nothing to be done. "And how well things were going up till now! how well we got on! She was contented and happy in her children; I never interfered with her in anything; I let her manage the children and the house just as she liked. It's true it's bad *her* having been a governess in our house. That's bad! There's something common, vulgar, in flirting with one's governess. But what a governess!" (He vividly recalled the roguish black eyes of Mlle Roland and her smile.) "But after all, while she was in the house, I kept myself in hand. And the worst of it all is that she's already . . . it seems as if ill-luck would have it so! Oh, oh! But what, what is to be done?"

There was no solution, but that universal solution which life gives to all questions, even the most complex and insoluble. That answer is: one must live in the needs of the day—that is, forget oneself. To forget himself in sleep was impossible now, at least till night-time; he could not go back now to the music sung by the decanter-women; so he must forget himself in the dream of daily life.

"Then we shall see," Stepan Arkadyevitch said to himself, and getting up he put on a gray dressing-gown lined with blue silk, tied the tassels in a knot, and, drawing a deep breath of air into his broad, bare chest, he walked to the window with his usual confident step, turning out his feet that carried his full frame so easily. He pulled up the blind and rang the bell loudly. It was at once answered by the appearance of an old friend, his valet, Matvey, carrying his clothes, his boots, and a telegram. Matvey was followed by the barber with all the necessaries for shaving.

"Are there any papers from the office?" asked Stepan Arkadyevitch, taking the telegram and seating himself at the looking-glass.

"On the table," replied Matvey, glancing with inquiring sympathy at his master; and, after a short pause, he added with a sly smile, "They've sent from the carriage-jobbers."

Stepan Arkadyevitch made no reply, he merely glanced at Matvey in the looking-glass. In the glance, in which their eyes met in the looking-glass, it was clear that they understood one another. Stepan Arkadyevitch's eyes asked: "Why do you tell me that? don't you know?"

Matvey put his hands in his jacket pockets, thrust out one leg, and gazed silently, good-humoredly, with a faint smile, at his master.

"I told them to come on Sunday, and till then not to trouble you or themselves for nothing," he said. He had obviously prepared the sentence beforehand.

Stepan Arkadyevitch saw Matvey wanted to make a joke and attract attention to himself. Tearing open the telegram, he read it through, guessing at the words, misspelt as they always are in telegrams, and his face brightened.

"Matvey, my sister Anna Arkadyevna will be here to-morrow," he said, checking for a minute the sleek, plump hand of the barber, cutting a pink path through his long, curly whiskers.

"Thank God!" said Matvey, showing by this response that he, like his master, realized the significance of this arrival—that is, that Anna Arkadyevna, the sister he was so fond of, might bring about a reconciliation between husband and wife.

"Alone, or with her husband?" inquired Matvey.

Stepan Arkadyevitch could not answer, as the barber was at work on his upper lip, and he raised one finger. Matvey nodded at the looking-glass.

"Alone. Is the room to be got ready up-stairs?"

"Inform Darya Alexandrovna: where she orders."

"Darya Alexandrovna?" Matvey repeated, as though in doubt.

"Yes, inform her. Here, take the telegram; give it to her, and then do what she tells you."

"You want to try it on," Matvey understood, but he only said, "Yes, sir."

Stepan Arkadyevitch was already washed and combed and ready to be dressed, when Matvey, stepping deliberately in his creaky boots, came back into the room with the telegram in his hand. The barber had gone.

"Darya Alexandrovna told me to inform you that she is going away. Let him do—that is you—as he likes," he said, laughing only with his eyes, and putting his hands in his pockets, he watched his master with his head on one side. Stepan Arkadye-

vitch was silent a minute. Then a good-humored and rather pitiful smile showed itself on his handsome face.

"Eh, Matvey?" he said, shaking his head.

"It's all right, sir; she will come round," said Matvey.

"Come round?"

"Yes, sir."

"Do you think so? Who's there?" asked Stepan Arkadyevitch,
hearing the rustle of a woman's dress at the door.

"It's I," said a firm, pleasant, woman's voice, and the stern,
pockmarked face of Matrona Philimonovna, the nurse, was thrust
in at the doorway.

"Well, what is it, Matrona?" queried Stepan Arkadyevitch,
going up to her at the door.

Although Stepan Arkadyevitch was completely in the wrong
as regards his wife, and was conscious of this himself, almost
every one in the house (even the nurse, Darya Alexandrovna's
chief ally) was on his side.

"Well, what now?" he asked disconsolately.

"Go to her, sir; own your fault again. Maybe God will aid you.
She is suffering so, it's sad to see her; and besides, everything in
the house is topsy-turvy. You must have pity, sir, on the children.
Beg her forgiveness, sir. There's no help for it! One must take
the consequences. . . ."

"But she won't see me."

"You do your part. God is merciful; pray to God, sir, pray to
God."

"Come, that'll do, you can go," said Stepan Arkadyevitch,
blushing suddenly. "Well now, do dress me." He turned to Matvey and threw off his dressing-gown decisively.

Matvey was already holding up the shirt like a horse's collar,
and, blowing off some invisible speck, he slipped it with obvious
pleasure over the well-groomed body of his master.

CHAPTER III

WHEN he was dressed, Stepan Arkadyevitch sprinkled some
scent on himself, pulled down his shirt-cuffs, distributed into his
pockets his cigarettes, pocketbook, matches, and watch with its

double chain and seals, and shaking out his handkerchief, feeling himself clean, fragrant, healthy, and physically at ease, in spite of his unhappiness, he walked with a slight swing on each leg into the dining-room, where coffee was already waiting for him, and beside the coffee, letters and papers from the office.

He read the letters. One was very unpleasant, from a merchant who was buying a forest on his wife's property. To sell this forest was absolutely essential; but at present, until he was reconciled with his wife, the subject could not be discussed. The most unpleasant thing of all was that his pecuniary interests should in this way enter into the question of his reconciliation with his wife. And the idea that he might be led on by his interests, that he might seek a reconciliation with his wife on account of the sale of the forest—that idea hurt him.

When he had finished his letters, Stepan Arkadyevitch moved the office-papers close to him, rapidly looked through two pieces of business, made a few notes with a big pencil, and pushing away the papers, turned to his coffee. As he sipped his coffee, he opened a still damp morning paper, and began reading it.

Stepan Arkadyevitch took in and read a liberal paper, not an extreme one, but one advocating the views held by the majority. And in spite of the fact that science, art, and politics had no special interest for him, he firmly held those views on all these subjects which were held by the majority and by his paper, and he only changed them when the majority changed them—or, more strictly speaking, he did not change them, but they imperceptibly changed of themselves within him.

Stepan Arkadyevitch had not chosen his political opinions or his views; these political opinions and views had come to him of themselves, just as he did not choose the shapes of his hat and coat, but simply took those that were being worn. And for him, living in a certain society—owing to the need, ordinarily developed at years of discretion, for some degree of mental activity—to have views was just as indispensable as to have a hat. If there was a reason for his preferring liberal to conservative views, which were held also by many of his circle, it arose not from his considering liberalism more rational, but from its being in closer accordance with his manner of life. The liberal party said that in Russia everything is wrong, and certainly Stepan Arkadyevitch had many debts and was decidedly short of money. The liberal party said that marriage is an institution quite out of date, and that it needs reconstruction; and family life certainly afforded Stepan Arkadyevitch little gratification, and forced him into lying and hypocrisy, which was so repulsive to his nature. The liberal party said, or rather allowed it to be understood, that religion is only a curb to keep in check the barbarous classes of the people; and Stepan Arkadyevitch could not get through even a short service without his legs aching from standing up, and could never make out what was the object of all the terrible and high-flown language about another world when life might be so very amusing in this world. And with all this, Stepan Arkadyevitch, who liked a joke, was fond of puzzling a plain man by saying that if he prided himself on his origin, he ought not to stop at Rurik and disown the first founder of his family—the monkey. And so liberalism had become a habit of Stepan Arkadyevitch's, and he liked his newspaper, as he did his cigar after dinner, for the slight fog it diffused in his brain. He read the leading article, in which it was maintained that it was quite senseless in our day to raise an outcry that radicalism was threatening to swallow up all conservative elements, and that the government ought to take measures to crush the revolutionary hydra; that, on the contrary, "in our opinion the danger lies not in that fantastic revolutionary hydra, but in the obstinacy of traditionalism clogging progress," etc., etc. He read another article, too, a financial one, which alluded to Bentham and Mill, and dropped some innuendoes reflecting on the ministry. With his characteristic quick-wittedness he caught the drift of each innuendo, divined whence it came, at whom and on what ground it was aimed, and that afforded him, as it always did, a certain satisfaction. But to-day that satisfaction was embittered by Matrona Philimonovna's advice and the unsatisfactory state of the household. He read, too, that Count Beist was rumored to have left for Wiesbaden, and that one need have no more gray hair, and of the sale of a light carriage, and of a young person seeking a situation; but these items of information did not give him, as usual, a quiet, ironical gratification. Having finished the paper, a second cup of coffee and a roll and butter, he got up, shaking the crumbs of the roll off his waistcoat; and, squaring his broad chest, he smiled joyously : not because there was anything particularly agreeable in his mind—the joyous smile was evoked by a good digestion.

But this joyous smile at once recalled everything to him, and he grew thoughtful.

Two childish voices (Stepan Arkadyevitch recognized the voices of Grisha, his youngest boy, and Tanya, his eldest girl) were heard outside the door. They were carrying something, and dropped it.

"I told you not to sit passengers on the roof," said the little girl in English; "there, pick them up!"

"Everything's in confusion," thought Stepan Arkadyevitch; "there are the children running about by themselves." And going to the door, he called them. They threw down the box, that represented a train, and came in to their father.

The little girl, her father's favorite, ran up boldly, embraced him, and hung laughingly on his neck, enjoying as she always did the smell of scent that came from his whiskers. At last the little girl kissed his face, which was flushed from his stooping posture and beaming with tenderness, loosed her hands, and was about to run away again; but her father held her back.

"How is mamma?" he asked, passing his hand over his daughter's smooth, soft little neck. "Good-morning," he said, smiling to the boy, who had come up to greet him. He was conscious that he loved the boy less, and always tried to be fair; but the boy felt it, and did not respond with a smile to his father's chilly smile.

"Mamma? She is up," answered the girl.

Stepan Arkadyevitch sighed. "That means that she's not slept again all night," he thought.

"Well, is she cheerful?"

The little girl knew that there was a quarrel between her father and mother, and that her mother could not be cheerful, and that her father must be aware of this, and that he was pretending when he asked about it so lightly. And she blushed for her father. He at once perceived it, and blushed too.

"I don't know," she said. "She did not say we must do our lessons, but she said we were to go for a walk with Miss Hoole to grandmamma's."

12

"Well, go, Tanya, my darling. Oh, wait a minute, though," he said, still holding her and stroking her soft little hand.

He took off the mantelpiece, where he had put it yesterday, a little box of sweets, and gave her two, picking out her favorites, a chocolate and a fondant.

"For Grisha?" said the little girl, pointing to the chocolate.

"Yes, yes." And still stroking her little shoulder, he kissed her on the roots of her hair and neck, and let her go.

"The carriage is ready," said Matvey; "but there's some one to see you with a petition."

"Been here long?" asked Stepan Arkadyevitch.

"Half an hour."

"How many times have I told you to tell me at once?"

"One must let you drink your coffee in peace, at least," said Matvey, in the affectionately gruff tone with which it was impossible to be angry.

"Well, show the person up at once," said Oblonsky, frowning with vexation.

The petitioner, the widow of a staff captain Kalinin, came with a request impossible and unreasonable; but Stepan Arkadyevitch, as he generally did, made her sit down, heard her to the end attentively without interrupting her, and gave her detailed advice as to how and to whom to apply, and even wrote her, in his large, sprawling, good and legible hand, a confident and fluent little note to a personage who might be of use to her. Having got rid of the staff captain's widow, Stepan Arkadyevitch took his hat and stopped to recollect whether he had forgotten anything. It appeared that he had forgotten nothing except what he wanted to forget—his wife.

"Ah, yes!" He bowed his head, and his handsome face assumed a harassed expression. "To go, or not to go!" he said to himself; and an inner voice told him he must not go, that nothing could come of it but falsity; that to amend, to set right their relations was impossible, because it was impossible to make her attractive again and able to inspire love, or to make him an old man, not susceptible to love. Except deceit and lying nothing could come of it now; and deceit and lying were opposed to his nature.

"It must be some time, though: it can't go on like this," he said, trying to give himself courage. He squared his chest, took out a cigarette, took two whiffs at it, flung it into a mother-of-pearl ash-tray, and with rapid steps walked through the drawing-room, and opened the other door into his wife's bedroom.

C H A P T E R   I V

DARYA ALEXANDROVNA, in a dressing jacket, and with her now scanty, once luxuriant and beautiful hair fastened up with hairpins on the nape of her neck, with a sunken, thin face and large, startled eyes, which looked prominent from the thinness of her face, was standing among a litter of all sorts of things scattered all over the room, before an open bureau, from which she was taking something. Hearing her husband's steps, she stopped, looking towards the door, and trying assiduously to give her features a severe and contemptuous expression. She felt she was afraid of him, and afraid of the coming interview. She was just attempting to do what she had attempted to do ten times already in these last three days—to sort out the children's things and her own, so as to take them to her mother's—and again she could not bring herself to do this; but now again, as each time before, she kept saying to herself, "that things cannot go on like this, that she must take some step" to punish him, put him to shame, avenge on him some little part at least of the suffering he had caused her. She still continued to tell herself that she should leave him, but she was conscious that this was impossible; it was impossible because she could not get out of the habit of regarding him as her husband and loving him. Besides this, she realized that if even here in her own house she could hardly manage to look after her five children properly, they would be still worse off where she was going with them all. As it was, even in the course of these three days, the youngest was unwell from being given unwholesome soup, and the others had almost gone without their dinner the day before. She was conscious that it was impossible to go away; but, cheating herself, she went on all the same sorting out her things and pretending she was going.

Seeing her husband, she dropped her hands into the drawer of the bureau as though looking for something, and only looked round at him when he had come quite up to her. But her face, to which she tried to give a severe and resolute expression, betrayed bewilderment and suffering.

"Dolly!" he said in a subdued and timid voice. He bent his head towards his shoulder and tried to look pitiful and humble, but for all that he was radiant with freshness and health. In a rapid glance she scanned his figure that beamed with health and freshness. "Yes, he is happy and content!" she thought; "while I . . . And that disgusting good nature, which every one likes him for and praises—I hate that good nature of his," she thought. Her mouth stiffened, the muscles of the cheek contracted on the right side of her pale, nervous face.

"What do you want?" she said in a rapid, deep, unnatural voice.

"Dolly!" he repeated, with a quiver in his voice. "Anna is coming to-day."

"Well, what is that to me? I can't see her!" she cried.

"But you must, really, Dolly. . . ."

"Go away, go away, go away!" she shrieked, not looking at him, as though this shriek were called up by physical pain.

Stepan Arkadyevitch could be calm when he thought of his wife, he could hope that she would *come round,* as Matvey expressed it, and could quietly go on reading his paper and drinking his coffee; but when he saw her tortured, suffering face, heard the tone of her voice, submissive to fate and full of despair, there was a catch in his breath and a lump in his throat, and his eyes began to shine with tears.

"My God! what have I done? Dolly! For God's sake! . . . You know . . ." He could not go on; there was a sob in his throat.

She shut the bureau with a slam, and glanced at him.

"Dolly, what can I say? . . . One thing: forgive . . . Remember, cannot nine years of my life atone for an instant . . ."

She dropped her eyes and listened, expecting what he would say, as it were beseeching him in some way or other to make her believe differently.

"—instant of passion?" . . . he said, and would have gone on, but at that word, as at a pang of physical pain, her lips stiffened again, and again the muscles of her right cheek worked.

15

"Go away, go out of the room!" she shrieked still more shrilly, "and don't talk to me of your passion and your loathsomeness."

She tried to go out, but tottered, and clung to the back of a chair to support herself. His face relaxed, his lips swelled, his eyes were swimming with tears.

"Dolly!" he said, sobbing now; "for mercy's sake, think of the children; they are not to blame! I am to blame, and punish me, make me expiate my fault. Anything I can do, I am ready to do anything! I am to blame, no words can express how much I am to blame! But, Dolly, forgive me!"

She sat down. He listened to her hard, heavy breathing, and he was unutterably sorry for her. She tried several times to begin to speak, but could not. He waited.

"You remember the children, Stiva, to play with them; but I remember them, and know that this means their ruin," she said —obviously one of the phrases she had more than once repeated to herself in the course of the last few days.

She had called him "Stiva," and he glanced at her with gratitude, and moved to take her hand, but she drew back from him with aversion.

"I think of the children, and for that reason I would do anything in the world to save them; but I don't myself know how to save them. By taking them away from their father, or by leaving them with a vicious father—yes, a vicious father. . . . Tell me, after what . . . has happened, can we live together? Is that possible? Tell me, eh, is it possible?" she repeated, raising her voice, "after my husband, the father of my children, enters into a love-affair with his own children's governess?"

"But what could I do? what could I do?" he kept saying in a pitiful voice, not knowing what he was saying, as his head sank lower and lower.

"You are loathsome to me, repulsive!" she shrieked, getting more and more heated. "Your tears mean nothing! You have never loved me; you have neither heart nor honorable feeling! You are hateful to me, disgusting, a stranger—yes, a complete stranger!" With pain and wrath she uttered the word so terrible to herself—*stranger*.

He looked at her, and the fury expressed in her face alarmed and amazed him. He did not understand how his pity for her exasperated her. She saw in him sympathy for her, but not love. "No, she hates me. She will not forgive me," he thought.

"It is awful! awful!" he said.

At that moment in the next room a child began to cry; probably it had fallen down. Darya Alexandrovna listened, and her face suddenly softened.

She seemed pulling herself together for a few seconds, as though she did not know where she was, and what she was doing, and getting up rapidly, she moved towards the door.

"Well, she loves my child," he thought, noticing the change of her face at the child's cry, "my child: how can she hate me?"

"Dolly, one word more," he said, following her.

"If you come near me, I will call in the servants, the children! They may all know you are a scoundrel! I am going away at once, and you may live here with your mistress!"

And she went out, slamming the door.

Stepan Arkadyevitch sighed, wiped his face, and with a subdued tread walked out of the room. "Matvey says she will come round; but how? I don't see the least chance of it. Ah, oh, how horrible it is! And how vulgarly she shouted," he said to himself, remembering her shriek and the words—"scoundrel" and "mistress." "And very likely the maids were listening! Horribly vulgar! horrible!" Stepan Arkadyevitch stood a few seconds alone, wiped his face, squared his chest, and walked out of the room.

It was Friday, and in the dining-room the German watchmaker was winding up the clock. Stepan Arkadyevitch remembered his joke about this punctual, bald watchmaker, "that the German was wound up for a whole lifetime himself, to wind up watches," and he smiled. Stepan Arkadyevitch was fond of a joke. "And maybe she will come round! That's a good expression, 'come round,'" he thought. "I must repeat that."

"Matvey!" he shouted. "Arrange everything with Darya in the sitting-room for Anna Arkadyevna," he said to Matvey when he came in.

"Yes, sir."

Stepan Arkadyevitch put on his fur coat and went out onto the steps.

"You won't dine at home?" said Matvey, seeing him off.

"That's as it happens. But here's for the housekeeping," he said, taking ten roubles from his pocketbook. "That'll be enough."

"Enough or not enough, we must make it do," said Matvey, slamming the carriage door and stepping back onto the steps.

Darya Alexandrovna meanwhile having pacified the child, and knowing from the sound of the carriage that he had gone off, went back again to her bedroom. It was her solitary refuge from the household cares which crowded upon her directly she went out from it. Even now, in the short time she had been in the nursery, the English governess and Matrona Philimonovna had succeeded in putting several questions to her, which did not admit of delay, and which only she could answer: "What were the children to put on for their walk? Should they have any milk? Should not a new cook be sent for?"

"Ah, let me alone, let me alone!" she said, and going back to her bedroom she sat down in the same place as she had sat when talking to her husband, clasping tightly her thin hands with the rings that slipped down on her bony fingers, and fell to going over in her memory all the conversation. "He has gone! But has he broken it off with her?" she thought. "Can it be he sees her? Why didn't I ask him! No, no, reconciliation is impossible. Even if we remain in the same house, we are strangers—strangers forever!" She repeated again with special significance the word so dreadful to her. "And how I loved him! my God, how I loved him! . . . How I loved him! And now don't I love him? Don't I love him more than before? The most horrible thing is," she began, but did not finish her thought, because Matrona Philimonovna put her head in at the door.

"Let us send for my brother," she said; "he can get a dinner anyway, or we shall have the children getting nothing to eat till six again, like yesterday."

"Very well, I will come directly and see about it. But did you send for some new milk?"

And Darya Alexandrovna plunged into the duties of the day, and drowned her grief in them for a time.

CHAPTER V

STEPAN ARKADYEVITCH had learned easily at school, thanks to his excellent abilities, but he had been idle and mischievous, and therefore was one of the lowest in his class. But in spite of his habitually dissipated mode of life, his inferior grade in the service, and his comparative youth, he occupied the honorable and lucrative position of president of one of the government boards at Moscow. This post he had received through his sister Anna's husband, Alexey Alexandrovitch Karenin, who held one of the most important positions in the ministry to whose department the Moscow office belonged. But if Karenin had not got his brother-in-law this berth, then through a hundred other personages—brothers, sisters, cousins, uncles, and aunts—Stiva Oblonsky would have received this post, or some other similar one, together with the salary of six thousand absolutely needful for him, as his affairs, in spite of his wife's considerable property, were in an embarrassed condition.

Half Moscow and Petersburg were friends and relations of Stepan Arkadyevitch. He was born in the midst of those who had been and are the powerful ones of this world. One-third of the men in the government, the older men, had been friends of his father's, and had known him in petticoats; another third were his intimate chums, and the remainder were friendly acquaintances. Consequently the distributors of earthly blessings in the shape of places, rents, shares, and such, were all his friends, and could not overlook one of their own set; and Oblonsky had no need to make any special exertion to get a lucrative post. He had only not to refuse things, not to show jealousy, not to be quarrelsome or take offense, all of which from his characteristic good nature he never did. It would have struck him as absurd if he had been told that he would not get a position with the salary he required, especially as he expected nothing out of the way; he only wanted what the men of his own age and standing did get, and he was no worse qualified for performing duties of the kind than any other man.

Stepan Arkadyevitch was not merely liked by all who knew

him for his good-humor, but for his bright disposition, and his unquestionable honesty. In him, in his handsome, radiant figure, his sparkling eyes, black hair and eyebrows, and the white and red of his face, there was something which produced a physical effect of kindliness and good-humor on the people who met him. "Aha! Stiva! Oblonsky! Here he is!" was almost always said with a smile of delight on meeting him. Even though it happened at times that after a conversation with him it seemed that nothing particularly delightful had happened, the next day, and the next, every one was just as delighted at meeting him again.

After filling for three years the post of president of one of the government boards at Moscow, Stepan Arkadyevitch had won the respect, as well as the liking, of his fellow-officials, subordinates, and superiors, and all who had had business with him. The principal qualities in Stepan Arkadyevitch which had gained him this universal respect in the service consisted, in the first place, of his extreme indulgence for others, founded on a consciousness of his own shortcomings; secondly, of his perfect liberalism—not the liberalism he read of in the papers, but the liberalism that was in his blood, in virtue of which he treated all men perfectly equally and exactly the same, whatever their fortune or calling might be; and thirdly—the most important point—his complete indifference to the business in which he was engaged, in consequence of which he was never carried away, and never made mistakes.

On reaching the offices of the board, Stepan Arkadyevitch, escorted by a deferential porter with a portfolio, went into his little private room, put on his uniform, and went into the board-room. The clerks and copyists all rose, greeting him with good-humored deference. Stepan Arkadyevitch moved quickly, as ever, to his place, shook hands with his colleagues, and sat down. He made a joke or two, and talked just as much as was consistent with due decorum, and began work. No one knew better than Stepan Arkadyevitch how to hit on the exact line between freedom, simplicity, and official stiffness necessary for the agreeable conduct of business. A secretary, with the good-humored deference common to every one in Stepan Arkadyevitch's office, came up with papers, and began to speak in the familiar and easy tone which had been introduced by Stepan Arkadyevitch.

"We have succeeded in getting the information from the government department of Penza. Here, would you care? . . ."

"You've got them at last?" said Stepan Arkadyevitch, laying his finger on the paper. "Now, gentlemen . . ."

And the sitting of the board began.

"If they knew," he thought, bending his head with a significant air as he listened to the report, "what a guilty little boy their president was half an hour ago." And his eyes were laughing during the reading of the report. Till two o'clock the sitting would go on without a break, and at two o'clock there would be an interval and luncheon.

It was not yet two, when the large glass doors of the board-room suddenly opened and some one came in.

All the officials sitting on the further side under the portrait of the Tsar and the eagle, delighted at any distraction, looked round at the door; but the doorkeeper standing at the door at once drove out the intruder, and closed the glass door after him.

When the case had been read through, Stepan Arkadyevitch got up and stretched, and by way of tribute to the liberalism of the times took out a cigarette in the board-room and went into his private room. Two of the members of the board, the old veteran in the service, Nikitin, and the *Kammerjunker* Grinevitch, went in with him.

"We shall have time to finish after lunch," said Stepan Arkadyevitch.

"To be sure we shall!" said Nikitin.

"A pretty sharp fellow this Fomin must be," said Grinevitch of one of the persons taking part in the case they were examining.

Stepan Arkadyevitch frowned at Grinevitch's words, giving him thereby to understand that it was improper to pass judgment prematurely, and made him no reply.

"Who was that came in?" he asked the doorkeeper.

"Some one, your excellency, crept in without permission directly my back was turned. He was asking for you. I told him: when the members come out, then . . ."

"Where is he?"

"Maybe he's gone into the passage, but here he comes anyway. That is he," said the doorkeeper, pointing to a strongly built, broad-shouldered man with a curly beard, who, without taking off his sheepskin cap, was running lightly and rapidly up the worn steps of the stone staircase. One of the members going down —a lean official with a portfolio—stood out of his way and looked disapprovingly at the legs of the stranger, then glanced inquiringly at Oblonsky.

Stepan Arkadyevitch was standing at the top of the stairs. His good-naturedly beaming face above the embroidered collar of his uniform beamed more than ever when he recognized the man coming up.

"Why, it's actually you, Levin, at last!" he said with a friendly mocking smile, scanning Levin as he approached. "How is it you have deigned to look me up in this den?" said Stepan Arkadyevitch, and not content with shaking hands, he kissed his friend. "Have you been here long?"

"I have just come, and very much wanted to see you," said

Levin, looking shyly and at the same time angrily and uneasily around.

"Well, let's go into my room," said Stepan Arkadyevitch, who knew his friend's sensitive and irritable shyness, and, taking his arm, he drew him along, as though guiding him through dangers.

Stepan Arkadyevitch was on familiar terms with almost all his acquaintances, and called almost all of them by their Christian names: old men of sixty, boys of twenty, actors, ministers, merchants, and adjutant-generals, so that many of his intimate chums were to be found at the extreme ends of the social ladder, and would have been very much surprised to learn that they had, through the medium of Oblonsky, something in common. He was the familiar friend of every one with whom he took a glass of champagne, and he took a glass of champagne with every one, and when in consequence he met any of his *disreputable* chums, as he used in joke to call many of his friends, in the presence of his subordinates, he well knew how, with his characteristic tact, to diminish the disagreeable impression made on them. Levin was not a disreputable chum, but Oblonsky, with his ready tact, felt that Levin fancied he might not care to show his intimacy with him before his subordinates, and so he made haste to take him off into his room.

Levin was almost of the same age as Oblonsky; their intimacy did not rest merely on champagne. Levin had been the friend and companion of his early youth. They were fond of one another in spite of the difference of their characters and tastes, as friends are fond of one another who have been together in early youth. But in spite of this, each of them—as is often the way with men who have selected careers of different kinds—though in discussion he would even justify the other's career, in his heart despised it. It seemed to each of them that the life he led himself was the only real life, and the life led by his friend was a mere phantasm. Oblonsky could not restrain a slight mocking smile at the sight of Levin. How often he had seen him come up to Moscow from the country where he was doing something, but what precisely Stepan Arkadyevitch could never quite make out, and indeed he took no interest in the matter. Levin arrived in Moscow always excited and in a hurry, rather ill at ease and irritated by his own want of ease, and for the most part with a perfectly new, unexpected view of things. Stepan Arkadyevitch laughed at this, and liked it. In the same way Levin in his heart despised the town mode of life of his friend, and his official duties, which he laughed at, and regarded as trifling. But the difference was that Oblonsky, as he was doing the same as every one did, laughed complacently and good-humoredly, while Levin laughed without complacency and sometimes angrily.

"We have long been expecting you," said Stepan Arkadyevitch, going into his room and letting Levin's hand go as though to show that here all danger was over. "I am very, very glad to see you," he went on. "Well, how are you? Eh? When did you come?"

Levin was silent, looking at the unknown faces of Oblonsky's two companions, and especially at the hand of the elegant Grinevitch, which had such long white fingers, such long yellow filbert-shaped nails, and such huge shining studs on the shirt-cuff, that apparently they absorbed all his attention, and allowed him no freedom of thought. Oblonsky noticed this at once, and smiled.

"Ah, to be sure, let me introduce you," he said. "My colleagues: Philip Ivanitch Nikitin, Mihail Stanislavitch Grinevitch"—and turning to Levin—"a district councilor, a modern district council man, a gymnast who lifts thirteen stone with one hand, a cattle-breeder and sportsman, and my friend, Konstantin Dmitrievitch Levin, the brother of Sergey Ivanovitch Koznishev."

"Delighted," said the veteran.

"I have the honor of knowing your brother, Sergey Ivanovitch," said Grinevitch, holding out his slender hand with its long nails.

Levin frowned, shook hands coldly, and at once turned to Oblonsky. Though he had a great respect for his half-brother, an author well known to all Russia, he could not endure it when people treated him not as Konstantin Levin, but as the brother of the celebrated Koznishev.

"No, I am no longer a district councilor. I have quarreled with them all, and don't go to the meetings any more," he said, turning to Oblonsky.

"You've been quick about it!" said Oblonsky with a smile. "But how? why?"

"It's a long story. I will tell you some time," said Levin, but he began telling him at once. "Well, to put it shortly, I was convinced that nothing was really done by the district councils, or ever could be," he began, as though some one had just insulted him. "On one side it's a plaything; they play at being a parliament, and I'm neither young enough nor old enough to find amusement in playthings; and on the other side" (he stammered) "it's a means for the coterie of the district to make money. Formerly they had wardships, courts of justice, now they have the district council—not in the form of bribes, but in the form of unearned salary," he said, as hotly as though some one of those present had opposed his opinion.

"Aha! You're in a new phase again, I see—a conservative," said Stepan Arkadyevitch. "However, we can go into that later."

"Yes, later. But I wanted to see you," said Levin, looking with hatred at Grinevitch's hand.

Stepan Arkadyevitch gave a scarcely perceptible smile.

"How was it you used to say you would never wear European dress again?" he said, scanning his new suit, obviously cut by a French tailor. "Ah! I see: a new phase."

Levin suddenly blushed, not as grown men blush, slightly, without being themselves aware of it, but as boys blush, feeling that they are ridiculous through their shyness, and consequently ashamed of it and blushing still more, almost to the point of tears. And it was so strange to see this sensible, manly face in such a childish plight, that Oblonsky left off looking at him.

"Oh, where shall we meet? You know I want very much to talk to you," said Levin.

Oblonsky seemed to ponder.

"I'll tell you what: let's go to Gurin's to lunch, and there we can talk. I am free till three."

"No," answered Levin, after an instant's thought, "I have got to go on somewhere else."

"All right, then, let's dine together."

"Dine together? But I have nothing very particular, only a few words to say, and a question I want to ask you, and we can have a talk afterwards."

"Well, say the few words, then, at once, and we'll gossip after dinner."

"Well, it's this," said Levin; "but it's of no importance, however."

His face all at once took an expression of anger from the effort he was making to surmount his shyness.

"What are the Shtcherbatskys doing? Everything as it used to be?" he said.

Stepan Arkadyevitch, who had long known that Levin was in love with his sister-in-law, Kitty, gave a hardly perceptible smile, and his eyes sparkled merrily.

"You said a few words, but I can't answer in a few words, because . . . Excuse me a minute. . . ."

A secretary came in, with respectful familiarity and the modest consciousness, characteristic of every secretary, of superiority to his chief in the knowledge of their business; he went up to Oblonsky with some papers, and began, under pretense of asking a question, to explain some objection. Stepan Arkadyevitch, without hearing him out, laid his hand genially on the secretary's sleeve.

"No, you do as I told you," he said, softening his words with a smile, and with a brief explanation of his view of the matter he turned away from the papers, and said: "So do it in that way, if you please, Zahar Nikititch."

The secretary retired in confusion. During the consultation with the secretary Levin had completely recovered from his embarrassment. He was standing with his elbows on the back of a chair, and on his face was a look of ironical attention.

"I don't understand it, I don't understand it," he said.

"What don't you understand?" said Oblonsky, smiling as brightly as ever, and picking up a cigarette. He expected some queer outburst from Levin.

"I don't understand what you are doing," said Levin, shrugging his shoulders. "How can you do it seriously?"

"Why not?"

"Why, because there's nothing in it."

"You think so, but we're overwhelmed with work."

"On paper. But, there, you've a gift for it," added Levin.

"That's to say, you think there's a lack of something in me?"

"Perhaps so," said Levin. "But all the same I admire your grandeur, and am proud that I've a friend such a great person. You've not answered my question, though," he went on, with a desperate effort looking Oblonsky straight in the face.

"Oh, that's all very well. You wait a bit, and you'll come to this yourself. It's very nice for you to have over six thousand acres in the Karazinsky district, and such muscles, and the freshness of a girl of twelve; still you'll be one of us one day. Yes, as to your question, there is no change, but it's a pity you've been away so long."

"Oh, why so?" Levin queried, panic-stricken.

"Oh, nothing," responded Oblonsky. "We'll talk it over. But what's brought you up to town?"

"Oh, we'll talk about that, too, later on," said Levin, reddening again up to his ears.

"All right. I see," said Stepan Arkadyevitch. "I should ask you to come to us, you know, but my wife's not quite the thing. But I tell you what; if you want to see them, they're sure now to be at the Zoological Gardens from four to five. Kitty skates. You drive along there, and I'll come and fetch you, and we'll go and dine somewhere together."

"Capital. So good-bye till then."

"Now mind, you'll forget, I know you, or rush off home to the country!" Stepan Arkadyevitch called out laughing.

"No, truly!"

And Levin went out of the room, only when he was in the doorway remembering that he had forgotten to take leave of Oblonsky's colleagues.

"That gentleman must be a man of great energy," said Grinevitch, when Levin had gone away.

"Yes, my dear boy," said Stepan Arkadyevitch, nodding his head, "he's a lucky fellow! Over six thousand acres in the Karazinsky district; everything before him; and what youth and vigor! Not like some of us."

"You have a great deal to complain of, haven't you, Stepan Arkadyevitch?"

"Ah, yes, I'm in a poor way, a bad way," said Stepan Arkadyevitch with a heavy sigh.

CHAPTER VI

WHEN Oblonsky asked Levin what had brought him to town, Levin blushed, and was furious with himself for blushing, because he could not answer, "I have come to make your sister-in-law an offer," though that was precisely what he had come for.

The families of the Levins and the Shtcherbatskys were old, noble Moscow families, and had always been on intimate and friendly terms. This intimacy had grown still closer during Levin's student-days. He had both prepared for the university with the young Prince Shtcherbatsky, the brother of Kitty and Dolly, and had entered at the same time with him. In those days Levin used often to be in the Shtcherbatskys' house, and he was in love with the Shtcherbatsky household. Strange as it may appear, it was with the household, the family, that Konstantin Levin was in love, especially with the feminine half of the household. Levin did not remember his own mother, and his only sister was older than he was, so that it was in the Shtcherbatskys' house that he saw for the first time that inner life of an old, noble, cultivated, and honorable family of which he had been deprived by the death of his father and mother. All the members of that family, especially the feminine half, were pictured by him, as it were, wrapped about with a mysterious poetical veil, and he not only perceived no defects whatever in them, but under the poetical veil that shrouded them he assumed the existence of the loftiest sentiments and every possible perfection. Why it was the three young ladies had one day to speak French, and the next English; why it was that at certain hours they played by turns on the piano, the sounds of which were audible in their brother's room above, where the students used to work; why they were visited by those professors of French literature, of music, of drawing, of dancing; why at certain hours all the three young ladies, with Mademoiselle Linon, drove in the coach to the Tversky boulevard, dressed in their satin cloaks, Dolly in a long one, Natalia in a half-long one, and Kitty in one so short that her shapely legs in tightly-drawn red stockings were visible to all beholders; why it was they had to walk about the Tversky boulevard escorted by a footman with a gold cockade in his hat—all this and much more that was done in their mysterious world he did not understand, but he was sure that everything that was done there was very good, and he was in love precisely with the mystery of the proceedings.

In his student-days he had all but been in love with the eldest, Dolly, but she was soon married to Oblonsky. Then he began being in love with the second. He felt, as it were, that he had to be in love with one of the sisters, only he could not quite make out which. But Natalia, too, had hardly made her appearance in the world when she married the diplomat Lvov. Kitty was still a child when Levin left the university. Young Shtcherbatsky went into the navy, was drowned in the Baltic, and Levin's relations with the Shtcherbatskys, in spite of his friendship with Oblonsky, became less intimate. But when early in the winter of this year Levin came to Moscow, after a year in the country, and saw the Shtcherbatskys, he realized which of the three sisters he was indeed destined to love.

One would have thought that nothing could be simpler than for him, a man of good family, rather rich than poor, and thirty-two years old, to make the young Princess Shtcherbatskaya an offer of marriage; in all likelihood he would at once have been looked upon as a good match. But Levin was in love, and so it seemed to him that Kitty was so perfect in every respect that she was a creature far above everything earthly; and that he was a creature so low and so earthly that it could not even be conceived that other people and she herself could regard him as worthy of her.

After spending two months in Moscow in a state of enchantment, seeing Kitty almost every day in society, into which he went so as to meet her, he abruptly decided that it could not be, and went back to the country.

Levin's conviction that it could not be was founded on the idea that in the eyes of her family he was a disadvantageous and worthless match for the charming Kitty, and that Kitty herself could not love him. In her family's eyes he had no ordinary, definite career and position in society, while his contemporaries by this time, when he was thirty-two, were already, one a colonel, and another a professor, another director of a bank and railways, or president of a board like Oblonsky. But he (he knew very well how he must appear to others) was a country gentleman, occupied in breeding cattle, shooting game, and building barns; in other words, a fellow of no ability, who had not turned out well, and who was doing just what, according to the ideas of the world, is done by people fit for nothing else.

The mysterious, enchanting Kitty herself could not love such an ugly person as he conceived himself to be, and, above all, such an ordinary, in no way striking person. Moreover, his attitude to Kitty in the past—the attitude of a grown-up person to a child, arising from his friendship with her brother—seemed to him yet another obstacle to love. An ugly, good-natured man, as he considered himself, might, he supposed, be liked as a friend; but to be loved with such a love as that with which he loved Kitty, one would need to be a handsome and, still more, a distinguished man.

He had heard that women often did care for ugly and ordinary men, but he did not believe it, for he judged by himself, and he could not himself have loved any but beautiful, mysterious, and exceptional women.

But after spending two months alone in the country, he was convinced that this was not one of those passions of which he had had experience in his early youth; that this feeling gave him not an instant's rest; that he could not live without deciding the question, would she or would she not be his wife, and that his despair had arisen only from his own imaginings, that he had no sort of proof that he would be rejected. And he had now come to Moscow with a firm determination to make an offer, and get married if he were accepted. Or . . . he could not conceive what would become of him if he were rejected.

CHAPTER VII

ON ARRIVING in Moscow by a morning train, Levin had put up at the house of his elder half-brother, Koznishev. After changing his clothes he went down to his brother's study, intending to talk to him at once about the object of his visit, and to ask his advice; but his brother was not alone. With him there was a well-known professor of philosophy, who had come from Harkov expressly to clear up a difference that had arisen between them on a very important philosophical question. The professor was carrying on a hot crusade against materialists. Sergey Koznishev had been following this crusade with interest, and after reading the professor's last article, he had written him a letter stating his objections. He accused the professor of making too great concessions to the materialists. And the professor had promptly appeared to argue the matter out. The point in discussion was the question then in vogue: Is there a line to be drawn between psychological and physiological phenomena in man? and if so, where?

Sergey Ivanovitch met his brother with the smile of chilly friendliness he always had for every one, and introducing him to the professor, went on with the conversation.

A little man in spectacles, with a narrow forehead, tore himself from the discussion for an instant to greet Levin, and then went on talking without paying any further attention to him. Levin sat down to wait till the professor should go, but he soon began to get interested in the subject under discussion.

Levin had come across the magazine articles about which they were disputing, and had read them, interested in them as a development of the first principles of science, familiar to him as a natural science student at the university. But he had never connected these scientific deductions as to the origin of man as an animal, as to reflex action, biology, and sociology, with those questions as to the meaning of life and death to himself, which had of late been more and more often in his mind.

As he listened to his brother's argument with the professor, he noticed that they connected these scientific questions with those spiritual problems, that at times they almost touched on the latter; but every time they were close upon what seemed to him the chief point, they promptly beat a hasty retreat, and plunged again into a sea of subtle distinctions, reservations, quotations, allusions, and appeals to authorities, and it was with difficulty that he understood what they were talking about.

"I cannot admit it," said Sergey Ivanovitch, with his habitual clearness, precision of expression, and elegance of phrase. "I cannot in any case agree with Keiss that my whole conception of the external world has been derived from perceptions. The most fundamental idea, the idea of existence, has not been received by me through sensation; indeed, there is no special sense-organ for the transmission of such an idea."

"Yes, but they—Wurt, and Knaust, and Pripasov—would answer that your consciousness of existence is derived from the conjunction of all your sensations, that that consciousness of existence is the result of your sensations. Wurt, indeed, says plainly that, assuming there are no sensations, it follows that there is no idea of existence."

"I maintain the contrary," began Sergey Ivanovitch.

But here it seemed to Levin that just as they were close upon the real point of the matter, they were again retreating, and he made up his mind to put a question to the professor.

"According to that, if my senses are annihilated, if my body is dead, I can have no existence of any sort?" he queried.

The professor, in annoyance, and, as it were, mental suffering at the interruption, looked round at the strange inquirer, more like a bargeman than a philosopher, and turned his eyes upon Sergey Ivanovitch, as though to ask: What's one to say to him? But Sergey Ivanovitch, who had been talking with far less heat and one-sidedness than the professor, and who had sufficient breadth of mind to answer the professor, and at the same time to comprehend the simple and natural point of view from which the question was put, smiled and said:

"That question we have no right to answer as yet."

"We have not the requisite data," chimed in the professor, and he went back to his argument. "No," he said; "I would point out the fact that if, as Pripasov directly asserts, perception is based on sensation, then we are bound to distinguish sharply between these two conceptions."

Levin listened no more, and simply waited for the professor to go.

CHAPTER VIII

WHEN the professor had gone, Sergey Ivanovitch turned to his brother.

"Delighted that you've come. For some time, is it? How's your farming getting on?"

Levin knew that his elder brother took little interest in farming, and only put the question in deference to him, and so he only told him about the sale of his wheat and money matters.

Levin had meant to tell his brother of his determination to get married, and to ask his advice; he had indeed firmly resolved to do so. But after seeing his brother, listening to his conversation with the professor, hearing afterwards the unconsciously patronizing tone in which his brother questioned him about agricultural matters (their mother's property had not been divided, and Levin took charge of both their shares), Levin felt that he could not for some reason begin to talk to him of his intention of marrying. He felt that his brother would not look at it as he would have wished him to.

"Well, how is your district council doing?" asked Sergey Ivanovitch, who was greatly interested in these local boards and attached great importance to them.

"I really don't know."

"What! Why, surely you're a member of the board?"

"No, I'm not a member now; I've resigned," answered Levin, "and I no longer attend the meetings."

"What a pity!" commented Sergey Ivanovitch, frowning.

Levin in self-defense began to describe what took place in the meetings in his district.

"That's how it always is!" Sergey Ivanovitch interrupted him. "We Russians are always like that. Perhaps it's our strong point, really, the faculty of seeing our own shortcomings; but we overdo it, we comfort ourselves with irony which we always have on the tip of our tongues. All I say is, give such rights as our local self-government to any other European people—why, the Germans or the English would have worked their way to freedom from them, while we simply turn them into ridicule."

"But how can it be helped?" said Levin penitently. "It was my last effort. And I did try with all my soul. I can't. I'm no good at it."

"It's not that you're no good at it," said Sergey Ivanovitch; "it is that you don't look at it as you should."

"Perhaps not," Levin answered dejectedly.

"Oh! do you know brother Nikolay's turned up again?"

This brother Nikolay was the elder brother of Konstantin Levin, and half-brother of Sergey Ivanovitch; a man utterly ruined, who had dissipated the greater part of his fortune, was living in the strangest and lowest company, and had quarreled with his brothers.

"What did you say?" Levin cried with horror. "How do you know?"

"Prokofy saw him in the street."

"Here in Moscow? Where is he? Do you know?" Levin got up from his chair, as though on the point of starting off at once.

"I am sorry I told you," said Sergey Ivanovitch, shaking his head at his younger brother's excitement. "I sent to find out where he is living, and sent him his I O U to Trubin, which I paid. This is the answer he sent me."

And Sergey Ivanovitch took a note from under a paperweight and handed it to his brother.

Levin read in the queer, familiar handwriting: "I humbly beg you to leave me in peace. That's the only favor I ask of my gracious brothers.—NIKOLAY LEVIN."

Levin read it, and without raising his head stood with the note in his hands opposite Sergey Ivanovitch.

There was a struggle in his heart between the desire to forget his unhappy brother for the time, and the consciousness that it would be base to do so.

"He obviously wants to offend me," pursued Sergey Ivanovitch; "but he cannot offend me, and I should have wished with all my heart to assist him, but I know it's impossible to do that."

"Yes, yes," repeated Levin. "I understand and appreciate your attitude to him; but I shall go and see him."

"If you want to, do; but I shouldn't advise it," said Sergey Ivanovitch. "As regards myself, I have no fear of your doing so; he will not make you quarrel with me; but for your own sake, I should say you would do better not to go. You can't do him any good; still, do as you please."

"Very likely I can't do any good, but I feel—especially at such a moment—but that's another thing—I feel I could not be at peace."

"Well, that I don't understand," said Sergey Ivanovitch. "One thing I do understand," he added; "it's a lesson in humility. I have come to look very differently and more charitably on what is called infamous since brother Nikolay has become what he is . . . you know what he did. . . ."

"Oh, it's awful, awful!" repeated Levin.

After obtaining his brother's address from Sergey Ivanovitch's footman, Levin was on the point of setting off at once to see him, but on second thought he decided to put off his visit till the evening. The first thing to do to set his heart at rest was to accomplish what he had come to Moscow for. From his brother's Levin went to Oblonsky's office, and on getting news of the Shtcherbatskys from him, he drove to the place where he had been told he might find Kitty.

CHAPTER IX

AT FOUR o'clock, conscious of his throbbing heart, Levin stepped out of a hired sledge at the Zoological Gardens, and turned along the path to the frozen mounds and the skating-ground, knowing that he would certainly find her there, as he had seen the Shtcherbatskys' carriage at the entrance.

It was a bright, frosty day. Rows of carriages, sledges, drivers, and policemen were standing in the approach. Crowds of well-dressed people, with hats bright in the sun, swarmed about the entrance and along the well-swept little paths between the little houses adorned with carving in the Russian style. The old curly birches of the gardens, all their twigs laden with snow, looked as though freshly decked in sacred vestments.

He walked along the path towards the skating-ground, and kept saying to himself—"You mustn't be excited, you must be calm. What's the matter with you? What do you want? Be quiet, stupid," he conjured his heart. And the more he tried to compose himself, the more breathless he found himself. An acquaintance met him and called him by his name, but Levin did not even recognize him. He went towards the mounds, whence came the clank of the chains of sledges as they slipped down or were dragged up, the rumble of the sliding sledges, and the sounds of merry voices. He walked on a few steps, and the skating-ground lay open before his eyes, and at once, amidst all the skaters, he knew her.

He knew she was there by the rapture and the terror that seized on his heart. She was standing talking to a lady at the opposite end of the ground. There was apparently nothing striking either in her dress or her attitude. But for Levin she was as easy to find in that crowd, as a rose among nettles. Everything was made bright by her. She was the smile that shed light on all round her. "Is it possible I can go over there on the ice, go up to her?" he thought. The place where she stood seemed to him a holy shrine, unapproachable, and there was one moment when he was almost retreating, so overwhelmed was he with terror. He had to make an effort to master himself, and to remind himself that people of all sorts were moving about her, and that he too might come there to skate. He walked down, for a long while avoiding looking at her as at the sun, but seeing her, as one does the sun, without looking.

On that day of the week and at that time of day people of one set, all acquainted with one another, used to meet on the ice. There were crack skaters there, showing off their skill, and learners clinging to chairs with timid, awkward movements, boys, and elderly people skating with hygienic motives. They seemed to Levin an elect band of blissful beings because they were here, near her. All the skaters, it seemed, with perfect self-possession, skated towards her, skated by her, even spoke to her, and were happy, quite apart from her, enjoying the capital ice and the fine weather.

Nikolay Shtcherbatsky, Kitty's cousin, in a short jacket and tight trousers, was sitting on a garden seat with his skates on. Seeing Levin, he shouted to him:

"Ah, the first skater in Russia! Been here long? First-rate ice —do put your skates on."

"I haven't got my skates," Levin answered, marveling at this boldness and ease in her presence, and not for one second losing sight of her, though he did not look at her. He felt as though the sun were coming near him. She was in a corner, and turning out her slender feet in their high boots with obvious timidity, she skated towards him. A boy in Russian dress, desperately waving his arms and bowed down to the ground, overtook her. She skated a little uncertainly; taking her hands out of the little muff that hung on a cord, she held them ready for emergency, and looking towards Levin, whom she had recognized, she smiled at him, and at her own fears. When she had got round the turn, she gave herself a push off with one foot, and skated straight up to Shtcherbatsky. Clutching at his arm, she nodded smiling to Levin. She was more splendid than he had imagined her.

When he thought of her, he could call up a vivid picture of her to himself, especially the charm of that little fair head, so freely set on the shapely girlish shoulders, and so full of childish brightness and good-humor. The childishness of her expression, together with the delicate beauty of her figure, made up her special charm, and that he fully realized. But what always struck him in her as something unlooked for, was the expression of her eyes, soft, serene, and truthful, and above all, her smile, which always transported Levin to an enchanted world, where he felt himself softened and tender, as he remembered himself in some days of his early childhood.

"Have you been here long?" she said, giving him her hand. "Thank you," she added, as he picked up the handkerchief that had fallen out of her muff.

"I? I've not long . . . yesterday . . . I mean to-day . . . I arrived," answered Levin, in his emotion not at once understanding her question. "I was meaning to come and see you," he said; and then, recollecting with what intention he was trying to see her, he was promptly overcome with confusion and blushed.

"I didn't know you could skate, and skate so well."

She looked at him earnestly, as though wishing to make out the cause of his confusion.

"Your praise is worth having. The tradition is kept up here that you are the best of skaters," she said, with her little black-gloved hand brushing a grain of hoarfrost off her muff.

"Yes, I used once to skate with passion; I wanted to reach perfection."

"You do everything with passion, I think," she said smiling. "I should so like to see how you skate. Put on skates, and let us skate together."

"Skate together! Can that be possible?" thought Levin, gazing at her.

"I'll put them on directly," he said.

And he went off to get skates.

"It's a long while since we've seen you here, sir," said the attendant, supporting his foot, and screwing on the heel of the skate. "Except you, there's none of the gentlemen first-rate skaters. Will that be all right?" said he, tightening the strap.

"Oh, yes, yes; make haste, please," answered Levin, with difficulty restraining the smile of rapture which would overspread his face. "Yes," he thought, "this now is life, this is happiness! *Together,* she said; *let us skate together!* Speak to her now? But that's just why I'm afraid to speak—because I'm happy now, happy in hope, anyway. . . . And then? . . . But I must! I must! I must! Away with weakness!"

Levin rose to his feet, took off his overcoat, and scurrying over the rough ice round the hut, came out on the smooth ice and skated without effort, as it were, by simple exercise of will, increasing and slackening speed and turning his course. He approached with timidity, but again her smile reassured him.

She gave him her hand, and they set off side by side, going faster and faster, and the more rapidly they moved the more tightly she grasped his hand.

"With you I should soon learn; I somehow feel confidence in you," she said to him.

"And I have confidence in myself when you are leaning on me," he said, but was at once panic-stricken at what he had said, and blushed. And indeed, no sooner had he uttered these words, when all at once, like the sun going behind a cloud, her face lost all its friendliness, and Levin detected the familiar change in her expression that denoted the working of thought; a crease showed on her smooth brow.

"Is there anything troubling you?—though I've no right to ask such a question," he said hurriedly.

"Oh, why so? . . . No, I have nothing to trouble me," she

responded coldly; and she added immediately: "You haven't seen Mlle Linon, have you?"

"Not yet."

"Go and speak to her, she likes you so much."

"What's wrong? I have offended her. Lord help me!" thought Levin, and he flew towards the old Frenchwoman with the gray ringlets, who was sitting on a bench. Smiling and showing her false teeth, she greeted him as an old friend.

"Yes, you see we're growing up," she said to him, glancing towards Kitty, "and growing old. *Tiny bear* has grown big now!" pursued the Frenchwoman, laughing, and she reminded him of his joke about the three young ladies whom he had compared to the three bears in the English nursery tale. "Do you remember that's what you used to call them?"

He remembered absolutely nothing, but she had been laughing at the joke for ten years now, and was fond of it.

"Now, go and skate, go and skate. Our Kitty has learned to skate nicely, hasn't she?"

When Levin darted up to Kitty her face was no longer stern; her eyes looked at him with the same sincerity and friendliness, but Levin fancied that in her friendliness there was a certain note of deliberate composure. And he felt depressed. After talking a little of her old governess and her peculiarities, she questioned him about his life.

"Surely you must be dull in the country in the winter, aren't you?" she said.

"No, I'm not dull, I am very busy," he said, feeling that she was holding him in check by her composed tone, which he would not have the force to break through, just as it had been at the beginning of the winter.

"Are you going to stay in town long?" Kitty questioned him.

"I don't know," he answered, not thinking of what he was saying. The thought that if he were held in check by her tone of quiet friendliness he would end by going back again without deciding anything came into his mind, and he resolved to make a struggle against it.

"How is it you don't know?"

"I don't know. It depends upon you," he said, and was immediately horror-stricken at his own words.

Whether it was that she had heard his words, or that she did not want to hear them, she made a sort of stumble, twice struck out, and hurriedly skated away from him. She skated up to Mlle Linon, said something to her, and went towards the pavilion where the ladies took off their skates.

"My God! what have I done! Merciful God! help me, guide me," said Levin, praying inwardly, and at the same time, feeling a need of violent exercise, he skated about, describing inner and outer circles.

At that moment one of the young men, the best of the skaters of the day, came out of the coffee-house in his skates, with a cigarette in his mouth. Taking a run, he dashed down the steps in his skates, crashing and bounding up and down. He flew down, and without even changing the position of his hands, skated away over the ice.

"Ah, that's a new trick!" said Levin, and he promptly ran up to the top to do this new trick.

"Don't break your neck! it needs practice!" Nikolay Shtcherbatsky shouted after him.

Levin went to the steps, took a run from above as best he could, and dashed down, preserving his balance in this unwonted movement with his hands. On the last step he stumbled, but barely touching the ice with his hand, with a violent effort recovered himself, and skated off, laughing.

"How splendid, how nice he is!" Kitty was thinking at that time, as she came out of the pavilion with Mlle Linon, and looked towards him with a smile of quiet affection, as though he were a favorite brother. "And can it be my fault, can I have done anything wrong? They talk of flirtation. I know it's not he that I love; but still I am happy with him, and he's so jolly. Only, why did he say that? . . ." she mused.

Catching sight of Kitty going away, and her mother meeting her at the steps, Levin, flushed from his rapid exercise, stood still and pondered a minute. He took off his skates, and overtook the mother and daughter at the entrance of the gardens.

"Delighted to see you," said Princess Shtcherbatskaya. "On Thursdays we are home, as always."

"To-day, then?"

"We shall be pleased to see you," the princess said stiffly.

This stiffness hurt Kitty, and she could not resist the desire to smooth over her mother's coldness. She turned her head, and with a smile said:

"Good-bye till this evening."

At that moment Stepan Arkadyevitch, his hat cocked on one side, with beaming face and eyes, strode into the garden like a conquering hero. But as he approached his mother-in-law, he responded in a mournful and crestfallen tone to her inquiries about Dolly's health. After a little subdued and dejected conversation with his mother-in-law, he threw out his chest again, and put his arm in Levin's.

"Well, shall we set off?" he asked. "I've been thinking about you all this time, and I'm very, very glad you've come," he said, looking him in the face with a significant air.

"Yes, come along," answered Levin in ecstasy, hearing unceasingly the sound of that voice saying, "Good-bye till this evening," and seeing the smile with which it was said.

"To the England or the Hermitage?"

"I don't mind which."

"All right, then, the England," said Stepan Arkadyevitch, selecting that restaurant because he owed more there than at the Hermitage, and consequently considered it mean to avoid it.

41

"Have you got a sledge? That's first-rate, for I sent my carriage home."

The friends hardly spoke all the way. Levin was wondering what that change in Kitty's expression had meant, and alternately assuring himself that there was hope, and falling into despair, seeing clearly that his hopes were insane, and yet all the while he felt himself quite another man, utterly unlike what he had been before her smile and those words, "Good-bye till this evening."

Stepan Arkadyevitch was absorbed during the drive in composing the menu of the dinner.

"You like turbot, don't you?" he said to Levin as they were arriving.

"Eh?" responded Levin. "Turbot? Yes, I'm *awfully* fond of turbot."

CHAPTER X

WHEN Levin went into the restaurant with Oblonsky, he could not help noticing a certain peculiarity of expression, as it were, a restrained radiance, about the face and whole figure of Stepan Arkadyevitch. Oblonsky took off his overcoat, and with his hat over one ear walked into the dining-room, giving directions to the Tatar waiters, who were clustered about him in evening coats, bearing napkins. Bowing to right and left to the people he met, and here as everywhere joyously greeting acquaintances, he went up to the sideboard for a preliminary appetizer of fish and vodka, and said to the painted Frenchwoman decked in ribbons, lace, and ringlets, behind the counter, something so amusing that even that Frenchwoman was moved to genuine laughter. Levin for his part refrained from taking any vodka simply because he felt such a loathing of that Frenchwoman, all made up, it seemed, of false hair, *poudre de riz,* and *vinaigre de toilette.* He made haste to move away from her, as from a dirty place. His whole soul was filled with memories of Kitty, and there was a smile of triumph and happiness shining in his eyes.

"This way, your excellency, please. Your excellency won't be disturbed here," said a particularly pertinacious, white-headed old Tatar with immense hips and coat-tails gaping widely behind. "Walk in, your excellency," he said to Levin; by way of showing his respect to Stepan Arkadyevitch, being attentive to his guest as well.

Instantly flinging a fresh cloth over the round table under the bronze chandelier, though it already had a table-cloth on it, he pushed up velvet chairs, and came to a standstill before Stepan Arkadyevitch with a napkin and a bill of fare in his hands, awaiting his commands.

"If you prefer it, your excellency, a private room will be free directly; Prince Golitsin with a lady. Fresh oysters have come in."

"Ah! oysters."

Stepan Arkadyevitch became thoughtful.

"How if we were to change our program, Levin?" he said keeping his finger on the bill of fare. And his face expressed serious hesitation. "Are the oysters good? Mind now."

"They're Flensburg, your excellency. We've no Ostend."

"Flensburg will do, but are they fresh?"

"Only arrived yesterday."

"Well, then, how if we were to begin with oysters, and so change the whole program? Eh?"

"It's all the same to me. I should like cabbage soup and porridge better than anything; but of course there's nothing like that here."

"*Porridge à la Russe,* your honor would like?" said the Tatar, bending down to Levin, like a nurse speaking to a child.

"No, joking apart, whatever you choose is sure to be good. I've been skating, and I'm hungry. And don't imagine," he added, detecting a look of dissatisfaction on Oblonsky's face, "that I shan't appreciate your choice. I am fond of good things."

"I should hope so! After all, it's one of the pleasures of life," said Stepan Arkadyevitch. "Well, then, my friend, you give us two—or better say three—dozen oysters, clear soup with vegetables. . . ."

"*Printanière,*" prompted the Tatar. But Stepan Arkadyevitch apparently did not care to allow him the satisfaction of giving the French names of the dishes.

"With vegetables in it, you know. Then turbot with thick

sauce, then . . . roast beef; and mind it's good. Yes, and capons, perhaps, and then sweets."

The Tatar, recollecting that it was Stepan Arkadyevitch's way not to call the dishes by the names in the French bill of fare, did not repeat them after him, but could not resist rehearsing the whole menu to himself according to the bill:— *"Soupe printanière, turbot, sauce Beaumarchais, poulard à l'estragon, macédoine de fruits* . . . etc.,"* and then instantly, as though worked by springs, laying down one bound bill of fare, he took up another, the list of wines, and submitted it to Stepan Arkadyevitch.

"What shall we drink?"

"What you like, only not too much. Champagne," said Levin.

"What! to start with? You're right though, I dare say. Do you like the white seal?"

"Cachet blanc," prompted the Tatar.

"Very well, then, give us that brand with the oysters, and then we'll see."

"Yes, sir. And what table wine?"

"You can give us Nuits. Oh, no, better the classic Chablis."

"Yes, sir. And *your* cheese, your excellency?"

"Oh, yes, Parmesan. Or would you like another?"

"No, it's all the same to me," said Levin, unable to suppress a smile.

And the Tatar ran off with flying coat-tails, and in five minutes darted in with a dish of opened oysters on mother-of-pearl shells, and a bottle between his fingers.

Stepan Arkadyevitch crushed the starchy napkin, tucked it into his waistcoat, and settling his arms comfortably, started on the oysters.

"Not bad," he said, stripping the oysters from the pearly shell with a silver fork, and swallowing them one after another. "Not bad," he repeated, turning his dewy, brilliant eyes from Levin to the Tatar.

Levin ate the oysters indeed, though white bread and cheese would have pleased him better. But he was admiring Oblonsky. Even the Tatar, uncorking the bottle and pouring the sparkling wine into the delicate glasses, glanced at Stepan Arkadyevitch, and settled his white cravat with a perceptible smile of satisfaction.

"You don't care much for oysters, do you?" said Stepan Arkadyevitch, emptying his wine-glass, "or you're worried about something. Eh?"

He wanted Levin to be in good spirits. But it was not that Levin was not in good spirits; he was ill at ease. With what he had in his soul, he felt sore and uncomfortable in the restaurant, in the midst of private rooms where men were dining with ladies, in all this fuss and bustle; the surroundings of bronzes, looking-glasses, gas, and waiters—all of it was offensive to him. He was afraid of sullying what his soul was brimful of.

"I? Yes, I am; but besides, all this bothers me," he said. "You can't conceive how queer it all seems to a country person like me, as queer as that gentleman's nails I saw at your place. . . ."

"Yes, I saw how much interested you were in poor Grinevitch's nails," said Stepan Arkadyevitch, laughing.

"It's too much for me," responded Levin. "Do try, now, and put yourself in my place, take the point of view of a country person. We in the country try to bring our hands into such a state as will be most convenient for working with. So we cut our nails; sometimes we turn up our sleeves. And here people purposely let their nails grow as long as they will, and link on small saucers by way of studs, so that they can do nothing with their hands."

Stepan Arkadyevitch smiled gaily.

"Oh, yes, that's just a sign that he has no need to do coarse work. His work is with the mind. . . ."

"Maybe. But still it's queer to me, just as at this moment it seems queer to me that we country folks try to get our meals over as soon as we can, so as to be ready for our work, while here are we trying to drag out our meal as long as possible, and with that object eating oysters. . . ."

"Why, of course," objected Stepan Arkadyevitch. "But that's just the aim of civilization—to make everything a source of enjoyment."

"Well, if that's its aim, I'd rather be a savage."

"And so you are a savage. All you Levins are savages."

Levin sighed. He remembered his brother Nikolay, and felt

ashamed and sore, and he scowled; but Oblonsky began speaking of a subject which at once drew his attention.

"Oh, I say, are you going to-night to our people, the Shtcherbatskys', I mean?" he said, his eyes sparkling significantly as he pushed away the empty rough shells, and drew the cheese towards him.

"Yes, I shall certainly go," replied Levin; "though I fancied the princess was not very warm in her invitation."

"What nonsense! That's her manner. . . . Come, boy, the soup! . . . That's her manner—*grande dame*," said Stepan Arkadyevitch. "I'm coming, too, but I have to go to the Countess Bonina's rehearsal. Come, isn't it true that you're a savage? How do you explain the sudden way in which you vanished from Moscow? The Shtcherbatskys were continually asking me about you, as though I ought to know. The only thing I know is that you always do what no one else does."

"Yes," said Levin, slowly and with emotion, "you're right. I am a savage. Only, my savageness is not in having gone away, but in coming now. Now I have come . . ."

"Oh, what a lucky fellow you are!" broke in Stepan Arkadyevitch, looking into Levin's eyes.

"Why?"

> *"I know a gallant steed by tokens sure,*
> *And by his eyes I know a youth in love,"*

declaimed Stepan Arkadyevitch. "Everything is before you."

"Why, is it over for you already?"

"No; not over exactly, but the future is yours, and the present is mine, and the present—well, it's not all that it might be."

"How so?"

"Oh, things go wrong. But I don't want to talk of myself, and besides I can't explain it all," said Stepan Arkadyevitch. "Well, why have you come to Moscow, then? . . . Hi! take away!" he called to the Tatar.

"You guess?" responded Levin, his eyes like deep wells of light fixed on Stepan Arkadyevitch.

"I guess, but I can't be the first to talk about it. You can see by that whether I guess right or wrong," said Stepan Arkadyevitch, gazing at Levin with a subtle smile.

"Well, and what have you to say to me?" said Levin in a quivering voice, feeling that all the muscles of his face were quivering too. "How do you look at the question?"

Stepan Arkadyevitch slowly emptied his glass of Chablis, never taking his eyes off Levin.

"I?" said Stepan Arkadyevitch, "there's nothing I desire so much as that—nothing! It would be the best thing that could be."

"But you're not making a mistake? You know what we're speaking of?" said Levin, piercing him with his eyes. "You think it's possible?"

"I think it's possible. Why not possible?"

"No! do you really think it's possible? No, tell me all you think! Oh, but if . . . if refusal's in store for me! . . . Indeed I feel sure . . ."

"Why should you think that?" said Stepan Arkadyevitch, smiling at his excitement.

"It seems so to me sometimes. That will be awful for me, and for her too."

"Oh, well, anyway there's nothing awful in it for a girl. Every girl's proud of an offer."

"Yes, every girl, but not she."

Stepan Arkadyevitch smiled. He so well knew that feeling of Levin's, that for him all the girls in the world were divided into two classes: one class—all the girls in the world except her, and those girls with all sorts of human weaknesses, and very ordinary girls: the other class—she alone, having no weaknesses of any sort and higher than all humanity.

"Stay, take some sauce," he said, holding back Levin's hand as it pushed away the sauce.

Levin obediently helped himself to sauce, but would not let Stepan Arkadyevitch go on with his dinner.

"No, stop a minute, stop a minute," he said. "You must understand that it's a question of life and death for me. I have never spoken to any one of this. And there's no one I could speak of it to, except you. You know we're utterly unlike each other, different tastes and views and everything; but I know you're fond of me and understand me, and that's why I like you awfully. But for God's sake, be quite straight-forward with me."

"I tell you what I think," said Stepan Arkadyevitch, smiling. "But I'll say more: my wife is a wonderful woman . . ." Stepan Arkadyevitch sighed, remembering his position with his wife, and, after a moment's silence, resumed—"She has a gift of fore-seeing things. She sees right through people; but that's not all; she knows what will come to pass, especially in the way of marriages. She foretold, for instance, that Princess Shahovskaya would marry Brenteln. No one would believe it, but it came to pass. And she's on your side."

"How do you mean?"

"It's not only that she likes you—she says that Kitty is certain to be your wife."

At these words Levin's face suddenly lighted up with a smile, a smile not far from tears of emotion.

"She says that!" cried Levin. "I always said she was exquisite, your wife. There, that's enough, enough said about it," he said, getting up from his seat.

"All right, but do sit down."

But Levin could not sit down. He walked with his firm tread twice up and down the little cage of a room, blinked his eyelids that his tears might not fall, and only then sat down to the table.

"You must understand," said he, "it's not love. I've been in love, but it's not that. It's not my feeling, but a sort of force outside me has taken possession of me. I went away, you see, because I made up my mind that it could never be, you understand, as a happiness that does not come on earth; but I've struggled with myself, I see there's no living without it. And it must be settled."

"What did you go away for?"

"Ah, stop a minute! Ah, the thoughts that come crowding on one! The questions one must ask oneself! Listen. You can't im-agine what you've done for me by what you said. I'm so happy that I've become positively hateful; I've forgotten everything. I heard to-day that my brother Nikolay . . . you know, he's here . . . I had even forgotten him. It seems to me that he's happy too. It's a sort of madness. But one thing's awful. . . . Here, you've been married, you know the feeling . . . it's awful that we—old—with a past . . . not of love, but of sins . . . are brought all at once so near to a creature pure and innocent; it's loathsome, and that's why one can't help feeling oneself unworthy."

"Oh, well, you've not many sins on your conscience."

"Alas! all the same," said Levin, "when with loathing I go over my life, I shudder and curse and bitterly regret it. . . . Yes."

"What would you have? The world's made so," said Stepan Arkadyevitch.

"The one comfort is like that prayer, which I always liked: 'Forgive me not according to my unworthiness, but according to Thy loving-kindness.' That's the only way she can forgive me."

CHAPTER XI

Levin emptied his glass, and they were silent for a while.

"There's one other thing I ought to tell you. Do you know Vronsky?" Stepan Arkadyevitch asked Levin.

"No, I don't. Why do you ask?"

"Give us another bottle," Stepan Arkadyevitch directed the Tatar, who was filling up their glasses and fidgeting round them just when he was not wanted.

"Why you ought to know Vronsky is that he's one of your rivals."

"Who's Vronsky?" said Levin, and his face was suddenly transformed from the look of childlike ecstasy which Oblonsky had just been admiring to an angry and unpleasant expression.

"Vronsky is one of the sons of Count Kirill Ivanovitch Vronsky, and one of the finest specimens of the gilded youth of Petersburg. I made his acquaintance in Tver when I was there on official business, and he came there for the levy of recruits. Fearfully rich, handsome, great connections, an aide-de-camp, and with all that a very nice, good-natured fellow. But he's more than simply a good-natured fellow, as I've found out here—he's a cultivated man, too, and very intelligent; he's a man who'll make his mark."

49

Levin scowled and was dumb.

"Well, he turned up here soon after you'd gone, and as I can see, he's over head and ears in love with Kitty, and you know that her mother . . ."

"Excuse me, but I know nothing," said Levin, frowning gloomily. And immediately he recollected his brother Nikolay and how hateful he was to have been able to forget him.

"You wait a bit, wait a bit," said Stepan Arkadyevitch, smiling and touching his hand. "I've told you what I know, and I repeat that in this delicate and tender matter, as far as one can conjecture, I believe the chances are in your favor."

Levin dropped back in his chair; his face was pale.

"But I would advise you to settle the thing as soon as may be," pursued Oblonsky, filling up his glass.

"No, thanks, I can't drink any more," said Levin, pushing away his glass. "I shall be drunk. . . . Come, tell me how are you getting on?" he went on, obviously anxious to change the conversation.

"One word more: in any case I advise you to settle the question soon. To-night I don't advise you to speak," said Stepan Arkadyevitch. "Go round to-morrow morning, make an offer in due form, and God bless you. . . ."

"Oh, do you still think of coming to me for some shooting? Come next spring, do," said Levin.

Now his whole soul was full of remorse that he had begun this conversation with Stepan Arkadyevitch. A feeling such as his was profaned by talk of the rivalry of some Petersburg officer, of the suppositions and the counsels of Stepan Arkadyevitch.

Stepan Arkadyevitch smiled. He knew what was passing in Levin's soul.

"I'll come some day," he said. "But women, my boy, they're the pivot everything turns upon. Things are in a bad way with me, very bad. And it's all through women. Tell me frankly now," he pursued, picking up a cigar and keeping one hand on his glass; "give me your advice."

"Why, what is it?"

"I'll tell you. Suppose you're married, you love your wife, but you're fascinated by another woman. . . ."

"Excuse me, but I'm absolutely unable to comprehend how

. . . just as I can't comprehend how I could now, after my dinner, go straight to a baker's shop and steal a roll."

Stepan Arkadyevitch's eyes sparkled more than usual. "Why not? A roll will sometimes smell so good one can't resist it.

> *"Himmlisch ist's, wenn ich bezwungen*
> *Meine irdische Begier;*
> *Aber doch wenn's nicht gelungen*
> *Hatt' ich auch recht hübsch Plaisir!"*

As he said this, Stepan Arkadyevitch smiled subtly. Levin, too, could not help smiling.

"Yes, but joking apart," resumed Stepan Arkadyevitch, "you must understand that the woman is a sweet, gentle, loving creature, poor and lonely, and has sacrificed everything. Now, when the thing's done, don't you see, can one possibly cast her off? Even supposing one parts from her, so as not to break up one's family life, still, can one help feeling for her, setting her on her feet, softening her lot?"

"Well, you must excuse me there. You know to me all women are divided into two classes . . . at least no . . . truer to say: there are women and there are . . . I've never seen exquisite fallen beings, and I never shall see them, but such creatures as that painted Frenchwoman at the counter with the ringlets are vermin to my mind, and all fallen women are the same."

"But the Magdalen?"

"Ah, drop that! Christ would never have said those words if He had known how they would be abused. Of all the Gospel those words are the only ones remembered. However, I'm not saying so much what I think, as what I feel. I have a loathing for fallen women. You're afraid of spiders, and I of these vermin. Most likely you've not made a study of spiders and don't know their character; and so it is with me."

"It's very well for you to talk like that; it's very much like that gentleman in Dickens who used to fling all difficult questions over his right shoulder. But to deny the facts is no answer. What's to be done—you tell me that, what's to be done? Your wife gets older, while you're full of life. Before you've time to look round, you feel that you can't love your wife with love,

51

however much you may esteem her. And then all at once love turns up, and you're done for, done for," Stepan Arkadyevitch said with weary despair.

Levin half smiled.

"Yes, you're done for," resumed Oblonsky. "But what's to be done?"

"Don't steal rolls."

Stepan Arkadyevitch laughed outright.

"Oh, moralist! But you must understand, there are two women; one insists only on her rights, and those rights are your love, which you can't give her; and the other sacrifices everything for you and asks for nothing. What are you to do? How are you to act? There's a fearful tragedy in it."

"If you care for my profession of faith as regards that, I'll tell you that I don't believe there was any tragedy about it. And this is why. To my mind, love . . . both the sorts of love, which you remember Plato defines in his Banquet, served as the test of men. Some men only understand one sort, and some only the other. And those who only know the non-platonic love have no need to talk of tragedy. In such love there can be no sort of tragedy. 'I'm much obliged for the gratification, my humble respects'—that's all the tragedy. And in platonic love there can be no tragedy, because in that love all is clear and pure, because . . ."

At that instant Levin recollected his own sins and the inner conflict he had lived through. And he added unexpectedly:

"But perhaps you are right. Very likely. . . . I don't know, I don't know."

"It's this, don't you see," said Stepan Arkadyevitch, "you're very much all of a piece. That's your strong point and your failing. You have a character that's all of a piece, and you want the whole of life to be of a piece too—but that's not how it is. You despise public official work because you want the reality to be invariably corresponding all the while with the aim—and that's not how it is. You want a man's work, too, always to have a defined aim, and love and family life always to be undivided—and that's not how it is. All the variety, all the charm, all the beauty of life is made up of light and shadow."

Levin sighed and made no reply. He was thinking of his own affairs, and did not hear Oblonsky.

And suddenly both of them felt that though they were friends, though they had been dining and drinking together, which should have drawn them closer, yet each was thinking only of his own affairs, and they had nothing to do with one another. Oblonsky had more than once experienced this extreme sense of aloofness, instead of intimacy, coming on after dinner, and he knew what to do in such cases.

"Bill!" he called, and he went into the next room, where he promptly came across an aide-de-camp of his acquaintance and dropped into conversation with him about an actress and her protector. And at once in the conversation with the aide-de-camp Oblonsky had a sense of relaxation and relief after the conversation with Levin, which always put him to too great a mental and spiritual strain.

When the Tatar appeared with a bill for twenty-six roubles and odd kopecks, besides a tip for himself, Levin, who would another time have been horrified, like any one from the country, at his share of fourteen roubles, did not notice it, paid, and set off homewards to dress and go to the Shtcherbatskys' there to decide his fate.

CHAPTER XII

THE young Princess Kitty Shtcherbatskaya was eighteen. It was the first winter that she had been out in the world. Her success in society had been greater than that of either of her elder sisters, and greater even than her mother had anticipated. To say nothing of the young men who danced at the Moscow balls being almost all in love with Kitty, two serious suitors had already this first winter made their appearance: Levin, and immediately after his departure, Count Vronsky.

Levin's appearance at the beginning of the winter, his frequent visits, and evident love for Kitty, had led to the first serious conversations between Kitty's parents as to her future, and to disputes between them. The prince was on Levin's side; he said he wished for nothing better for Kitty. The princess for her part, going round the question in the manner peculiar to women, maintained that Kitty was too young, that Levin had done nothing to prove that he had serious intentions, that Kitty felt no great attraction to him, and other side issues; but she did not state the principal point, which was that she looked for a better match for her daughter, and that Levin was not to her liking, and she did not understand him. When Levin had abruptly departed, the princess was delighted, and said to her husband triumphantly: "You see I was right." When Vronsky appeared on the scene, she was still more delighted, confirmed in her opinion that Kitty was to make not simply a good, but a brilliant match.

In the mother's eyes there could be no comparison between Vronsky and Levin. She disliked in Levin his strange and uncompromising opinions and his shyness in society, founded, as she supposed, on his pride and his queer sort of life, as she considered it, absorbed in cattle and peasants. She did not very much like it that he, who was in love with her daughter, had kept coming to the house for six weeks, as though he were waiting for something, inspecting, as though he were afraid he might be doing them too great an honor by making an offer, and did not realize that a man, who continually visits at a house where there is a young unmarried girl, is bound to make his intentions clear. And suddenly, without doing so, he disappeared. "It's as well he's not attractive enough for Kitty to have fallen in love with him," thought the mother.

Vronsky satisfied all the mother's desires. Very wealthy, clever, of aristocratic family, on the highroad to a brilliant career in the army and at court, and a fascinating man. Nothing better could be wished for.

Vronsky openly flirted with Kitty at balls, danced with her, and came continually to the house; consequently there could be no doubt of the seriousness of his intentions. But, in spite of that, the mother had spent the whole of that winter in a state of terrible anxiety and agitation.

Princess Shtcherbatskaya had herself been married thirty years ago, her aunt arranging the match. Her husband, about whom everything was well known beforehand, had come, looked at his future bride, and been looked at. The matchmaking aunt had ascertained and communicated their mutual impression.

That impression had been favorable. Afterwards, on a day fixed beforehand, the expected offer was made to her parents, and accepted. All had passed very simply and easily. So it seemed, at least, to the princess. But over her own daughters she had felt how far from simple and easy is the business, apparently so common-place, of marrying off one's daughters. The panics that had been lived through, the thoughts that had been brooded over, the money that had been wasted, and the disputes with her husband over marrying the two elder girls, Darya and Natalia! Now, since the youngest had come out, she was going through the same terrors, the same doubts, and still more violent quarrels with her husband than she had over the elder girls. The old prince, like all fathers indeed, was exceedingly punctilious on the score of the honor and reputation of his daughters. He was irrationally jeal-ous over his daughters, especially over Kitty, who was his favor-ite. At every turn he had scenes with the princess for compromis-ing her daughter. The princess had grown accustomed to this already with her other daughters, but now she felt that there was more ground for the prince's touchiness. She saw that of late years much was changed in the manners of society, that a mother's duties had become still more difficult. She saw that girls of Kitty's age formed some sort of clubs, went to some sort of lectures, mixed freely in men's society; drove about the streets alone, many of them did not curtsey, and, what was the most im-portant thing, all the girls were firmly convinced that to choose their husbands was their own affair, and not their parents'. "Mar-riages aren't made nowadays as they used to be," was thought and said by all these young girls, and even by their elders. But how marriages were made now, the princess could not learn from any one. The French fashion—of the parents arranging their children's future—was not accepted; it was condemned. The English fashion of the complete independence of girls was also not accepted, and not possible in Russian society. The Russian fashion of matchmaking by the offices of intermediate persons was for some reason considered unseemly; it was ridiculed by every one, and by the princess herself. But how girls were to be married, and how parents were to marry them, no one knew. Every one with whom the princess had chanced to discuss the matter said the same thing: "Mercy on us, it's high time in our day to cast off all that old-fashioned business. It's the young people have to marry, and not their parents; and so we ought to leave the young people to arrange it as they choose." It was very easy for any one to say that who had no daughters, but the princess realized that in the process of getting to know each other, her daughter might fall in love, and fall in love with some one who did not care to marry her or who was quite unfit to be her husband. And, however much it was instilled into the princess that in our times young people ought to arrange their lives for themselves, she was unable to believe it, just as she would have been unable to believe that, at any time whatever, the most suitable playthings for children five years old ought to be loaded pistols. And so the princess was more uneasy over Kitty than she had been over her elder sisters.

Now she was afraid that Vronsky might confine himself to simply flirting with her daughter. She saw that her daughter was in love with him, but tried to comfort herself with the thought that he was an honorable man, and would not do this. But at the same time she knew how easy it is, with the freedom of manners of to-day, to turn a girl's head, and how lightly men generally regard such a crime. The week before, Kitty had told her mother of a conversation she had with Vronsky during a mazurka. This conversation had partly reassured the princess; but perfectly at ease she could not be. Vronsky had told Kitty that both he and his brother were so used to obeying their mother that they never made up their minds to any important undertaking without consulting her. "And just now, I am impatiently awaiting my mother's arrival from Petersburg, as peculiarly fortunate," he told her.

Kitty had repeated this without attaching any significance to the words. But her mother saw them in a different light. She knew that the old lady was expected from day to day, that she would be pleased at her son's choice, and she felt it strange that he should not make his offer through fear of vexing his mother. However, she was so anxious for the marriage itself, and still more for relief from her fears, that she believed it was so. Bitter as it was for the princess to see the unhappiness of her eldest daughter, Dolly, on the point of leaving her husband, her anxiety over the decision of her youngest daughter's fate engrossed all her feelings. To-day, with Levin's reappearance, a fresh source of anxiety arose. She was afraid that her daughter, who had at one time, as she fancied, a feeling for Levin, might, from extreme sense of honor, refuse Vronsky, and that Levin's arrival might generally complicate and delay the affair so near being concluded.

"Why, has he been here long?" the princess asked about Levin, as they returned home.

"He came to-day, mamma."

"There's one thing I want to say . . ." began the princess, and from her serious and alert face, Kitty guessed what it would be.

"Mamma," she said, flushing hotly and turning quickly to her, "please, please don't say anything about that. I know, I know all about it."

She wished for what her mother wished for, but the motives of her mother's wishes wounded her.

"I only want to say that to raise hopes . . ."

"Mamma, darling, for goodness' sake, don't talk about it. It's so horrible to talk about it."

"I won't," said her mother, seeing the tears in her daughter's eyes; but one thing, my love; you promised me you would have no secrets from me. You won't?"

"Never, mamma, none," answered Kitty, flushing a little, and looking her mother straight in the face, "but there's no use in my telling you anything, and I . . . I . . . if I wanted to, I don't know what to say or how. . . . I don't know. . . ."

"No, she could not tell an untruth with those eyes," thought the mother, smiling at her agitation and happiness. The princess smiled that what was taking place just now in her soul seemed to the poor child so immense and so important.

CHAPTER XIII

AFTER dinner, and till the beginning of the evening, Kitty was feeling a sensation akin to the sensation of a young man before a battle. Her heart throbbed violently, and her thoughts would not rest on anything.

She felt that this evening, when they would both meet for the first time, would be a turning-point in her life. And she was continually picturing them to herself, at one moment each separately, and then both together. When she mused on the past, she dwelt with pleasure, with tenderness, on the memories of her relations with Levin. The memories of childhood and of Levin's friendship with her dead brother gave a special poetic charm to her relations with him. His love for her, of which she felt certain, was flattering and delightful to her; and it was pleasant for her to think of Levin. In her memories of Vronsky there always entered a certain element of awkwardness, though he was in the highest degree well-bred and at ease, as though there were some false note—not in Vronsky, he was very simple and nice, but in herself, while with Levin she felt perfectly simple and clear. But, on the other hand, directly she thought of the future with Vronsky, there arose before her a perspective of brilliant happiness; with Levin the future seemed misty.

When she went up-stairs to dress, and looked into the looking-glass, she noticed with joy that it was one of her good days, and that she was in complete possession of all her forces,—she needed this so for what lay before her : she was conscious of external composure and free grace in her movements.

At half-past seven she had only just gone down into the drawing-room, when the footman announced, "Konstantin Dmitrievitch Levin." The princess was still in her room, and the prince had not come in. "So it is to be," thought Kitty, and all the blood seemed to rush to her heart. She was horrified at her paleness, as she glanced into the looking-glass. At that moment she knew beyond doubt that he had come early on purpose to find her alone and to make her an offer. And only then for the first time the whole thing presented itself in a new, different aspect; only then she realized that the question did not affect her only—with whom she would be happy, and whom she loved—but that she would have that moment to wound a man whom she liked. And to wound him cruelly. What for? Because he, dear fellow, loved her, was in love with her. But there was no help for it, so it must be, so it would have to be.

"My God! shall I myself really have to say it to him?" she thought. "Can I tell him I don't love him? That will be a lie. What am I to say to him? That I love some one else? No, that's impossible. I'm going away, I'm going away."

She had reached the door, when she heard his step. "No! it's not honest. What have I to be afraid of? I have done nothing wrong. What is to be, will be! I'll tell the truth. And with him one can't be ill at ease. Here he is," she said to herself, seeing his powerful, shy figure, with his shining eyes fixed on her. She looked straight into his face, as though imploring him to spare her, and gave her hand.

"It's not time yet; I think I'm too early," he said glancing round the empty drawing-room. When he saw that his expectations were realized, that there was nothing to prevent him from speaking, his face became gloomy.

"Oh, no," said Kitty, and sat down to the table.

"But this was just what I wanted, to find you alone," he began, not sitting down, and not looking at her, so as not to lose courage.

"Mamma will be down directly. She was very much tired. . . . Yesterday . . ."

She talked on, not knowing what her lips were uttering, and not taking her supplicating and caressing eyes off him.

He glanced at her; she blushed, and ceased speaking.

"I told you I did not know whether I should be here long . . . that it depended on you. . . ."

She dropped her head lower and lower, not knowing herself what answer she should make to what was coming.

"That it depended on you," he repeated. "I meant to say . . . I meant to say . . . I came for this . . . to be my wife!" he brought out, not knowing what he was saying; but feeling that the most terrible thing was said, he stopped short and looked at her. . . .

She was breathing heavily, not looking at him. She was feeling ecstasy. Her soul was flooded with happiness. She had never anticipated that the utterance of love would produce such a powerful effect on her. But it lasted only an instant. She remembered Vronsky. She lifted her clear, truthful eyes, and seeing his desperate face, she answered hastily:

"That cannot be . . . forgive me."

A moment ago, and how close she had been to him, of what importance in his life! And how aloof and remote from him she had become now!

"It was bound to be so," he said, not looking at her.

He bowed, and was meaning to retreat.

CHAPTER XIV

BUT at that very moment the princess came in. There was a look of horror on her face when she saw them alone, and their disturbed faces. Levin bowed to her, and said nothing. Kitty did not speak nor lift her eyes. "Thank God, she has refused him," thought the mother, and her face lighted up with the habitual smile with which she greeted her guests on Thursdays. She sat down and began questioning Levin about his life in the country. He sat down again, waiting for other visitors to arrive, in order to retreat unnoticed.

Five minutes later there came in a friend of Kitty's, married the preceding winter, Countess Nordston.

She was a thin, sallow, sickly, and nervous woman, with brilliant black eyes. She was fond of Kitty, and her affection for her showed itself, as the affection of married women for girls always does, in the desire to make a match for Kitty after her own ideal of married happiness; she wanted her to marry Vronsky. Levin she had often met at the Shtcherbatskys' early in the winter, and she had always disliked him. Her invariable and favorite pursuit, when they met, consisted in making fun of him.

"I do like it when he looks down at me from the height of his

grandeur, or breaks off his learned conversation with me because I'm a fool, or is condescending to me. I like that so; to see him condescending! I am so glad he can't bear me," she used to say of him.

She was right, for Levin actually could not bear her, and despised her for what she was proud of and regarded as a fine characteristic—her nervousness, her delicate contempt and indifference for everything coarse and earthly.

The Countess Nordston and Levin had got into that relation with one another not seldom seen in society, when two persons, who remain externally on friendly terms, despise each other to such a degree that they cannot even take each other seriously, and cannot even be offended by each other.

The Countess Nordston pounced upon Levin at once.

"Ah, Konstantin Dmitrievitch! So you've come back to our corrupt Babylon," she said, giving him her tiny, yellow hand, and recalling what he had chanced to say early in the winter, that Moscow was a Babylon. "Come, is Babylon reformed, or have you degenerated?" she added, glancing with a simper at Kitty.

"It's very flattering for me, countess, that you remember my words so well," responded Levin, who had succeeded in recovering his composure, and at once from habit dropped into his tone of joking hostility to the Countess Nordston. "They must certainly make a great impression on you."

"Oh, I should think so! I always note them all down. Well, Kitty, have you been skating again? . . ."

And she began talking to Kitty. Awkward as it was for Levin to withdraw now, it would still have been easier for him to perpetrate this awkwardness than to remain all the evening and see Kitty, who glanced at him now and then and avoided his eyes. He was on the point of getting up, when the princess, noticing that he was silent, addressed him.

"Shall you be long in Moscow? You're busy with the district council, though, aren't you, and can't be away for long?"

"No, princess, I'm no longer a member of the council," he said. "I have come up for a few days."

"There's something the matter with him," thought Countess Nordston, glancing at his stern, serious face. "He isn't in his old argumentative mood. But I'll draw him out. I do love making a fool of him before Kitty, and I'll do it."

"Konstantin Dmitrievitch," she said to him, "do explain to me, please, what's the meaning of it. You know all about such things. At home in our village of Kaluga all the peasants and all the women have drunk up all they possessed, and now they can't pay us any rent. What's the meaning of that? You always praise the peasants so."

At that instant another lady came into the room, and Levin got up.

"Excuse me, countess, but I really know nothing about it, and can't tell you anything," he said, and looked round at the officer who came in behind the lady.

"That must be Vronsky," thought Levin, and, to be sure of it, glanced at Kitty. She had already had time to look at Vronsky, and looked round at Levin. And simply from the look in her eyes, that grew unconsciously brighter, Levin knew that she loved that man, knew it as surely as if she had told him so in words. But what sort of a man was he? Now, whether for good or for ill, Levin could not choose but remain; he must find out what the man was like whom she loved.

There are people who, on meeting a successful rival, no matter in what, are at once disposed to turn their backs on everything good in him, and to see only what is bad. There are people, on the other hand, who desire above all to find in that lucky rival the qualities by which he has outstripped them, and seek with a throbbing ache at heart only what is good. Levin belonged to the second class. But he had no difficulty in finding what was good and attractive in Vronsky. It was apparent at the first glance. Vronsky was a squarely built, dark man, not very tall, with a good-humored, handsome, and exceedingly calm and resolute face. Everything about his face and figure, from his short-cropped black hair and freshly shaven chin down to his loosely fitting, brand-new uniform, was simple and at the same time elegant. Making way for the lady who had come in, Vronsky went up to the princess and then to Kitty.

As he approached her, his beautiful eyes shone with a specially tender light, and with a faint, happy, and modestly triumphant smile (so it seemed to Levin), bowing carefully and respectfully over her, he held out his small broad hand to her.

Greeting and saying a few words to every one, he sat down without once glancing at Levin, who had never taken his eyes off him.

"Let me introduce you," said the princess, indicating Levin. "Konstantin Dmitrievitch Levin, Count Alexey Kirillovitch Vronsky."

Vronsky got up and, looking cordially at Levin, shook hands with him.

"I believe I was to have dined with you this winter," he said, smiling his simple and open smile; "but you had unexpectedly left for the country."

"Konstantin Dmitrievitch despises and hates town and us townspeople," said Countess Nordston.

"My words must make a deep impression on you, since you remember them so well," said Levin, and, suddenly conscious that he had said just the same thing before, he reddened.

Vronsky looked at Levin and Countess Nordston, and smiled.

"Are you always in the country?" he inquired. "I should think it must be dull in the winter."

"It's not dull if one has work to do; besides, one's not dull by oneself," Levin replied abruptly.

"I am fond of the country," said Vronsky, noticing, and affecting not to notice, Levin's tone.

"But I hope, count, you would not consent to live in the country always," said Countess Nordston.

"I don't know; I have never tried for long. I experienced a queer feeling once," he went on. "I never longed so for the country, Russian country, with bast shoes and peasants, as when I was spending a winter with my mother in Nice. Nice itself is dull enough, you know. And indeed, Naples and Sorrento are only pleasant for a short time. And it's just there that Russia comes back to me most vividly, and especially the country. It's as though . . ."

He talked on, addressing both Kitty and Levin, turning his serene, friendly eyes from one to the other, and saying obviously just what came into his head.

Noticing that Countess Nordston wanted to say something, he stopped short without finishing what he had begun, and listened attentively to her.

63

The conversation did not flag for an instant, so that the princess, who always kept in reserve, in case a subject should be lacking, two heavy guns—the relative advantages of classical and of modern education, and universal military service—had not to move out either of them, while Countess Nordston had not a chance of chaffing Levin.

Levin wanted to, and could not, take part in the general conversation ; saying to himself every instant, "Now go," he still did not go, as though waiting for something.

The conversation fell upon table-turning and spirits, and Countess Nordston, who believed in spiritualism, began to describe the marvels she had seen.

"Ah, countess, you really must take me, for pity's sake do take me to see them! I have never seen anything extraordinary, though I am always on the lookout for it everywhere," said Vronsky, smiling.

"Very well, next Saturday," answered Countess Nordston. "But you, Konstantin Dmitrievitch, do you believe in it?" she asked Levin.

"Why do you ask me? You know what I shall say."

"But I want to hear your opinion."

"My opinion," answered Levin, "is only that this table-turning simply proves that educated society—so called—is no higher than the peasants. They believe in the evil eye, and in witchcraft and omens, while we . . ."

"Oh, then you don't believe in it?"

"I can't believe in it, countess."

"But if I've seen it myself?"

"The peasant women too tell us they have seen goblins."

"Then you think I tell a lie?"

And she laughed a mirthless laugh.

"Oh, no, Masha, Konstantin Dmitrievitch said he could not believe in it," said Kitty, blushing for Levin, and Levin saw this, and, still more exasperated, would have answered, but Vronsky with his bright frank smile rushed to the support of the conversation, which was threatening to become disagreeable.

"You do not admit the conceivability at all?" he queried. "But why not? We admit the existence of electricity, of which we know nothing. Why should there not be some new force, still unknown to us, which . . ."

"When electricity was discovered," Levin interrupted hurriedly, "it was only the phenomenon that was discovered, and it was unknown from what it proceeded and what were its effects, and ages passed before its applications were conceived. But the spiritualists have begun with tables writing for them, and spirits appearing to them, and have only later started saying that it is an unknown force."

Vronsky listened attentively to Levin, as he always did listen, obviously interested in his words.

"Yes, but the spiritualists say we don't know at present what this force is, but there is a force, and these are the conditions in which it acts. Let the scientific men find out what the force consists in. No, I don't see why there should not be a new force, if it . . ."

"Why, because with electricity," Levin interrupted again, "every time you rub tar against wool, a recognized phenomenon is manifested, but in this case it does not happen every time, and so it follows it is not a natural phenomenon."

Feeling probably that the conversation was taking a tone too serious for a drawing-room, Vronsky made no rejoinder, but by way of trying to change the conversation, he smiled brightly, and turned to the ladies.

"Do let us try at once, countess," he said; but Levin would finish saying what he thought.

"I think," he went on, "that this attempt of the spiritualists to explain their marvels as some sort of new natural force is most futile. They boldly talk of spiritual force, and then try to subject it to material experiment."

Every one was waiting for him to finish, and he felt it.

"And I think you would be a first-rate medium," said Countess Nordston; "there's something enthusiastic in you."

Levin opened his mouth, was about to say something, reddened, and said nothing.

"Do let us try table-turning at once, please," said Vronsky. "Princess, will you allow it?"

And Vronsky stood up, looking about for a little table.

Kitty got up to fetch a table, and as she passed, her eyes met Levin's. She felt for him with her whole heart, the more because she was pitying him for suffering of which she was herself the cause. "If you can forgive me, forgive me," said her eyes, "I am so happy."

"I hate them all, and you, and myself," his eyes responded, and he took up his hat. But he was not destined to escape. Just as they were arranging themselves round the table, and Levin was on the point of retiring, the old prince came in, and after greeting the ladies, addressed Levin.

"Ah!" he began joyously. "Been here long, my boy? I didn't even know you were in town. Very glad to see you." The old prince embraced Levin, and talking to him did not observe Vronsky, who had risen, and was serenely waiting till the prince should turn to him.

Kitty felt how distasteful her father's warmth was to Levin after what had happened. She saw, too, how coldly her father responded at last to Vronsky's bow, and how Vronsky looked with amiable perplexity at her father, as though trying and failing to understand how and why any one could be hostilely disposed towards him, and she flushed.

"Prince, let us have Konstantin Dmitrievitch," said Countess Nordston; "we want to try an experiment."

"What experiment? Table-turning? Well, you must excuse me, ladies and gentlemen, but to my mind it is better fun to play the ring game," said the old prince, looking at Vronsky, and guessing that it had been his suggestion. "There's some sense in that, anyway."

Vronsky looked wonderingly at the prince with his resolute eyes, and, with a faint smile, began immediately talking to Countess Nordston of the great ball that was to come off next week.

"I hope you will be there?" he said to Kitty. As soon as the old prince turned away from him, Levin went out unnoticed, and the last impression he carried away with him of that evening was the smiling, happy face of Kitty answering Vronsky's inquiry about the ball.

AT THE end of the evening Kitty told her mother of her conversation with Levin, and in spite of all the pity she felt for Levin,
she was glad at the thought that she had received an *offer*. She
had no doubt that she had acted rightly. But after she had gone
to bed, for a long while she could not sleep. One impression pursued her relentlessly. It was Levin's face, with his scowling brows,
and his kind eyes looking out in dark dejection below them, as
he stood listening to her father, and glancing at her and at Vronsky. And she felt so sorry for him that tears came into her eyes.
But immediately she thought of the man for whom she had given
him up. She vividly recalled his manly, resolute face, his noble
self-possession, and the good-nature conspicuous in everything
towards every one. She remembered the love for her of the man
she loved, and once more all was gladness in her soul, and she lay
on the pillow, smiling with happiness. "I'm sorry, I'm sorry; but
what could I do? It's not my fault," she said to herself; but an
inner voice told her something else. Whether she felt remorse at
having won Levin's love, or at having refused him, she did not
know. But her happiness was poisoned by doubts. "Lord, have
pity on us; Lord, have pity on us; Lord, have pity on us!" she
repeated to herself, till she fell asleep.

Meanwhile there took place below, in the prince's little library,
one of the scenes so often repeated between the parents on account
of their favorite daughter.

"What? I'll tell you what!" shouted the prince, waving his
arms, and at once wrapping his squirrel-lined dressing-gown
round him again. "That you've no pride, no dignity; that you're
disgracing, ruining your daughter by this vulgar, stupid matchmaking!"

"But, really, for mercy's sake, prince, what have I done?" said
the princess, almost crying.

She, pleased and happy after her conversation with her daughter, had gone to the prince to say good-night as usual, and though
she had no intention of telling him of Levin's offer and Kitty's
refusal, still she hinted to her husband that she fancied things

were practically settled with Vronsky, and that he would declare himself so soon as his mother arrived. And thereupon, at those words, the prince had all at once flown into a passion, and began to use unseemly language.

"What have you done? I'll tell you what. First of all, you're trying to catch an eligible gentleman, and all Moscow will be talking of it, and with good reason. If you have evening parties, invite every one, don't pick out the possible suitors. Invite all the young bucks. Engage a piano-player, and let them dance, and not as you do things nowadays, hunting up good matches. It makes me sick, sick to see it, and you've gone on till you've turned the poor wench's head. Levin's a thousand times the better man. As for this little Petersburg swell, they're turned out by machinery, all on one pattern, and all precious rubbish. But if he were a prince of the blood, my daughter need not run after any one."

"But what have I done?"

"Why, you've . . ." The prince was crying wrathfully.

"I know if one were to listen to you," interrupted the princess, "we should never marry our daughter. If it's to be so, we'd better go into the country."

"Well, and we had better."

"But do wait a minute. Do I try and catch them? I don't try to catch them in the least. A young man, and a very nice one, has fallen in love with her, and she, I fancy . . ."

"Oh, yes, you fancy! And how if she really is in love, and he's no more thinking of marriage than I am! . . . Oh, that I should live to see it! . . . Ah! spiritualism! Ah! Nice! Ah! the ball!" And the prince, imagining that he was mimicking his wife, made a mincing curtsey at each word. "And this is how we're preparing wretchedness for Kitty; and she's really got the notion into her head . . ."

"But what makes you suppose so?"

"I don't suppose; I know. We have eyes for such things, though women-folk haven't. I see a man who has serious intentions, that's Levin: and I see a peacock, like this feather-head, who's only amusing himself."

"Oh, well, when once you get an idea into your head! . . ."

"Well, you'll remember my words, but too late, just as with Dolly."

"Well, well, we won't talk of it," the princess stopped him, recollecting her unlucky Dolly.

"By all means, and good-night!"

And signing each other with the cross, the husband and wife parted with a kiss, feeling that they each remained of their own opinion.

The princess had at first been quite certain that that evening had settled Kitty's future, and that there could be no doubt of Vronsky's intentions, but her husband's words had disturbed her. And returning to her own room, in terror before the unknown future, she, too, like Kitty, repeated several times in her heart, "Lord, have pity; Lord, have pity; Lord, have pity."

CHAPTER XVI

VRONSKY had never had a real home-life. His mother had been in her youth a brilliant society woman, who had had during her married life, and still more afterwards, many love-affairs notorious in the whole fashionable world. His father he scarcely remembered, and he had been educated in the Corps of Pages.

Leaving the school very young as a brilliant officer, he had at once got into the circle of wealthy Petersburg army men. Although he did go more or less into Petersburg society, his love-affairs had always hitherto been outside it.

In Moscow he had for the first time felt, after his luxurious and coarse life at Petersburg, all the charm of intimacy with a sweet and innocent girl of his own rank, who cared for him. It never even entered his head that there could be any harm in his relations with Kitty. At balls he danced principally with her. He was a constant visitor at their house. He talked to her as people commonly do talk in society—all sorts of nonsense, but nonsense to which he could not help attaching a special meaning in her case. Although he said nothing to her that he could not have said before everybody, he felt that she was becoming more and more dependent upon him, and the more he felt this, the better he liked it, and the tenderer was his feeling for her. He did not know that this mode of behavior in relation to Kitty had a definite character, that it is courting young girls with no intention of marriage, and that such courting is one of the evil actions common among brilliant young men such as he was. It seemed to him that he was the first who had discovered this pleasure, and he was enjoying his discovery.

If he could have heard what her parents were saying that evening, if he could have put himself at the point of view of the family and have heard that Kitty would be unhappy if he did not marry her, he would have been greatly astonished, and would not have believed it. He could not believe that what gave such great and delicate pleasure to him, and above all to her, could be wrong. Still less could he have believed that he ought to marry.

Marriage had never presented itself to him as a possibility. He not only disliked family life, but a family, and especially a husband was, in accordance with the views general in the bachelor world in which he lived, conceived as something alien, repellent, and, above all, ridiculous.

But though Vronsky had not the least suspicion what the parents were saying, he felt on coming away from the Shtcherbatskys' that the secret spiritual bond which existed between him and Kitty had grown so much stronger that evening that some step must be taken. But what step could and ought to be taken he could not imagine.

"What is so exquisite," he thought, as he returned from the Shtcherbatskys', carrying away with him, as he always did, a delicious feeling of purity and freshness, arising partly from the fact that he had not been smoking for a whole evening, and with it a new feeling of tenderness at her love for him—"what is so exquisite is that not a word has been said by me or by her, but we understand each other so well in this unseen language of looks and tones, that this evening more clearly than ever she told me she loves me. And how secretly, simply, and most of all, how trustfully! I feel myself better, purer. I feel that I have a heart, and that there is a great deal of good in me. Those sweet, loving eyes! When she said: 'Indeed I do. . . .'

"Well, what then? Oh, nothing. It's good for me, and good for her." And he began wondering where to finish the evening.

He passed in review the places he might go to. "Club? a game of bezique, champagne with Ignatov? No, I'm not going. Château des Fleurs; there I shall find Oblonsky, songs, the cancan. No,

I'm sick of it. That's why I like the Shtcherbatskys', that I'm growing better. I'll go home." He went straight to his room at Dussot's Hotel, ordered supper, and then undressed, and as soon as his head touched the pillow, fell into a sound sleep.

CHAPTER XVII

NEXT day at eleven o'clock in the morning Vronsky drove to the station of the Petersburg railway to meet his mother, and the first person he came across on the great flight of steps was Oblonsky, who was expecting his sister by the same train.

"Ah! your excellency!" cried Oblonsky, "whom are you meeting?"

"My mother," Vronsky responded, smiling, as every one did who met Oblonsky. He shook hands with him, and together they ascended the steps. "She is to be here from Petersburg to-day."

"I was looking out for you till two o'clock last night. Where did you go after the Shtcherbatskys'?"

"Home," answered Vronsky. "I must own I felt so well content yesterday after the Shtcherbatskys' that I didn't care to go anywhere."

> *"I know a gallant steed by tokens sure,*
> *And by his eyes I know a youth in love,"*

declaimed Stepan Arkadyevitch, just as he had done before to Levin.

Vronsky smiled with a look that seemed to say that he did not deny it, but he promptly changed the subject.

"And whom are you meeting?" he asked.

"I? I've come to meet a pretty woman," said Oblonsky.

"You don't say so!"

"Honi soit qui mal y pense! My sister Anna."

"Ah! that's Madame Karenina," said Vronsky.

"You know her, no doubt?"

"I think I do. Or perhaps not . . . I really am not sure," Vronsky answered heedlessly, with a vague recollection of something stiff and tedious evoked by the name Karenina.

"But Alexey Alexandrovitch, my celebrated brother-in-law, you surely must know. All the world knows him."

"I know him by reputation and by sight. I know that he's clever, learned, religious somewhat. . . . But you know that's not . . . *not in my line,*" said Vronsky in English.

"Yes, he's a very remarkable man; rather a conservative, but a splendid man," observed Stepan Arkadyevitch, "a splendid man."

"Oh, well, so much the better for him," said Vronsky, smiling. "Oh, you've come," he said, addressing a tall old footman of his mother's, standing at the door; "come here."

Besides the charm Oblonsky had in general for every one, Vronsky had felt of late specially drawn to him by the fact that in his imagination he was associated with Kitty.

"Well, what do you say? Shall we give a supper on Sunday for the *diva?*" he said to him with a smile, taking his arm.

"Of course. I'm collecting subscriptions. Oh, did you make the acquaintance of my friend Levin?" asked Stepan Arkadyevitch.

"Yes; but he left rather early."

"He's a capital fellow," pursued Oblonsky. "Isn't he?"

"I don't know why it is," responded Vronsky, "in all Moscow people—present company of course excepted," he put in jestingly, "there's something uncompromising. They are all on the defensive, lose their tempers, as though they all want to make one feel something. . . ."

"Yes, that's true, it is so," said Stepan Arkadyevitch, laughing good-humoredly.

"Will the train soon be in?" Vronsky asked a railway official.

"The train's signaled," answered the man.

The approach of the train was more and more evident by the preparatory bustle in the station, the rush of porters, the movement of policemen and attendants, and people meeting the train. Through the frosty vapor could be seen workmen in short sheepskins and soft felt boots crossing the rails of the curving line. The hiss of the boiler could be heard on the distant rails, and the rumble of something heavy.

"No," said Stepan Arkadyevitch, who felt a great inclination to tell Vronsky of Levin's intentions in regard to Kitty. "No, you've not got a true impression of Levin. He's a very nervous man, and is sometimes out of humor, it's true, but then he is often very nice. He's such a true, honest nature, and a heart of gold. But yesterday there were special reasons," pursued Stepan Arkadyevitch, with a meaning smile, totally oblivious of the genuine sympathy he had felt the day before for his friend, and feeling the same sympathy now, only for Vronsky. "Yes, there were reasons why he could not help being either particularly happy or particularly unhappy."

Vronsky stood still and asked directly: "How so? Do you mean he made your *belle-sœur* an offer yesterday?"

"Maybe," said Stepan Arkadyevitch. "I fancied something of the sort yesterday. Yes, if he went away early, and was out of humor too, it must mean it. . . . He's been so long in love, and I'm very sorry for him."

"So that's it! . . . I should imagine, though, she might reckon on a better match," said Vronsky, drawing himself up and walking about again, "though I don't know him, of course," he added. "Yes, that is a hateful position! That's why most fellows prefer to have to do with Klaras. If you don't succeed with them it only proves that you've not enough cash, but in this case one's dignity's at stake. But here's the train."

The engine had already whistled in the distance. A few instants later the platform was quivering, and with puffs of steam hanging low in the air from the frost, the engine rolled up, with the lever of the middle wheel rhythmically moving up and down, and the stooping figure of the engine-driver covered with frost. Behind the tender, setting the platform more and more slowly swaying, came the luggage-van with a dog whining in it. At last the passenger carriages rolled in, oscillating before coming to a standstill.

A smart guard jumped out, giving a whistle, and after him one by one the impatient passengers began to get down: an officer of the guards, holding himself erect, and looking severely about him; a nimble little merchant with a satchel, smiling gaily; a peasant with a sack over his shoulder.

Vronsky, standing beside Oblonsky, watched the carriages and the passengers, totally oblivious of his mother. What he had just heard about Kitty excited and delighted him. Unconsciously he arched his chest, and his eyes flashed. He felt himself a conqueror.

"Countess Vronskaya is in that compartment," said the smart guard, going up to Vronsky.

The guard's words roused him, and forced him to think of his mother and his approaching meeting with her. He did not in his heart respect his mother, and without acknowledging it to himself, he did not love her, though in accordance with the ideas of the set in which he lived, and with his own education, he could not have conceived of any behavior to his mother not in the highest degree respectful and obedient, and the more externally obedient and respectful his behavior, the less in his heart he respected and loved her.

C H A P T E R   X V I I I

VRONSKY followed the guard to the carriage, and at the door of the compartment he stopped short to make room for a lady who was getting out.

With the insight of a man of the world, from one glance at this lady's appearance Vronsky classified her as belonging to the best society. He begged pardon, and was getting into the carriage, but felt he must glance at her once more; not that she was very beautiful, not on account of the elegance and modest grace which were apparent in her whole figure, but because in the expression of her charming face, as she passed close by him, there was something peculiarly caressing and soft. As he looked round, she too turned her head. Her shining gray eyes, that looked dark from the thick lashes, rested with friendly attention on his face, as though she were recognizing him, and then promptly turned away to the passing crowd, as though seeking some one. In that brief look Vronsky had time to notice the suppressed eagerness which played over her face, and flitted between the brilliant eyes and the faint smile that curved her red lips. It was as though her nature were so brimming over with something that against her will it showed itself now in the flash of her eyes, and now in her smile. Deliberately she shrouded the light in her eyes, but it shone against her will in the faintly perceptible smile.

Vronsky stepped into the carriage. His mother, a dried-up old lady with black eyes and ringlets, screwed up her eyes, scanning her son, and smiled slightly with her thin lips. Getting up from the seat and handing her maid a bag, she gave her little wrinkled hand to her son to kiss, and lifting his head from her hand, kissed him on the cheek.

"You got my telegram? Quite well? Thank God."

"You had a good journey?" said her son, sitting down beside her, and involuntarily listening to a woman's voice outside the door. He knew it was the voice of the lady he had met at the door.

"All the same I don't agree with you," said the lady's voice.

"It's the Petersburg view, madame."

"Not Petersburg, but simply feminine," she responded.

"Well, well, allow me to kiss your hand."

"Good-bye, Ivan Petrovitch. And would you see if my brother is here, and send him to me?" said the lady in the doorway, and stepped back again into the compartment.

"Well, have you found your brother?" said Countess Vronskaya, addressing the lady.

Vronsky understood now that this was Madame Karenina.

"Your brother is here," he said, standing up. "Excuse me, I did not know you, and, indeed, our acquaintance was so slight," said Vronsky bowing, "that no doubt you do not remember me."

"Oh, no," said she, "I should have known you because your mother and I have been talking, I think, of nothing but you all the way." As she spoke she let the eagerness that would insist on coming out show itself in her smile. "And still no sign of my brother."

"Do call him, Alexey," said the old countess. Vronsky stepped out onto the platform and shouted:

"Oblonsky! Here!"

Madame Karenina, however, did not wait for her brother, but catching sight of him she stepped out with her light, resolute step. And as soon as her brother had reached her, with a gesture that struck Vronsky by its decision and its grace, she flung her left arm around his neck, drew him rapidly to her, and kissed him warmly. Vronsky gazed, never taking his eyes from her, and smiled, he could not have said why. But recollecting that his mother was waiting for him, he went back again into the carriage.

"She's very sweet, isn't she?" said the countess of Madame Karenina. "Her husband put her with me, and I was delighted to

have her. We've been talking all the way. And so you, I hear . . .
vous filez le parfait amour. Tant mieux, mon cher, tant mieux."

"I don't know what you are referring to, maman," he answered
coldly. "Come, maman, let us go."

Madame Karenina entered the carriage again to say good-bye
to the countess.

"Well, countess, you have met your son, and I my brother,"
she said. "And all my gossip is exhausted. I should have nothing
more to tell you."

"Oh, no," said the countess, taking her hand. "I could go all
around the world with you and never be dull. You are one of those
delightful women in whose company it's sweet to be silent as well
as to talk. Now please don't fret over your son; you can't expect
never to be parted."

Madame Karenina stood quite still, holding herself very erect,
and her eyes were smiling.

"Anna Arkadyevna," the countess said in explanation to her
son, "has a little son eight years old, I believe, and she has never
been parted from him before, and she keeps fretting over leaving
him."

"Yes, the countess and I have been talking all the time, I of my
son and she of hers," said Madame Karenina, and again a smile
lighted up her face, a caressing smile intended for him.

"I am afraid that you must have been dreadfully bored," he
said, promptly catching the ball of coquetry she had flung him.
But apparently she did not care to pursue the conversation in that
strain, and she turned to the old countess.

"Thank you so much. The time has passed so quickly. Good-
bye, countess."

"Good-bye, my love," answered the countess. "Let me have a
kiss of your pretty face. I speak plainly, at my age, and I tell you
simply that I've lost my heart to you."

Stereotyped as the phrase was, Madame Karenina obviously
believed it and was delighted by it. She flushed, bent down
slightly, and put her cheek to the countess's lips, drew herself up
again, and with the same smile fluttering between her lips and
her eyes, she gave her hand to Vronsky. He pressed the little hand
she gave him, and was delighted, as though at something special,

by the energetic squeeze with which she freely and vigorously shook his hand. She went out with the rapid step which bore her rather fully-developed figure with such strange lightness.

"Very charming," said the countess.

That was just what her son was thinking. His eyes followed her till her graceful figure was out of sight, and then the smile remained on his face. He saw out of the window how she went up to her brother, put her arm in his, and began telling him something eagerly, obviously something that had nothing to do with him, Vronsky, and at that he felt annoyed.

"Well, maman, are you perfectly well?" he repeated, turning to his mother.

"Everything has been delightful. Alexander has been very good, and Marie has grown very pretty. She's very interesting."

And she began telling him again of what interested her most —the christening of her grandson, for which she had been staying in Petersburg, and the special favor shown her elder son by the Tsar.

"Here's Lavrenty," said Vronsky, looking out of the window; "now we can go, if you like."

The old butler who had traveled with the countess, came to the carriage to announce that everything was ready, and the countess got up to go.

"Come; there's not such a crowd now," said Vronsky.

The maid took a hand-bag and the lap-dog, the butler and a porter the other baggage. Vronsky gave his mother his arm; but just as they were getting out of the carriage several men ran suddenly by with panic-stricken faces. The station-master, too, ran by in his extraordinary colored cap. Obviously something unusual had happened. The crowd who had left the train were running back again.

"What? . . . What? . . . Where? . . . Flung himself! . . . Crushed! . . ." was heard among the crowd. Stepan Arkadyevitch, with his sister on his arm, turned back. They too looked scared, and stopped at the carriage door to avoid the crowd.

The ladies got in, while Vronsky and Stepan Arkadyevitch followed the crowd to find out details of the disaster.

A guard, either drunk or too much muffled up in the bitter

frost, had not heard the train moving back, and had been crushed.

Before Vronsky and Oblonsky came back the ladies heard the facts from the butler.

Oblonsky and Vronsky had both seen the mutilated corpse. Oblonsky was evidently upset. He frowned and seemed ready to cry.

"Ah, how awful! Ah, Anna, if you had seen it! Ah, how awful!" he said.

Vronsky did not speak; his handsome face was serious, but perfectly composed.

"Oh, if you had seen it, countess," said Stepan Arkadyevitch. "And his wife was there. . . . It was awful to see her! . . . She flung herself on the body. They say he was the only support of an immense family. How awful!"

"Couldn't one do anything for her?" said Madame Karenina in an agitated whisper.

Vronsky glanced at her, and immediately got out of the carriage.

"I'll be back directly, maman," he remarked, turning round in the doorway.

When he came back a few minutes later, Stepan Arkadyevitch was already in conversation with the countess about the new singer, while the countess was impatiently looking towards the door, waiting for her son.

"Now let us be off," said Vronsky, coming in. They went out together; Vronsky was in front with his mother. Behind walked Madame Karenina with her brother. Just as they were going out of the station the station-master overtook Vronsky.

"You gave my assistant two hundred roubles. Would you kindly explain for whose benefit you intend them?"

"For the widow," said Vronsky, shrugging his shoulders. "I should have thought there was no need to ask."

"You gave that?" cried Oblonsky, behind, and, pressing his sister's hand, he added: "Very nice, very nice! Isn't he a splendid fellow? Good-bye, countess."

And he and his sister stood still, looking for her maid.

When they went out the Vronskys' carriage had already driven away. People coming in were still talking of what happened.

"What a horrible death!" said a gentleman, passing by. "They say he was cut in two pieces."

"On the contrary, I think it's the easiest—instantaneous," observed another.

"How is it they don't take proper precautions?" said a third.

Madame Karenina seated herself in the carriage, and Stepan Arkadyevitch saw with surprise that her lips were quivering, and she was with difficulty restraining her tears.

"What is it, Anna?" he asked, when they had driven a few hundred yards.

"It's an omen of evil," she said.

"What nonsense!" said Stepan Arkadyevitch. "You've come, that's the chief thing. You can't conceive how I'm resting my hopes on you."

"Have you known Vronsky long?" she asked.

"Yes. You know we're hoping he will marry Kitty."

"Yes?" said Anna softly. "Come now, let us talk of you," she added, tossing her head, as though she would physically shake off something superfluous oppressing her. "Let us talk of your affairs. I got your letter, and here I am."

"Yes, all my hopes are in you," said Stepan Arkadyevitch.

"Well, tell me all about it."

And Stepan Arkadyevitch began to tell his story.

On reaching home Oblonsky helped his sister out, sighed, pressed her hand, and set off to his office.

CHAPTER XIX

WHEN Anna went into the room, Dolly was sitting in the little drawing-room with a white-headed fat little boy, already like his father, giving him a lesson in French reading. As the boy read, he kept twisting and trying to tear off a button that was nearly off his jacket. His mother had several times taken his hand from it, but the fat little hand went back to the button again. His mother pulled the button off and put it in her pocket.

"Keep your hands still, Grisha," she said, and she took up her work, a coverlet she had long been making. She always set to

work on it at depressed moments, and now she knitted at it nervously, twitching her fingers and counting the stitches. Though she had sent word the day before to her husband that it was nothing to her whether his sister came or not, she had made everything ready for her arrival, and was expecting her sister-in-law with emotion.

Dolly was crushed by her sorrow, utterly swallowed up by it. Still she did not forget that Anna, her sister-in-law, was the wife of one of the most important personages in Petersburg, and was a Petersburg *grande dame*. And, thanks to this circumstance, she did not carry out her threat to her husband—that is to say, she remembered that her sister-in-law was coming. "And, after all, Anna is in no wise to blame," thought Dolly. "I know nothing of her except the very best, and I have seen nothing but kindness and affection from her towards myself." It was true that as far as she could recall her impressions at Petersburg at the Karenins', she did not like their household itself; there was something artificial in the whole framework of their family life. "But why should I not receive her? If only she doesn't take it into her head to console me!" thought Dolly. "All consolation and counsel and Christian forgiveness, all that I have thought over a thousand times, and it's all no use."

All these days Dolly had been alone with her children. She did not want to talk of her sorrow, but with that sorrow in her heart she could not talk of outside matters. She knew that in one way or another she would tell Anna everything, and she was alternately glad at the thought of speaking freely, and angry at the necessity of speaking of her humiliation with her, his sister, and of hearing her ready-made phrases of good advice and comfort. She had been on the lookout for her, glancing at her watch every minute, and, as often happens, let slip just that minute when her visitor arrived, so that she did not hear the bell.

Catching a sound of skirts and light steps at the door, she looked round, and her care-worn face unconsciously expressed not gladness, but wonder. She got up and embraced her sister-in-law.

"What, here already!" she said as she kissed her.

"Dolly, how glad I am to see you!"

"I am glad, too," said Dolly, faintly smiling, and trying by the expression of Anna's face to find out whether she knew. "Most likely she knows," she thought, noticing the sympathy in Anna's face. "Well, come along, I'll take you to your room," she went on, trying to defer as long as possible the moment of confidences.

"Is this Grisha? Heavens, how he's grown!" said Anna; and kissing him, never taking her eyes off Dolly, she stood still and flushed a little. "No, please, let us stay here."

She took off her kerchief and her hat, and catching it in a lock of her black hair, which was a mass of curls, she tossed her head and shook her hair down.

"You are radiant with health and happiness!" said Dolly, almost with envy.

"I? . . . Yes," said Anna. "Merciful heavens, Tanya! You're the same age as my Seryozha," she added, addressing the little girl as she ran in. She took her in her arms and kissed her. "Delightful child, delightful! Show me them all."

She mentioned them, not only remembering the names, but the years, months, characters, illnesses of all the children, and Dolly could not but appreciate that.

"Very well, we will go to them," she said. "It's a pity Vassya's asleep."

After seeing the children, they sat down, alone now, in the drawing-room, to coffee. Anna took the tray, and then pushed it away from her.

"Dolly," she said, "he has told me."

Dolly looked coldly at Anna; she was waiting now for phrases of conventional sympathy, but Anna said nothing of the sort.

"Dolly, dear," she said, "I don't want to speak for him to you, nor to try to comfort you; that's impossible. But, darling, I'm simply sorry, sorry from my heart for you!"

Under the thick lashes of her shining eyes tears suddenly glittered. She moved nearer to her sister-in-law and took her hand in her vigorous little hand. Dolly did not shrink away, but her face did not lose its frigid expression. She said:

"To comfort me's impossible. Everything's lost after what has happened, everything's over!"

And directly she had said this, her face suddenly softened. Anna lifted the wasted, thin hand of Dolly, kissed it and said:

"But, Dolly, what's to be done, what's to be done? How is it best to act in this awful position—that's what you must think of."

"All's over, and there's nothing more," said Dolly. "And the worst of it all is, you see, that I can't cast him off: there are the children, I am tied. And I can't live with him! it's a torture to me to see him."

"Dolly, darling, he has spoken to me, but I want to hear it from you: tell me all about it."

Dolly looked at her inquiringly.

Sympathy and love unfeigned were visible on Anna's face.

"Very well," she said all at once. "But I will tell you it from the beginning. You know how I was married. With the education mamma gave us I was more than innocent, I was stupid. I knew nothing. I know they say men tell their wives of their former lives, but Stiva"—she corrected herself—"Stepan Arkadyevitch told me nothing. You'll hardly believe it, but till now I imagined that I was the only woman he had known. So I lived eight years. You must understand that I was so far from suspecting infidelity, I regarded it as impossible, and then—try to imagine it—with such ideas, to find out suddenly all the horror, all the loathsomeness. . . . You must try and understand me. To be fully convinced of one's happiness, and all at once . . ." continued Dolly, holding back her sobs, "to get a letter . . . his letter to his mistress, my governess. No, it's too awful!" She hastily pulled out her handkerchief and hid her face in it. "I can understand being carried away by feeling," she went on after a brief silence, "but deliberately, slyly deceiving me . . . and with whom? . . . To go on being my husband together with her . . . it's awful! You can't understand . . ."

"Oh, yes, I understand! I understand! Dolly, dearest, I do understand," said Anna, pressing her hand.

"And do you imagine he realizes all the awfulness of my position?" Dolly resumed. "Not the slightest! He's happy and contented."

"Oh, no!" Anna interposed quickly. "He's to be pitied, he's weighed down by remorse . . ."

"Is he capable of remorse?" Dolly interrupted, gazing intently into her sister-in-law's face.

"Yes. I know him. I could not look at him without feeling sorry for him. We both know him. He's good-hearted, but he's proud, and now he's so humiliated. What touched me most . . ." (and here Anna guessed what would touch Dolly most) "he's tortured by two things: that he's ashamed for the children's sake, and that, loving you—yes, yes, loving you beyond everything on earth," she hurriedly interrupted Dolly, who would have answered—"he has hurt you, pierced you to the heart. 'No, no, she cannot forgive me,' he keeps saying."

Dolly looked dreamily away beyond her sister-in-law as she listened to her words.

"Yes, I can see that his position is awful; it's worse for the guilty than the innocent," she said, "if he feels that all the misery comes from his fault. But how am I to forgive him, how am I to be his wife again after her? For me to live with him now would be torture, just because I love my past love for him. . . ."

And sobs cut short her words. But as though of set design, each time she was softened she began to speak again of what exasperated her.

"She's young, you see, she's pretty," she went on. "Do you know, Anna, my youth and my beauty are gone, taken by whom? By him and his children. I have worked for him, and all I had has gone in his service, and now of course any fresh, vulgar creature has more charm for him. No doubt they talked of me together, or, worse still, they were silent. Do you understand?"

Again her eyes glowed with hatred.

"And after that he will tell me . . . What! can I believe him?

Never! No, everything is over, everything that once made my comfort, the reward of my work, and my sufferings. . . . Would you believe it, I was teaching Grisha just now: once this was a joy to me, now it is a torture. What have I to strive and toil for? Why are the children here? What's so awful is that all at once my heart's turned, and instead of love and tenderness, I have nothing but hatred for him; yes, hatred. I could kill him."

"Darling Dolly, I understand, but don't torture yourself. You are so distressed, so overwrought, that you look at many things mistakenly."

Dolly grew calmer, and for two minutes both were silent.

"What's to be done? Think for me, Anna, help me. I have thought over everything, and I see nothing."

Anna could think of nothing, but her heart responded instantly to each word, to each change of expression of her sister-in-law.

"One thing I would say," began Anna. "I am his sister, I know his character, that faculty of forgetting everything, everything" (she waved her hand before her forehead), "that faculty for being completely carried away, but for completely repenting too. He cannot believe it, he cannot comprehend now how he can have acted as he did."

"No; he understands, he understood!" Dolly broke in. "But I . . . you are forgetting me . . . does it make it easier for me?"

"Wait a minute. When he told me, I will own I did not realize all the awfulness of your position. I saw nothing but him, and that the family was broken up. I felt sorry for him, but after talking to you, I see it, as a woman, quite differently. I see your agony, and I can't tell you how sorry I am for you! But, Dolly, darling, I fully realize your sufferings, only there is one thing I don't know; I don't know . . . I don't know how much love there is still in your heart for him. That you know—whether there is enough for you to be able to forgive him. If there is, forgive him!"

"No," Dolly was beginning, but Anna cut her short, kissing her hand once more.

"I know more of the world than you do," she said. "I know how men like Stiva look at it. You speak of his talking of you with her. That never happened. Such men are unfaithful, but their own home and wife are sacred to them. Somehow or other these women are still looked on with contempt by them, and do not touch on their feeling for their family. They draw a sort of line that can't be crossed between them and their families. I don't understand it, but it is so."

"Yes, but he has kissed her . . ."

"Dolly, hush, darling. I saw Stiva when he was in love with you. I remember the time when he came to me and cried, talking of you, and all the poetry and loftiness of his feeling for you, and I know that the longer he has lived with you the loftier you have been in his eyes. You know we have sometimes laughed at him for putting in at every word: 'Dolly's a marvelous woman.' You have always been a divinity for him, and you are that still, and this has not been an infidelity of the heart. . . ."

"But if it is repeated?"

"It cannot be, as I understand it. . . ."

"Yes, but could you forgive it?"

"I don't know, I can't judge. . . . Yes, I can," said Anna, thinking a moment; and grasping the position in her thought and weighing it in her inner balance, she added: "Yes, I can, I can, I can. Yes, I could forgive it. I could not be the same, no; but I could forgive it, and forgive it as though it had never been, never been at all. . . ."

"Oh, of course," Dolly interposed quickly, as though saying what she had more than once thought, "else it would not be forgiveness. If one forgives, it must be completely, completely. Come, let us go; I'll take you to your room," she said, getting up, and on the way she embraced Anna. "My dear, how glad I am you came. It has made things better, ever so much better."

CHAPTER XX

THE whole of that day Anna spent at home, that's to say at the Oblonskys', and received no one, though some of her acquaintances had already heard of her arrival, and came to call the same day. Anna spent the whole morning with Dolly and the children. She merely sent a brief note to her brother to tell him that he must not fail to dine at home. "Come, God is merciful," she wrote.

Oblonsky did dine at home: the conversation was general, and his wife, speaking to him, addressed him as "Stiva," as she had not done before. In the relations of the husband and wife the same estrangement still remained, but there was no talk now of separation, and Stepan Arkadyevitch saw the possibility of explanation and reconciliation.

Immediately after dinner Kitty came in. She knew Anna Arkadyevna, but only very slightly, and she came now to her sister's with some trepidation at the prospect of meeting this fashionable Petersburg lady, whom every one spoke so highly of. But she made a favorable impression on Anna Arkadyevna— she saw that at once. Anna was unmistakably admiring her love-liness and her youth: before Kitty knew where she was she found herself not merely under Anna's sway, but in love with her, as young girls do fall in love with older and married women. Anna was not like a fashionable lady, nor the mother of a boy of eight years old. In the elasticity of her movements, the freshness and the unflagging eagerness which persisted in her face and broke out in her smile and her glance, she would rather have passed for a girl of twenty, had it not been for a serious and at times mourn-ful look in her eyes, which struck and attracted Kitty. Kitty felt that Anna was perfectly simple and was concealing nothing, but that she had another higher world of interests inaccessible to her, complex and poetic.

After dinner, when Dolly went away to her own room, Anna rose quickly and went up to her brother, who was just lighting a cigar.

"Stiva," she said to him, winking gaily, crossing him, and glancing towards the door, "go, and God help you."

He threw down the cigar, understanding her, and departed through the doorway.

When Stepan Arkadyevitch had disappeared, she went back to the sofa where she had been sitting, surrounded by the children. Either because the children saw that their mother was fond of this aunt, or that they felt a special charm in her themselves, the two elder ones, and the younger following their lead, as children so often do, had clung about their new aunt since before dinner, and would not leave her side. And it had become a sort of game among them to sit as close as possible to their aunt, to touch her, hold her little hand, kiss it, play with her ring, or even touch the flounce of her skirt.

"Come, come, as we were sitting before," said Anna Arkadyevna, sitting down in her place.

And again Grisha poked his little face under her arm, and nestled with his head on her gown, beaming with pride and happiness.

"And when is your next ball?" she asked Kitty.

"Next week, and a splendid ball. One of those balls where one always enjoys oneself."

"Why, are there balls where one always enjoys oneself?" Anna said, with tender irony.

"It's strange, but there are. At the Bobrishtchevs' one always enjoys oneself, and at the Nikitins' too, while at the Mezhkovs' it's always dull. Haven't you noticed it?"

"No, my dear, for me there are no balls now where one enjoys oneself," said Anna, and Kitty detected in her eyes that mysterious world which was not open to her. "For me there are some less dull and tiresome."

"How can *you* be dull at a ball?"

"Why should not *I* be dull at a ball?" inquired Anna.

Kitty perceived that Anna knew what answer would follow.

"Because you always look nicer than any one."

Anna had the faculty of blushing. She blushed a little, and said:

"In the first place it's never so; and secondly, if it were, what difference would it make to me?"

"Are you coming to this ball?" asked Kitty.

"I imagine it won't be possible to avoid going. Here, take it," she said to Tanya, who was pulling the loosely-fitting ring off her white, slender-tipped finger.

"I shall be so glad if you go. I should so like to see you at a ball."

"Anyway, if I do go, I shall comfort myself with the thought that it's a pleasure to you. . . . Grisha, don't pull my hair. It's untidy enough without that," she said, putting up a straying lock, which Grisha had been playing with.

"I imagine you at the ball in lilac."

"And why in lilac precisely?" asked Anna, smiling. "Now, children, run along, run along. Do you hear? Miss Hoole is calling you to tea," she said, tearing the children from her, and sending them off to the dining-room.

"I know why you press me to come to the ball. You expect a great deal of this ball, and you want every one to be there to take part in it."

"How do you know? Yes."

"Oh! what a happy time you are at," pursued Anna. "I remember, and I know that blue haze like the mist on the mountains in Switzerland. That mist which covers everything in that blissful time when childhood is just ending, and out of that vast circle, happy and gay, there is a path growing narrower and narrower, and it is delightful and alarming to enter the ballroom, bright and splendid as it is. . . . Who has not been through it?"

Kitty smiled without speaking. "But how did she go through it? How I should like to know all her love-story!" thought Kitty, recalling the unromantic appearance of Alexey Alexandrovitch, her husband.

"I know something. Stiva told me, and I congratulate you. I liked him so much," Anna continued. "I met Vronsky at the railway station."

"Oh, was he there?" asked Kitty, blushing. "What was it Stiva told you?"

"Stiva gossiped about it all. And I should be so glad. . . . I traveled yesterday with Vronsky's mother," she went on; "and his mother talked without a pause of him, he's her favorite. I know mothers are partial, but . . ."

"What did his mother tell you?"

"Oh, a great deal! And I know that he's her favorite; still one can see how chivalrous he is . . . Well, for instance, she told me that he had wanted to give up all his property to his brother, that he had done something extraordinary when he was quite a child, saved a woman out of the water. He's a hero, in fact," said Anna, smiling and recollecting the two hundred roubles he had given at the station.

But she did not tell Kitty about the two hundred roubles. For some reason it was disagreeable to her to think of it. She felt that there was something that had to do with her in it, and something that ought not to have been.

"She pressed me very much to go and see her," Anna went on; "and I shall be glad to go to see her to-morrow. Stiva is staying a long while in Dolly's room, thank God," Anna added, changing the subject, and getting up, Kitty fancied, displeased with something.

"No, I'm first! No, I!" screamed the children, who had finished tea, running up to their Aunt Anna.

"All together," said Anna, and she ran laughing to meet them, and embraced and swung round all the throng of swarming children, shrieking with delight.

CHAPTER XXI

DOLLY came out of her room to the tea of the grown-up people. Stepan Arkadyevitch did not come out. He must have left his wife's room by the other door.

"I am afraid you'll be cold up-stairs," observed Dolly, addressing Anna; "I want to move you down-stairs, and we shall be nearer."

"Oh, please, don't trouble about me," answered Anna, looking intently into Dolly's face, trying to make out whether there had been a reconciliation or not.

"It will be lighter for you here," answered her sister-in-law.

"I assure you that I sleep everywhere, and always like a marmot."

. "What's the question?" inquired Stepan Arkadyevitch, coming out of his room and addressing his wife.

From his tone both Kitty and Anna knew that a reconciliation had taken place.

"I want to move Anna down-stairs, but we must hang up blinds. No one knows how to do it; I must see to it myself," answered Dolly addressing him.

"God knows whether they are fully reconciled," thought Anna, hearing her tone, cold and composed.

"Oh, nonsense, Dolly, always making difficulties," answered her husband. "Come, I'll do it all, if you like. . . ."

"Yes, they must be reconciled," thought Anna.

"I know how you do everything," answered Dolly. "You tell Matvey to do what can't be done, and go away yourself, leaving him to make a muddle of everything," and her habitual, mocking smile curved the corners of Dolly's lips as she spoke.

"Full, full reconciliation, full," thought Anna; "thank God!" and rejoicing that she was the cause of it, she went up to Dolly and kissed her.

"Not at all. Why do you always look down on me and Matvey?" said Stepan Arkadyevitch, smiling hardly perceptibly, and addressing his wife.

The whole evening Dolly was, as always, a little mocking in her tone to her husband, while Stepan Arkadyevitch was happy and cheerful, but not so as to seem as though, having been forgiven, he had forgotten his offense.

At half-past nine o'clock a particularly joyful and pleasant family conversation over the tea-table at the Oblonskys' was broken up by an apparently simple incident. But this simple incident for some reason struck every one as strange. Talking about common acquaintances in Petersburg, Anna got up quickly.

"She is in my album," she said; "and, by the way, I'll show you my Seryozha," she added, with a mother's smile of pride.

Towards ten o'clock, when she usually said good-night to her son, and often before going to a ball put him to bed herself, she felt depressed at being so far from him; and whatever she was talking about, she kept coming back in thought to her curly-headed Seryozha. She longed to look at his photograph and talk of him. Seizing the first pretext, she got up, and with her light, resolute step went for her album. The stairs up to her room came out on the landing of the great warm main staircase.

Just as she was leaving the drawing-room, a ring was heard in the hall.

"Who can that be?" said Dolly.

"It's early for me to be fetched, and for any one else it's late," observed Kitty.

"Sure to be some one with papers for me," put in Stepan Arkadyevitch. When Anna was passing the top of the staircase, a servant was running up to announce the visitor, while the visitor himself was standing under a lamp. Anna glancing down at once recognized Vronsky, and a strange feeling of pleasure and at the same time of dread of something stirred in her heart. He was standing still, not taking off his coat, pulling something out of his pocket. At the instant when she was just facing the stairs, he raised his eyes, caught sight of her, and into the expression of his face there passed a shade of embarrassment and dismay. With a slight inclination of her head she passed, hearing behind her Stepan Arkadyevitch's loud voice calling him to come up, and the quiet, soft, and composed voice of Vronsky refusing.

When Anna returned with the album, he was already gone, and Stepan Arkadyevitch was telling them that he had called to inquire about the dinner they were giving next day to a celebrity who had just arrived. "And nothing would induce him to come up. What a queer fellow he is!" added Stepan Arkadyevitch.

Kitty blushed. She thought that she was the only person who knew why he had come, and why he would not come up. "He has been at home," she thought, "and didn't find me, and thought I should be here, but he did not come up because he thought it late, and Anna's here."

All of them looked at each other, saying nothing, and began to look at Anna's album.

There was nothing either exceptional or strange in a man's calling at half-past nine on a friend to inquire details of a proposed dinner-party and not coming in, but it seemed strange to all of them. Above all, it seemed strange and not right to Anna.

CHAPTER XXII

THE ball was only just beginning as Kitty and her mother walked up the great staircase, flooded with light, and lined with flowers and footmen in powder and red coats. From the rooms came a constant, steady hum, as from a hive, and the rustle of movement; and while on the landing between plants they gave last touches to their hair and dresses before the mirror, they heard from the ballroom the careful, distinct notes of the fiddles of the orchestra beginning the first waltz. A little old man in civilian dress, arranging his gray curls before another mirror, and diffusing an odor of scent, stumbled against them on the stairs, and stood aside, evidently admiring Kitty, whom he did not know. A beardless youth, one of those society youths whom the old Prince Shtcherbatsky called "young bucks," in an exceedingly open waistcoat, straightening his white tie as he went, bowed to them, and after running by, came back to ask Kitty for a quadrille. As the first quadrille had already been given to Vronsky, she had to promise this youth the second. An officer, buttoning his glove, stood aside in the doorway, and, stroking his mustache, admired rosy Kitty.

Although her dress, her coiffure, and all the preparations for the ball had cost Kitty great trouble and consideration, at this moment she walked into the ballroom in her elaborate tulle dress over a pink slip as easily and simply as though all the rosettes and lace, all the minute details of her attire, had not cost her or her family a moment's attention, as though she had been born in that tulle and lace, with her hair done up high on her head, and a rose and two leaves on the top of it.

When, just before entering the ballroom, the princess, her mother, tried to turn right side out the ribbon of her sash, Kitty had drawn back a little. She felt that everything must be right of itself, and graceful, and nothing could need setting straight.

92

It was one of Kitty's best days. Her dress was not uncomfortable anywhere; her lace berthe did not droop anywhere; her rosettes were not crushed nor torn off; her pink slippers with high, hollowed-out heels did not pinch, but gladdened her feet; and the thick rolls of fair chignon kept up on her head as if they were her own hair. All the three buttons buttoned up without tearing on the long glove that covered her hand without concealing its lines. The black velvet of her locket nestled with special softness round her neck. That velvet was delicious; at home, looking at her neck in the looking-glass, Kitty had felt that that velvet was speaking. About all the rest there might be a doubt, but the velvet was delicious. Kitty smiled here too, at the ball, when she glanced at it in the glass. Her bare shoulders and arms gave Kitty a sense of chill marble, a feeling she particularly liked. Her eyes sparkled, and her rosy lips could not keep from smiling from the consciousness of her own attractiveness. She had scarcely entered the ballroom and reached the throng of ladies, all tulle, ribbons, lace, and flowers, waiting to be asked to dance—Kitty was never one of that throng—when she was asked for a waltz, and asked by the best partner, the first star in the hierarchy of the ballroom, a renowned director of dances, a married man, handsome and well-built, Yegorushka Korsunsky. He had only just left the Countess Bonina, with whom he had danced the first half of the waltz, and, scanning his kingdom—that is to say, a few couples who had started dancing—he caught sight of Kitty, entering, and flew up to her with that peculiar, easy amble which is confined to directors of balls. Without even asking her if she cared to dance, he put out his arm to encircle her slender waist. She looked round for some one to give her fan to, and their hostess, smiling to her, took it.

"How nice you've come in good time," he said to her, embracing her waist; "such a bad habit to be late." Bending her left hand, she laid it on his shoulder, and her little feet in their pink slippers began swiftly, lightly, and rhythmically moving over the slippery floor in time to the music.

"It's a rest to waltz with you," he said to her, as they fell into the first slow steps of the waltz. "It's exquisite—such lightness, precision." He said to her the same thing he said to almost all his partners whom he knew well.

She smiled at his praise, and continued to look about the room over his shoulder. She was not like a girl at her first ball, for whom all faces in the ballroom melt into one vision of fairyland. And she was not a girl who had gone the stale round of balls till every face in the ballroom was familiar and tiresome. But she was in the middle stage between these two; she was excited, and at the same time she had sufficient self-possession to be able to observe. In the left corner of the ballroom she saw the cream of society gathered together. There—incredibly naked—was the beauty Lidi, Korsunsky's wife; there was the lady of the house; there shone the bald head of Krivin, always to be found where the best people were. In that direction gazed the young men, not venturing to approach. There, too, she descried Stiva, and there she saw the exquisite figure and head of Anna in a black velvet gown. And *he* was there. Kitty had not seen him since the evening she refused Levin. With her long-sighted eyes, she knew him at once, and was even aware that he was looking at her.

"Another turn, eh? You're not tired?" said Korsunsky, a little out of breath.

"No, thank you!"

"Where shall I take you?"

"Madame Karenina's here, I think . . . take me to her."

"Wherever you command."

And Korsunsky began waltzing with measured steps straight towards the group in the left corner, continually saying, "Pardon, mesdames, pardon, pardon, mesdames"; and steering his course through the sea of lace, tulle, and ribbon, and not disarranging a feather, he turned his partner sharply round, so that her slim ankles, in light, transparent stockings, were exposed to view, and her train floated out in fan shape and covered Krivin's knees. Korsunsky bowed, set straight his open shirt-front, and gave her his arm to conduct her to Anna Arkadyevna. Kitty, flushed, took her train from Krivin's knees, and, a little giddy, looked round, seeking Anna. Anna was not in lilac, as Kitty had so urgently wished, but in a black, low-cut, velvet gown, showing her full throat and shoulders, that looked as though carved in old ivory, and her rounded arms, with tiny, slender wrists. The whole gown was trimmed with Venetian guipure. On her head, among her black hair—her own, with no false additions—was a little wreath of pansies, and a bouquet of the same in the black ribbon of her sash among white lace. Her coiffure was not striking. All that was noticeable was the little wilful tendrils of her curly hair that would always break free about her neck and temples. Round her well-cut, strong neck was a thread of pearls.

Kitty had been seeing Anna every day; she adored her, and had pictured her invariably in lilac. But now seeing her in black, she felt that she had not fully seen her charm. She saw her now as some one quite new and surprising to her. Now she understood that Anna could not have been in lilac, and that her charm was just that she always stood out against her attire, that her dress could never be noticeable on her. And her black dress, with its sumptuous lace, was not noticeable on her; it was only the frame, and all that was seen was she—simple, natural, elegant, and at the same time gay and eager.

She was standing holding herself, as always, very erect, and when Kitty drew near the group she was speaking to the master of the house, her head slightly turned towards him.

"No, I don't throw stones," she was saying, in answer to something, "though I can't understand it," she went on, shrugging her shoulders, and she turned at once with a soft smile of protection towards Kitty. With a flying, feminine glance she scanned her attire, and made a movement of her head, hardly perceptible, but understood by Kitty, signifying approval of her dress and her looks. "You came into the room dancing," she added.

"This is one of my most faithful supporters," said Korsunsky, bowing to Anna Arkadyevna, whom he had not yet seen. "The princess helps to make balls happy and successful. Anna Arkadyevna, a waltz?" he said, bending down to her.

"Why, have you met?" inquired their host.

"Is there any one we have not met? My wife and I are like white wolves—every one knows us," answered Korsunsky. "A waltz, Anna Arkadyevna?"

"I don't dance when it's possible not to dance," she said.

"But to-night it's impossible," answered Korsunsky.

At that instant Vronsky came up.

"Well, since it's impossible to-night, let us start," she said, not noticing Vronsky's bow, and she hastily put her hand on Korsunsky's shoulder.

"What is she vexed with him about?" thought Kitty, discerning that Anna had intentionally not responded to Vronsky's bow. Vronsky went up to Kitty reminding her of the first quadrille, and expressing his regret that he had not seen her all this time. Kitty gazed in admiration at Anna waltzing, and listened to him. She expected him to ask her for a waltz, but he did not, and she glanced wonderingly at him. He flushed slightly, and hurriedly asked her to waltz, but he had only just put his arm round her waist and taken the first step when the music suddenly stopped. Kitty looked into his face, which was so close to her own, and long afterwards—for several years after—that look, full of love, to which he made no response, cut her to the heart with an agony of shame.

"Pardon! pardon! Waltz! waltz!" shouted Korsunsky from the other side of the room, and seizing the first young lady he came across he began dancing himself.

CHAPTER XXIII

VRONSKY and Kitty waltzed several times round the room. After the first waltz Kitty went to her mother, and she had hardly time to say a few words to Countess Nordston when Vronsky came up again for the first quadrille. During the quadrille nothing of any significance was said : there was disjointed talk between them of the Korsunskys, husband and wife, whom he described very amusingly, as delightful children at forty, and of the future town theater ; and only once the conversation touched her to the quick, when he asked her about Levin, whether he was here, and added that he liked him so much. But Kitty did not expect much from the quadrille. She looked forward with a thrill at her heart to the mazurka. She fancied that in the mazurka everything must be decided. The fact that he did not during the quadrille ask her for the mazurka did not trouble her. She felt sure she would dance the mazurka with him as she had done at former balls, and refused five young men, saying she was engaged for the mazurka.

The whole ball up to the last quadrille was for Kitty an enchanted vision of delightful colors, sounds, and motions. She only sat down when she felt too tired and begged for a rest. But as she was dancing the last quadrille with one of the tiresome young men whom she could not refuse, she chanced to be *vis-à-vis* with Vronsky and Anna. She had not been near Anna again since the beginning of the evening, and now again she saw her suddenly quite new and surprising. She saw in her the signs of that excitement of success she knew so well in herself; she saw that she was intoxicated with the delighted admiration she was exciting. She knew that feeling and knew its signs, and saw them in Anna; saw the quivering, flashing light in her eyes, and the smile of happiness and excitement unconsciously playing on her lips, and the deliberate grace, precision, and lightness of her movements.

"Who?" she asked herself. "All or one?" And not assisting the harassed young man she was dancing with in the conversation, the thread of which he had lost and could not pick up again, she obeyed with external liveliness the peremptory shouts of Korsunsky starting them all into the *grand rond,* and then into the *chaîne,* and at the same time she kept watch with a growing pang at her heart. "No, it's not the admiration of the crowd has intoxicated her, but the adoration of one. And that one? can it be he?" Every time he spoke to Anna the joyous light flashed into her eyes, and the smile of happiness curved her red lips. She seemed to make an effort to control herself, to try not to show these signs of delight, but they came out on her face of themselves. "But what of him?" Kitty looked at him and was filled with terror. What was pictured so clearly to Kitty in the mirror of

Anna's face she saw in him. What had become of his always self-possessed resolute manner, and the carelessly serene expression of his face? Now every time he turned to her, he bent his head, as though he would have fallen at her feet, and in his eyes there was nothing but humble submission and dread. "I would not offend you," his eyes seemed every time to be saying, "but I want to save myself, and I don't know how." On his face was a look such as Kitty had never seen before.

They were speaking of common acquaintances, keeping up the most trivial conversation, but to Kitty it seemed that every word they said was determining their fate and hers. And strange it was that they were actually talking of how absurd Ivan Ivanovitch was with his French, and how the Eletskaya girl might have made a better match, yet these words had all the while consequence for them, and they were feeling just as Kitty did. The whole ball, the whole world, everything seemed lost in fog in Kitty's soul. Nothing but the stern discipline of her bringing-up supported her and forced her to do what was expected of her, that is, to dance, to answer questions, to talk, even to smile. But before the mazurka, when they were beginning to rearrange the chairs and a few couples moved out of the smaller rooms into the big room, a moment of despair and horror came for Kitty. She had refused five partners, and now she was not dancing the mazurka. She had not even a hope of being asked for it, because she was so successful in society that the idea would never occur to any one that she had remained disengaged till now. She would have to tell her mother she felt ill and go home, but she had not the strength to do this. She felt crushed. She went to the furthest end of the little drawing-room and sank into a low chair. Her light, transparent skirts rose like a cloud about her slender waist; one bare, thin, soft, girlish arm, hanging listlessly, was lost in the folds of her pink tunic; in the other she held her fan, and with rapid, short strokes fanned her burning face. But while she looked like a butterfly, clinging to a blade of grass, and just about to open its rainbow wings for fresh flight, her heart ached with a horrible despair.

"But perhaps I am wrong, perhaps it was not so?" And again she recalled all she had seen.

"Kitty, what is it?" said Countess Nordston, stepping noiselessly over the carpet towards her. "I don't understand it."

Kitty's lower lip began to quiver; she got up quickly.

"Kitty, you're not dancing the mazurka?"

"No, no," said Kitty in a voice shaking with tears.

"He asked her for the mazurka before me," said Countess Nordston, knowing Kitty would understand who were "he" and "her."

"She said: 'Why, aren't you going to dance it with Princess Shtcherbatskaya?'"

"Oh, I don't care!" answered Kitty.

No one but she herself understood her position; no one knew that she had just refused the man whom perhaps she loved, and refused him because she had put her faith in another.

Countess Nordston found Korsunsky, with whom she was to dance the mazurka, and told him to ask Kitty.

Kitty danced in the first couple, and luckily for her she had not to talk, because Korsunsky was all the time running about directing the figure. Vronsky and Anna sat almost opposite her. She saw them with her long-sighted eyes, and saw them, too, close by, when they met in the figures, and the more she saw of them the more convinced was she that her unhappiness was complete. She saw that they felt themselves alone in that crowded room. And on Vronsky's face, always so firm and independent, she saw that look that had struck her, of bewilderment and humble submissiveness, like the expression of an intelligent dog when it has done wrong.

Anna smiled, and her smile was reflected by him. She grew thoughtful, and he became serious. Some supernatural force drew Kitty's eyes to Anna's face. She was fascinating in her simple black dress, fascinating were her round arms with their bracelets, fascinating was her firm neck with its thread of pearls, fascinating the straying curls of her loose hair, fascinating the graceful, light movements of her little feet and hands, fascinating was that lovely face in its eagerness, but there was something terrible and cruel in her fascination.

Kitty admired her more than ever, and more and more acute was her suffering. Kitty felt overwhelmed, and her face showed it. When Vronsky saw her, coming across her in the mazurka, he did not at once recognize her, she was so changed.

"Delightful ball!" he said to her, for the sake of saying something.

"Yes," she answered.

In the middle of the mazurka, repeating a complicated figure, newly invented by Korsunsky, Anna came forward into the center of the circle, chose two gentlemen, and summoned a lady and Kitty. Kitty gazed at her in dismay as she went up. Anna looked at her with drooping eyelids, and smiled, pressing her hand. But, noticing that Kitty only responded to her smile by a look of despair and amazement, she turned away from her, and began gaily talking to the other lady.

"Yes, there is something uncanny, devilish and fascinating in her," Kitty said to herself.

Anna did not mean to stay to supper, but the master of the house began to press her to do so.

"Nonsense, Anna Arkadyevna," said Korsunsky, drawing her bare arm under the sleeve of his dress coat, "I've such an idea for a *cotillon! Un bijou!*"

And he moved gradually on, trying to draw her along with him. Their host smiled approvingly.

"No, I am not going to stay," answered Anna, smiling, but in spite of her smile, both Korsunsky and the master of the house saw from her resolute tone that she would not stay.

"No; why, as it is, I have danced more at your ball in Moscow than I have all the winter in Petersburg," said Anna, looking round at Vronsky, who stood near her. "I must rest a little before my journey."

"Are you certainly going to-morrow then?" asked Vronsky.

"Yes, I suppose so," answered Anna, as it were wondering at the boldness of his question; but the irrepressible, quivering brilliance of her eyes and her smile set him on fire as she said it.

Anna Arkadyevna did not stay to supper, but went home.

CHAPTER XXIV

"Yes, there is something in me hateful, repulsive," thought Levin, as he came away from the Shtcherbatskys', and walked in the direction of his brother's lodgings. "And I don't get on with

100

other people. Pride, they say. No, I have no pride. If I had any pride, I should not have put myself in such a position." And he pictured to himself Vronsky, happy, good-natured, clever, and self-possessed, certainly never placed in the awful position in which he had been that evening. "Yes, she was bound to choose him. So it had to be, and I cannot complain of any one or anything. I am myself to blame. What right had I to imagine she would care to join her life to mine? Who am I and what am I? A nobody, not wanted by any one, nor of use to anybody." And he recalled his brother Nikolay, and dwelt with pleasure on the thought of him. "Isn't he right that everything in the world is base and loathsome? And are we fair in our judgment of brother Nikolay? Of course, from the point of view of Prokofy, seeing him in a torn cloak and tipsy, he's a despicable person. But I know him differently. I know his soul, and know that we are like him. And I, instead of going to seek him out, went out to dinner, and came here." Levin walked up to a lamp-post, read his brother's address, which was in his pocketbook, and called a sledge. All the long way to his brother's, Levin vividly recalled all the facts familiar to him of his brother Nikolay's life. He remembered how his brother, while at the university, and for a year afterwards, had, in spite of the jeers of his companions, lived like a monk, strictly observing all religious rites, services, and fasts, and avoiding every sort of pleasure, especially women. And afterwards, how he had all at once broken out: he had associated with the most horrible people, and rushed into the most senseless debauchery. He remembered later the scandal over a boy, whom he had taken from the country to bring up, and, in a fit of rage, had so violently beaten that proceedings were brought against him for unlawfully wounding. Then he recalled the scandal with a sharper, to whom he had lost money, and given a promissory note, and against whom he had himself lodged a complaint, asserting that he had cheated him. (This was the money Sergey Ivanovitch had paid.) Then he remembered how he had spent a night in the lockup for disorderly conduct in the street. He remembered the shameful proceedings he had tried to get up against his brother Sergey Ivanovitch, accusing him of not having paid him his share of his mother's fortune, and the last scandal, when he had gone to a western province in an official capacity, and there had got into trouble for assaulting a village elder. . . . It was all horribly disgusting, yet to Levin it appeared not at all in the same disgusting light as it inevitably would to those who did not know Nikolay, did not know all his story, did not know his heart.

Levin remembered that when Nikolay had been in the devout stage, the period of fasts and monks and church services, when he was seeking in religion a support and a curb for his passionate temperament, every one, far from encouraging him, had jeered at him, and he, too, with the others. They had teased him, called him Noah and Monk; and, when he had broken out, no one had helped him, but every one had turned away from him with horror and disgust.

Levin felt that, in spite of all the ugliness of his life, his brother Nikolay, in his soul, in the very depths of his soul, was no more in the wrong than the people who despised him. He was not to blame for having been born with his unbridled temperament and his somehow limited intelligence. But he had always wanted to be good. "I will tell him everything, without reserve, and I will make him speak without reserve, too, and I'll show him that I love him, and so understand him," Levin resolved to himself, as, towards eleven o'clock, he reached the hotel of which he had the address.

"At the top, 12 and 13," the porter answered Levin's inquiry.

"At home?"

"Sure to be at home."

The door of No. 12 was half open, and there came out into the streak of light thick fumes of cheap, poor tobacco, and the sound of a voice, unknown to Levin; but he knew at once that his brother was there; he heard his cough.

As he went in at the door, the unknown voice was saying:

"It all depends with how much judgment and knowledge the thing's done."

Konstantin Levin looked in at the door, and saw that the speaker was a young man with an immense shock of hair, wearing a Russian jerkin, and that a pockmarked woman in a woolen gown, without collar or cuffs, was sitting on the sofa. His brother was not to be seen. Konstantin felt a sharp pang at his heart at the thought of the strange company in which his brother spent his life. No one had heard him, and Konstantin, taking off his goloshes, listened to what the gentleman in the jerkin was saying. He was speaking of some enterprise.

"Well, the devil flay them, the privileged classes," his brother's voice responded, with a cough. "Masha! get us some supper and some wine if there's any left; or else go and get some."

The woman rose, came out from behind the screen, and saw Konstantin.

"There's some gentleman, Nikolay Dmitrievitch," she said.

"Whom do you want?" said the voice of Nikolay Levin, angrily.

"It's I," answered Konstantin Levin, coming forward into the light.

"Who's *I?*" Nikolay's voice said again, still more angrily. He could be heard getting up hurriedly, stumbling against something, and Levin saw, facing him in the doorway, the big, scared eyes, and the huge, thin, stooping figure of his brother, so familiar, and yet astonishing in its weirdness and sickliness.

He was even thinner than three years before, when Konstantin Levin had seen him last. He was wearing a short coat, and his hands and big bones seemed huger than ever. His hair had grown thinner, the same straight mustaches hid his lips, the same eyes gazed strangely and naïvely at his visitor.

"Ah, Kostya!" he exclaimed suddenly, recognizing his brother, and his eyes lighted up with joy. But the same second he looked round at the young man, and gave the nervous jerk of his head and neck that Konstantin knew so well, as if his neckband hurt him; and a quite different expression, wild, suffering, and cruel, rested on his emaciated face.

"I wrote to you and Sergey Ivanovitch both that I don't know you and don't want to know you. What is it you want?"

He was not at all same as Konstantin had been fancying him. The worst and most tiresome part of his character, what made all relations with him so difficult, had been forgotten by Konstantin Levin when he thought of him, and now, when he saw his face, and especially that nervous twitching of his head, he remembered it all.

"I didn't want to see you for anything," he answered timidly. "I've simply come to see you."

His brother's timidity obviously softened Nikolay. His lips twitched.

"Oh, so that's it?" he said. "Well, come in; sit down. Like some supper? Masha, bring supper for three. No, stop a minute. Do you know who this is?" he said, addressing his brother, and indicating the gentleman in the jerkin: "This is Mr. Kritsky, my friend from Kiev, a very remarkable man. He's persecuted by the police, of course, because he's not a scoundrel."

And he looked round in the way he always did at every one in the room. Seeing that the woman standing in the doorway was moving to go, he shouted to her, "Wait a minute, I said." And with the inability to express himself, the incoherence that Konstantin knew so well, he began, with another look round at every one, to tell his brother Kritsky's story: how he had been expelled from the university for starting a benefit society for the poor students and Sunday-schools; and how he had afterwards been a teacher in a peasant school, and how he had been driven out of that too, and had afterwards been condemned for something.

"You're of the Kiev university?" said Konstantin Levin to Kritsky, to break the awkward silence that followed.

"Yes, I was of Kiev," Kritsky replied angrily, his face darkening.

"And this woman," Nikolay Levin interrupted him, pointing to her, "is the partner of my life, Marya Nikolaevna. I took her out of a bad house," and he jerked his neck saying this; "but I love her and respect her, and any one who wants to know me," he added, raising his voice and knitting his brows, "I beg to love her and respect her. She's just the same as my wife, just the same. So now you know whom you've got to do with. And if you think you're lowering yourself, well, here's the floor, there's the door."

And again his eyes traveled inquiringly over all of them.

"Why I should be lowering myself, I don't understand."

"Then, Masha, tell them to bring supper; three portions, spirits and wine. . . . No, wait a minute. . . . No, it doesn't matter. . . . Go along."

"So you see," pursued Nikolay Levin, painfully wrinkling his forehead and twitching.

It was obviously difficult for him to think of what to say and do.

"Here, do you see?" . . . He pointed to some sort of iron bars, fastened together with strings, lying in a corner of the room. "Do you see that? That's the beginning of a new thing we're going into. It's a productive association. . . ."

Konstantin scarcely heard him. He looked into his sickly, consumptive face, and he was more and more sorry for him, and he could not force himself to listen to what his brother was telling him about the association. He saw that this association was a mere anchor to save him from self-contempt. Nikolay Levin went on talking:

"You know that capital oppresses the laborer. The laborers with us, the peasants, bear all the burden of labor, and are so placed that however much they work they can't escape from their position of beasts of burden. All the profits of labor, on which they might improve their position, and gain leisure for themselves, and after that education, all the surplus values are taken from them by the capitalists. And society's so constituted that the harder they work, the greater the profit of the merchants and landowners, while they stay beasts of burden to the end. And that state of things must be changed," he finished up, and he looked questioningly at his brother.

"Yes, of course," said Konstantin, looking at the patch of red that had come out on his brother's projecting cheek-bones.

"And so we're founding a locksmiths' association, where all the production and profit and the chief instruments of production will be in common."

"Where is the association to be?" asked Konstantin Levin.

"In the village of Vozdrem, Kazan government."

"But why in a village? In the villages, I think, there is plenty of work as it is. Why a locksmiths' association in a village?"

"Why? Because the peasants are just as much slaves as they

ever were, and that's why you and Sergey Ivanovitch don't like people to try and get them out of their slavery," said Nikolay Levin, exasperated by the objection.

Konstantin Levin sighed, looking meanwhile about the cheerless and dirty room. This sigh seemed to exasperate Nikolay still more.

"I know your and Sergey Ivanovitch's aristocratic views. I know that he applies all the power of his intellect to justify existing evils."

"No; and what do you talk of Sergey Ivanovitch for?" said Levin, smiling.

"Sergey Ivanovitch? I'll tell you what for!" Nikolay Levin shrieked suddenly at the name of Sergey Ivanovitch. "I'll tell you what for. . . . But what's the use of talking? There's only one thing. . . . What did you come to me for? You look down on this, and you're welcome to,—and go away, in God's name go away!" he shrieked, getting up from his chair. "And go away, and go away!"

"I don't look down on it at all," said Konstantin Levin timidly. "I don't even dispute it."

At that instant Marya Nikolaevna came back. Nikolay Levin looked round angrily at her. She went quickly to him, and whispered something.

"I'm not well; I've grown irritable," said Nikolay Levin, getting calmer and breathing painfully; "and then you talk to me of Sergey Ivanovitch and his article. It's such rubbish, such lying, such self-deception. What can a man write of justice who knows nothing of it? Have you read his article?" he asked Kritsky, sitting down again at the table, and moving back off half of it the scattered cigarettes, so as to clear a space.

"I've not read it," Kritsky responded gloomily, obviously not desiring to enter into the conversation.

"Why not?" said Nikolay Levin, now turning with exasperation upon Kritsky.

"Because I didn't see the use of wasting my time over it."

"Oh, but excuse me, how did you know it would be wasting your time? That article's too deep for many people—that's to say it's over their heads. But with me, it's another thing; I see through his ideas, and I know where its weakness lies."

Every one was mute. Kritsky got up deliberately and reached his cap.

"Won't you have supper? All right, good-bye! Come round to-morrow with the locksmith."

Kritsky had hardly gone out when Nikolay Levin smiled and winked.

"He's no good either," he said. "I see, of course . . ."

But at that instant Kritsky, at the door, called him. . . .

"What do you want now?" he said, and went out to him in the passage. Left alone with Marya Nikolaevna, Levin turned to her.

"Have you been long with my brother?" he said to her.

"Yes, more than a year. Nikolay Dmitrievitch's health has become very poor. Nikolay Dmitrievitch drinks a great deal," she said.

"That is . . . how does he drink?"

"Drinks vodka, and it's bad for him."

"And a great deal?" whispered Levin.

"Yes," she said, looking timidly towards the doorway, where Nikolay Levin had reappeared.

"What were you talking about?" he said, knitting his brows, and turning his scared eyes from one to the other. "What was it?"

"Oh, nothing," Konstantin answered in confusion.

"Oh, if you don't want to say, don't. Only it's no good your talking to her. She's a wench, and you're a gentleman," he said with a jerk of the neck. "You understand everything, I see, and have taken stock of everything, and look with commiseration on my shortcomings," he began again, raising his voice.

"Nikolay Dmitrievitch, Nikolay Dmitrievitch," whispered Marya Nikolaevna, again going up to him.

"Oh, very well, very well! . . . But where's the supper? Ah, here it is," he said, seeing a waiter with a tray. "Here, set it here," he added angrily, and promptly seizing the vodka, he poured out a glassful and drank it greedily. "Like a drink?" he turned to his brother, and at once became better humored.

"Well, enough of Sergey Ivanovitch. I'm glad to see you, anyway. After all's said and done, we're not strangers. Come, have a drink. Tell me what you're doing," he went on, greedily munching a piece of bread, and pouring out another glassful. "How are you living?"

"I live alone in the country, as I used to. I'm busy looking after the land," answered Konstantin, watching with horror the greediness with which his brother ate and drank, and trying to conceal that he noticed it.

"Why don't you get married?"

"It hasn't happened so," Konstantin answered, reddening a little.

"Why not? For me now . . . everything's at an end! I've made a mess of my life. But this I've said, and I say still, that if my share had been given me when I needed it, my whole life would have been different."

Konstantin made haste to change the conversation.

"Do you know your little Vanya's with me, a clerk in the counting-house at Pokrovskoe."

Nikolay jerked his neck, and sank into thought.

"Yes, tell me what's going on at Pokrovskoe. Is the house standing still, and the birch-trees, and our schoolroom? And Philip the gardener, is he living? How I remember the arbor and the seat! Now mind and don't alter anything in the house, but make haste and get married, and make everything as it used to be again. Then I'll come and see you, if your wife is nice."

"But come to me now," said Levin. "How nicely we would arrange it!"

"I'd come and see you if I were sure I should not find Sergey Ivanovitch."

"You wouldn't find him there. I live quite independently of him."

"Yes, but say what you like, you will have to choose between me and him," he said, looking timidly into his brother's face.

This timidity touched Konstantin.

"If you want to hear my confession of faith on the subject, I tell you that in your quarrel with Sergey Ivanovitch I take neither side. You're both wrong. You're more wrong externally, and he inwardly."

"Ah, ah! You see that, you see that!" Nikolay shouted joyfully.

"But I personally value friendly relations with you more because . . . ."

"Why, why?"

Konstantin could not say that he valued it more because Nikolay was unhappy, and needed affection. But Nikolay knew that this was just what he meant to say, and scowling he took up the vodka again.

"Enough, Nikolay Dmitrievitch!" said Marya Nikolaevna, stretching out her plump, bare arm towards the decanter.

"Let it be! Don't insist! I'll beat you!" he shouted.

Marya Nikolaevna smiled a sweet and good-humored smile, which was at once reflected on Nikolay's face, and she took the bottle.

"And do you suppose she understands nothing?" said Nikolay. "She understands it all better than any of us. Isn't it true there's something good and sweet in her?"

"Were you never before in Moscow?" Konstantin said to her, for the sake of saying something.

"Only you mustn't be polite and stiff with her. It frightens her. No one ever spoke to her so but the justices of the peace who tried her for trying to get out of a house of ill-fame. Mercy on us, the senselessness in the world!" he cried suddenly. "These new institutions, these justices of the peace, rural councils, what hideousness it all is!"

And he began to enlarge on his encounters with the new institutions.

Konstantin Levin heard him, and the disbelief in the sense of all public institutions, which he shared with him, and often expressed, was distasteful to him now from his brother's lips.

"In another world we shall understand it all," he said lightly.

"In another world! Ah, I don't like that other world! I don't like it," he said, letting his scared eyes rest on his brother's eyes. "Here one would think that to get out of all the baseness and the mess, one's own and other people's, would be a good thing, and yet I'm afraid of death, awfully afraid of death." He shuddered. "But do drink something. Would you like some champagne? Or shall we go somewhere? Let's go to the Gypsies! Do you know I have got so fond of the Gypsies and Russian songs."

His speech had begun to falter, and he passed abruptly from one subject to another. Konstantin with the help of Masha persuaded him not to go out anywhere, and got him to bed hopelessly drunk.

Masha promised to write to Konstantin in case of need, and to persuade Nikolay Levin to go and stay with his brother.

CHAPTER XXVI

In the morning Konstantin Levin left Moscow, and towards evening he reached home. On the journey in the train he talked to his neighbors about politics and the new railways, and, just as in Moscow, he was overcome by a sense of confusion of ideas, dissatisfaction with himself, shame of something or other. But when he got out at his own station, when he saw his one-eyed coachman, Ignat, with the collar of his coat turned up; when, in the dim light reflected by the station fires, he saw his own sledge, his own horses with their tails tied up, in their harness trimmed with rings and tassels; when the coachman Ignat, as he put in his luggage, told him the village news, that the contractor had arrived, and that Pava had calved,—he felt that little by little the confusion was clearing up, and the shame and self-dissatisfaction were passing away. He felt this at the mere sight of Ignat and the horses; but when he had put on the sheepskin brought for him, had sat down wrapped up in the sledge, and had driven off pondering on the work that lay before him in the village, and staring at the side-horse, that had been his saddle-horse, past his prime now, but a spirited beast from the Don, he began to see what had happened to him in quite a different light. He felt himself, and did not want to be any one else. All he wanted now was to be better than before. In the first place he resolved that from that day he would give up hoping for any extraordinary happiness, such as marriage must have given him, and consequently he would not so disdain what he really had. Secondly, he would never again let himself give way to low passion, the memory of which had so tortured him when he had been making up his mind to make an offer. Then remembering his brother Nikolay, he resolved to himself that he would never allow himself to forget him, that he would follow him up, and not lose sight of him, so as to be ready to help when things should go ill with him. And

110

that would be soon, he felt. Then, too, his brother's talk of communism, which he had treated so lightly at the time, now made him think. He considered a revolution in economic conditions nonsense. But he always felt the injustice of his own abundance in comparison with the poverty of the peasants, and now he determined that so as to feel quite in the right, though he had worked hard and lived by no means luxuriously before, he would now work still harder, and would allow himself even less luxury. And all this seemed to him so easy a conquest over himself that he spent the whole drive in the pleasantest day-dreams. With a resolute feeling of hope in a new, better life, he reached home before nine o'clock at night.

The snow of the little quadrangle before the house was lit up by a light in the bedroom windows of his old nurse, Agafea Mihalovna, who performed the duties of housekeeper in his house. She was not yet asleep. Kouzma, waked up by her, came sidling sleepily out onto the steps. A setter bitch, Laska, ran out too, almost upsetting Kouzma, and whining, turned round about Levin's knees, jumping up and longing, but not daring, to put her forepaws on his chest.

"You're soon back again, sir," said Agafea Mihalovna.

"I got tired of it, Agafea Mihalovna. With friends, one is well; but at home, one is better," he answered, and went into his study.

The study was slowly lit up as the candle was brought in. The familiar details came out: the stag's horns, the bookshelves, the looking-glass, the stove with its ventilator, which had long wanted mending, his father's sofa, a large table, on the table an open book, a broken ash-tray, a manuscript-book with his handwriting. As he saw all this, there came over him for an instant a doubt of the possibility of arranging the new life, of which he had been dreaming on the road. All these traces of his life seemed to clutch him, and to say to him: "No, you're not going to get away from us, and you're not going to be different, but you're going to be the same as you've always been; with doubts, everlasting dissatisfaction with yourself, vain efforts to amend, and falls, and everlasting expectation, of a happiness which you won't get, and which isn't possible for you."

This the things said to him, but another voice in his heart was telling him that he must not fall under the sway of the past, and that one can do anything with oneself. And hearing that voice, he went into the corner where stood his two heavy dumb-bells, and began brandishing them like a gymnast, trying to restore his confident temper. There was a creak of steps at the door. He hastily put down the dumb-bells.

The bailiff came in, and said everything, thank God, was doing well; but informed him that the buckwheat in the new drying-machine had been a little scorched. This piece of news irritated Levin. The new drying-machine had been constructed and partly invented by Levin. The bailiff had always been against the drying-machine, and now it was with suppressed triumph that he announced that the buckwheat had been scorched. Levin was firmly convinced that if the buckwheat had been scorched, it was only because the precautions had not been taken, for which he had hundreds of times given orders. He was annoyed, and reprimanded the bailiff. But there had been an important and joyful event: Pava, his best cow, an expensive beast, bought at a show, had calved.

"Kouzma, give me my sheepskin. And you tell them to take a lantern. I'll come and look at her," he said to the bailiff.

The cowhouse for the more valuable cows was just behind the house. Walking across the yard, passing a snowdrift by the lilac-tree, he went into the cowhouse. There was the warm, steamy smell of dung when the frozen door was opened, and the cows, astonished at the unfamiliar light of the lantern, stirred on the fresh straw. He caught a glimpse of the broad, smooth, black and piebald back of Hollandka. Berkoot, the bull, was lying down with his ring in his lip, and seemed about to get up, but thought better of it, and only gave two snorts as they passed by him. Pava, a perfect beauty, huge as a hippopotamus, with her back turned to them, prevented their seeing the calf, as she sniffed her all over.

Levin went into the pen, looked Pava over, and lifted the red and spotted calf onto her long, tottering legs. Pava, uneasy, began lowing, but when Levin put the calf close to her she was soothed, and, sighing heavily, began licking her with her rough tongue. The calf, fumbling, poked her nose under her mother's udder, and stiffened her tail out straight.

"Here, bring the light, Fyodor, this way," said Levin, examining the calf. "Like the mother! though the color takes after the father; but that's nothing. Very good. Long and broad in the haunch. Vassily Fedorovitch, isn't she splendid?" he said to the bailiff, quite forgiving him for the buckwheat under the influence of his delight in the calf.

"How could she fail to be? Oh, Semyon the contractor came the day after you left. You must settle with him, Konstantin Dmitrievitch," said the bailiff. "I did inform you about the machine."

This question was enough to take Levin back to all the details of his work on the estate, which was on a large scale, and complicated. He went straight from the cowhouse to the counting-house, and after a little conversation with the bailiff and Semyon the contractor, he went back to the house and straight up-stairs to the drawing-room.

CHAPTER XXVII

THE house was big and old-fashioned, and Levin, though he lived alone, had the whole house heated and used. He knew that this was stupid, he knew that it was positively not right, and contrary to his present new plans, but this house was a whole world to Levin. It was the world in which his father and mother had lived and died. They had lived just the life that to Levin seemed the ideal of perfection, and that he had dreamed of beginning with his wife, his family.

Levin scarcely remembered his mother. His conception of her was for him a sacred memory, and his future wife was bound to be in

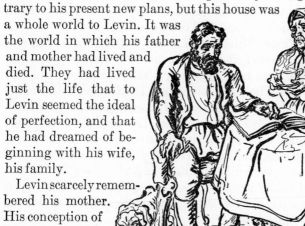

his imagination a repetition of that exquisite, holy ideal of a woman that his mother had been.

He was so far from conceiving of love for woman apart from marriage that he positively pictured to himself first the family, and only secondarily the woman who would give him a family. His ideas of marriage were, consequently, quite unlike those of the great majority of his acquaintances, for whom getting married was one of the numerous facts of social life. For Levin it was the chief affair of life, on which its whole happiness turned. And now he had to give up that.

When he had gone into the little drawing-room, where he always had tea, and had settled himself in his armchair with a book, and Agafea Mihalovna had brought him tea, and with her usual, "Well, I'll stay a while, sir," had taken a chair in the window, he felt that, however strange it might be, he had not parted from his day-dreams, and that he could not live without them. Whether with her, or with another, still it would be. He was reading a book, and thinking of what he was reading, and stopping to listen to Agafea Mihalovna, who gossiped away without flagging, and yet with all that, all sorts of pictures of family life and work in the future rose disconnectedly before his imagination. He felt that in the depth of his soul something had been put in its place, settled down, and laid to rest.

He heard Agafea Mihalovna talking of how Prohor had forgotten his duty to God, and with the money Levin had given him to buy a horse, had been drinking without stopping, and had beaten his wife till he'd half killed her. He listened, and read his book, and recalled the whole train of ideas suggested by his reading. It was Tyndall's *Treatise on Heat*. He recalled his own criticisms of Tyndall for his complacent satisfaction in the cleverness of his experiments, and for his lack of philosophic insight. And suddenly there floated into his mind the joyful thought: "In two years' time I shall have two Dutch cows; Pava herself will perhaps still be alive, a dozen young daughters of Berkoot and the three others—how lovely!"

He took up his book again. "Very good, electricity and heat are the same thing; but is it possible to substitute the one quantity for the other in the equation for the solution of any problem? No. Well, then what of it? The connection between all the forces of nature is felt instinctively. . . . It's particularly nice if Pava's daughter should be a red-spotted cow, and all the herd will take after her, and the other three, too! Splendid! To go out with my wife and visitors to meet the herd. . . . My wife says, 'Kostya and I looked after that calf like a child.' 'How can it interest you so much?' says a visitor. 'Everything that interests him, interests me.' But who will she be?" And he remembered what had happened at Moscow. . . . "Well, there's nothing to be done. . . . It's not my fault. But now everything shall go on in a new way. It's nonsense to pretend that life won't let one, that the past won't let one. One must struggle to live better, much better." . . . He raised his head, and fell to dreaming. Old Laska, who had not yet fully digested her delight at his return, and had run out into the yard to bark, came back wagging her tail, and crept up to him, bringing in the scent of the fresh air, put her head under his hand, and whined plaintively, asking to be stroked.

"There, who'd have thought it?" said Agafea Mihalovna. "The dog now . . . why, she understands that her master's come home, and that he's low-spirited."

"Why low-spirited?"

"Do you suppose I don't see it, sir? It's high time I should know the gentry. Why, I've grown up from a little thing with them. It's nothing, sir, so long as there's health and a clear conscience."

Levin looked intently at her, surprised at how well she knew his thought.

"Shall I fetch you another cup?" said she, and taking his cup she went out.

Laska kept poking her head under his hand. He stroked her, and she promptly curled up at his feet, laying her head on a hind-paw. And in token of all now being well and satisfactory, she opened her mouth a little, smacked her lips, and settling her sticky lips more comfortably about her old teeth, she sank into blissful repose. Levin watched all her movements attentively.

"That's what I'll do," he said to himself; "that's what I'll do! Nothing's amiss. . . . All's well."

AFTER the ball, early next morning, Anna Arkadyevna sent her husband a telegram that she was leaving Moscow the same day.

"No, I must go, I must go"; she explained to her sister-in-law the change in her plans in a tone that suggested that she had to remember so many things that there was no enumerating them: "no, it had really better be to-day!"

Stepan Arkadyevitch was not dining at home, but he promised to come and see his sister off at seven o'clock.

Kitty, too, did not come, sending a note that she had a head-ache. Dolly and Anna dined alone with the children and the English governess. Whether it was that the children were fickle, or that they had acute senses, and felt that Anna was quite different that day from what she had been when they had taken such a fancy to her, that she was not now interested in them,—but they had abruptly dropped their play with their aunt, and their love for her, and were quite indifferent that she was going away. Anna was absorbed the whole morning in preparations for her departure. She wrote notes to her Moscow acquaintances, put down her accounts, and packed. Altogether Dolly fancied she was not in a placid state of mind, but in that worried mood, which Dolly knew well with herself, and which does not come without cause, and for the most part covers dissatisfaction with self. After dinner, Anna went up to her room to dress, and Dolly followed her.

"How queer you are to-day!" Dolly said to her.

"I? Do you think so? I'm not queer, but I'm nasty. I am like that sometimes. I keep feeling as if I could cry. It's very stupid, but it'll pass off," said Anna quickly, and she bent her flushed face over a tiny bag in which she was packing a nightcap and some cambric handkerchiefs. Her eyes were particularly bright, and were continually swimming with tears. "In the same way I didn't want to leave Petersburg, and now I don't want to go away from here."

"You came here and did a good deed," said Dolly, looking in-tently at her.

Anna looked at her with eyes wet with tears.

"Don't say that, Dolly. I've done nothing, and could do nothing. I often wonder why people are all in league to spoil me. What have I done, and what could I do? In your heart there was found love enough to forgive. . . ."

"If it had not been for you, God knows what would have happened! How happy you are, Anna!" said Dolly. "Everything is clear and good in your heart."

"Every heart has its own *skeletons,* as the English say."

"You have no sort of *skeleton,* have you? Everything is so clear in you."

"I have!" said Anna suddenly, and, unexpectedly after her tears, a sly, ironical smile curved her lips.

"Come, he's amusing, anyway, your *skeleton,* and not depressing," said Dolly, smiling.

"No, he's depressing. Do you know why I'm going to-day instead of to-morrow? It's a confession that weighs on me; I want to make it to you," said Anna, letting herself drop definitely into an armchair, and looking straight into Dolly's face.

And to her surprise Dolly saw that Anna was blushing up to her ears, up to the curly black ringlets on her neck.

"Yes," Anna went on. "Do you know why Kitty didn't come to dinner? She's jealous of me. I have spoiled . . . I've been the cause of that ball being a torture to her instead of a pleasure. But truly, truly, it's not my fault, or only my fault a little bit," she said, daintily drawling the words "a little bit."

"Oh, how like Stiva you said that!" said Dolly, laughing.

Anna was hurt.

"Oh no, oh no! I'm not Stiva," she said, knitting her brows. "That's why I'm telling you, just because I could never let myself doubt myself for an instant," said Anna.

But at the very moment she was uttering the words, she felt that they were not true. She was not merely doubting herself, she felt emotion at the thought of Vronsky, and was going away sooner than she had meant, simply to avoid meeting him.

"Yes, Stiva told me you danced the mazurka with him, and that he . . ."

"You can't imagine how absurdly it all came about. I only meant to be matchmaking, and all at once it turned out quite differently. Possibly against my own will . . ."

She crimsoned and stopped.

"Oh, they feel it directly!" said Dolly.

"But I should be in despair if there were anything serious in it on his side," Anna interrupted her. "And I am certain it will all be forgotten, and Kitty will leave off hating me."

"All the same, Anna, to tell you the truth, I'm not very anxious for this marriage for Kitty. And it's better it should come to nothing, if he, Vronsky, is capable of falling in love with you in a single day."

"Oh, heavens, that would be too silly!" said Anna, and again a deep flush of pleasure came out on her face, when she heard the idea, that absorbed her, put into words. "And so here I am going away, having made an enemy of Kitty, whom I liked so much! Ah, how sweet she is! But you'll make it right, Dolly? Eh?"

Dolly could scarcely suppress a smile. She loved Anna, but she enjoyed seeing that she too had her weaknesses.

"An enemy? That can't be."

"I did so want you all to care for me, as I do for you, and now I care for you more than ever," said Anna, with tears in her eyes. "Ah, how silly I am to-day!"

She passed her handkerchief over her face and began dressing.

At the very moment of starting Stepan Arkadyevitch arrived, late, rosy and good-humored, smelling of wine and cigars.

Anna's emotionalism infected Dolly, and when she embraced her sister-in-law for the last time, she whispered: "Remember, Anna, what you've done for me—I shall never forget. And remember that I love you, and shall always love you as my dearest friend!"

"I don't know why," said Anna, kissing her and hiding her tears.

"You understood me, and you understand. Good-bye, my darling!"

CHAPTER XXIX

"Come, it's all over, and thank God!" was the first thought that came to Anna Arkadyevna, when she had said good-bye for the last time to her brother, who had stood blocking up the entrance to the carriage till the third bell rang. She sat down on her lounge beside Annushka, and looked about her in the twilight of the sleeping-carriage. "Thank God! to-morrow I shall see Seryozha and Alexey Alexandrovitch, and my life will go on in the old way, all nice and as usual."

Still in the same anxious frame of mind, as she had been all that day, Anna took pleasure in arranging herself for the journey with great care. With her little deft hands she opened and shut her little red bag, took out a cushion, laid it on her knees, and carefully wrapping up her feet, settled herself comfortably. An invalid lady had already lain down to sleep. Two other ladies began talking to Anna, and a stout elderly lady tucked up her feet, and made observations about the heating of the train. Anna answered a few words, but not foreseeing any entertainment from the conversation, she asked Annushka to get a lamp, hooked it onto the arm of her seat, and took from her bag a paper-knife and an English novel. At first her reading made no progress. The fuss and bustle were disturbing; then when the train had started, she could not help listening to the noises; then the snow beating on the left window and sticking to the pane, and the sight of the muffled guard passing by, covered with snow on one side, and the conversations about the terrible snowstorm raging outside, distracted her attention. Further on, it was continually the same again and again: the same shaking and rattling, the same snow on the window, the same rapid transitions from steaming heat to cold, and back again to heat, the same passing glimpses of the same figures in the twilight, and the same voices, and Anna began to read and to understand what she read. Annushka was already dozing, the red bag on her lap, clutched by her broad hands, in gloves, of which one was torn. Anna Arkadyevna read and understood; but it was distasteful to her to read, that is, to follow the reflection of other people's lives. She had too great a desire to live herself. If she read that the heroine of the novel was nursing a sick man, she longed to move with noiseless steps about the room of a sick man; if she read of a member of Parliament making a speech, she longed to be delivering the speech; if she read of how Lady Mary had ridden after the hounds, and had provoked her sister-in-law, and had surprised every one by her boldness, she too wished to be doing the same. But there was no chance of doing anything; and twisting the smooth paper-knife in her little hands, she forced herself to read.

The hero of the novel was already almost reaching his English happiness, a baronetcy and an estate, and Anna was feeling a desire to go with him to the estate, when she suddenly felt that *he* ought to feel ashamed, and that she was ashamed of the same thing. But what had he to be ashamed of? "What have I to be ashamed of?" she asked herself in injured surprise. She laid down the book and sank against the back of the chair, tightly gripping the paper-cutter in both hands. There was nothing. She went over all her Moscow recollections. All were good, pleasant. She remembered the ball, remembered Vronsky and his face of slavish adoration, remembered all her conduct with him: there was nothing shameful. And for all that, at the same point in her memories, the feeling of shame was intensified, as though some inner voice, just at the point when she thought of Vronsky, were saying to her, "Warm, very warm, hot." "Well, what is it?" she said to herself resolutely, shifting her seat in the lounge. "What does it mean? Am I afraid to look it straight in the face? Why, what is it? Can it be that between me and this officer boy there exist, or can exist, any other relations than such as are common with every acquaintance?" She laughed contemptuously and took up her book again; but now she was definitely unable to follow what she read. She passed the paper-knife over the window-pane, then laid its smooth, cool surface to her cheek, and almost laughed aloud at the feeling of delight that all at once without cause came over her. She felt as though her nerves were strings being strained tighter and tighter on some sort of screwing peg. She felt her eyes opening wider and wider, her fingers and toes twitching nervously, something within oppressing her breathing, while all shapes and sounds seemed in the uncertain half-light to strike her with unaccustomed vividness. Moments of doubt were continually coming upon her, when she was uncertain whether the train were going forwards or backwards, or were standing still altogether; whether it were Annushka at her side or a stranger. "What's that on the arm of the chair, a fur cloak or some beast? And what am I myself? Myself or some other woman?" She was afraid of giving away to this delirium. But something drew her towards it, and she could yield to it or resist it at will. She got up to rouse herself, and slipped off her plaid and the cape of her warm dress. For a moment she regained her self-possession, and realized that the thin peasant who had come in wearing a long overcoat, with buttons missing from it, was the stoveheater, that he was looking at the thermometer, that it was the wind and snow bursting in after him at the door; but then everything grew blurred again. . . . That peasant with the long waist seemed to be gnawing something on the wall, the old lady began stretching her legs the whole length of the carriage, and filling it with a black cloud; then there was a fearful shrieking and banging, as though some one were being torn to pieces; then there was a blinding dazzle of red fire before her eyes and a wall seemed to rise up and hide everything. Anna felt as though she were sinking down. But it was not terrible, but delightful. The voice of a man muffled up and covered with snow shouted something in her ear. She got up and pulled herself together; she realized that they had reached a station and that this was the guard. She asked Annushka to hand her the cape she had taken off and her shawl, put them on and moved towards the door.

"Do you wish to get out?" asked Annushka.

"Yes, I want a little air. It's very hot in here." And she opened the door. The driving snow and the wind rushed to meet her and struggled with her over the door. But she enjoyed the struggle.

She opened the door and went out. The wind seemed as though lying in wait for her; with gleeful whistle it tried to snatch her up and bear her off, but she clung to the cold door-post, and holding her skirt got down onto the platform and under the shelter of the carriages. The wind had been powerful on the steps, but on the platform, under the lee of the carriages, there was a lull. With enjoyment she drew deep breaths of the frozen, snowy air, and standing near the carriage looked about the platform and the lighted station.

CHAPTER XXX

THE raging tempest rushed whistling between the wheels of the carriages, about the scaffolding, and round the corner of the station. The carriages, posts, people, everything that was to be seen was covered with snow on one side, and was getting more and more thickly covered. For a moment there would come a lull in the storm, but then it would swoop down again with such onslaughts that it seemed impossible to stand against it. Meanwhile men ran to and fro, talking merrily together, their steps crackling on the platform as they continually opened and closed the big doors. The bent shadow of a man glided by at her feet, and she heard sounds of a hammer upon iron. "Hand over that telegram!" came an angry voice out of the stormy darkness on the other side. "This way! No. 28!" several different voices shouted again, and muffled figures ran by covered with snow. Two gentlemen with lighted cigarettes passed by her. She drew one more deep breath of the fresh air, and had just put her hand out of her muff to take hold of the door-post and get back into the carriage, when another man in a military overcoat, quite close beside her, stepped between her and the flickering light of the lamp-post. She looked round, and the same instant recognized Vronsky's face. Putting his hand to the peak of his cap, he bowed to her and asked, Was there anything she wanted? Could he be of any service to her? She gazed rather a long while at him without answering, and, in spite of the shadow in which he was standing, she saw, or fancied she saw, both the expression of his face and his eyes. It was again that expression of reverential ecstasy which had so worked upon her the day before. More than once she had told herself during the past few days, and again only a few moments before, that Vronsky was for her only one of the hundreds of young men, forever exactly the same, that are met everywhere, that she would never allow herself to bestow a thought upon him. But now at the first instant of meeting him, she was seized by a feeling of joyful pride. She had no need to ask why he had come. She knew as certainly as if he had told her that he was here to be where she was.

"I didn't know you were going. What are you coming for?" she said, letting fall the hand with which she had grasped the door-post. And irrepressible delight and eagerness shone in her face.

"What am I coming for?" he repeated, looking straight into her eyes. "You know that I have come to be where you are," he said; "I can't help it."

At that moment the wind, as it were, surmounting all obstacles, sent the snow flying from the carriage roofs, and clanked some sheet of iron it had torn off, while the hoarse whistle of the engine roared in front, plaintively and gloomily. All the awfulness of the storm seemed to her more splendid now. He had said what her soul longed to hear, though she feared it with her reason. She made no answer, and in her face he saw conflict.

"Forgive me, if you dislike what I said," he said humbly.

He had spoken courteously, deferentially, yet so firmly, so stubbornly, that for a long while she could make no answer.

"It's wrong, what you say, and I beg you, if you're a good man, to forget what you've said, as I forget it," she said at last.

"Not one word, not one gesture of yours shall I, could I, ever forget. . . ."

"Enough, enough!" she cried, trying assiduously to give a stern expression to her face, into which he was gazing greedily. And clutching at the cold door-post, she clambered up the steps and got rapidly into the corridor of the carriage. But in the little corridor she paused, going over in her imagination what had happened. Though she could not recall her own words or his, she realized instinctively that that momentary conversation had brought them fearfully closer; and she was panic-stricken and blissful at it. After standing still a few seconds, she went into the carriage and sat down in her place. The overstrained condition which had tormented her before did not only come back, but was intensified, and reached such a pitch that she was afraid every minute that something would snap within her from the excessive tension. She did not sleep all night. But in that nervous tension, and in the visions that filled her imagination, there was nothing disagreeable or gloomy: on the contrary there was something blissful, glowing, and exhilarating. Towards morning Anna sank into a doze, sitting in her place, and when she waked it was daylight and the train was near Petersburg. At once thoughts of home, of husband and of son, and the details of that day and the following came upon her.

At Petersburg, as soon as the train stopped and she got out, the first person that attracted her attention was her husband. "Oh, mercy! why do his ears look like that?" she thought, looking at his frigid and imposing figure, and especially the ears that struck her at the moment as propping up the brim of his round hat. Catching sight of her, he came to meet her, his lips falling into their habitual sarcastic smile, and his big, tired eyes looking straight at her. An unpleasant sensation gripped at her heart when she met his obstinate and weary glance, as though she had expected to see him different. She was especially struck by the feeling of dissatisfaction with herself that she experienced on meeting him. That feeling was an intimate, familiar feeling, like a consciousness of hypocrisy, which she experienced in her relations with her husband. But hitherto she had not taken note of the feeling, now she was clearly and painfully aware of it.

"Yes, as you see, your tender spouse, as devoted as the first year after marriage, burned with impatience to see you," he said in his deliberate, high-pitched voice, and in that tone which he almost always took with her, a tone of jeering at any one who should say in earnest what he said.

"Is Seryozha quite well?" she asked.

"And is this all the reward," said he, "for my ardor? He's quite well. . . ."

CHAPTER XXXI

VRONSKY had not even tried to sleep all that night. He sat in his armchair, looking straight before him or scanning the people who got in and out. If he had indeed on previous occasions struck and impressed people who did not know him by his air of unhesitating composure, he seemed now more haughty and self-possessed than ever. He looked at people as if they were things. A nervous young man, a clerk in a law-court, sitting opposite him, hated him for that look. The young man asked him for a light, and entered into conversation with him, and even pushed against him, to make him feel that he was not a thing, but a person. But Vronsky gazed at him exactly as he did at the lamp, and the young man made a wry face, feeling that he was losing his self-possession under the oppression of this refusal to recognize him as a person.

Vronsky saw nothing and no one. He felt himself a king, not because he believed that he had made an impression on Anna—

he did not yet believe that—but because the impression she had made on him gave him happiness and pride.

What would come of it all he did not know, he did not even think. He felt that all his forces, hitherto dissipated, wasted, were centered on one thing, and bent with fearful energy on one blissful goal. And he was happy at it. He knew only that he had told her the truth, that he had come where she was, that all the happiness of his life, the only meaning in life for him, now lay in seeing and hearing her. And when he got out of the carriage at Bologova to get some seltzer water, and caught sight of Anna, involuntarily his first word had told her just what he thought. And he was glad he had told her it, that she knew it now and was thinking of it. He did not sleep all night. When he was back in the carriage, he kept unceasingly going over every position in which he had seen her, every word she had uttered, and before his fancy, making his heart faint with emotion, floated pictures of a possible future.

When he got out of the train at Petersburg, he felt after his sleepless night as keen and fresh as after a cold bath. He paused near his compartment, waiting for her to get out. "Once more," he said to himself, smiling unconsciously, "once more I shall see her walk, her face; she will say something, turn her head, glance, smile, maybe." But before he caught sight of her, he saw her husband, whom the station-master was deferentially escorting through the crowd. "Ah, yes! The husband." Only now for the first time did Vronsky realize clearly the fact that there was a person attached to her, a husband. He knew that she had a husband, but had hardly believed in his existence, and only now fully believed in him, with his head and shoulders, and his legs clad in black trousers; especially when he saw this husband calmly take her arm with a sense of property.

Seeing Alexey Alexandrovitch with his Petersburg face and severely self-confident figure, in his round hat, with his rather prominent spine, he believed in him, and was aware of a disagreeable sensation, such as a man might feel tortured by thirst, who, on reaching a spring, should find a dog, a sheep, or a pig, who has drunk of it and muddied the water. Alexey Alexandrovitch's manner of walking, with a swing of the hips and flat feet, particularly annoyed Vronsky. He could recognize in no one but himself an indubitable right to love her. But she was still the same, and the sight of her affected him the same way, physically reviving him, stirring him, and filling his soul with rapture. He told his German valet, who ran up to him from the second-class, to take his things and go on, and he himself went up to her. He saw the first meeting between the husband and wife, and noted with a lover's insight the signs of slight reserve with which she spoke to her husband. "No, she does not love him and cannot love him," he decided to himself.

At the moment when he was approaching Anna Arkadyevna he noticed too with joy that she was conscious of his being near, and looked round, and seeing him, turned again to her husband. "Have you passed a good night?" he asked, bowing to her and her husband together, and leaving it up to Alexey Alexandrovitch to accept the bow on his own account, and to recognize it or not, as he might see fit.

"Thank you, very good," she answered.

Her face looked weary, and there was not that play of eagerness in it, peeping out in her smile and her eyes; but for a single instant, as she glanced at him, there was a flash of something in her eyes, and although the flash died away at once, he was happy for that moment. She glanced at her husband to find out whether he knew Vronsky. Alexey Alexandrovitch looked at Vronsky with displeasure, vaguely recalling who this was. Vronsky's composure and self-confidence here struck, like a scythe against a stone, upon the cold self-confidence of Alexey Alexandrovitch.

"Count Vronsky," said Anna.

"Ah! We are acquainted, I believe," said Alexey Alexandrovitch indifferently, giving his hand.

"You set off with the mother and you return with the son," he said, articulating each syllable, as though each were a separate favor he was bestowing.

"You're back from leave, I suppose?" he said, and without waiting for a reply, he turned to his wife in his jesting tone: "Well, were a great many tears shed at Moscow at parting?"

By addressing his wife like this he gave Vronsky to understand that he wished to be left alone, and, turning slightly towards him, he touched his hat; but Vronsky turned to Anna Arkadyevna.

"I hope I may have the honor of calling on you," he said.

Alexey Alexandrovitch glanced with his weary eyes at Vronsky.

"Delighted," he said coldly. "On Mondays we're at home. Most fortunate," he said to his wife, dismissing Vronsky altogether, "that I should just have half an hour to meet you, so that I can prove my devotion," he went on in the same jesting tone.

"You lay too much stress on your devotion for me to value it much," she responded in the same jesting tone, involuntarily listening to the sound of Vronsky's steps behind them. "But what has it to do with me?" she said to herself, and she began asking her husband how Seryozha had got on without her.

"Oh, capitally! Mariette says he has been very good, and . . . I must disappoint you . . . but he has not missed you as your husband has. But once more *merci,* my dear, for giving me a day. Our dear *Samovar* will be delighted." (He used to call the Countess Lidia Ivanovna, well known in society, a samovar, because she was always bubbling over with excitement.) "She has been continually asking after you. And, do you know, if I may venture to advise you, you should go and see her to-day. You know how she takes everything to heart. Just now, with all her own cares, she's anxious about the Oblonskys being brought together."

The Countess Lidia Ivanovna was a friend of her husband's, and the center of that one of the coteries of the Petersburg world with which Anna was, through her husband, in the closest relations.

"But you know I wrote to her?"

127

"Still she'll want to hear details. Go and see her, if you're not too tired, my dear. Well, Kondraty will take you in the carriage, while I go to my committee. I shall not be alone at dinner again," Alexey Alexandrovitch went on, no longer in a sarcastic tone. "You wouldn't believe how I've missed . . ." And with a long pressure of her hand and a meaning smile, he put her in her carriage.

CHAPTER XXXII

THE first person to meet Anna at home was her son. He dashed down the stairs to her, in spite of the governess's call, and with desperate joy shrieked: "Mother! mother!" Running up to her, he hung on her neck.

"I told you it was mother!" he shouted to the governess. "I knew!"

And her son, like her husband, aroused in Anna a feeling akin to disappointment. She had imagined him better than he was in reality. She had to let herself drop down to the reality to enjoy him as he really was. But even as he was, he was charming, with his fair curls, his blue eyes, and his plump, graceful little legs in tightly pulled-up stockings. Anna experienced almost physical pleasure in the sensation of his nearness and his caresses, and moral soothing, when she met his simple, confiding, and loving glance, and heard his naïve questions. Anna took out the presents Dolly's children had sent him, and told her son what sort of little girl was Tanya at Moscow, and how Tanya could read, and even taught the other children.

"Why, am I not so nice as she?" asked Seryozha.

"To me you're nicer than any one in the world."

"I know that," said Seryozha, smiling.

Anna had not had time to drink her coffee when the Countess Lidia Ivanovna was announced. The Countess Lidia Ivanovna was a tall, stout woman, with an unhealthily sallow face and splendid, pensive black eyes. Anna liked her, but to-day she seemed to be seeing her for the first time with all her defects.

128

"Well, my dear, so you took the olive branch?" inquired Countess Lidia Ivanovna, as soon as she came into the room.

"Yes, it's all over, but it was all much less serious than we had supposed," answered Anna. "My *belle-sœur* is in general too hasty."

But Countess Lidia Ivanovna, though she was interested in everything that did not concern her, had a habit of never listening to what interested her; she interrupted Anna:

"Yes, there's plenty of sorrow and evil in the world. I am so worried to-day."

"Oh, why?" asked Anna, trying to suppress a smile.

"I'm beginning to be weary of fruitlessly championing the truth, and sometimes I'm quite unhinged by it. The Society of the Little Sisters" (this was a religiously-patriotic, philanthropic institution) "was going splendidly, but with these gentlemen it's impossible to do anything," added Countess Lidia Ivanovna in a tone of ironical submission to destiny. "They pounce on the idea, and distort it, and then work it out so pettily and unworthily. Two or three people, your husband among them, understand all the importance of the thing, but the others simply drag it down. Yesterday Pravdin wrote to me . . ."

Pravdin was a well-known Panslavist abroad, and Countess Lidia Ivanovna described the purport of his letter.

Then the countess told her of more disagreements and intrigues against the work of the unification of the churches, and departed in haste, as she had that day to be at the meeting of some society and also at the Slavonic committee.

"It was all the same before, of course; but why was it I didn't notice it before?" Anna asked herself. "Or has she been very much irritated to-day? It's really ludicrous; her object is doing good; she's a Christian, yet she's always angry; and she always has enemies, and always enemies in the name of Christianity and doing good."

After Countess Lidia Ivanovna another friend came, the wife of a chief secretary, who told her all the news of the town. At three o'clock she too went away, promising to come to dinner. Alexey Alexandrovitch was at the ministry. Anna, left alone, spent the time till dinner in assisting at her son's dinner (he dined apart from his parents) and in putting her things in order, and in reading and answering the notes and letters which had accumulated on her table.

The feeling of causeless shame, which she had felt on the journey, and her excitement, too, had completely vanished. In the habitual conditions of her life she felt again resolute and irreproachable.

She recalled with wonder her state of mind on the previous day. "What was it? Nothing. Vronsky said something silly, which it was easy to put a stop to, and I answered as I ought to have done. To speak of it to my husband would be unnecessary and out of the question. To speak of it would be to attach importance to what has no importance." She remembered how she had told her husband of what was almost a declaration made her at Petersburg by a young man, one of her husband's subordinates, and how Alexey Alexandrovitch had answered that every woman living in the world was exposed to such incidents, but that he had the fullest confidence in her tact, and could never lower her and himself by jealousy. "So then there's no reason to speak of it? And indeed, thank God, there's nothing to speak of," she told herself.

CHAPTER XXXIII

ALEXEY ALEXANDROVITCH came back from the meeting of the ministers at four o'clock, but as often happened, he had not time to come in to her. He went into his study to see the people waiting for him with petitions, and to sign some papers brought him by his chief secretary. At dinner-time (there were always a few people dining with the Karenins) there arrived an old lady, a cousin of Alexey Alexandrovitch, the chief secretary of the department and his wife, and a young man who had been recommended to Alexey Alexandrovitch for the service. Anna went into the drawing-room to receive these guests. Precisely at five o'clock, before the bronze Peter the First clock had struck the fifth stroke, Alexey Alexandrovitch came in, wearing a white tie and evening coat with two stars, as he had to go out directly after dinner. Every minute of Alexey Alexandrovitch's life was portioned out and occupied. And to make time to get through all

that lay before him every day, he adhered to the strictest punc-
tuality. "Unhasting and unresting," was his motto. He came into
the dining-hall, greeted every one, and hurriedly sat down, smiling to his wife.

"Yes, my solitude is over. You wouldn't believe how uncomfortable" (he laid stress on the word *uncomfortable*) "it is to
dine alone."

At dinner he talked a little to his wife about Moscow matters,
and, with a sarcastic smile, asked her after Stepan Arkadyevitch;
but the conversation was for the most part general, dealing with
Petersburg official and public news. After dinner he spent half
an hour with his guests, and again, with a smile, pressed his
wife's hand, withdrew, and drove off to the council. Anna did
not go out that evening either to the Princess Betsy Tverskaya,
who, hearing of her return, had invited her, nor to the theater,
where she had a box for that evening. She did not go out principally because the dress she had reckoned upon was not ready.
Altogether, Anna, on turning, after the departure of her guests,
to the consideration of her attire, was very much annoyed. She
was generally a mistress of the art of dressing well without great
expense, and before leaving Moscow she had given her dressmaker three dresses to transform. The dresses had to be altered
so that they could not be recognized, and they ought to have been
ready three days before. It appeared that two dresses had not
been done at all, while the other one had not been altered as Anna
had intended. The dressmaker came to explain, declaring that it
would be better as she had done it, and Anna was so furious that
she felt ashamed when she thought of it afterwards. To regain
her serenity completely she went into the nursery, and spent the
whole evening with her son, put him to bed herself, signed him
with the cross, and tucked him up. She was glad she had not
gone out anywhere, and had spent the evening so well. She felt
so light-hearted and serene, she saw so clearly that all that had
seemed to her so important on her railway journey was only one
of the common trivial incidents of fashionable life, and that she
had no reason to feel ashamed before any one else or before herself. Anna sat down at the hearth with an English novel and
waited for her husband. Exactly at half-past nine she heard his
ring, and he came into the room.

"Here you are at last!" she observed, holding out her hand to him.

He kissed her hand and sat down beside her.

"Altogether then, I see your visit was a success," he said to her.

"Oh, yes," she said, and she began telling him about everything from the beginning: her journey with Countess Vronskaya, her arrival, the accident at the station. Then she described the pity she had felt, first for her brother, and afterwards for Dolly.

"I imagine one cannot exonerate such a man from blame, though he is your brother," said Alexey Alexandrovitch severely.

Anna smiled. She knew that he said that simply to show that family considerations could not prevent him from expressing his genuine opinion. She knew that characteristic in her husband, and liked it.

"I am glad it has all ended so satisfactorily, and that you are back again," he went on. "Come, what do they say about the new act I have got passed in the council?"

Anna had heard nothing of this act, and she felt conscience-stricken at having been able so readily to forget what was to him of such importance.

"Here, on the other hand, it has made a great sensation," he said, with a complacent smile.

She saw that Alexey Alexandrovitch wanted to tell her something pleasant to him about it, and she brought him by questions to telling it. With the same complacent smile he told her of the ovations he had received in consequence of the act he had passed.

"I was very, very glad. It shows that at last a reasonable and steady view of the matter is becoming prevalent among us."

Having drunk his second cup of tea with cream, and bread, Alexey Alevandrovitch got up, and was going towards his study.

"And you've not been anywhere this evening? You've been dull, I expect?" he said.

"Oh, no!" she answered, getting up after him and accompanying him across the room to his study. "What are you reading now?" she asked.

"Just now I'm reading Duc de Lille, *Poésie des Enfers*," he answered. "A very remarkable book."

Anna smiled, as people smile at the weaknesses of those they love, and, putting her hand under his, she escorted him to the door of the study. She knew his habit, that had grown into a necessity, of reading in the evening. She knew, too, that in spite of his official duties, which swallowed up almost the whole of his time, he considered it his duty to keep up with everything of note that appeared in the intellectual world. She knew, too, that he was really interested in books dealing with politics, philosophy, and theology, that art was utterly foreign to his nature; but, in spite of this, or rather, in consequence of it, Alexey Alexandrovitch never missed over anything in the world of art, but made it his duty to read everything. She knew that in politics, in philosophy, in theology, Alexey Alexandrovitch often had doubts, and made investigations; but on questions of art and poetry, and, above all, of music, of which he was totally devoid of understanding, he had the most distinct and decided opinions. He was fond of talking about Shakespeare, Raphael, Beethoven, of the significance of new schools of poetry and music, all of which were classified by him with very conspicuous consistency.

"Well, God be with you," she said at the door of the study, where a shaded candle and a decanter of water were already put by his armchair. "And I'll write to Moscow."

He pressed her hand, and again kissed it.

"All the same he's a good man; truthful, good-hearted, and remarkable in his own line," Anna said to herself going back to her room, as though she were defending him to some one who had attacked him and said that one could not love him. "But why is it his ears stick out so strangely? Or has he had his hair cut?"

Precisely at twelve o'clock, when Anna was still sitting at her writing-table, finishing a letter to Dolly, she heard the sound of measured steps in slippers, and Alexey Alexandrovitch, freshly washed and combed, with a book under his arm, came in to her.

"It's time, it's time," said he, with a meaning smile, and he went into their bedroom.

"And what right had he to look at him like that?" thought Anna, recalling Vronsky's glance at Alexey Alexandrovitch.

Undressing, she went into the bedroom; but her face had none of the eagerness which, during her stay at Moscow, had fairly flashed from her eyes and her smile; on the contrary, now the fire seemed quenched in her, hidden somewhere far away.

WHEN Vronsky went to Moscow from Petersburg, he had left his large set of rooms in Morskaia to his friend and favorite comrade Petritsky.

Petritsky was a young lieutenant, not particularly well-connected, and not merely not wealthy, but always hopelessly in debt. Towards evening he was always drunk, and he had often been locked up after all sorts of ludicrous and disgraceful scandals, but he was a favorite both of his comrades and his superior officers. On arriving at twelve o'clock from the station at his flat, Vronsky saw, at the outer door, a hired carriage familiar to him. While still outside his own door, as he rang, he heard masculine laughter, the lisp of a feminine voice, and Petritsky's voice. "If that's one of the villains, don't let him in!" Vronsky told the servant not to announce him, and slipped quietly into the first room. Baroness Shilton, a friend of Petritsky's, with a rosy little face and flaxen hair, resplendent in a lilac satin gown, and filling the whole room, like a canary, with her Parisian chatter, sat at the round table making coffee. Petritsky, in his overcoat, and the cavalry captain Kamerovsky, in full uniform, probably just come from duty, were sitting each side of her.

"Bravo! Vronsky!" shouted Petritsky, jumping up, scraping his chair. "Our host himself! Baroness, some coffee for him out of the new coffee-pot. Why, we didn't expect you! Hope you're satisfied with the ornament of your study," he said, indicating the baroness. "You know each other, of course?"

"I should think so," said Vronsky, with a bright smile, pressing the baroness's little hand. "What next! I'm an old friend."

"You're home after a journey," said the baroness, "so I'm flying. Oh, I'll be off this minute, if I'm in the way."

"You're home, wherever you are, baroness," said Vronsky. "How do you do, Kamerovsky?" he added, coldly shaking hands with Kamerovsky.

"There, you never know how to say such pretty things," said the baroness, turning to Petritsky.

"No; what's that for? After dinner I say things quite as good."

"After dinner there's no credit in them! Well, then, I'll make you some coffee, so go and wash and get ready," said the baroness, sitting down again, and anxiously turning the screw in the new coffee-pot. "Pierre, give me the coffee," she said, addressing Petritsky, whom she called Pierre as a contraction of his surname, making no secret of her relations with him. "I'll put it in."

"You'll spoil it!"

"No, I won't spoil it! Well, and your wife?" said the baroness suddenly, interrupting Vronsky's conversation with his comrade. "We've been marrying you here. Have you brought your wife?"

"No, baroness. I was born a Bohemian, and a Bohemian I shall die."

"So much the better, so much the better. Shake hands on it."

And the baroness, detaining Vronsky, began telling him, with many jokes, about her last new plans of life, asking his advice.

"He persists in refusing to give me a divorce! Well, what am I to do?" (*He* was her husband.) "Now I want to begin a suit against him. What do you advise? Kamerovsky, look after the coffee; it's boiling over. You see, I'm engrossed with business! I want a lawsuit, because I must have my property. Do you understand the folly of it, that on the pretext of my being unfaithful to him," she said contemptuously, "he wants to get the benefit of my fortune."

Vronsky heard with pleasure this light-hearted prattle of a pretty woman, agreed with her, gave her half-joking counsel, and altogether dropped at once into the tone habitual to him in talking to such women. In his Petersburg world all people were divided into utterly opposed classes. One, the lower class, vulgar, stupid, and, above all, ridiculous people, who believe that one husband ought to live with the one wife whom he has lawfully married; that a girl should be innocent, a woman modest, and a man manly, self-controlled, and strong; that one ought to bring up one's children, earn one's bread, and pay one's debts; and various similar absurdities. This was the class of old-fashioned and ridiculous people. But there was another class of people, the real people. To this class they all belonged, and in it the great thing was to be elegant, generous, plucky, gay, to abandon oneself without a blush to every passion, and to laugh at everything else.

For the first moment only, Vronsky was startled after the impressions of a quite different world that he had brought with him from Moscow. But immediately as though slipping his feet into old slippers, he dropped back into the light-hearted, pleasant world he had always lived in.

The coffee was never really made, but spluttered over every one, and boiled away, doing just what was required of it—that is, providing cause for much noise and laughter, and spoiling a costly rug and the baroness's gown.

"Well now, good-bye, or you'll never get washed, and I shall have on my conscience the worst sin a gentleman can commit. So you would advise a knife to his throat?"

"To be sure, and manage that your hand may not be far from his lips. He'll kiss your hand, and all will end satisfactorily," answered Vronsky.

"So at the Français!" and, with a rustle of her skirts, she vanished.

Kamerovsky got up too, and Vronsky, not waiting for him to go, shook hands and went off to his dressing-room.

While he was washing, Petritsky described to him in brief outlines his position, as far as it had changed since Vronsky had left Petersburg. No money at all. His father said he wouldn't give him any and pay his debts. His tailor was trying to get him locked up, and another fellow, too, was threatening to get him locked up. The colonel of the regiment had announced that if these scandals did not cease he would have to leave. As for the baroness, he was sick to death of her, especially since she'd taken to offering continually to lend him money. But he had found a girl—he'd show her to Vronsky—a marvel, exquisite, in the strict Oriental style, "genre of the slave Rebecca, don't you know." He'd had a row, too, with Berkoshov, and was going to send seconds to him, but of course it would come to nothing. Altogether everything was supremely amusing and jolly. And, not letting his comrade enter into further details of his position, Petritsky proceeded to tell him all the interesting news. As he listened to Petritsky's familiar stories in the familiar setting of the rooms he had spent the last three years in, Vronsky felt a delightful sense of coming back to the careless Petersburg life that he was used to.

"Impossible!" he cried, letting down the pedal of the washing basin in which he had been sousing his healthy red neck. "Impossible!" he cried, at the news that Laura had flung over Fertinghof and had made up to Mileev. "And is he as stupid and pleased as ever? Well, and how's Buzulukov?"

"Oh, there is a tale about Buzulukov—simply lovely!" cried Petritsky. "You know his weakness for balls, and he never misses a single court ball. He went to a big ball in a new helmet. Have you seen the new helmets? Very nice, lighter. Well, so he's standing . . . No, I say, do listen."

"I am listening," answered Vronsky, rubbing himself with a rough towel.

"Up comes the Grand-Duchess with some ambassador or other, and, as ill-luck would have it, she begins talking to him about the new helmets. The Grand-Duchess positively wanted to show the new helmet to the ambassador. They see our friend standing there." (Petritsky mimicked how he was standing with the helmet.) "The Grand-Duchess asked him to give her the helmet; he doesn't give it her. What do you think of that? Well, every one's winking at him, nodding, frowning—give it to her, do! He doesn't give it to her. He's mute as a fish. Only picture it! . . . Well, the . . . what's his name, whatever he was . . . tries to take the helmet from him . . . he won't give it up! . . . He pulls it from him, and hands it to the Grand-Duchess. 'Here, your Highness,' says he, 'is the new helmet.' She turned the helmet the other side up, and—just picture it!—plop went a pear and sweetmeats out of it, two pounds of sweetmeats! . . . He'd been storing them up, the darling!"

Vronsky burst into roars of laughter. And long afterwards, when he was talking of other things, he broke out into his healthy laugh, showing his strong, close rows of teeth, when he thought of the helmet.

Having heard all the news, Vronsky, with the assistance of his valet, got into his uniform, and went off to report himself. He intended, when he had done that, to drive to his brother's, and to Betsy's, and to pay several visits with a view to beginning to go into that society where he might meet Madame Karenina. As he always did in Petersburg, he left home not meaning to return till late at night.

Part Two

CHAPTER I

At the end of the winter, in the Shtcherbatskys' house, a consultation was being held, which was to pronounce on the state of Kitty's health and the measures to be taken to restore her failing strength. She had been ill, and as spring came on she grew worse. The family doctor gave her cod-liver oil, then iron, then nitrate of silver, but as the first and the second and the third were alike in doing no good, and as his advice when spring came was to go abroad, a celebrated physician was called in. The celebrated physician, a very handsome man, still youngish, asked to examine the patient. He maintained, with peculiar satisfaction, it seemed, that maiden modesty is a mere relic of barbarism, and that nothing could be more natural than for a man still youngish to handle a young girl naked. He thought it natural because he did it every day, and felt and thought, as it seemed to him, no harm as he did it and consequently he considered modesty in the girl not merely as a relic of barbarism, but also as an insult to himself.

There was nothing for it but to submit, since, although all the doctors had studied in the same school, had read the same books, and learned the same science, and though some people said this celebrated doctor was a bad doctor, in the princess's household and circle it was for some reason accepted that this celebrated doctor alone had some special knowledge, and that he alone could save Kitty. After a careful examination and sounding of the bewildered patient, dazed with shame, the celebrated doctor, having scrupulously washed his hands, was standing in the drawing-room talking to the prince. The prince frowned and coughed, listening to the doctor. As a man who had seen something of life, and neither a fool nor an invalid, he had no faith in medicine, and in his heart was furious at the whole farce, specially as he was perhaps the only one who fully comprehended the cause of Kitty's illness. "Conceited blockhead!" he thought, as he listened to the celebrated doctor's chatter about his daughter's symptoms. The doctor was meantime with difficulty restraining the expression of his contempt for this old gentleman, and with difficulty condescending to the level of his intelligence. He perceived that it was no good talking to the old man, and that the principal person in the house was the mother. Before her he decided to scatter

his pearls. At that instant the princess came into the drawing-room with the family doctor. The prince withdrew, trying not to show how ridiculous he thought the whole performance. The princess was distracted, and did not know what to do. She felt she had sinned against Kitty.

"Well, doctor, decide our fate," said the princess. "Tell me everything."

"Is there hope?" she meant to say, but her lips quivered, and she could not utter the question. "Well, doctor?"

"Immediately, princess. I will talk it over with my colleague, and then I will have the honor of laying my opinion before you."

"So we had better leave you?"

"As you please."

The princess went out with a sigh.

When the doctors were left alone, the family doctor began timidly explaining his opinion, that there was a commencement of tuberculous trouble, but . . . and so on. The celebrated doctor listened to him, and in the middle of his sentence looked at his big gold watch.

"Yes," said he. "But . . ."

The family doctor respectfully ceased in the middle of his observations.

"The commencement of the tuberculous process we are not, as you are aware, able to define; till there are cavities, there is nothing definite. But we may suspect it. And there are indications; malnutrition, nervous excitability, and so on. The question stands thus: in presence of indications of tuberculous process, what is to be done to maintain nutrition?"

"But, you know, there are always moral, spiritual causes at the back in these cases," the family doctor permitted himself to interpolate with a subtle smile.

"Yes, that's an understood thing," responded the celebrated physician, again glancing at his watch. "Beg pardon, is the Yausky bridge done yet, or shall I have to drive round?" he asked. "Ah! it is. Oh, well, then I can do it in twenty minutes. So we were saying the problem may be put thus: to maintain nutrition and to give tone to the nerves. The one is in close connection with the other, one must attack both sides at once."

"And how about a tour abroad?" asked the family doctor.

"I've no liking to foreign tours. And take note: if there is an early stage of tuberculous process, of which we cannot be certain, a foreign tour will be of no use. What is wanted is means of improving nutrition, and not for lowering it." And the celebrated doctor expounded his plan of treatment with Soden waters, a remedy obviously prescribed primarily on the ground that they could do no harm.

The family doctor listened attentively and respectfully.

"But in favor of foreign travel I would urge the change of habits, the removal from conditions calling up reminiscences. And then the mother wishes it," he added.

"Ah! Well, in that case, to be sure, let them go. Only, those German quacks are mischievous. . . . They ought to be persuaded. . . . Well, let them go then."

He glanced once more at his watch.

"Oh! time's up already," and he went to the door. The celebrated doctor announced to the princess (a feeling of what was due from him dictated his doing so) that he ought to see the patient once more.

"What! another examination!" cried the mother, with horror.

"Oh, no, only a few details, princess."

"Come this way."

And the mother, accompanied by the doctor, went into the drawing-room to Kitty. Wasted and flushed, with a peculiar glitter in her eyes, left there by the agony of shame she had been put through, Kitty stood in the middle of the room. When the doctor came in she flushed crimson, and her eyes filled with tears. All her illness and treatment struck her as a thing so stupid, ludicrous even! Doctoring her seemed to her as absurd as putting together the pieces of a broken vase. Her heart was broken. Why would they try to cure her with pills and powders? But she could not grieve her mother, especially as her mother considered herself to blame.

"May I trouble you to sit down, princess?" the celebrated doctor said to her.

He sat down with a smile, facing her, felt her pulse, and again began asking her tiresome questions. She answered him, and all at once got up furious.

"Excuse me, doctor, but there is really no object in this. This is the third time you've asked me the same thing."

The celebrated doctor did not take offense.

"Nervous irritability," he said to the princess, when Kitty had left the room. "However, I had finished. . . ."

And the doctor began scientifically explaining to the princess, as an exceptionally intelligent woman, the condition of the young princess, and concluded by insisting on the drinking of the waters, which were certainly harmless. At the question: Should they go abroad? the doctor plunged into deep meditation, as though resolving a weighty problem. Finally his decision was pronounced: they were to go abroad, but to put no faith in foreign quacks, and to apply to him in any need.

It seemed as though some piece of good fortune had come to pass after the doctor had gone. The mother was much more cheerful when she went back to her daughter, and Kitty pretended to be more cheerful. She had often, almost always, to be pretending now.

"Really, I'm quite well, mamma. But if you want to go abroad, let's go!" she said, and trying to appear interested in the proposed tour, she began talking of the preparations for the journey.

CHAPTER II

Soon after the doctor, Dolly had arrived. She knew that there was to be a consultation that day, and though she was only just up after her confinement (she had another baby, a little girl, born at the end of the winter), though she had trouble and anxiety enough of her own, she had left her tiny baby and a sick child, to come and hear Kitty's fate, which was to be decided that day.

"Well, well?" she said, coming into the drawing-room, without taking off her hat. "You're all in good spirits. Good news, then?"

They tried to tell her what the doctor had said, but it appeared that though the doctor had talked distinctly enough and at great length, it was utterly impossible to report what he had said. The only point of interest was that it was settled they should go abroad.

Dolly could not help sighing. Her dearest friend, her sister, was going away. And her life was not a cheerful one. Her relations with Stepan Arkadyevitch after their reconciliation had become humiliating. The union Anna had cemented turned out to be of no solid character, and family harmony was breaking down again at the same point. There had been nothing definite, but Stepan Arkadyevitch was hardly ever at home; money, too, was hardly ever forthcoming, and Dolly was continually tortured by suspicions of infidelity, which she tried to dismiss, dreading the agonies of jealousy she had been through, already. The first onslaught of jealousy, once lived through, could never come back again, and even the discovery of infidelities could never now affect her as it had the first time. Such a discovery now would only mean breaking up family habits, and she let herself be deceived, despising him and still more herself, for the weakness. Besides this, the care of her large family was a constant worry to her: first, the nursing of her young baby did not go well, then the nurse had gone away, now one of the children had fallen ill.

"Well, how are all of you?" asked her mother.

"Ah, mamma, we have plenty of troubles of our own. Lili is ill, and I'm afraid it's scarlatina. I have come here now to hear about Kitty, and then I shall shut myself up entirely, if—God forbid—it should be scarlatina."

The old prince too had come in from his study after the doctor's departure, and after presenting his cheek to Dolly, and saying a few words to her, he turned to his wife:

"How have you settled it? you're going? Well, and what do you mean to do with me?"

"I suppose you had better stay here, Alexander," said his wife.

"That's as you like."

"Mamma, why shouldn't father come with us?" said Kitty. "It would be nicer for him and for us as well."

The old prince got up and stroked Kitty's hair. She lifted her head and looked at him with a forced smile. It always seemed to her that he understood her better than any one in the family, though he did not say much about her. Being the youngest, she was her father's favorite, and she fancied that his love gave him insight. When now her glance met his blue kindly eyes looking intently at her, it seemed to her that he saw right through her, and understood all that was not good that was passing within her. Reddening, she stretched out towards him expecting a kiss, but he only patted her hair and said:

"These stupid chignons! There's no getting at the real daughter, one simply strokes the bristles of dead women. Well, Dolinka," he turned to his elder daughter, "what's your young buck about, hey?"

"Nothing, father," answered Dolly, understanding that her husband was meant. "He's always out; I scarcely ever see him," she could not resist adding with a sarcastic smile.

"Why, hasn't he gone into the country yet—to see about selling that forest?"

"No, he's still getting ready for the journey."

"Oh, that's it!" said the prince. "And so am I to be getting ready for a journey too? At your service," he said to his wife, sitting down. "And I tell you what, Katia," he went on to his younger daughter, "you must wake up one fine day and say to yourself: Why, I'm quite well, and merry, and going out again with father for an early morning walk in the frost. Hey?"

What her father said seemed simple enough, yet at these words Kitty became confused and overcome like a detected criminal. "Yes, he sees it all, he understands it all, and in these words he's telling me that though I'm ashamed, I must get over my shame." She could not pluck up spirit to make any answer. She tried to begin, and all at once burst into tears, and rushed out of the room.

"See what comes of your jokes!" the princess pounced down on her husband. "You're always . . ." she began a string of reproaches.

The prince listened to the princess's scolding rather a long while without speaking, but his face was more and more frowning.

"She's so much to be pitied, poor child, so much to be pitied, and you don't feel how it hurts her to hear the slightest reference to the cause of it. Ah! to be so mistaken in people!" said the princess, and by the change in her tone both Dolly and the prince knew she was speaking of Vronsky. "I don't know why there aren't laws against such base, dishonorable people."

"Ah, I can't bear to hear you!" said the prince gloomily, getting up from his low chair, and seeming anxious to get away, yet stopping in the doorway. "There are laws, madam, and since you've challenged me to it, I'll tell you who's to blame for it all: you and you, you and nobody else. Laws against such young gallants there have always been, and there still are! Yes, if there has been nothing that ought not to have been, old as I am, I'd have called him out to the barrier, the young dandy. Yes, and now you physic her and call in these quacks."

The prince apparently had plenty more to say, but as soon as the princess heard his tone she subsided at once, and became penitent, as she always did on serious occasions.

"Alexander, Alexander," she whispered, moving to him and beginning to weep.

As soon as she began to cry the prince too calmed down. He went up to her.

"There, that's enough, that's enough! You're wretched too, I know. It can't be helped. There's no great harm done. God is merciful . . . thanks . . ." he said, not knowing what he was saying, as he responded to the tearful kiss of the princess that he felt on his hand. And the prince went out of the room.

Before this, as soon as Kitty went out of the room in tears, Dolly, with her motherly, family instincts, had promptly perceived that here a woman's work lay before her, and she prepared to do it. She took off her hat, and, morally speaking, tucked up her sleeves and prepared for action. While her mother was attacking her father, she tried to restrain her mother, so far as filial reverence would allow. During the prince's outburst she was silent; she felt ashamed for her mother, and tender towards her father for so quickly being kind again. But when her father left them she made ready for what was the chief thing needful—to go to Kitty and console her.

"I'd been meaning to tell you something for a long while, mamma: did you know that Levin meant to make Kitty an offer when he was here the last time? He told Stiva so."

"Well, what then? I don't understand. . . ."

"So did Kitty perhaps refuse him? . . . She didn't tell you so?"

"No, she has said nothing to me either of one or the other; she's too proud. But I know it's all on account of the other."

"Yes, but suppose she has refused Levin, and she wouldn't have refused him if it hadn't been for the other, I know. And then, he has deceived her so horribly."

It was too terrible for the princess to think how she had sinned against her daughter, and she broke out angrily.

"Oh, I really don't understand! Nowadays they will all go their own way, and mothers haven't a word to say in anything, and then . . ."

"Mamma, I'll go up to her."

"Well, do. Did I tell you not to?" said her mother.

CHAPTER III

WHEN she went into Kitty's little room, a pretty, pink little room, full of knick-knacks in *vieux saxe,* as fresh, and pink, and white, and gay as Kitty herself had been two months ago, Dolly remembered how they had decorated the room the year before together, with what love and gaiety. Her heart turned cold when she saw Kitty sitting on a low chair near the door, her eyes fixed immovably on a corner of the rug. Kitty glanced at her sister, and the cold, rather ill-tempered, expression of her face did not change.

"I'm just going now, and I shall have to keep in and you won't be able to come to see me," said Dolly, sitting down beside her. "I want to talk to you."

"What about?" Kitty asked swiftly, lifting her head in dismay.

"What should it be, but your trouble?"

"I have no trouble."

"Nonsense, Kitty. Do you suppose I could help knowing? I know all about it. And believe me, it's of so little consequence. . . . We've all been through it."

Kitty did not speak, and her face had a stern expression.

"He's not worth your grieving over him," pursued Darya Alexandrovna, coming straight to the point.

"No, because he has treated me with contempt," said Kitty, in a breaking voice. "Don't talk of it! Please, don't talk of it!"

"But who can have told you so? No one has said that. I'm certain he was in love with you, and would still be in love with you, if it hadn't . . ."

"Oh, the most awful thing of all for me is this sympathizing!" shrieked Kitty, suddenly flying into a passion. She turned round on her chair, flushed crimson, and rapidly moving her fingers, pinched the clasp of her belt first with one hand and then with the other. Dolly knew this trick her sister had of clenching her hands when she was much excited; she knew, too, that in moments of excitement Kitty was capable of forgetting herself and saying a great deal too much, and Dolly would have soothed her, but it was too late.

"What, what is it you want to make me feel, eh?" said Kitty quickly. "That I've been in love with a man who didn't care a straw for me, and that I'm dying of love for him? And this is said to me by my own sister, who imagines that . . . that . . . that she's sympathizing with me! . . . I don't want these condolences and this humbug!"

"Kitty, you're unjust."

"Why are you tormenting me?"

"But I . . . quite the contrary . . . I see you're unhappy. . . ."

But Kitty in her fury did not hear her.

"I've nothing to grieve over and be comforted about. I am too proud ever to allow myself to care for a man who does not love me."

"Yes, I don't say so either. . . . Only one thing. Tell me the truth," said Darya Alexandrovna, taking her by the hand: "tell me, did Levin speak to you? . . ."

The mention of Levin's name seemed to deprive Kitty of the last vestige of self-control. She leaped up from her chair, and flinging her clasp on the ground, she gesticulated rapidly with her hands and said:

"Why bring Levin in too? I can't understand what you want to torment me for. I've told you, and I say it again, that I have some pride, and never, *never* would I do as you're doing—go back to a man who's deceived you, who has cared for another woman. I can't understand it! You may, but I can't!"

And saying these words she glanced at her sister, and seeing that Dolly sat silent, her head mournfully bowed, Kitty, instead of running out of the room, as she had meant to do, sat down near the door, and hid her face in her handkerchief.

The silence lasted for two minutes: Dolly was thinking of herself. That humiliation of which she was always conscious came back to her with a peculiar bitterness when her sister reminded her of it. She had not looked for such cruelty in her sister, and she was angry with her. But suddenly she heard the rustle of a skirt, and with it the sound of heart-rending, smothered sobbing, and felt arms about her neck. Kitty was on her knees before her.

"Dolinka, I am so, so wretched!" she whispered penitently. And the sweet face covered with tears hid itself in Darya Alexandrovna's skirt.

As though tears were the indispensable oil, without which the machinery of mutual confidence could not run smoothly between the two sisters, the sisters after their tears talked, not of what was uppermost in their minds, but, though they talked of outside matters, they understood each other. Kitty knew that the words she had uttered in anger about her husband's infidelity and her humiliating position had cut her poor sister to the heart, but that she had forgiven her. Dolly for her part knew all she had wanted to find out. She felt certain that her surmises were correct; that Kitty's misery, her inconsolable misery, was due precisely to the fact that Levin had made her an offer and she had refused him, and Vronsky had deceived her, and that she was fully prepared to love Levin and to detest Vronsky. Kitty said not a word of that; she talked of nothing but her spiritual condition.

"I have nothing to make me miserable," she said, getting calmer; "but can you understand that everything has become hateful, loathsome, coarse to me, and I myself most of all? You can't imagine what loathsome thoughts I have about everything."

"Why, whatever loathsome thoughts can you have?" asked Dolly, smiling.

"The most utterly loathsome and coarse: I can't tell you. It's

151

not unhappiness, or low spirits, but much worse. As though everything that was good in me was all hidden away, and nothing was left but the most loathsome. Come, how am I to tell you?" she went on, seeing the puzzled look in her sister's eyes. "Father began saying something to me just now. . . . It seems to me he thinks all I want is to be married. Mother takes me to a ball: it seems to me she only takes me to get me married off as soon as may be, and be rid of me. I know it's not the truth, but I can't drive away such thoughts. Eligible suitors, as they call them—I can't bear to see them. It seems to me they're taking stock of me and summing me up. In old days to go anywhere in a ball-dress was a simple joy to me, I admired myself; now I feel ashamed and awkward. And then! The doctor . . . Then . . ." Kitty hesitated; she wanted to say further that ever since this change had taken place in her, Stepan Arkadyevitch had become insufferably repulsive to her, and that she could not see him without the grossest and most hideous conceptions rising before her imagination.

"Oh, well, everything presents itself to me, in the coarsest, most loathsome light," she went on. "That's my illness. Perhaps it will pass off."

"But you mustn't think about it."

"I can't help it. I'm never happy except with the children at your house."

"What a pity you can't be with me!"

"Oh, yes, I'm coming. I've had scarlatina, and I'll persuade mamma to let me."

Kitty insisted on having her way, and went to stay at her sister's and nursed the children all through the scarlatina, for scarlatina it turned out to be. The two sisters brought all the six children successfully through it, but Kitty was no better in health, and in Lent the Shtcherbatskys went abroad.

CHAPTER IV

THE highest Petersburg society is essentially one: in it every one knows every one else, every one even visits every one else. But this great set has its subdivisions. Anna Arkadyevna Kare-

nina had friends and close ties in three different circles of this highest society. One circle was her husband's government official set, consisting of his colleagues and subordinates, brought together in the most various and capricious manner, and belonging to different social strata. Anna found it difficult now to recall the feeling of almost awe-stricken reverence which she had at first entertained for these persons. Now she knew all of them as people know one another in a country town; she knew their habits and weaknesses, and where the shoe pinched each one of them. She knew their relations with one another and with the head authorities, knew who was for whom, and how each one maintained his position, and where they agreed and disagreed. But that circle of political, masculine interests had never interested her, in spite of Countess Lidia Ivanovna's influence, and she avoided it.

Another little set with which Anna was in close relations was the one by means of which Alexey Alexandrovitch had made his career. The center of this circle was the Countess Lidia Ivanovna. It was a set made up of elderly, ugly, benevolent, and godly women, and clever, learned, and ambitious men. One of the clever people belonging to the set had called it "the conscience of Petersburg society." Alexey Alexandrovitch had the highest esteem for this circle; and Anna with her special gift for getting on with every one, had in the early days of her life in Petersburg made friends in this circle also. Now, since her return from Moscow, she had come to feel this set insufferable. It seemed to her that both she and all of them were insincere, and she felt so bored and ill at ease in that world that she went to see the Countess Lidia Ivanovna as little as possible.

The third circle with which Anna had ties was preëminently the fashionable world—the world of balls, of dinners, of sumptuous dresses, the world that hung on to the court with one hand, so as to avoid sinking to the level of the demi-monde. For the demi-monde the members of that fashionable world believed that they despised, though their tastes were not merely similar, but in fact identical. Her connection with this circle was kept up through Princess Betsy Tverskaya, her cousin's wife, who had an income of a hundred and twenty thousand roubles, and who had taken a great fancy to Anna ever since she first came out, showed her much attention, and drew her into her set, making fun of Countess Lidia Ivanovna's coterie.

"When I'm old and ugly I'll be the same," Betsy used to say; "but for a pretty young woman like you it's early days for that house of charity."

Anna had at first avoided as far as she could Princess Tverskaya's world, because it necessitated an expenditure beyond her means, and besides in her heart she preferred the first circle. But since her visit to Moscow she had done quite the contrary. She avoided her serious-minded friends, and went out into the fashionable world. There she met Vronsky, and experienced an agitating joy at those meetings. She met Vronsky specially often at Betsy's, for Betsy was a Vronsky by birth and his cousin. Vronsky was everywhere where he had any chance of meeting Anna, and speaking to her, when he could, of his love. She gave him no encouragement, but every time she met him there surged up in her heart that same feeling of quickened life that had come upon her that day in the railway carriage when she saw him for the first time. She was conscious herself that her delight sparkled in her eyes and curved her lips into a smile, and she could not quench the expression of this delight.

At first Anna sincerely believed that she was displeased with him for daring to pursue her. Soon after her return from Moscow, on arriving at a soirée where she had expected to meet him, and not finding him there, she realized distinctly from the rush of disappointment that she had been deceiving herself, and that this pursuit was not merely not distasteful to her, but that it made the whole interest of her life.

A celebrated singer was singing for the second time, and all the fashionable world was in the theater. Vronsky, seeing his cousin from his stall in the front row, did not wait till the *entr'-acte,* but went to her box.

"Why didn't you come to dinner?" she said to him. "I marvel at the second-sight of lovers," she added with a smile, so that no one but he could hear; *"she wasn't there.* But come after the opera."

Vronsky looked inquiringly at her. She nodded. He thanked her by a smile, and sat down beside her.

"But how I remember your jeers!" continued Princess Betsy, who took a peculiar pleasure in following up this passion to a successful issue. "What's become of all that? You're caught, my dear boy."

"That's my one desire, to be caught," answered Vronsky, with his serene, good-humored smile. "If I complain of anything it's only that I'm not caught enough, to tell the truth. I begin to lose hope."

"Why, whatever hope can you have?" said Betsy, offended on behalf of her friend. *"Entendons nous. . . ."* But in her eyes there were gleams of light that betrayed that she understood perfectly and precisely as he did what hope he might have.

"None whatever," said Vronsky, laughing and showing his even rows of teeth. "Excuse me," he added, taking an opera-glass out of her hand, and proceeding to scrutinize, over her bare shoulder, the row of boxes facing them. "I'm afraid I'm becoming ridiculous."

He was very well aware that he ran no risk of being ridiculous in the eyes of Betsy or any other fashionable people. He was very well aware that in their eyes the position of an unsuccessful lover of a girl, or of any woman free to marry, might be ridiculous. But the position of a man pursuing a married woman, and, regardless of everything, staking his life on drawing her into adultery, has something fine and grand about it, and can never be ridiculous; and so it was with a proud and gay smile under his mustaches that he lowered the opera-glass and looked at his cousin.

"But why was it you didn't come to dinner?" she said, admiring him.

"I must tell you about that. I was busily employed, and doing what, do you suppose? I'll give you a hundred guesses, a thousand . . . you'd never guess. I've been reconciling a husband with a man who'd insulted his wife. Yes, really!"

"Well, did you succeed?"

"Almost."

"You really must tell me about it," she said, getting up. "Come to me in the next *entr'acte.*"

"I can't; I'm going to the French theater."

"From Nilsson?" Betsy queried in horror, though she could not herself have distinguished Nilsson's voice from any chorus girl's.

"Can't help it. I've an appointment there, all to do with my mission of peace."

" 'Blessed are the peacemakers; theirs is the kingdom of heaven,' " said Betsy, vaguely recollecting she had heard some similar saying from some one. "Very well, then, sit down, and tell me what it's all about."

And she sat down again.

C H A P T E R   V

"THIS is rather indiscreet, but it's so good, it's an awful temptation to tell the story," said Vronsky, looking at her with his laughing eyes. "I'm not going to mention any names."

"But I shall guess, so much the better."

"Well, listen : two festive young men were driving . . ."

"Officers of your regiment, of course?"

"I didn't say they were officers,—two young men who had been lunching."

"In other words, drinking."

"Possibly. They were driving on their way to dinner with a friend in the most festive state of mind. And they beheld a pretty woman in a hired sledge; she overtakes them, looks round at them, and, so they fancy anyway, nods to them and laughs. They, of course, follow her. They gallop at full speed. To their amazement, the fair one alights at the entrance of the very house to which they were going. The fair one darts up-stairs to the top story. They get a glimpse of red lips under a short veil, and exquisite little feet."

"You describe it with such feeling that I fancy you must be one of the two."

"And after what you said, just now! Well, the young men go in to their comrade's; he was giving a farewell dinner. There they certainly did drink a little too much, as one always does at farewell dinners. And at dinner they inquire who lives at the top in that house. No one knows; only their host's valet, in answer to

156

their inquiry whether any 'young ladies' are living on the top floor, answered that there were a great many of them about there. After dinner the two young men go into their host's study, and write a letter to the unknown fair one. They compose an ardent epistle, a declaration in fact, and they carry the letter up-stairs themselves, so as to elucidate whatever might appear not perfectly intelligible in the letter."

"Why are you telling me these horrible stories? Well?"

"They ring. A maid-servant opens the door, they hand her the letter, and assure the maid that they're both so in love that they'll die on the spot at the door. The maid, stupefied, carries in their messages. All at once a gentleman appears with whiskers like sausages, as red as a lobster, announces that there is no one living in that flat except his wife, and sends them both about their business."

"How do you know he had whiskers like sausages, as you say?"

"Ah, you shall hear. I've just been to make peace between them."

"Well, and what then?"

"That's the most interesting part of the story. It appears that it's a happy couple, a government clerk and his lady. The government clerk lodges a complaint, and I became a mediator, and such a mediator! . . . I assure you Talleyrand couldn't hold a candle to me."

"Why, where was the difficulty?"

"Ah, you shall hear. . . . We apologize in due form: we are in despair, we entreat forgiveness for the unfortunate misunderstanding. The government clerk with the sausages begins to melt, but he, too, desires to express his sentiments, and as soon as ever he begins to express them, he begins to get hot and say nasty things, and again I'm obliged to trot out all my diplomatic talents. I allowed that their conduct was bad, but I urged him to take into consideration their heedlessness, their youth; then, too, the young men had only just been lunching together. 'You understand. They regret it deeply, and beg you to overlook their misbehavior.' The government clerk was softened once more. 'I consent, count, and am ready to overlook it; but you perceive that my wife—my wife's a respectable woman—has been exposed to the persecution, and insults, and effrontery of young upstarts, scoundrels. . . .' And you must understand, the young upstarts are present all the while, and I have to keep the peace between them. Again I call out all my diplomacy, and again as soon as the thing was about at an end, our friend the government clerk gets hot and red, and his sausages stand on end with wrath, and once more I launch out into diplomatic wiles."

"Ah, he must tell you this story!" said Betsy, laughing, to a lady who came into her box. "He has been making me laugh so."

"Well, *bonne chance!*" she added, giving Vronsky one finger of the hand in which she held her fan, and with a shrug of her shoulders she twitched down the bodice of her gown that had worked up, so as to be duly naked as she moved forward towards the footlights into the light of the gas, and the sight of all eyes.

Vronsky drove to the French theater, where he really had to see the colonel of his regiment, who never missed a single performance there. He wanted to see him, to report on the result of his mediation, which had occupied and amused him for the last three days. Petritsky, whom he liked, was implicated in the affair, and the other culprit was a capital fellow and first-rate comrade, who had lately joined the regiment, the young Prince Kedrov. And what was most important, the interests of the regiment were involved in it too.

Both the young men were in Vronsky's company. The colonel of the regiment was waited upon by the government clerk, Venden, with a complaint against his officers, who had insulted his wife. His young wife, so Venden told the story—he had been married half a year—was at church with her mother, and suddenly overcome by indisposition, arising from her interesting condition, she could not remain standing, she drove home in the first sledge, a smart-looking one, she came across. On the spot the officers set off in pursuit of her; she was alarmed, and feeling still more unwell, ran up the staircase home. Venden himself, on returning from his office, heard a ring at their bell and voices, went out, and seeing the intoxicated officers with a letter, he had turned them out. He asked for exemplary punishment.

"Yes, it's all very well," said the colonel to Vronsky, whom he had invited to come and see him. "Petritsky's becoming impossible. Not a week goes by without some scandal. This government clerk won't let it drop, he'll go on with the thing."

Vronsky saw all the thanklessness of the business, and that there could be no question of a duel in it, that everything must be done to soften the government clerk, and hush the matter up. The colonel had called in Vronsky just because he knew him to be an honorable and intelligent man, and, more than all, a man who cared for the honor of the regiment. They talked it over, and decided that Petritsky and Kedrov must go with Vronsky to Venden's to apologize. The colonel and Vronsky were both fully aware that Vronsky's name and rank would be sure to contribute greatly to the softening of the injured husband's feelings.

And these two influences were not in fact without effect; though the result remained, as Vronsky had described, uncertain.

On reaching the French theater, Vronsky retired to the foyer with the colonel, and reported to him his success, or non-success. The colonel, thinking it all over, made up his mind not to pursue the matter further, but then for his own satisfaction proceeded to cross-examine Vronsky about his interview; and it was a long while before he could restrain his laughter, as Vronsky described how the government clerk, after subsiding for a while, would suddenly flare up again, as he recalled the details, and how Vronsky, at the last half word of conciliation, skillfully manœuvred a retreat, shoving Petritsky out before him.

"It's a disgraceful story, but killing. Kedrov really can't fight the gentleman! Was he so awfully hot?" he commented, laughing. "But what do you say to Claire to-day? She's marvelous," he went on, speaking of a new French actress. "However often you see her, every day she's different. It's only the French who can do that."

CHAPTER VI

Princess Betsy drove home from the theater, without waiting for the end of the last act. She had only just time to go into her dressing-room, sprinkle her long, pale face with powder, rub it, set her dress to rights, and order tea in the big drawing-room, when one after another carriages drove up to her huge house in Bolshaia Morskaia. Her guests stepped out at the wide entrance, and the stout porter, who used to read the newspapers in the mornings behind the glass door, to the edification of the passers-by, noiselessly opened the immense door, letting the visitors pass by him into the house.

Almost at the same instant the hostess, with freshly arranged coiffure and freshened face, walked in at one door and her guests at the other door of the drawing-room, a large room with dark walls, downy rugs, and a brightly lighted table, gleaming with the light of candles, white cloth, silver samovar, and transparent china tea-things.

The hostess sat down at the table and took off her gloves. Chairs were set with the aid of footmen, moving almost imperceptibly about the room; the party settled itself, divided into two groups: one round the samovar near the hostess, the other at the opposite end of the drawing-room, round the handsome wife of an ambassador, in black velvet, with sharply defined black eyebrows. In both groups conversation wavered, as it always does, for the first few minutes, broken up by meetings, greetings, offers of tea, and as it were, feeling about for something to rest upon.

"She's exceptionally good as an actress; one can see she's studied Kaulbach," said a diplomatic attaché in the group round the ambassador's wife. "Did you notice how she fell down? . . ."

"Oh, please, don't let us talk about Nilsson! No one can possibly say anything new about her," said a fat, red-faced, flaxen-headed lady, without eyebrows and chignon, wearing an old silk dress. This was Princess Myakaya, noted for her simplicity and the roughness of her manners, and nicknamed *enfant terrible*. Princess Myakaya, sitting in the middle between the two groups, and listening to both, took part in the conversation first of one and then of the other. "Three people have used that very phrase about Kaulbach to me to-day already, just as though they had made a compact about it. And I can't see why they liked that remark so."

The conversation was cut short by this observation, and a new subject had to be thought of again.

"Do tell me something amusing but not spiteful," said the ambassador's wife, a great proficient in the art of that elegant conversation called by the English, *small-talk*. She addressed the attaché, who was at a loss now what to begin upon.

"They say that that's a difficult task, that nothing's amusing that isn't spiteful," he began with a smile. "But I'll try. Get me a subject. It all lies in the subject. If a subject's given me, it's easy to spin something round it. I often think that the celebrated talkers of last century would have found it difficult to talk cleverly now. Everything clever is so stale . . ."

"That has been said long ago," the ambassador's wife interrupted him, laughing.

The conversation began amiably, but just because it was too amiable, it came to a stop again. They had to have recourse to the sure, never-failing topic—gossip.

"Don't you think there's something Louis Quinze about Tushkevitch?" he said, glancing towards a handsome, fair-haired young man, standing at the table.

"Oh, yes! He's in the same style as the drawing-room, and that's why it is he's so often here."

This conversation was maintained, since it rested on allusions to what could not be talked of in that room—that is to say, of the relations of Tushkevitch with their hostess.

Round the samovar and the hostess the conversation had been meanwhile vacillating in just the same way between three inevitable topics: the latest piece of public news, the theater, and scandal. It, too, came finally to rest on the last topic, that is, ill-natured gossip.

"Have you heard the Maltishtcheva woman—the mother, not the daughter—has ordered a costume in *diable rose* color?"

"Nonsense! No, that's too lovely!"

"I wonder that with her sense—for she's not a fool, you know—that she doesn't see how funny she is."

Every one had something to say in censure or ridicule of the luckless Madame Maltishtcheva, and the conversation crackled merrily, like a burning fagot-stack.

The husband of Princess Betsy, a good-natured fat man, an ardent collector of engravings, hearing that his wife had visitors, came into the drawing-room before going to his club. Stepping noiselessly over the thick rugs, he went up to Princess Myakaya.

"How did you like Nilsson?" he asked.

"Oh, how can you steal upon any one like that! How you startled me!" she responded. "Please don't talk to me about the opera; you know nothing about music. I'd better meet you on your own ground, and talk about your majolica and engravings. Come now, what treasure have you been buying lately at the old curiosity shops?"

"Would you like me to show you? But you don't understand such things."

"Oh, do show me! I've been learning about them at those—what's their names? . . the bankers . . . they've some splendid engravings. They showed them to us."

"Why, have you been at the Schützburgs'?" asked the hostess from the samovar.

"Yes, *ma chère*. They asked my husband and me to dinner, and told us the sauce at that dinner cost a hundred pounds," Princess Myakaya said, speaking loudly, and conscious every one was listening; "and very nasty sauce it was, some green mess. We had to ask them, and I made them sauce for eighteenpence, and everybody was very much pleased with it. I can't run to hundred-pound sauces."

"She's unique!" said the lady of the house.

"Marvelous!" said some one.

The sensation produced by Princess Myakaya's speeches was always unique, and the secret of the sensation she produced lay in the fact that though she spoke not always appropriately, as now, she said simple things with some sense in them. In the society in which she lived such plain statements produced the effect of the wittiest epigram. Princess Myakaya could never see why it had that effect, but she knew it had, and took advantage of it.

As every one had been listening while Princess Myakaya spoke, and so the conversation around the ambassador's wife had dropped, Princess Betsy tried to bring the whole party together, and she turned to the ambassador's wife.

"Will you really not have tea? You should come over here by us."

"No, we're very happy here," the ambassador's wife responded with a smile, and she went on with the conversation that had been begun.

It was a very agreeable conversation. They were criticizing the Karenins, husband and wife.

"Anna is quite changed since her stay in Moscow. There's something strange about her," said her friend.

"The great change is that she brought back with her the shadow of Alexey Vronsky," said the ambassador's wife.

"Well, what of it? There's a fable of Grimm's about a man without a shadow, a man who's lost his shadow. And that's his punishment for something. I never could understand how it was a punishment. But a woman must dislike being without a shadow."

"Yes, but women with a shadow usually come to a bad end," said Anna's friend.

"Bad luck to your tongue!" said Princess Myakaya suddenly. "Madame Karenina's a splendid woman. I don't like her husband, but I like her very much."

"Why don't you like her husband? He's such a remarkable man," said the ambassador's wife. "My husband says there are few statesmen like him in Europe."

"And my husband tells me just the same, but I don't believe it," said Princess Myakaya. "If our husbands didn't talk to us, we should see the facts as they are. Alexey Alexandrovitch, to my thinking, is simply a fool. I say it in a whisper . . . but doesn't it really make everything clear? Before, when I was told to consider him clever, I kept looking for his ability, and thought myself a fool for not seeing it; but directly I said, *he's a fool,* though only in a whisper, everything's explained, isn't it?"

"How spiteful you are to-day!"

"Not a bit. I'd no other way out of it. One of the two had to be a fool. And, well, you know one can't say that of oneself."

" 'No one is satisfied with his fortune, and every one is satisfied with his wit.' " The attaché repeated the French saying.

"That's just it, just it," Princess Myakaya turned to him. "But the point is that I won't abandon Anna to your mercies. She's so nice, so charming. How can she help it if they're all in love with her, and follow her about like shadows?"

"Oh, I had no idea of blaming her for it," Anna's friend said in self-defense.

"If no one follows us about like a shadow, that's no proof that we've any right to blame her."

And having duly disposed of Anna's friend, the Princess Myakaya got up, and together with the ambassador's wife, joined the group at the table, where the conversation was dealing with the king of Prussia.

"What wicked gossip were you talking over there?" asked Betsy.

"About the Karenins. The princess gave us a sketch of Alexey Alexandrovitch," said the ambassador's wife with a smile, as she sat down at the table.

"Pity we didn't hear it!" said Princess Betsy, glancing towards the door. "Ah, here you are at last!" she said, turning with a smile to Vronsky, as he came in.

Vronsky was not merely acquainted with all the persons whom he was meeting here; he saw them all every day; and so he came in with the quiet manner with which one enters a room full of people from whom one has only just parted.

"Where do I come from?" he said, in answer to a question from the ambassador's wife. "Well, there's no help for it, I must confess. From the *opéra bouffe.* I do believe I've seen it a hundred times, and always with fresh enjoyment. It's exquisite! I know it's disgraceful, but I go to sleep at the opera, and I sit out the *opéra bouffe* to the last minute, and enjoy it. This evening . . ."

He mentioned a French actress, and was going to tell something about her; but the ambassador's wife, with playful horror, cut him short.

"Please don't tell us about that horror."

"All right, I won't, especially as every one knows those horrors."

"And we should all go to see them if it were accepted as the correct thing, like the opera," chimed in Princess Myakaya.

CHAPTER VII

STEPS were heard at the door, and Princess Betsy, knowing it was Madame Karenina, glanced at Vronsky. He was looking towards the door, and his face wore a strange new expression. Joyfully, intently, and at the same time timidly, he gazed at the approaching figure, and slowly he rose to his feet. Anna walked into the drawing-room. Holding herself extremely erect, as always, looking straight before her, and moving with her swift, resolute, and light step, that distinguished her from all other society women, she crossed the short space to her hostess, shook hands with her, smiled, and with the same smile looked around at Vronsky. Vronsky bowed low and pushed a chair up for her.

She acknowledged this only by a slight nod, flushed a little, and frowned. But immediately, while rapidly greeting her acquaintances, and shaking the hands proffered to her, she addressed Princess Betsy:

"I have been at Countess Lidia's, and meant to have come here earlier, but I stayed on. Sir John was there. He's very interesting."

"Oh, that's this missionary?"

"Yes; he told us about the life in India, most interesting things."

The conversation, interrupted by her coming in, flickered up again like the light of a lamp being blown out.

"Sir John! Yes, Sir John; I've seen him. He speaks well. The Vlassieva girl's quite in love with him."

"And is it true the younger Vlassieva girl's to marry Topov?"

"Yes, they say it's quite a settled thing."

"I wonder at the parents! They say it's a marriage for love."

"For love? What antediluvian notions you have! Can one talk of love in these days?" said the ambassador's wife.

"What's to be done? It's a foolish old fashion that's kept up still," said Vronsky.

"So much the worse for those who keep up the fashion. The only happy marriages I know are marriages of prudence."

"Yes, but then how often the happiness of these prudent marriages flies away like dust just because that passion turns up that they have refused to recognize," said Vronsky.

"But by marriages of prudence we mean those in which both parties have sown their wild oats already. That's like scarlatina—one has to go through it and get it over."

"Then they ought to find out how to vaccinate for love, like smallpox."

"I was in love in my young days with a deacon," said the Princess Myakaya. "I don't know that it did me any good."

"No; I imagine, joking apart, that to know love, one must make mistakes and then correct them," said Princess Betsy.

"Even after marriage?" said the ambassador's wife playfully.

"'It's never too late to mend.'" The attaché repeated the English proverb.

"Just so," Betsy agreed; "one must make mistakes and correct them. What do you think about it?" She turned to Anna, who, with a faintly perceptible resolute smile on her lips, was listening in silence to the conversation.

"I think," said Anna, playing with the glove she had taken off, "I think . . . if so many men, so many minds, certainly so many hearts, so many kinds of love."

Vronsky was gazing at Anna, and with a fainting heart waiting for what she would say. He sighed as after a danger escaped when she uttered these words.

Anna suddenly turned to him.

"Oh, I have had a letter from Moscow. They write me that Kitty Shtcherbatskaya's very ill."

"Really?" said Vronsky, knitting his brows.

Anna looked sternly at him.

"That doesn't interest you?"

"On the contrary, it does, very much. What was it exactly they told you, if I may know?" he questioned.

Anna got up and went to Betsy.

"Give me a cup of tea," she said, standing at her table.

While Betsy was pouring out the tea, Vronsky went up to Anna.

"What is it they write to you?" he repeated.

"I often think men have no understanding of what's not honorable though they're always talking of it," said Anna, without answering him. "I've wanted to tell you so a long while," she added, and moving a few steps away, she sat down at a table in a corner covered with albums.

"I don't quite understand the meaning of your words," he said, handing her the cup.

She glanced towards the sofa beside her, and he instantly sat down.

"Yes, I have been wanting to tell you," she said, not looking at him. "You behaved wrongly, very wrongly."

"Do you suppose I don't know that I've acted wrongly? But who was the cause of my doing so?"

"What do you say that to me for?" she said, glancing severely at him.

"You know what for," he answered boldly and joyfully, meeting her glance and not dropping his eyes.

Not he, but she, was confused.

"That only shows you have no heart," she said. But her eyes said that she knew he had a heart, and that was why she was afraid of him.

"What you spoke of just now was a mistake, and not love."

"Remember that I have forbidden you to utter that word, that hateful word," said Anna, with a shudder. But at once she felt that by that very word "forbidden" she had shown that she acknowledged certain rights over him, and by that very fact was encouraging him to speak of love. "I have long meant to tell you this," she went on, looking resolutely into his eyes, and hot all over from the burning flush on her cheeks. "I've come on purpose this evening, knowing I should meet you. I have come to tell you that this must end. I have never blushed before any one, and you force me to feel to blame for something."

He looked at her and was struck by a new spiritual beauty in her face.

"What do you wish of me?" he said simply and seriously.

"I want you to go to Moscow and ask for Kitty's forgiveness," she said.

"You don't wish that?" he said.

He saw she was saying what she forced herself to say, not what she wanted to say.

"If you love me, as you say," she whispered, "do so that I may be at peace."

His face grew radiant.

"Don't you know that you're all my life to me? But I know no peace, and I can't give it to you; all myself—and love . . . yes. I can't think of you and myself apart. You and I are one to me. And I see no chance before us of peace for me or for you. I see a chance of despair, of wretchedness . . . or I see a chance of bliss, what bliss! . . . Can it be there's no chance of it?" he murmured with his lips; but she heard.

She strained every effort of her mind to say what ought to be said. But instead of that she let her eyes rest on him, full of love, and made no answer.

"It's come!" he thought in ecstasy. "When I was beginning to despair, and it seemed there would be no end—it's come! She loves me! She owns it!"

"Then do this for me: never say such things to me, and let us be friends," she said in words; but her eyes spoke quite differently.

"Friends we shall never be, you know that yourself. Whether we shall be the happiest or the wretchedest of people—that's in your hands."

She would have said something, but he interrupted her.

"I ask one thing only: I ask for the right to hope, to suffer as I do. But if even that cannot be, command me to disappear, and I disappear. You shall not see me if my presence is distasteful to you."

"I don't want to drive you away."

"Only don't change anything, leave everything as it is," he said in a shaky voice. "Here's your husband."

At that instant Alexey Alexandrovitch did in fact walk into the room with his calm, awkward gait.

Glancing at his wife and Vronsky, he went up to the lady of

the house, and sitting down for a cup of tea, began talking in his deliberate, always audible voice, in his habitual tone of banter, ridiculing some one.

"Your Rambouillet is in full conclave," he said, looking round at all the party; "the graces and the muses."

But Princess Betsy could not endure that tone of his—"sneering," as she called it, using the English word, and like a skillful hostess she at once brought him into a serious conversation on the subject of universal conscription. Alexey Alexandrovitch was immediately interested in the subject, and began seriously defending the new imperial decree against Princess Betsy, who had attacked it.

Vronsky and Anna still sat at the little table.

"This is getting indecorous," whispered one lady, with an expressive glance at Madame Karenina, Vronsky, and her husband.

"What did I tell you?" said Anna's friend.

But not only those ladies, almost every one in the room, even the Princess Myakaya and Betsy herself, looked several times in the direction of the two who had withdrawn from the general circle, as though that were a disturbing fact. Alexey Alexandrovitch was the only person who did not once look in that direction, and was not diverted from the interesting discussion he had entered upon.

Noticing the disagreeable impression that was being made on every one, Princess Betsy slipped some one else into her place to listen to Alexey Alexandrovitch, and went up to Anna.

"I'm always amazed at the clearness and precision of your husband's language," she said. "The most transcendental ideas seem to be within my grasp when he's speaking."

"Oh, yes!" said Anna, radiant with a smile of happiness, and not understanding a word of what Betsy had said. She crossed over to the big table and took part in the general conversation.

Alexey Alexandrovitch, after staying half an hour, went up to his wife and suggested that they should go home together. But she answered, not looking at him, that she was staying to supper. Alexey Alexandrovitch made his bows and withdrew.

The fat old Tatar, Madame Karenina's coachman, was with difficulty holding one of her pair of grays, chilled with the cold and rearing at the entrance. A footman stood opening the carriage door. The hall porter stood holding open the great door of the house. Anna Arkadyevna, with her quick little hand, was unfastening the lace of her sleeve, caught in the hook of her fur cloak, and with bent head listening with rapture to the words Vronsky murmured as he escorted her down.

"You've said nothing, of course, and I ask nothing," he was saying; "but you know that friendship's not what I want: that there's only one happiness in life for me, that word that you dislike so . . . yes, love! . . ."

"Love," she repeated slowly, in an inner voice, and suddenly, at the very instant she unhooked the lace, she added, "Why I don't like the word is that it means too much to me, far more than you can understand," and she glanced into his face. *"Au revoir!"*

She gave him her hand, and with her rapid, springy step she passed by the porter and vanished into the carriage.

Her glance, the touch of her hand, set him aflame. He kissed the palm of his hand where she had touched it, and went home, happy in the sense that he had got nearer to the attainment of his aims that evening than during the two last months.

CHAPTER VIII

ALEXEY ALEXANDROVITCH had seen nothing striking or improper in the fact that his wife was sitting with Vronsky at a table apart, in eager conversation with him about something. But he noticed that to the rest of the party this appeared something striking and improper, and for that reason it seemed to him too to be improper. He made up his mind that he must speak of it to his wife.

On reaching home Alexey Alexandrovitch went to his study, as he usually did, seated himself in his low chair, opened a book on the Papacy at the place where he had laid the paper-knife in it, and read till one o'clock, just as he usually did. But from time to time he rubbed his high forehead and shook his head, as though to drive away something. At his usual time he got up and made his toilet for the night. Anna Arkadyevna had not yet come in. With a book under his arm he went up-stairs. But this evening, instead of his usual thoughts and meditations upon official details, his thoughts were absorbed by his wife and something disagreeable connected with her. Contrary to his usual habit, he did not get into bed, but fell to walking up and down the rooms with his hands clasped behind his back. He could not go to bed, feeling that it was absolutely needful for him first to think thoroughly over the position that had just arisen.

When Alexey Alexandrovitch had made up his mind that he must talk to his wife about it, it had seemed a very easy and simple matter. But now, when he began to think over the question that had just presented itself, it seemed to him very complicated and difficult.

Alexey Alexandrovitch was not jealous. Jealousy according to his notions was an insult to one's wife, and one ought to have confidence in one's wife. Why one ought to have confidence—that is to say, complete conviction that his young wife would always love him—he did not ask himself. But he had had no experience of lack of confidence, because he had confidence in her, and told himself that he ought to have it. Now, though his conviction, that jealousy was a shameful feeling and that one ought to feel confidence, had not broken down, he felt that he was standing face to face with something illogical and irrational, and did not know what was to be done. Alexey Alexandrovitch was standing face to face with life, with the possibility of his wife's loving some one other than himself, and this seemed to him very irrational and incomprehensible because it was life itself. All his life Alexey Alexandrovitch had lived and worked in official spheres, having to do with the reflection of life. And every time he had stumbled against life itself he had shrunk away from it. Now he experienced a feeling akin to that of a man who, while calmly crossing a precipice by a bridge, should suddenly discover that the bridge is broken, and that there is a chasm below. That chasm was life itself, the bridge that artificial life in which Alexey Alexandrovitch had lived. For the first time the question presented itself to him of the possibility of his wife's loving some one else, and he was horrified at it.

He did not undress, but walked up and down with his regular tread over the resounding parquet of the dining-room, where one lamp was burning, over the carpet of the dark drawing-room, in which the light was reflected on the big new portrait of himself

171

hanging over the sofa, and across her boudoir, where two candles burned, lighting up the portraits of her parents and woman friends, and the pretty knick-knacks of her writing-table, that he knew so well. He walked across her boudoir to the bedroom door, and turned back again. At each turn in his walk, especially at the parquet of the lighted dining-room, he halted and said to himself, "Yes, this I must decide and put a stop to; I must express my view of it and my decision." And he turned back again. "But express what—what decision?" he said to himself in the drawing-room, and he found no reply. "But after all," he asked himself before turning into the boudoir, "what has occurred? Nothing. She was talking a long while with him. But what of that? Surely women in society can talk to whom they please. And then, jealousy means lowering both myself and her," he told himself as he went into her boudoir; but this dictum, which had always had such weight with him before, had now no weight and no mean-

ing at all. And from the bedroom door he turned back again; but as he entered the dark drawing-room some inner voice told him that it was not so, and that if others noticed it that showed that there was something. And he said to himself again in the dining-room, "Yes, I must decide and put a stop to it, and express my view of it. . . ."And again at the turn in the drawing-room he asked himself, "Decide how?" And again he asked himself, "What had occurred?" and answered, "Nothing," and recollected that jealousy was a feeling insulting to his wife; but again in the drawing-room he was convinced that something had happened. His thoughts, like his body, went round a complete circle, without coming upon anything new. He noticed this, rubbed his forehead, and sat down in her boudoir.

There, looking at her table, with the malachite blotting-case lying at the top and an unfinished letter, his thoughts suddenly changed. He began to think of her, of what she was thinking and feeling. For the first time he pictured vividly to himself her personal life, her ideas, her desires, and the idea that she could and should have a separate life of her own seemed to him so alarming that he made haste to dispel it. It was the chasm which he was afraid to peep into. To put himself in thought and feeling in another person's place was a spiritual exercise not natural to Alexey Alexandrovitch. He looked on this spiritual exercise as a harmful and dangerous abuse of the fancy.

"And the worst of it all," thought he, "is that just now, at the very moment when my great work is approaching completion" (he was thinking of the project he was bringing forward at the time), "when I stand in need of all my mental peace and all my energies, just now this stupid worry should fall foul of me. But what's to be done? I'm not one of those men who submit to uneasiness and worry without having the force of character to face them."

"I must think it over, come to a decision, and put it out of my mind," he said aloud.

"The question of her feelings, of what has passed and may be passing in her soul, that's not my affair; that's the affair of her conscience, and falls under the head of religion," he said to himself, feeling consolation in the sense that he had found to which division of regulating principles this new circumstance could be properly referred.

"And so," Alexey Alexandrovitch said to himself, "questions as to her feelings, and so on, are questions for her conscience, with which I can have nothing to do. My duty is clearly defined. As the head of the family, I am a person bound in duty to guide her, and consequently, in part the person responsible; I am bound to point out the danger I perceive, to warn her, even to use my authority. I ought to speak plainly to her." And everything that he would say to-night to his wife took clear shape in Alexey Alexandrovitch's head. Thinking over what he would say, he somewhat regretted that he should have to use his time and mental powers for domestic consumption, with so little to show for it, but, in spite of that, the form and contents of the speech before

173

him shaped itself as clearly and distinctly in his head as a ministerial report.

"I must say and express fully the following points: first, exposition of the value to be attached to public opinion and to decorum; secondly, exposition of religious significance of marriage; thirdly, if need be, reference to the calamity possibly ensuing to our son; fourthly, reference to the unhappiness likely to result to herself." And, interlacing his fingers, Alexey Alexandrovitch stretched them, and the joints of the fingers cracked. This trick, a bad habit, the cracking of his fingers, always soothed him, and gave precision to his thoughts, so needful to him at this juncture.

There was the sound of a carriage driving up to the front door. Alexey Alexandrovitch halted in the middle of the room.

A woman's step was heard mounting the stairs. Alexey Alexandrovitch, ready for his speech, stood compressing his crossed fingers, waiting to see if the crack would not come again. One joint cracked.

Already, from the sound of light steps on the stairs, he was aware that she was close, and though he was satisfied with his speech, he felt frightened of the explanation confronting him.

CHAPTER IX

ANNA came in with hanging head, playing with the tassels of her hood. Her face was brilliant and glowing; but this glow was not one of brightness; it suggested the fearful glow of a conflagration in the midst of a dark night. On seeing her husband, Anna raised her head and smiled, as though she had just waked up.

"You're not in bed? What a wonder!" she said, letting fall her hood, and, without stopping, she went on into the dressing-room. "It's late, Alexey Alexandrovitch," she said, when she had gone through the doorway.

"Anna, it's necessary for me to have a talk with you."

"With me?" she said, wonderingly. She came out from behind the door of the dressing-room, and looked at him. "Why, what

174

is it? What about?" she asked, sitting down. "Well, let's talk, if it's so necessary. But it would be better to get to sleep."

Anna said what came to her lips, and marveled, hearing herself, at her own capacity for lying. How simple and natural were her words, and how likely that she was simply sleepy! She felt herself clad in an impenetrable armor of falsehood. She felt that some unseen force had come to her aid and was supporting her.

"Anna, I must warn you," he began.

"Warn me?" she said. "Of what?"

She looked at him so simply, so brightly, that any one who did not know her as her husband knew her could not have noticed anything unnatural, either in the sound or the sense of her words. But to him, knowing her, knowing that whenever he went to bed five minutes later than usual, she noticed it, and asked him the reason; to him, knowing that every joy, every pleasure and pain that she felt she communicated to him at once; to him, now to see that she did not care to notice his state of mind, that she did not care to say a word about herself, meant a great deal. He saw that the inmost recesses of her soul, that had always hitherto lain open before him, were closed against him. More than that, he saw from her tone that she was not even perturbed at that, but as it were said straight out to him: "Yes, it's shut up, and so it must be, and will be in future." Now he experienced a feeling such as a man might have, returning home and finding his own house locked up. "But perhaps the key may yet be found," thought Alexey Alexandrovitch.

"I want to warn you," he said in a low voice, "that through thoughtlessness and lack of caution you may cause yourself to be talked about in society. Your too animated conversation this evening with Count Vronsky" (he enunciated the name firmly and with deliberate emphasis) "attracted attention."

He talked and looked at her laughing eyes, which frightened him now with their impenetrable look, and, as he talked, he felt all the uselessness and idleness of his words.

"You're always like that," she answered as though completely misapprehending him, and of all he had said only taking in the last phrase. "One time you don't like my being dull, and another time you don't like my being lively. I wasn't dull. Does that offend you?"

175

Alexey Alexandrovitch shivered, and bent his hands to make the joints crack.

"Oh, please, don't do that, I do so dislike it," she said.

"Anna, is this you?" said Alexey Alexandrovitch, quietly making an effort over himself, and restraining the motion of his fingers.

"But what is it all about?" she said, with such genuine and droll wonder. "What do you want of me?"

Alexey Alexandrovitch paused, and rubbed his forehead and his eyes. He saw that instead of doing as he had intended—that is to say, warning his wife against a mistake in the eyes of the world—he had unconsciously become agitated over what was the affair of her conscience, and was struggling against the barrier he fancied between them.

"This is what I meant to say to you," he went on coldly and composedly, "and I beg you to listen to it. I consider jealousy, as you know, a humiliating and degrading feeling, and I shall never allow myself to be influenced by it; but there are certain rules of decorum which cannot be disregarded with impunity. This evening it was not I observed it, but judging by the impression made on the company, every one observed that your conduct and deportment were not altogether what could be desired."

"I positively don't understand," said Anna, shrugging her shoulders.—"He doesn't care," she thought. "But other people noticed it, and that's what upsets him."—"You're not well, Alexey Alexandrovitch," she added, and she got up, and would have gone towards the door; but he moved forward as though he would stop her.

His face was ugly and forbidding, as Anna had never seen him. She stopped, and bending her head back and on one side, began with her rapid hand taking out her hairpins.

"Well, I'm listening to what's to come," she said, calmly and ironically; "and indeed I listen with interest, for I should like to understand what's the matter."

She spoke, and marveled at the confident, calm, and natural tone in which she was speaking, and the choice of the words she used.

"To enter into all the details of your feelings I have no right, and besides, I regard that as useless and even harmful," began

Alexey Alexandrovitch. "Ferreting in one's soul, one often ferrets out something that might have lain there unnoticed. Your feelings are an affair of your own conscience; but I am in duty bound to you, to myself, and to God, to point out to you your duties. Our life has been joined, not by man, but by God. That union can only be severed by a crime, and a crime of that nature brings its own chastisement."

"I don't understand a word. And, oh dear! how sleepy I am, unluckily," she said, rapidly passing her hand through her hair, feeling for the remaining hairpins.

"Anna, for God's sake don't speak like that!" he said gently. "Perhaps I am mistaken, but believe me, what I say, I say as much for myself as for you. I am your husband, and I love you."

For an instant her face fell, and the mocking gleam in her eyes died away; but the word love threw her into revolt again. She thought: "Love? Can he love? If he hadn't heard there was such a thing as love, he would never have used the word. He doesn't even know what love is."

"Alexey Alexandrovitch, really I don't understand," she said. "Define what it is you find . . ."

"Pardon, let me say all I have to say. I love you. But I am not speaking of myself; the most important persons in this matter are our son and yourself. It may very well be, I repeat, that my words seem to you utterly unnecessary and out of place; it may be that they are called forth by my mistaken impression. In that case, I beg you to forgive me. But if you are conscious yourself of even the smallest foundation for them, then I beg you to think a little, and if your heart prompts you, to speak out to me. . . ."

Alexey Alexandrovitch was unconsciously saying something utterly unlike what he had prepared.

"I have nothing to say. And besides," she said hurriedly, with difficulty repressing a smile, "it's really time to be in bed."

Alexey Alexandrovitch sighed, and, without saying more, went into the bedroom.

When she came into the bedroom, he was already in bed. His lips were sternly compressed, and his eyes looked away from her. Anna got into her bed, and lay expecting every minute that he would begin to speak to her again. She both feared his speaking and wished for it. But he was silent. She waited for a long while without moving, and had forgotten about him. She thought of that other; she pictured him, and felt how her heart was flooded with emotion and guilty delight at the thought of him. Suddenly she heard an even, tranquil snore. For the first instant Alexey Alexandrovitch seemed, as it were, appalled at his own snoring, and ceased; but after an interval of two breathings the snore sounded again, with a new tranquil rhythm.

"It's late, it's late," she whispered with a smile. A long while she lay, not moving, with open eyes, whose brilliance she almost fancied she could herself see in the darkness.

CHAPTER X

From that time a new life began for Alexey Alexandrovitch and for his wife. Nothing special happened. Anna went out into society, as she had always done, was particularly often at Princess Betsy's, and met Vronsky everywhere. Alexey Alexandrovitch saw this, but could do nothing. All his efforts to draw her into open discussion she confronted with a barrier which he could not penetrate, made up of a sort of amused perplexity. Outwardly everything was the same, but their inner relations were completely changed. Alexey Alexandrovitch, a man of great power in the world of politics, felt himself helpless in this. Like an ox with head bent, submissively he awaited the blow which he felt was lifted over him. Every time he began to think about it, he felt that he must try once more, that by kindness, tenderness, and persuasion there was still hope of saving her, of bringing her back to herself, and every day he made ready to talk to her. But every time he began talking to her, he felt that the spirit of evil and deceit, which had taken possession of her, had possession of him too, and he talked to her in a tone quite unlike that in which he had meant to talk. Involuntarily he talked to her in his habitual tone of jeering at any one who should say what he was saying. And in that tone it was impossible to say what needed to be said to her.

. . . . . .

THAT which for Vronsky had been almost a whole year the one absorbing desire of his life, replacing all his old desires; that which for Anna had been an impossible, terrible, and even for that reason more entrancing dream of bliss, that desire had been fulfilled. He stood before her, pale, his lower jaw quivering, and besought her to be calm, not knowing how or why.

"Anna! Anna!" he said with a choking voice, "Anna, for pity's sake! . . ."

But the louder he spoke, the lower she dropped her once proud and gay, now shame-stricken head, and she bowed down and sank from the sofa where she was sitting, down on the floor, at his feet; she would have fallen on the carpet if he had not held her.

"My God! Forgive me!" she said, sobbing, pressing his hands to her bosom.

She felt so sinful, so guilty, that nothing was left her but to humiliate herself and beg forgiveness; and as now there was no one in her life but him, to him she addressed her prayer for forgiveness. Looking at him, she had a physical sense of her humiliation, and she could say nothing more. He felt what a murderer must feel, when he sees the body he has robbed of life. That body, robbed by him of life, was their love, the first stage of their love. There was something awful and revolting in the memory of what had been bought at this fearful price of shame. Shame at their spiritual nakedness crushed her and infected him. But in spite of all the murderer's horror before the body of his victim, he must hack it to pieces, hide the body, must use what he has gained by his murder.

And with fury, as it were with passion, the murderer falls on the body, and drags it and hacks at it; so he covered her face and shoulders with kisses. She held his hand, and did not stir. "Yes, these kisses—that is what has been bought by this shame. Yes, and one hand, which will always be mine—the hand of my accomplice." She lifted up that hand and kissed it. He sank on his knees and tried to see her face; but she hid it, and said nothing. At last, as though making an effort over herself, she got up and

179

pushed him away. Her face was still as beautiful, but it was only the more pitiful for that.

"All is over," she said; "I have nothing but you. Remember that."

"I can never forget what is my whole life. For one instant of this happiness . . ."

"Happiness!" she said with horror and loathing and her horror unconsciously infected him. "For pity's sake, not a word, not a word more."

She rose quickly and moved away from him.

"Not a word more," she repeated, and with a look of chill despair, incomprehensible to him, she parted from him. She felt that at that moment she could not put into words the sense of shame, of rapture, and of horror at this stepping into a new life, and she did not want to speak of it, to vulgarize this feeling by inappropriate words. But later too, and the next day and the third day, she still found no words in which she could express the complexity of her feelings; indeed, she could not even find thoughts in which she could clearly think out all that was in her soul.

She said to herself: "No, just now I can't think of it, later on, when I am calmer." But this calm for thought never came; every time the thought rose of what she had done and what would happen to her, and what she ought to do, a horror came over her and she drove those thoughts away.

"Later, later," she said—"when I am calmer."

But in dreams, when she had no control over her thoughts, her position presented itself to her in all its hideous nakedness. One dream haunted her almost every night. She dreamed that both were her husbands at once, that both were lavishing caresses on her. Alexey Alexandrovitch was weeping, kissing her hands, and saying, "How happy we are now!" And Alexey Vronsky was there too, and he too was her husband. And she was marveling that it had once seemed impossible to her, was explaining to them, laughing, that this was ever so much simpler, and that now both of them were happy and contented. But this dream weighed on her like a nightmare, and she awoke from it in terror.

CHAPTER XII

In the early days after his return from Moscow, whenever Levin shuddered and grew red, remembering the disgrace of his rejection, he said to himself: "This was just how I used to shudder and blush, thinking myself utterly lost, when I was plucked in physics and did not get my remove; and how I thought myself utterly ruined after I had mismanaged that affair of my sister's that was intrusted to me. And yet, now that years have passed, I recall it and wonder that it could distress me so much. It will be the same thing too with this trouble. Time will go by and I shall not mind about this either."

But three months had passed and he had not left off minding about it; and it was as painful for him to think of it as it had been those first days. He could not be at peace because after dreaming so long of family life, and feeling himself so ripe for it, he was still not married, and was further than ever from marriage. He was painfully conscious himself, as were all about him, that at his years it is not well for man to be alone. He remembered how before starting for Moscow he had once said to his cowman Nikolay, a simple-hearted peasant, whom he liked talking to: "Well, Nikolay! I mean to get married," and how Nikolay had promptly answered, as of a matter on which there could be no possible doubt: "And high time too, Konstantin Dmitrievitch." But marriage had now become further off than ever. The place was taken, and whenever he tried to imagine any of the girls he knew in that place, he felt that it was utterly impossible. Moreover, the recollection of the rejection and the part he had played in the affair tortured him with shame. However often he told himself that he was in no wise to blame in it, that recollection, like other humiliating reminiscences of a similar kind, made him twinge and blush. There had been in his past, as in every man's, actions, recognized by him as bad, for which his conscience ought to have tormented him; but the memory of these evil actions was far from causing him so much suffering as those trivial but humiliating reminiscences. These wounds never healed. And with these memories was now ranged his rejection and the pitiful position in

181

which he must have appeared to others that evening. But time and work did their part. Bitter memories were more and more covered up by the incidents—paltry in his eyes, but really important—of his country life. Every week he thought less often of Kitty. He was impatiently looking forward to the news that she was married, or just going to be married, hoping that such news would, like having a tooth out, completely cure him.

Meanwhile spring came on, beautiful and kindly, without the delays and treacheries of spring,—one of those rare springs in which plants, beasts, and man rejoice alike. This lovely spring roused Levin still more, and strengthened him in his resolution of renouncing all his past and building up his lonely life firmly and independently. Though many of the plans with which he had returned to the country had not been carried out, still his most important resolution—that of purity—had been kept by him. He was free from that shame, which had usually harassed him after a fall; and he could look every one straight in the face. In February he had received a letter from Marya Nikolaevna telling him that his brother Nikolay's health was getting worse, but that he would not take advice, and in consequence of this letter Levin went to Moscow to his brother's, and succeeded in persuading him to see a doctor and to go to a watering-place abroad. He succeeded so well in persuading his brother, and in lending him money for the journey without irritating him, that he was satisfied with himself in that matter. In addition to his farming, which called for special attention in spring, and in addition to reading, Levin had begun that winter a work on agriculture, the plan of which turned on taking into account the character of the laborer on the land as one of the unalterable data of the question, like the climate and the soil, and consequently deducing all the principles of scientific culture, not simply from the data of soil and climate, but from the data of soil, climate, and a certain unalterable character of the laborer. Thus, in spite of his solitude, or in consequence of his solitude, his life was exceedingly full. Only rarely he suffered from an unsatisfied desire to communicate his stray ideas to some one besides Agafea Mihalovna. With her indeed he not infrequently fell into discussions upon physics, the theory of agriculture, and especially philosophy; philosophy was Agafea Mihalovna's favorite subject.

Spring was slow in unfolding. For the last few weeks it had been steadily fine frosty weather. In the daytime it thawed in the sun, but at night there were even seven degrees of frost. There was such a frozen surface on the snow that they drove the wagons anywhere off the roads. Easter came in the snow. Then all of a sudden, on Easter Monday, a warm wind sprang up, storm-clouds swooped down, and for three days and three nights the warm, driving rain fell in streams. On Thursday the wind dropped, and a thick gray fog brooded over the land as though hiding the mysteries of the transformations that were being wrought in nature. Behind the fog there was the flowing of water, the cracking and floating of ice, the swift rush of turbid, foaming torrents; and on the following Monday, in the evening, the fog parted, the storm-clouds split up into little curling crests of cloud, the sky cleared, and the real spring had come. In the morning the sun rose brilliant and quickly wore away the thin layer of ice that covered the water, and all the warm air was quivering with the steam that rose up from the quickened earth. The old grass looked greener, and the young grass thrust up its tiny blades; the buds of the guelder-rose and of the currant and the sticky birch-buds were swollen with sap, and an exploring bee was humming about the golden blossoms that studded the willow. Larks trilled unseen above the velvety green fields and the ice-covered stubble-land; peewits wailed over the low lands and marshes flooded by the pools; cranes and wild geese flew high across the sky uttering their spring calls. The cattle, bald in patches where the new hair had not grown yet, lowed in the pastures; the bow-legged lambs frisked round their bleating mothers. Nimble children ran about the drying paths, covered with the prints of bare feet. There was a merry chatter of peasant women over their linen at the pond, and the ring of axes in the yard, where the peasants were repairing ploughs and harrows. The real spring had come.

CHAPTER XIII

LEVIN put on his big boots, and, for the first time, a cloth jacket, instead of his fur cloak, and went out to look after his farm, stepping over streams of water that flashed in the sunshine and dazzled his eyes, and treading one minute on ice and the next into sticky mud.

Spring is the time of plans and projects. And, as he came out into the farmyard, Levin, like a tree in spring that knows not what form will be taken by the young shoots and twigs imprisoned in its swelling buds, hardly knew what undertakings he was going to begin upon now in the farm-work that was so dear to him. But he felt that he was full of the most splendid plans and projects. First of all he went to the cattle. The cows had been let out into their paddock, and their smooth sides were already shining with their new, sleek, spring coats; they basked in the sunshine and lowed to go to the meadow. Levin gazed admiringly at the cows he knew so intimately to the minutest detail of their condition, and gave orders for them to be driven out into the meadow, and the calves to be let into the paddock. The herdsman ran gaily to get ready for the meadow. The cowherd girls, picking up their petticoats, ran splashing through the mud with bare legs, still white, not yet brown from the sun, waving brushwood in their hands, chasing the calves that frolicked in the mirth of spring.

After admiring the young ones of that year, who were particularly fine—the early calves were the size of a peasant's cow, and Pava's daughter, at three months old, was as big as a yearling—Levin gave orders for a trough to be brought out and for them to be fed in the paddock. But it appeared that as the paddock had not been used during the winter, the hurdles made in the autumn for it were broken. He sent for the carpenter, who, according to his orders, ought to have been at work at the thrashing-machine. But it appeared that the carpenter was repairing the harrows, which ought to have been repaired before Lent. This was very annoying to Levin. It was annoying to come upon that everlasting slovenliness in the farm-work against which he had been striving with all his might for so many years. The hurdles, as he ascertained, being not wanted in winter, had been carried to the cart-horses' stable, and there broken, as they were of light construction, only meant for folding calves. Moreover, it was apparent also that the harrows and all the agricultural implements, which he had directed to be looked over and repaired in the winter, for which very purpose he had hired three carpenters, had not been put into repair, and the harrows were being repaired when they ought to have been harrowing the field. Levin sent for his bailiff, but immediately went off himself to look for him. The bailiff, beaming all over, like every one that day, in a sheepskin bordered with astrachan, came out of the barn, twisting a bit of straw in his hands.

"Why isn't the carpenter at the thrashing-machine?"

"Oh, I meant to tell you yesterday, the harrows want repairing. Here it's time they got to work in the fields."

"But what were they doing in the winter, then?"

"But what did you want the carpenter for?"

"Where are the hurdles for the calves' paddock?"

"I ordered them to be got ready. What would you have with those peasants!" said the bailiff, with a wave of his hand.

"It's not those peasants but this bailiff!" said Levin, getting angry. "Why, what do I keep you for?" he cried. But, bethinking himself that this would not help matters, he stopped short in the middle of a sentence, and merely sighed. "Well, what do you say? Can sowing begin?" he asked, after a pause.

"Behind Turkin to-morrow or next day they might begin."

"And the clover?"

"I've sent Vassily and Mishka; they're sowing. Only I don't know if they'll manage to get through; it's so slushy."

"How many acres?"

"About fifteen."

"Why not sow all?" cried Levin.

That they were only sowing the clover on fifteen acres, not on all the forty-five, was still more annoying to him. Clover, as he knew, both from books and from his own experience, never did well except when it was sown as early as possible, almost in the snow. And yet Levin could never get this done.

"There's no one to send. What would you have with such a set of peasants? Three haven't turned up. And there's Semyon . . ."

"Well, you should have taken some men from the thatching."

"And so I have, as it is."

"Where are the peasants, then?"

"Five are making *compôte*" (which meant compost), "four are shifting the oats for fear of a touch of mildew, Konstantin Dmitrievitch."

Levin knew very well that "a touch of mildew" meant that his English seed oats were already ruined. Again they had not done as he had ordered.

"Why, but I told you during Lent to put in pipes," he cried.

"Don't put yourself out; we shall get it all done in time."

Levin waved his hand angrily, went into the granary to glance at the oats, and then to the stable. The oats were not yet spoiled. But the peasants were carrying the oats in spades when they might simply let them slide down into the lower granary; and arranging for this to be done, and taking two workmen from there for sowing clover, Levin got over his vexation with the bailiff. Indeed, it was such a lovely day that one could not be angry.

"Ignat!" he called to the coachman, who, with his sleeves tucked up, was washing the carriage wheels, "saddle me . . ."

"Which, sir?"

"Well, let it be Kolpik."

"Yes, sir."

While they were saddling his horse, Levin again called up the bailiff, who was hanging about in sight, to make it up with him, and began talking to him about the spring operations before them, and his plans for the farm.

The wagons were to begin carting manure earlier, so as to get all done before the early mowing. And the ploughing of the further land to go on without a break so as to let it ripen lying fallow. And the mowing to be all done by hired labor, not on half-profits. The bailiff listened attentively, and obviously made an effort to approve of his employer's projects. But still he had that look Levin knew so well that always irritated him, a look of hopelessness and despondency. That look said: "That's all very well, but as God wills."

Nothing mortified Levin so much as that tone. But it was the tone common to all the bailiffs he had ever had. They had all taken up that attitude to his plans, and so now he was not angered by it, but mortified, and felt all the more roused to struggle against this, as it seemed, elemental force continually ranged against him, for which he could find no other expression than "as God wills."

"If we can manage it, Konstantin Dmitrievitch," said the bailiff.

"Why ever shouldn't you manage it?"

"We positively must have another fifteen laborers. And they don't turn up. There were some here to-day asking seventy roubles for the summer."

Levin was silent. Again he was brought face to face with that opposing force. He knew that however much they tried, they could not hire more than forty—thirty-seven perhaps or thirty-eight—laborers for a reasonable sum. Some forty had been taken on, and there were no more. But still he could not help struggling against it.

"Send to Sury, to Tchefirovka; if they don't come we must look for them."

"Oh, I'll send, to be sure," said Vassily Fedorovitch despondently. "But there are the horses too, they're not good for much."

"We'll get some more. I know, of course," Levin added laughing, "you always want to do with as little and as poor quality as possible; but this year I'm not going to let you have things your own way. I'll see to everything myself."

"Why, I don't think you take much rest as it is. It cheers us up to work under the master's eye. . . ."

"So they're sowing clover behind the Birch Dale? I'll go and have a look at them," he said, getting on to the little bay cob, Kolpik, who was led up by the coachman.

"You can't get across the streams, Konstantin Dmitrievitch," the coachman shouted.

"All right, I'll go by the forest."

And Levin rode through the slush of the farmyard to the gate and out into the open country, his good little horse, after his long inactivity, stepping out gallantly, snorting over the pools, and asking, as it were, for guidance. If Levin had felt happy before in the cattle-pens and farmyard, he felt happier yet in the open country. Swaying rhythmically with the ambling paces of his good little cob, drinking in the warm yet fresh scent of the snow and the air, as he rode through his forest over the crumbling, wasted snow, still left in parts, and covered with dissolving tracks, he rejoiced over every tree, with the moss reviving on its bark and

187

the buds swelling on its shoots. When he came out of the forest, in the immense plain before him, his grass fields stretched in an unbroken carpet of green, without one bare place or swamp, only spotted here and there in the hollows with patches of melting snow. He was not put out of temper even by the sight of the peasants' horses and colts trampling down his young grass (he told a peasant he met to drive them out), nor by the sarcastic and stupid reply of the peasant Ipat, whom he met on the way, and asked, "Well, Ipat, shall we soon be sowing?" "We must get the ploughing done first, Konstantin Dmitrievitch," answered Ipat. The further he rode, the happier he became, and plans for the land rose to his mind each better than the last; to plant all his fields with hedges along the southern borders, so that the snow should not lie under them; to divide them up into six fields of arable and three of pasture and hay; to build a cattle-yard at the further end of the estate, and to dig a pond and to construct movable pens for the cattle as a means of manuring the land. And then eight hundred acres of wheat, three hundred of potatoes, and four hundred of clover, and not one acre exhausted.

Absorbed in such dreams, carefully keeping his horse by the hedges, so as not to trample his young crops, he rode up to the laborers who had been sent to sow clover. A cart with the seed in it was standing, not at the edge, but in the middle of the crop, and the winter-corn had been torn up by the wheels and trampled by the horse. Both the laborers were sitting in the hedge, probably smoking a pipe together. The earth in the cart, with which the seed was mixed, was not crushed to powder, but crusted together or adhering in clods. Seeing the master, the laborer, Vassily, went towards the cart, while Mishka set to work sowing. This was not as it should be, but with the laborers Levin seldom lost his temper. When Vassily came up, Levin told him to lead the horse to the hedge.

"It's all right, sir, it'll spring up again," responded Vassily.

"Please don't argue," said Levin, "but do as you're told."

"Yes, sir," answered Vassily, and he took the horse's head. "What a sowing, Konstantin Dmitrievitch," he said, hesitating; "first rate. Only it's a work to get about! You drag a ton of earth on your shoes."

"Why is it you have earth that's not sifted?" said Levin.

"Well, we crumble it up," answered Vassily, taking up some seed and rolling the earth in his palms.

Vassily was not to blame for their having filled up his cart with unsifted earth, but still it was annoying.

Levin had more than once already tried a way he knew for stifling his anger, and turning all that seemed dark right again, and he tried that way now. He watched how Mishka strode along, swinging the huge clods of earth that clung to each foot; and getting off his horse, he took the sieve from Vassily and started sowing himself.

"Where did you stop?"

Vassily pointed to the mark with his foot, and Levin went forward as best he could, scattering the seed on the land. Walking was as difficult as on a bog, and by the time Levin had ended the row he was in a great heat, and he stopped and gave up the sieve to Vassily.

"Well, master, when summer's here, mind you don't scold me for these rows," said Vassily.

"Eh?" said Levin cheerily, already feeling the effect of his method.

"Why, you'll see in the summer-time. It'll look different. Look you where I sowed last spring. How I did work at it! I do my best, Konstantin Dmitrievitch, d'ye see, as I would for my own father. I don't like bad work myself, nor would I let another man do it. What's good for the master's good for us too. To look out yonder now," said Vassily, pointing, "it does one's heart good."

"It's a lovely spring, Vassily."

"Why, it's a spring such as the old men don't remember the like of. I was up home; an old man up there has sown wheat too, about an acre of it. He was saying you wouldn't know it from rye."

"Have you been sowing wheat long?"

"Why, sir, it was you taught us the year before last. You gave me two measures. We sold about eight bushels and sowed a rood."

"Well, mind you crumble up the clods," said Levin, going towards his horse, "and keep an eye on Mishka. And if there's a good crop you shall have half a rouble for every acre."

"Humbly thankful. We are very well content, sir, as it is."

189

Levin got on his horse and rode towards the field where was last year's clover, and the one which was ploughed ready for the spring corn.

The crop of clover coming up in the stubble was magnificent. It had survived everything, and stood up vividly green through the broken stalks of last year's wheat. The horse sank in up to the pasterns, and he drew each hoof with a sucking sound out of the half-thawed ground. Over the ploughland riding was utterly impossible; the horse could only keep a foothold where there was ice, and in the thawing furrows he sank deep in at each step. The ploughland was in splendid condition; in a couple of days it would be fit for harrowing and sowing. Everything was capital, everything was cheering. Levin rode back across the streams, hoping the water would have gone down. And he did in fact get across, and startled two ducks. "There must be snipe too," he thought, and just as he reached the turning homewards he met the forest-keeper, who confirmed his theory about the snipe.

Levin went home at a trot, so as to have time to eat his dinner and get his gun ready for the evening.

CHAPTER XIV

As HE rode up to the house in the happiest frame of mind, Levin heard the bell ring at the side of the principal entrance of the house.

"Yes, that's some one from the railway station," he thought, "just the time to be here from the Moscow train. . . . Who could it be? What if it's brother Nikolay? He did say: 'Maybe I'll go to the waters, or maybe I'll come down to you.' " He felt dismayed and vexed for the first minute, that his brother Nikolay's presence should come to disturb his happy mood of spring. But he felt ashamed of the feeling, and at once he opened, as it were, the arms of his soul, and with a softened feeling of joy and expectation, now he hoped with all his heart that it was his brother. He pricked up his horse, and riding out from behind the acacias he saw a hired three-horse sledge from the railway station, and a gentleman in a fur coat. It was not his brother. "Oh, if it were only some nice person one could talk to a little!" he thought.

"Ah," cried Levin joyfully, flinging up both his hands. "Here's a delightful visitor! Ah, how glad I am to see you!" he shouted, recognizing Stepan Arkadyevitch.

"I shall find out for certain whether she's married, or when she's going to be married," he thought. And on that delicious spring day he felt that the thought of her did not hurt him at all.

"Well, you didn't expect me, eh?" said Stepan Arkadyevitch, getting out of the sledge, splashed with mud on the bridge of his nose, on his cheek, and on his eyebrows, but radiant with health and good spirits. "I've come to see you in the first place," he said, embracing and kissing him, "to have some stand-shooting second, and to sell the forest at Ergushovo third."

"Delightful! What a spring we're having! How ever did you get along in a sledge?"

"In a cart it would have been worse still, Konstantin Dmitrievitch," answered the driver, who knew him.

"Well, I'm very, very glad to see you," said Levin, with a genuine smile of childlike delight.

Levin led his friend to the room set apart for visitors, where Stepan Arkadyevitch's things were carried also—a bag, a gun in a case, a satchel for cigars. Leaving him there to wash and change his clothes, Levin went off to the counting-house to speak about the ploughing and clover. Agafea Mihalovna, always very anxious for the credit of the house, met him in the hall with inquiries about dinner.

"Do just as you like, only let it be as soon as possible," he said, and went to the bailiff.

When he came back, Stepan Arkadyevitch, washed and combed, came out of his room with a beaming smile, and they went up-stairs together.

"Well, I am glad I managed to get away to you! Now I shall understand what the mysterious business is that you are always absorbed in here. No, really, I envy you. What a house, how nice it all is! So bright, so cheerful!" said Stepan Arkadyevitch, forgetting that it was not always spring and fine weather like that day. "And your nurse is simply charming! A pretty maid in an apron might be even more agreeable, perhaps; but for your severe monastic style it does very well."

Stepan Arkadyevitch told him many interesting pieces of news; especially interesting to Levin was the news that his brother, Sergey Ivanovitch, was intending to pay him a visit in the summer.

Not one word did Stepan Arkadyevitch say in reference to Kitty and the Shtcherbatskys; he merely gave him greetings from his wife. Levin was grateful to him for his delicacy, and was very glad of his visitor. As always happened with him during his solitude, a mass of ideas and feelings had been accumulating within him, which he could not communicate to those about him. And now he poured out upon Stepan Arkadyevitch his poetic joy in the spring, and his failures and plans for the land, and his thoughts and criticisms on the books he had been reading, and the idea of his own book, the basis of which really was, though he was unaware of it himself, a criticism of all the old books on agriculture. Stepan Arkadyevitch, always charming, understanding everything at the slightest reference, was particularly charming on this visit, and Levin noticed in him a special tenderness, as it were, and a new tone of respect that flattered him.

The efforts of Agafea Mihalovna and the cook, that the dinner should be particularly good, only ended in the two famished friends attacking the preliminary course, eating a great deal of bread-and-butter, salt goose and salted mushrooms, and in Levin's finally ordering the soup to be served without the accompaniment of little pies, with which the cook had particularly meant to impress their visitor. But though Stepan Arkadyevitch was accustomed to very different dinners, he thought everything excellent: the herb-brandy, and the bread, and the butter, and above all the salt goose and the mushrooms, and the nettle soup, and the chicken in white sauce, and the white Crimean wine— everything was superb and delicious.

"Splendid, splendid!" he said, lighting a fat cigar after the roast. "I feel as if, coming to you, I had landed on a peaceful shore after the noise and jolting of a steamer. And so you maintain that the laborer himself is an element to be studied and to regulate the choice of methods in agriculture. Of course, I'm an ignorant outsider; but I should fancy theory and its application will have its influence on the laborer too."

"Yes, but wait a bit. I'm not talking of political economy, I'm talking of the science of agriculture. It ought to be like the natural sciences, and to observe given phenomena and the laborer in his economic, ethnographical . . ."

At that instant Agafea Mihalovna came in with jam.

"Oh, Agafea Mihalovna," said Stepan Arkadyevitch, kissing the tips of his plump fingers, "what salt goose, what herb-brandy! . . . What do you think, isn't it time to start, Kostya?" he added.

Levin looked out of the window at the sun sinking behind the bare tree-tops of the forest.

"Yes, it's time," he said. "Kouzma, get ready the trap," and he ran down-stairs.

Stepan Arkadyevitch, going down, carefully took the canvas cover off his varnished gun-case with his own hands, and opening it, began to get ready his expensive new-fashioned gun. Kouzma, who already scented a big tip, never left Stepan Arkadyevitch's side, and put on him both his stockings and boots, a task which Stepan Arkadyevitch readily left him.

"Kostya, give orders that if the merchant Ryabinin comes . . . I told him to come to-day, he's to be brought in and to wait for me . . ."

"Why, do you mean to say you're selling the forest to Ryabinin?"

"Yes. Do you know him?"

"To be sure I do. I have had to do business with him, 'positively and conclusively.' "

Stepan Arkadyevitch laughed. "Positively and conclusively" were the merchant's favorite words.

"Yes, it's wonderfully funny the way he talks. She knows where her master's going!" he added, patting Laska, who hung about Levin, whining and licking his hands, his boots, and his gun.

The trap was already at the steps when they went out.

"I told them to bring the trap round; or would you rather walk?"

"No, we'd better drive," said Stepan Arkadyevitch, getting into the trap. He sat down, tucked the tiger-skin rug round him, and lighted a cigar. "How is it you don't smoke? A cigar is a sort of thing, not exactly a pleasure, but the crown and outward sign of pleasure. Come, this is life! How splendid it is! This is how I should like to live!"

"Why, who prevents you?" said Levin, smiling.

"No, you're a lucky man! You've got everything you like. You like horses—and you have them; dogs—you have them; shooting—you have it; farming—you have it."

"Perhaps because I rejoice in what I have, and don't fret for what I haven't," said Levin, thinking of Kitty.

Stepan Arkadyevitch comprehended, looked at him, but said nothing.

Levin was grateful to Oblonsky for noticing, with his never-failing tact, that he dreaded conversation about the Shtcherbatskys, and so saying nothing about them. But now Levin was longing to find out what was tormenting him so, yet he had not the courage to begin.

"Come, tell me how things are going with you," said Levin, bethinking himself that it was not nice of him to think only of himself.

Stepan Arkadyevitch's eyes sparkled merrily.

"You don't admit, I know, that one can be fond of new rolls when one has had one's rations of bread—to your mind it's a crime; but I don't count life as life without love," he said, taking Levin's question in his own way. "What am I to do? I'm made that way. And really, one does so little harm to any one, and gives oneself so much pleasure . . ."

"What! is there something new, then?" queried Levin.

"Yes, my boy, there is! There, do you see, you know the type of Ossian's women . . . Women, such as one sees in dreams . . . Well, these women are sometimes to be met in reality . . . and these women are terrible. Woman, don't you know, is such a subject that however much you study it, it's always perfectly new."

"Well, then, it would be better not to study it."

"No. Some mathematician has said that enjoyment lies in the search for truth, not in the finding it."

Levin listened in silence, and in spite of all the efforts he made, he could not in the least enter into the feelings of his friend and understand his sentiments and the charm of studying such women.

CHAPTER XV

THE place fixed on for the stand-shooting was not far above a stream in a little aspen copse. On reaching the copse, Levin got out of the trap and led Oblonsky to a corner of a mossy, swampy glade, already quite free from snow. He went back himself to a double birch-tree on the other side, and leaning his gun on the fork of a dead lower branch, he took off his full overcoat, fastened his belt again, and worked his arms to see if they were free.

Gray old Laska, who had followed them, sat down warily opposite him and pricked up her ears. The sun was setting behind a thick forest, and in the glow of sunset the birch-trees, dotted about in the aspen copse, stood out clearly with their hanging twigs, and their buds swollen almost to bursting.

From the thickest parts of the copse, where the snow still remained, came the faint sound of narrow winding threads of water running away. Tiny birds twittered, and now and then fluttered from tree to tree.

In the pauses of complete stillness there came the rustle of last year's leaves, stirred by the thawing of the earth and the growth of the grass.

"Imagine! One can hear and see the grass growing!" Levin said to himself, noticing a wet, slate-colored aspen leaf moving beside a blade of young grass. He stood, listened, and gazed sometimes down at the wet mossy ground, sometimes at Laska listening all alert, sometimes at the sea of bare tree-tops that stretched on the slope below him, sometimes at the darkening sky, covered with white streaks of cloud.

A hawk flew high over a forest far away with slow sweep of its wings; another flew with exactly the same motion in the same direction and vanished. The birds twittered more and more loudly and busily in the thicket. An owl hooted not far off, and Laska, starting, stepped cautiously a few steps forward, and putting her head on one side, began to listen intently. Beyond the stream was heard the cuckoo. Twice she uttered her usual cuckoo-call, and then gave a hoarse, hurried call and broke down.

"Imagine! the cuckoo already!" said Stepan Arkadyevitch, coming out from behind a bush.

"Yes, I hear it," answered Levin, reluctantly breaking the stillness with his voice, which sounded disagreeable to himself. "Now it's coming!"

Stepan Arkadyevitch's figure again went behind the bush, and Levin saw nothing but the bright flash of a match, followed by the red glow and blue smoke of a cigarette.

"Tchk! tchk!" came the snapping sound of Stepan Arkadye-vitch cocking his gun.

"What's that cry?" asked Oblonsky, drawing Levin's attention to a prolonged cry, as though a colt were whinnying in a high voice, in play.

"Oh, don't you know it? That's the hare. But enough talking! Listen, it's flying!" almost shrieked Levin, cocking his gun.

They heard a shrill whistle in the distance, and in the exact time, so well-known to the sportsman, two seconds later—another, a third, and after the third whistle the hoarse, guttural cry could be heard.

Levin looked about him to right and to left, and there, just facing him against the dusky blue sky above the confused mass of tender shoots of the aspens, he saw the flying bird. It was flying straight towards him; the guttural cry, like the even tearing of some strong stuff, sounded close to his ear; the long beak and neck of the bird could be seen, and at the very instant when Levin was taking aim, behind the bush where Oblonsky stood, there was a flash of red lightning: the bird dropped like an arrow, and darted upwards again. Again came the red flash and the sound of a blow, and fluttering its wings as though trying to keep up in the air, the bird halted, stopped still an instant, and fell with a heavy splash on the slushy ground.

"Can I have missed it?" shouted Stepan Arkadyevitch, who could not see for the smoke.

"Here it is!" said Levin, pointing to Laska, who with one ear raised, wagging the end of her shaggy tail, came slowly back as though she would prolong the pleasure, and as it were smiling,

brought the dead bird to her master. "Well, I'm glad you were successful," said Levin, who, at the same time, had a sense of envy that he had not succeeded in shooting the snipe.

"It was a bad shot from the right barrel," responded Stepan Arkadyevitch, loading his gun. "Sh . . . it's flying!"

The shrill whistles rapidly following one another were heard again. Two snipe, playing and chasing one another, and only whistling, not crying, flew straight at the very heads of the sportsmen. There was the report of four shots, and like swallows the snipe turned swift somersaults in the air and vanished from sight.

. . . . . .

The stand-shooting was capital. Stepan Arkadyevitch shot two more birds and Levin two, of which one was not found. It began to get dark. Venus, bright and silvery, shone with her soft light low down in the west behind the birch-trees, and high up in the east twinkled the red lights of Arcturus. Over his head Levin made out the stars of the Great Bear and lost them again. The snipe had ceased flying; but Levin resolved to stay a little longer, till Venus, which he saw below a branch of birch, should be above it, and the stars of the Great Bear should be perfectly plain. Venus had risen above the branch, and the car of the Great

Bear with its shaft was now all plainly visible against the dark blue sky, yet still he waited.

"Isn't it time to go home?" said Stepan Arkadyevitch.

It was quite still now in the copse, and not a bird was stirring.

"Let's stay a little while," answered Levin.

"As you like."

They were standing now about fifteen paces from one another.

"Stiva!" said Levin unexpectedly; "how is it you don't tell me whether your sister-in-law's married yet, or when she's going to be?"

Levin felt so resolute and serene that no answer, he fancied, could affect him. But he had never dreamed of what Stepan Arkadyevitch replied.

"She's never thought of being married, and isn't thinking of it; but she's very ill, and the doctors have sent her abroad. They're positively afraid she may not live."

"What!" cried Levin. "Very ill? What is wrong with her? How has she . . . ?"

While they were saying this, Laska, with ears pricked up, was looking upwards at the sky, and reproachfully at them.

"They have chosen a time to talk," she was thinking. "It's on the wing . . . Here it is, yes, it is. They'll miss it," thought Laska.

But at that very instant both suddenly heard a shrill whistle which, as it were, smote on their ears, and both suddenly seized their guns and two flashes gleamed, and two bangs sounded at the very same instant. The snipe flying high above instantly folded its wings and fell into a thicket, bending down the delicate shoots.

"Splendid! Together!" cried Levin, and he ran with Laska into the thicket to look for the snipe.

"Oh, yes, what was it that was unpleasant?" he wondered. "Yes, Kitty's ill. . . . Well, it can't be helped; I'm very sorry," he thought.

"She's found it! Isn't she a clever thing?" he said, taking the warm bird from Laska's mouth and packing it into the almost full game-bag. "I've got it, Stiva!" he shouted.

CHAPTER XVI

ON THE way home Levin asked all details of Kitty's illness and the Shtcherbatskys' plans, and though he would have been ashamed to admit it, he was pleased at what he heard. He was pleased that there was still hope, and still more pleased that she should be suffering who had made him suffer so much. But when Stepan Arkadyevitch began to speak of the causes of Kitty's illness, and mentioned Vronsky's name, Levin cut him short.

"I have no right whatever to know family matters, and, to tell the truth, no interest in them either."

Stepan Arkadyevitch smiled hardly perceptibly, catching the instantaneous change he knew so well in Levin's face, which had become as gloomy as it had been bright a minute before.

"Have you quite settled about the forest with Ryabinin?" asked Levin.

"Yes, it's settled. The price is magnificent; thirty-eight thousand. Eight straight away, and the rest in six years. I've been bothering about it for ever so long. No one would give more."

"Then you've as good as given away your forest for nothing," said Levin gloomily.

"How do you mean for nothing?" said Stepan Arkadyevitch with a good-humored smile, knowing that nothing would be right in Levin's eyes now.

"Because the forest is worth at least a hundred and fifty roubles the acre," answered Levin.

"Oh, these farmers!" said Stepan Arkadyevitch playfully. "Your tone of contempt for us poor townsfolk! . . . But when it comes to business, we do it better than any one. I assure you I have reckoned it all out," he said, "and the forest is fetching a very good price—so much so that I'm afraid of this fellow's crying off, in fact. You know it's not 'timber,'" said Stepan Arkadyevitch, hoping by this distinction to convince Levin completely of the unfairness of his doubts. "And it won't run to more than twenty-five yards of fagots per acre, and he's giving me at the rate of seventy roubles the acre."

Levin smiled contemptuously. "I know," he thought, "that

fashion not only in him, but in all city people, who, after being twice in ten years in the country, pick up two or three phrases and use them in season and out of season, firmly persuaded that they know all about it. '*Timber, run to so many yards the acre.*' He says those words without understanding them himself."

"I wouldn't attempt to teach you what you write about in your office," said he, "and if need arose, I should come to you to ask about it. But you're so positive you know all the lore of the forest. It's difficult. Have you counted the trees?"

"How count the trees?" said Stepan Arkadyevitch, laughing, still trying to draw his friend out of his ill-temper. "Count the sands of the sea, number the stars. Some higher power might do it."

"Oh, well, the higher power of Ryabinin can. Not a single merchant ever buys a forest without counting the trees, unless they get it given them for nothing, as you're doing now. I know your forest. I go there every year shooting, and your forest's worth a hundred and fifty roubles an acre paid down, while he's giving you sixty by installments. So that in fact you're making him a present of thirty thousand."

"Come, don't let your imagination run away with you," said Stepan Arkadyevitch piteously. "Why was it none would give it, then?"

"Why, because he has an understanding with the merchants; he's bought them off. I've had to do with all of them; I know them. They're not merchants, you know: they're speculators. He wouldn't look at a bargain that gave him ten, fifteen per cent profit, but holds back to buy a rouble's worth for twenty kopecks."

"Well, enough of it! You're out of temper."

"Not the least," said Levin gloomily, as they drove up to the house.

At the steps there stood a trap tightly covered with iron and leather, with a sleek horse tightly harnessed with broad collar-straps. In the trap sat the chubby, tightly belted clerk who served Ryabinin as coachman. Ryabinin himself was already in the house, and met the friends in the hall. Ryabinin was a tall, thin-nish, middle-aged man, with mustache and a projecting clean-shaven chin, and prominent muddy-looking eyes. He was dressed in a long-skirted blue coat, with buttons below the waist at the back, and wore high boots wrinkled over the ankles and straight over the calf, with big goloshes drawn over them. He rubbed his face with his handkerchief, and wrapping round him his coat, which sat extremely well as it was, he greeted them with a smile, holding out his hand to Stepan Arkadyevitch, as though he wanted to catch something.

"So here you are," said Stepan Arkadyevitch, giving him his hand. "That's capital."

"I did not venture to disregard your excellency's commands, though the road was extremely bad. I positively walked the whole way, but I am here at my time. Konstantin Dmitrievitch, my respects"; he turned to Levin, trying to seize his hand too. But Levin, scowling, made as though he did not notice his hand, and took out the snipe. "Your honors have been diverting yourselves with the chase? What kind of bird may it be, pray?" added Ryabinin, looking contemptuously at the snipe: "a great delicacy, I suppose." And he shook his head disapprovingly, as though he had grave doubts whether this game were worth the candle.

"Would you like to go into my study?" Levin said in French to Stepan Arkadyevitch, scowling morosely. "Go into my study; you can talk there."

"Quite so, where you please," said Ryabinin with contemptuous dignity, as though wishing to make it felt that others might be in difficulties as to how to behave, but that he could never be in any difficulty about anything.

On entering the study Ryabinin looked about, as his habit was, as though seeking the holy picture, but when he had found it, he did not cross himself. He scanned the bookcases and bookshelves, and with the same dubious air with which he had regarded the snipe, he smiled contemptuously and shook his head disapprovingly, as though by no means willing to allow that this game were worth the candle.

"Well, have you brought the money?" asked Oblonsky. "Sit down."

"Oh, don't trouble about the money. I've come to see you to talk it over."

"What is there to talk over? But do sit down."

"I don't mind if I do," said Ryabinin, sitting down and leaning his elbows on the back of his chair in a position of the most intense discomfort to himself. "You must knock it down a bit, prince. It would be too bad. The money is ready conclusively to the last farthing. As to paying the money down, there'll be no hitch there."

Levin, who had meanwhile been putting his gun away in the cupboard, was just going out of the door, but catching the merchant's words, he stopped.

"Why, you've got the forest for nothing as it is," he said. "He came to me too late, or I'd have fixed the price for him."

Ryabinin got up, and in silence, with a smile, he looked Levin down and up.

"Very close about money is Konstantin Dmitrievitch," he said with a smile, turning to Stepan Arkadyevitch; "there's positively no dealing with him. I was bargaining for some wheat of him, and a pretty price I offered too."

"Why should I give you my goods for nothing? I didn't pick it up on the ground, nor steal it either."

"Mercy on us! nowadays there's no chance at all of stealing. With the open courts and everything done in style, nowadays there's no question of stealing. We are just talking things over like gentlemen. His excellency's asking too much for the forest. I can't make both ends meet over it. I must ask for a little concession."

"But is the thing settled between you or not? If it's settled, it's useless haggling; but if it's not," said Levin, "I'll buy the forest."

The smile vanished at once from Ryabinin's face. A hawk-like, greedy, cruel expression was left upon it. With rapid, bony fingers he unbuttoned his coat, revealing a shirt, bronze waistcoat buttons, and a watch-chain, and quickly pulled out a fat old pocketbook.

"Here you are, the forest is mine," he said, crossing himself quickly, and holding out his hand. "Take the money; it's my forest. That's Ryabinin's way of doing business; he doesn't haggle over every halfpenny," he added, scowling and waving the pocketbook.

"I wouldn't be in a hurry if I were you," said Levin.

"Come, really," said Oblonsky in surprise, "I've given my word, you know."

Levin went out of the room, slamming the door. Ryabinin looked towards the door and shook his head with a smile.

"It's all youthfulness—positively nothing but boyishness. Why, I'm buying it, upon my honor, simply, believe me, for the glory of it, that Ryabinin, and no one else, should have bought the copse of Oblonsky. And as to the profits, why, I must make what God gives. In God's name. If you would kindly sign the title-deed . . ."

Within an hour the merchant, stroking his big overcoat neatly down, and hooking up his jacket, with the agreement in his pocket, seated himself in his tightly covered trap, and drove homewards.

"Ugh, these gentlefolks!" he said to the clerk. "They—they're a nice lot!"

"That's so," responded the clerk, handing him the reins and buttoning the leather apron. "But I can congratulate you on the purchase, Mihail Ignatitch?"

"Well, well. . . ."

CHAPTER XVII

STEPAN ARKADYEVITCH went up-stairs with his pocket bulging with notes, which the merchant had paid him for three months in advance. The business of the forest was over, the money in his pocket; their shooting had been excellent, and Stepan Arkadye-vitch was in the happiest frame of mind, and so he felt specially anxious to dissipate the ill-humor that had come upon Levin. He wanted to finish the day at supper as pleasantly as it had been begun.

Levin certainly was out of humor, and in spite of all his desire to be affectionate and cordial to his charming visitor, he could not control his mood. The intoxication of the news that Kitty was not married had gradually begun to work upon him.

Kitty was not married, but ill, and ill from love for a man who had slighted her. This slight, as it were, rebounded upon him. Vronsky had slighted her, and she had slighted him, Levin. Consequently Vronsky had the right to despise Levin, and therefore he was his enemy. But all this Levin did not think out. He vaguely felt that there was something in it insulting to him, and he was not angry now at what had disturbed him, but he fell foul of everything that presented itself. The stupid sale of the forest, the fraud practised upon Oblonsky and concluded in his house, exasperated him.

"Well, finished?" he said, meeting Stepan Arkadyevitch upstairs. "Would you like supper?"

"Well, I wouldn't say no to it. What an appetite I get in the country! Wonderful! Why didn't you offer Ryabinin something?"

"Oh, damn him!"

"Still, how you do treat him!" said Oblonsky. "You didn't even shake hands with him. Why not shake hands with him?"

"Because I don't shake hands with a waiter, and a waiter's a hundred times better than he is."

"What a reactionist you are, really! What about the amalgamation of classes?" said Oblonsky.

"Any one who likes amalgamating is welcome to it, but it sickens me."

"You're a regular reactionist, I see."

"Really, I have never considered what I am. I am Konstantin Levin, and nothing else."

"And Konstantin Levin very much out of temper," said Stepan Arkadyevitch, smiling.

"Yes, I am out of temper, and do you know why? Because—excuse me—of your stupid sale. . . ."

Stepan Arkadyevitch frowned good-humoredly, like one who feels himself teased and attacked for no fault of his own.

"Come, enough about it!" he said. "When did anybody ever sell anything without being told immediately after the sale, 'It was worth much more'? But when one wants to sell, no one will give anything. . . . No, I see you've a grudge against that unlucky Ryabinin."

"Maybe I have. And do you know why? You'll say again that I'm a reactionist, or some other terrible word; but all the same it does annoy and anger me to see on all sides the impoverishing of the nobility to which I belong, and, in spite of the amalgamation of classes, I'm glad to belong. And their impoverishment is not due to extravagance—that would be nothing; living in good style

—that's the proper thing for noblemen: it's only the nobles who know how to do it. Now the peasants about us buy land, and I don't mind that. The gentleman does nothing, while the peasant works and supplants the idle man. That's as it ought to be. And I'm very glad for the peasant. But I do mind seeing the process of impoverishment from a sort of—I don't know what to call it—innocence. Here a Polish speculator bought for half its value a magnificent estate from a young lady who lives in Nice. And there a merchant will get three acres of land, worth ten roubles, as security for the loan of one rouble. Here, for no kind of reason, you've made that rascal a present of thirty thousand roubles."

"Well, what should I have done? Counted every tree?"

"Of course, they must be counted. You didn't count them, but Ryabinin did. Ryabinin's children will have means of livelihood and education, while yours maybe will not!"

"Well, you must excuse me, but there's something mean in this counting. We have our business and they have theirs, and they must make their profit. Anyway, the thing's done, and there's an end of it. And here come some poached eggs, my favorite dish. And Agafea Mihalovna will give us that marvelous herb-brandy. . . ."

Stepan Arkadyevitch sat down at the table and began joking with Agafea Mihalovna, assuring her that it was long since he had tasted such a dinner and such a supper.

"Well, you do praise it, anyway," said Agafea Mihalovna, "but Konstantin Dmitrievitch, give him what you will—a crust of bread—he'll eat it and walk away."

Though Levin tried to control himself, he was gloomy and silent. He wanted to put one question to Stepan Arkadyevitch, but he could not bring himself to the point, and could not find the words or the moment in which to put it. Stepan Arkadyevitch had gone down to his room, undressed, again washed, and attired in a night-shirt with goffered frills, he had got into bed, but Levin still lingered in his room, talking of various trifling matters, and not daring to ask what he wanted to know.

"How wonderfully they make this soap," he said gazing at a piece of soap he was handling, which Agafea Mihalovna had put ready for the visitor but Oblonsky had not used. "Only look; why, it's a work of art."

"Yes, everything's brought to such a pitch of perfection nowadays," said Stepan Arkadyevitch, with a moist and blissful yawn. "The theater, for instance, and the entertainments . . . a-a-a!" he yawned. "The electric light everywhere . . . a-a-a!"

"Yes, the electric light," said Levin. "Yes. Oh, and where's Vronsky now?" he asked suddenly, laying down the soap.

"Vronsky?" said Stepan Arkadyevitch, checking his yawn; "he's in Petersburg. He left soon after you did, and he's not once been in Moscow since. And do you know, Kostya, I'll tell you the truth," he went on, leaning his elbow on the table, and propping on his hand his handsome ruddy face, in which his moist, good-natured, sleepy eyes shone like stars. "It's your own fault. You took fright at the sight of your rival. But, as I told you at the time, I couldn't say which had the better chance. Why didn't you fight it out? I told you at the time that . . ." He yawned inwardly, without opening his mouth.

"Does he know, or doesn't he, that I did make an offer?" Levin wondered, gazing at him. "Yes, there's something humbugging, diplomatic in his face," and feeling he was blushing, he looked Stepan Arkadyevitch straight in the face without speaking.

"If there was anything on her side at that time, it was nothing but a superficial attraction," pursued Oblonsky. "His being such a perfect aristocrat, don't you know, and his future position in society, had an influence not with her, but with her mother."

Levin scowled. The humiliation of his rejection stung him to the heart, as though it were a fresh wound he had only just received. But he was at home, and the walls of home are a support.

"Stay, stay," he began, interrupting Oblonsky. "You talk of his being an aristocrat. But allow me to ask what it consists in, that aristocracy of Vronsky or of anybody else, beside which I can be looked down upon? You consider Vronsky an aristocrat, but I don't. A man whose father crawled up from nothing at all by intrigue, and whose mother—God knows whom she wasn't mixed up with. . . . No, excuse me, but I consider myself aristocratic, and people like me, who can point back in the past to three or four honorable generations of their family, of the highest degree of breeding (talent and intellect, of course that's another matter), and have never curried favor with any one, never depended on any one for anything, like my father and my grandfather. And I know many such. You think it mean of me to count the trees in my forest, while you make Ryabinin a present of thirty thousand; but you get rents from your lands and I don't know what, while I don't, and so I prize what's come to me from my ancestors or been won by hard work. . . . We are aristocrats, and not those who can only exist by favor of the powerful of this world, and who can be bought for twopence halfpenny."

"Well, but whom are you attacking? I agree with you," said Stepan Arkadyevitch, sincerely and genially; though he was aware that in the class of those who could be bought for twopence halfpenny Levin was reckoning him too. Levin's warmth gave him genuine pleasure. "Whom are you attacking? Though a good deal is not true that you say about Vronsky, but I won't talk about that. I tell you straight out, if I were you, I should go back with me to Moscow, and . . ."

"No; I don't know whether you know it or not, but I don't care. And I tell you—I did make an offer and was rejected, and Katerina Alexandrovna is nothing now to me but a painful and humiliating reminiscence."

"What ever for? What nonsense!"

"But we won't talk about it. Please forgive me, if I've been nasty," said Levin. Now that he had opened his heart, he became as he had been in the morning. "You're not angry with me, Stiva? Please don't be angry," he said, and smiling, he took his hand.

"Of course not; not a bit, and no reason to be. I'm glad we've spoken openly. And do you know, stand-shooting in the morning is usually good—why not go? I couldn't sleep the night anyway, but I might go straight from shooting to the station."

"Capital."

CHAPTER XVIII

ALTHOUGH all Vronsky's inner life was absorbed in his passion, his external life unalterably and inevitably followed along the old accustomed lines of his social and regimental ties and interests. The interests of his regiment took an important place in Vronsky's life, both because he was fond of the regiment, and because the regiment was fond of him. They were not only fond of Vronsky in his regiment, they respected him too, and were proud of him; proud that this man, with his immense wealth, his brilliant education and abilities, and the path open before him to every kind of success, distinction, and ambition, had disregarded all that, and of all the interests of life had the interests of his regiment and his comrades nearest to his heart. Vronsky was aware of his comrades' view of him, and in addition to his liking for the life, he felt bound to keep up that reputation.

It need not be said that he did not speak of his love to any of his comrades, nor did he betray his secret even in the wildest drinking bouts (though indeed he was never so drunk as to lose all control of himself). And he shut up any of his thoughtless comrades who attempted to allude to his connection. But in spite of that, his love was known to all the town; every one guessed with more or less confidence at his relations with Madame Karenina. The majority of the younger men envied him for just what was the most irksome factor in his love—the exalted position of Karenin, and the consequent publicity of their connection in society.

The greater number of the young women, who envied Anna and had long been weary of hearing her called *virtuous,* rejoiced at the fulfillment of their predictions, and were only waiting for a decisive turn in public opinion to fall upon her with all the weight of their scorn. They were already making ready their handfuls of mud to fling at her when the right moment arrived. The greater number of the middle-aged people and certain great personages were displeased at the prospect of the impending scandal in society.

Vronsky's mother, on hearing of his connection, was at first pleased at it, because nothing to her mind gave such a finishing-touch to a brilliant young man as a *liaison* in the highest society; she was pleased, too, that Madame Karenina, who had so taken her fancy, and had talked so much of her son, was, after all, just like all other pretty and well-bred women,—at least according to the Countess Vronskaya's ideas. But she had heard of late that her son had refused a position offered him of great importance to his career, simply in order to remain in the regiment, where he could be constantly seeing Madame Karenina. She learned that great personages were displeased with him on this account, and she changed her opinion. She was vexed, too, that from all she could learn of this connection it was not that brilliant, graceful, worldly *liaison* which she would have welcomed, but a sort of Wertherish, desperate passion, so she was told, which might well lead him into imprudence. She had not seen him since his abrupt departure from Moscow, and she sent her elder son to bid him come to see her.

This elder son, too, was displeased with his younger brother. He did not distinguish what sort of love his might be, big or little, passionate or passionless, lasting or passing (he kept a ballet-girl himself, though he was the father of a family, so he was lenient in these matters), but he knew that this love-affair was viewed with displeasure by those whom it was necessary to please, and therefore he did not approve of his brother's conduct.

Besides the service and society, Vronsky had another great interest—horses; he was passionately fond of horses.

That year races and a steeplechase had been arranged for the officers. Vronsky had put his name down, bought a thoroughbred English mare, and in spite of his love-affair, he was looking forward to the races with intense, though reserved, excitement. . . .

These two passions did not interfere with one another. On the contrary, he needed occupation and distraction quite apart from his love, so as to recruit and rest himself from the violent emotions that agitated him.

CHAPTER XIX

ON THE day of the races at Krasnoe Selo, Vronsky had come earlier than usually to eat beefsteak in the common mess-room of the regiment. He had no need to be strict with himself, as he had very quickly been brought down to the required light weight; but still he had to avoid gaining flesh, and so he eschewed farinaceous and sweet dishes. He sat with his coat unbuttoned over a white waistcoat, resting both elbows on the table, and while waiting for the steak he had ordered he looked at a French novel that lay open on his plate. He was only looking at the book to avoid conversation with the officers coming in and out; he was thinking.

He was thinking of Anna's promise to see him that day after the races. But he had not seen her for three days, and as her husband had just returned from abroad, he did not know whether she would be able to meet him to-day or not, and he did not know how to find out. He had had his last interview with her at his cousin Betsy's summer villa. He visited the Karenins' summer villa as rarely as possible. Now he wanted to go there, and he pondered the question how to do it.

"Of course I shall say Betsy has sent me to ask whether she's coming to the races. Of course, I'll go," he decided, lifting his head from the book. And as he vividly pictured the happiness of seeing her, his face lighted up.

"Send to my house, and tell them to have out the carriage and three horses as quick as they can," he said to the servant, who handed him the steak on a hot silver dish, and moving the dish up he began eating.

From the billiard-room next door came the sound of balls knocking, of talk and laughter. Two officers appeared at the entrance-door: one, a young fellow, with a feeble, delicate face, who had lately joined the regiment from the Corps of Pages; the other, a plump, elderly officer, with a bracelet on his wrist, and little eyes, lost in fat.

Vronsky glanced at them, frowned, and looking down at his book as though he had not noticed them, he proceeded to eat and read at the same time.

"What? Fortifying yourself for your work?" said the plump officer, sitting down beside him.

"As you see," responded Vronsky, knitting his brows, wiping his mouth, and not looking at the officer.

"So you're not afraid of getting fat?" said the latter, turning a chair round for the young officer.

"What?" said Vronsky angrily, making a wry face of disgust, and showing his even teeth.

"You're not afraid of getting fat?"

"Waiter, sherry!" said Vronsky, without replying, and moving the book to the other side of him, he went on reading.

The plump officer took up the list of wines and turned to the young officer.

"You choose what we're to drink," he said, handing him the card, and looking at him.

"Rhine wine, please," said the young officer, stealing a timid glance at Vronsky, and trying to pull his scarcely visible mustache. Seeing that Vronsky did not turn round, the young officer got up.

"Let's go into the billiard-room," he said.

The plump officer rose submissively, and they moved towards the door.

At that moment there walked into the room the tall and well-built Captain Yashvin. Nodding with an air of lofty contempt to the two officers, he went up to Vronsky.

"Ah! here he is!" he cried, bringing his big hand down heavily on his epaulet. Vronsky looked round angrily, but his face lighted up immediately with his characteristic expression of genial and manly serenity.

"That's it, Alexey," said the captain, in his loud baritone. "You must just eat a mouthful, now, and drink only one tiny glass."

"Oh, I'm not hungry."

"There go the inseparables," Yashvin dropped, glancing sarcastically at the two officers who were at that instant leaving the room. And he bent his long legs, swathed in tight riding-breeches, and sat down in the chair, too low for him, so that his knees were cramped up in a sharp angle.

"Why didn't you turn up at the Red Theater yesterday? Numerova wasn't at all bad. Where were you?"

"I was late at the Tverskoys'," said Vronsky.

"Ah!" responded Yashvin.

Yashvin, a gambler and a rake, a man not merely without moral principles, but of immoral principles, Yashvin was Vronsky's greatest friend in the regiment. Vronsky liked him both for his exceptional physical strength, which he showed for the most part by being able to drink like a fish, and do without sleep without being in the slightest degree affected by it; and for his great strength of character, which he showed in his relations with his comrades and superior officers, commanding both fear and respect, and also at cards, when he would play for tens of thousands and however much he might have drunk, always with such skill and decision that he was reckoned the best player in the English Club. Vronsky respected and liked Yashvin particularly because he felt Yashvin liked him, not for his name and his money, but for himself. And of all men he was the only one with whom Vronsky would have liked to speak of his love. He felt that Yashvin, in spite of his apparent contempt for every sort of feeling, was the only man who could, so he fancied, comprehend the intense passion which now filled his whole life. Moreover, he felt certain that Yashvin, as it was, took no delight in gossip and scandal, and interpreted his feeling rightly, that is to say, knew and believed that this passion was not a jest, not a pastime, but something more serious and important.

Vronsky had never spoken to him of his passion, but he was aware that he knew all about it, and that he put the right interpretation on it, and he was glad to see that in his eyes.

"Ah! yes," he said, to the announcement that Vronsky had been at the Tverskoys'; and his black eyes shining, he plucked at his left mustache, and began twisting it into his mouth, a bad habit he had.

"Well, and what did you do yesterday? Win anything?" asked Vronsky.

"Eight thousand. But three don't count; he won't pay up."

"Oh, then you can afford to lose over me," said Vronsky, laughing. (Yashvin had betted heavily on Vronsky in the races.)

"No chance of my losing. Mahotin's the only one that's risky."

And the conversation passed to forecasts of the coming race, the only thing Vronsky could think of just now.

"Come along, I've finished," said Vronsky, and getting up he went to the door. Yashvin got up too, stretching his long legs and his long back.

"It's too early for me to dine, but I must have a drink. I'll come along directly. Hi, wine!" he shouted, in his rich voice, that always rang out so loudly at drill, and set the windows shaking now.

"No, all right," he shouted again immediately after. "You're going home, so I'll go with you."

And he walked out with Vronsky.

CHAPTER XX

VRONSKY was staying in a roomy, clean, Finnish hut, divided into two by a partition. Petritsky lived with him in camp too. Petritsky was asleep when Vronsky and Yashvin came into the hut.

"Get up, don't go on sleeping," said Yashvin, going behind the partition and giving Petritsky, who was lying with ruffled hair and with his nose in the pillow, a prod on the shoulder.

Petritsky jumped up suddenly onto his knees and looked round.

"Your brother's been here," he said to Vronsky. "He waked me up, damn him, and said he'd look in again." And pulling up the rug he flung himself back on the pillow. "Oh, do shut up, Yashvin!" he said, getting furious with Yashvin, who was pulling the rug off him. "Shut up!" He turned over and opened his eyes. "You'd better tell me what to drink; such a nasty taste in my mouth, that . . ."

"Brandy's better than anything," boomed Yashvin. "Tereshtchenko! brandy for your master and cucumbers," he shouted, obviously taking pleasure in the sound of his own voice.

"Brandy do you think? Eh?" queried Petritsky, blinking and rubbing his eyes. "And you'll drink something? All right then, we'll have a drink together! Vronsky, have a drink?" said Petritsky, getting up and wrapping the tiger-skin rug round him. He went to the door of the partition wall, raised his hands, and hummed in French, "There was a king in Thule." "Vronsky, will you have a drink?"

"Go along," said Vronsky, putting on the coat his valet handed him.

"Where are you off to?" asked Yashvin. "Oh, here are your three horses," he added, seeing the carriage drive up.

"To the stables, and I've got to see Bryansky, too, about the horses," said Vronsky.

Vronsky had as a fact promised to call at Bryansky's, some eight miles from Peterhof, and to bring him some money owing for some horses; and he hoped to have time to get that in too.

But his comrades were at once aware that he was not only going there.

Petritsky, still humming, winked and made a pout with his lips, as though he would say : "Oh, yes, we know your Bryansky."

"Mind you're not late!" was Yashvin's only comment; and to change the conversation : "How's my roan? is he doing all right?" he inquired, looking out of the window at the middle one of the three horses, which he had sold Vronsky.

"Stop!" cried Petritsky to Vronsky as he was just going out. "Your brother left a letter and a note for you. Wait a bit; where are they?"

Vronsky stopped.

"Well, where are they?"

"Where are they? That's just the question!" said Petritsky solemnly, moving his forefinger upwards from his nose.

"Come, tell me; this is silly!" said Vronsky, smiling.

"I have not lighted the fire. Here somewhere about."

"Come, enough fooling! Where is the letter?"

"No, I've forgotten really. Or was it a dream? Wait a bit, wait a bit! But what's the use of getting in a rage. If you'd drunk four bottles yesterday as I did you'd forget where you were lying. Wait a bit, I'll remember!"

Petritsky went behind the partition and lay down on his bed.

"Wait a bit! This was how I was lying, and this was how he was standing. Yes—yes—yes. . . . Here it is!"—and Petritsky pulled a letter out from under the mattress, where he had hidden it.

Vronsky took the letter and his brother's note. It was the letter he was expecting—from his mother, reproaching him for not having been to see her—and the note was from his brother to say that he must have a little talk with him. Vronsky knew that it was all about the same thing. "What business is it of theirs!" thought Vronsky, and crumpling up the letters he thrust them between the buttons of his coat so as to read them carefully on the road. In the porch of the hut he was met by two officers; one of his regiment and one of another.

Vronsky's quarters were always a meeting-place for all the officers.

"Where are you off to?"

"I must go to Peterhof."

"Has the mare come from Tsarskoe?"

"Yes, but I've not seen her yet."

"They say Mahotin's Gladiator's lame."

"Nonsense! But however are you going to race in this mud?" said the other.

"Here are my saviors!" cried Petritsky, seeing them come in. Before him stood the orderly with a tray of brandy and salted cucumbers. "Here's Yashvin ordering me to drink a pick-me-up."

"Well, you did give it to us yesterday," said one of those who had come in; "you didn't let us get a wink of sleep all night."

"Oh, didn't we make a pretty finish!" said Petritsky. "Volkov climbed onto the roof and began telling us how sad he was. I said: 'Let's have music, the funeral march!' He fairly dropped asleep on the roof over the funeral march."

"Drink it up; you positively must drink the brandy, and then seltzer water and a lot of lemon," said Yashvin, standing over Petritsky like a mother making a child take medicine, "and then a little champagne—just a small bottle."

"Come, there's some sense in that. Stop a bit, Vronsky. We'll all have a drink."

"No; good-bye all of you. I'm not going to drink to-day."

"Why, are you gaining weight? All right, then we must have it alone. Give us the seltzer water and lemon."

"Vronsky!" shouted some one when he was already outside. "Well?"

"You'd better get your hair cut, it'll weigh you down, especially at the top."

Vronsky was in fact beginning, prematurely, to get a little bald. He laughed gaily, showing his even teeth, and pulling his cap over the thin place, went out and got into his carriage.

"To the stables!" he said, and was just pulling out the letters to read them through, but he thought better of it, and put off reading them so as not to distract his attention before looking at the mare. "Later!"

CHAPTER XXI

THE temporary stable, a wooden shed, had been put up close to the race-course, and there his mare was to have been taken the previous day. He had not yet seen her there.

During the last few days he had not ridden her out for exercise himself, but had put her in the charge of the trainer, and so now he positively did not know in what condition his mare had arrived yesterday and was to-day. He had scarcely got out of his carriage when his groom, the so-called "stable-boy," recognizing the carriage some way off, called the trainer. A dry-looking Englishman, in high boots and a short jacket, clean shaven, except for a tuft below his chin, came to meet him, walking with the uncouth gait of a jockey, turning his elbows out and swaying from side to side.

"Well, how's Frou-Frou?" Vronsky asked in English.

"All right, sir," the Englishman's voice responded somewhere in the inside of his throat. "Better not go in," he added, touching his hat. "I've put a muzzle on her, and the mare's fidgety. Better not go in, it'll excite the mare."

"No, I'm going in. I want to look at her."

"Come along, then," said the Englishman, frowning, and speaking with his mouth shut, and with swinging elbows, he went on in front with his disjointed gait.

They went into the little yard in front of the shed. A stable-boy, spruce and smart in his holiday attire, met them with a broom in his hand, and followed them. In the shed there were five horses in their separate stalls, and Vronsky knew that his chief rival, Gladiator, a very tall chestnut horse, had been brought there, and must be standing among them. Even more than his mare, Vronsky longed to see Gladiator, whom he had never seen. But he knew that by the etiquette of the race-course it was not merely impossible for him to see the horse, but improper even to ask questions about him. Just as he was passing along the passage, the boy opened the door into the second horse-box on the left, and Vronsky caught a glimpse of a big chestnut horse with white legs. He knew that this was Gladiator, but, with

the feeling of a man turning away from the sight of another man's open letter, he turned round and went into Frou-Frou's stall.

"The horse is here belonging to Mak . . . Mak . . . I never can say the name," said the Englishman, over his shoulder, pointing his big finger and dirty nail towards Gladiator's stall.

"Mahotin? Yes, he's my most serious rival," said Vronsky.

"If you were riding him," said the Englishman, "I'd bet on you."

"Frou-Frou's more nervous; he's stronger," said Vronsky, smiling at the compliment to his riding.

"In a steeplechase it all depends on riding and on pluck," said the Englishman.

Of pluck—that is, energy and courage—Vronsky did not merely feel that he had enough; what was of far more importance, he was firmly convinced that no one in the world could have more of this "pluck" than he had.

"Don't you think I want more thinning down?"

"Oh, no," answered the Englishman. "Please, don't speak loud. The mare's fidgety," he added, nodding towards the horse-box, before which they were standing, and from which came the sound of restless stamping in the straw.

He opened the door, and Vronsky went into the horse-box,

dimly lighted by one little window. In the horse-box stood a dark bay mare, with a muzzle on, picking at the fresh straw with her hoofs. Looking round him in the twilight of the horse-box, Vronsky unconsciously took in once more in a comprehensive glance all the points of his favorite mare. Frou-Frou was a beast of medium size, not altogether free from reproach, from a breeder's point of view. She was small-boned all over; though her chest was extremely prominent in front, it was narrow. Her hindquarters were a little drooping, and in her fore-legs, and still more in her hind-legs, there was a noticeable curvature. The muscles of both hind- and fore-legs were not very thick; but across her shoulders the mare was exceptionally broad, a peculiarity specially striking now that she was lean from training. The bones of her legs below the knees looked no thicker than a finger from in front, but were extraordinarily thick seen from the side. She looked altogether, except across the shoulders, as it were, pinched in at the sides and pressed out in depth. But she had in the highest degree the quality that makes all defects forgotten : that quality was *blood,* the blood *that tells,* as the English expression has it. The muscles stood up sharply under the network of sinews, covered with the delicate, mobile skin, soft as satin, and they were hard as bone. Her clean-cut head, with prominent, bright, spirited eyes, broadened out at the open nostrils, that showed the red blood in the cartilage within. About all her figure, and especially her head, there was a certain expression of energy, and, at the same time, of softness. She was one of those creatures which seem only not to speak because the mechanism of their mouth does not allow them to.

To Vronsky, at any rate, it seemed that she understood all he felt at that moment, looking at her.

Directly Vronsky went towards her, she drew in a deep breath, and, turning back her prominent eye till the white looked bloodshot, she started at the approaching figures from the opposite side, shaking her muzzle, and shifting lightly from one leg to the other.

"There, you see how fidgety she is," said the Englishman.

"There, darling! There!" said Vronsky, going up to the mare and speaking soothingly to her.

But the nearer he came, the more excited she grew. Only when he stood by her head, she was suddenly quieter, while the muscles quivered under her soft, delicate coat. Vronsky patted her strong neck, straightened over her sharp withers a stray lock of her mane that had fallen on the other side, and moved his face near her dilated nostrils, transparent as a bat's wing. She drew a loud breath and snorted out through her tense nostrils, started, pricked up her sharp ear, and put out her strong, black lip towards Vronsky, as though she would nip hold of his sleeve. But remembering the muzzle, she shook it and again began restlessly stamping one after the other her shapely legs.

"Quiet, darling, quiet!" he said, patting her again over her hind-quarters; and with a glad sense that his mare was in the best possible condition, he went out of the horse-box.

The mare's excitement had infected Vronsky. He felt that his heart was throbbing, and that he, too, like the mare, longed to move, to bite; it was both dreadful and delicious.

"Well, I rely on you, then," he said to the Englishman; "half-past six on the ground."

"All right," said the Englishman. "Oh, where are you going, my lord?" he asked suddenly, using the title "my lord," which he had scarcely ever used before.

Vronsky in amazement raised his head, and stared, as he knew how to stare, not into the Englishman's eyes, but at his forehead, astounded at the impertinence of his question. But realizing that in asking this the Englishman had been looking at him not as an employer, but as a jockey, he answered:

"I've got to go to Bryansky's; I shall be home within an hour."

"How often I'm asked that question to-day!" he said to himself, and he blushed, a thing which rarely happened to him. The Englishman looked gravely at him; and, as though he, too, knew where Vronsky was going, he added:

"The great thing's to keep quiet before a race," said he; "don't get out of temper or upset about anything."

"All right," answered Vronsky, smiling; and jumping into his carriage, he told the man to drive to Peterhof.

Before he had driven many paces away, the dark clouds that had been threatening rain all day broke, and there was a heavy downpour of rain.

"What a pity!" thought Vronsky, putting up the roof of the

carriage. "It was muddy before, now it will be a perfect swamp."
As he sat in solitude in the closed carriage, he took out his
mother's letter and his brother's note, and read them through.

Yes, it was the same thing over and over again. Everyone, his
mother, his brother, everyone thought fit to interfere in the
affairs of his heart. This interference aroused in him a feeling
of angry hatred—a feeling he had rarely known before. "What
business is it of theirs? Why does everybody feel called upon to
concern himself about me? And why do they worry me so? Just
because they see that this is something they can't understand.
If it were a common, vulgar, worldly intrigue, they would have
left me alone. They feel that this is something different, that
this is not a mere pastime, that this woman is dearer to me than
life. And this is incomprehensible, and that's why it annoys
them. Whatever our destiny is or may be, we have made it ourselves, and we do not complain of it," he said, in the word *we*
linking himself with Anna. "No, they must needs teach us how
to live. They haven't an idea of what happiness is; they don't
know that without our love, for us there is neither happiness nor
unhappiness—no life at all," he thought.

He was angry with all of them for their interference just because he felt in his soul that they, all these people, were right. He
felt that the love that bound him to Anna was not a momentary
impulse, which would pass, as worldly intrigues do pass, leaving
no other traces in the life of either but pleasant or unpleasant
memories. He felt all the torture of his own and her position, all
the difficulty there was for them, conspicuous as they were in the
eye of all the world, in concealing their love, in lying and deceiving; and in lying, deceiving, feigning, and continually
thinking of others, when the passion that united them was so
intense that they were both oblivious of everything else but their
love.

He vividly recalled all the constantly recurring instances of
inevitable necessity for lying and deceit, which were so against
his natural bent. He recalled particularly vividly the shame he
had more than once detected in her at this necessity for lying and
deceit. And he experienced the strange feeling that had sometimes come upon him since his secret love for Anna. This was a
feeling of loathing for something—whether for Alexey Alexan-

drovitch, or for himself, or for the whole world, he could not have said. But he always drove away this strange feeling. Now, too, he shook it off and continued the thread of his thoughts.

"Yes, she was unhappy before, but proud and at peace; and now she cannot be at peace and feel secure in her dignity, though she does not show it. Yes, we must put an end to it," he decided.

And for the first time the idea clearly presented itself that it was essential to put an end to this false position, and the sooner the better. "Throw up everything, she and I, and hide ourselves somewhere alone with our love," he said to himself.

CHAPTER XXII

THE rain did not last long, and by the time Vronsky arrived, his shaft-horse trotting at full speed and dragging the trace-horses galloping through the mud, with their reins hanging loose, the sun had peeped out again, the roofs of the summer villas and the old lime-trees in the gardens on both sides of the principal streets sparkled with wet brilliance, and from the twigs came a pleasant drip and from the roofs rushing streams of water. He thought no more of the shower spoiling the race-course, but was rejoicing now that—thanks to the rain—he would be sure to find her at home and alone, as he knew that Alexey Alexandrovitch, who had lately returned from a foreign watering-place, had not moved from Petersburg.

Hoping to find her alone, Vronsky alighted, as he always did, to avoid attracting attention, before crossing the bridge, and walked to the house. He did not go up the steps to the street door, but went into the court.

"Has your master come?" he asked a gardener.

"No, sir. The mistress is at home. But will you please go to the front door; there are servants there," the gardener answered. "They'll open the door."

"No, I'll go in from the garden."

And feeling satisfied that she was alone, and wanting to take her by surprise, since he had not promised to be there to-day, and she would certainly not expect him to come before the races, he walked, holding his sword and stepping cautiously over the sandy path, bordered with flowers, to the terrace that looked out upon the garden. Vronsky forgot now all that he had thought on the way of the hardships and difficulties of their position. He thought of nothing but that he would see her directly, not in imagination, but living, all of her, as she was in reality. He was just going in, stepping on his whole foot so as not to creak, up the worn steps of the terrace, when he suddenly remembered what he always forgot, and what caused the most torturing side of his relations with her, her son with his questioning—hostile, as he fancied—eyes.

This boy was more often than any one else a check upon their freedom. When he was present, both Vronsky and Anna did not merely avoid speaking of anything that they could not have repeated before every one; they did not even allow themselves to refer by hints to anything the boy did not understand. They had made no agreement about this, it had settled itself. They would have felt it wounding themselves to deceive the child. In his presence they talked like acquaintances. But in spite of this caution, Vronsky often saw the child's intent, bewildered glance fixed upon him, and a strange shyness, uncertainty, at one time friendliness, at another, coldness and reserve, in the boy's manner to him; as though the child felt that between this man and his mother there existed some important bond, the significance of which he could not understand.

As a fact, the boy did feel that he could not understand this relation, and he tried painfully, and was not able to make clear to himself what feeling he ought to have for this man. With a child's keen instinct for every manifestation of feeling, he saw distinctly that his father, his governess, his nurse,—all did not merely dislike Vronsky, but looked on him with horror and aversion, though they never said anything about him, while his mother looked on him as her greatest friend.

"What does it mean? Who is he? How ought I to love him? If I don't know, it's my fault; either I'm stupid or a naughty boy," thought the child. And this was what caused his dubious, inquiring, sometimes hostile, expression, and the shyness and uncertainty which Vronsky found so irksome. This child's presence always and infallibly called up in Vronsky that strange feeling of inexplicable loathing which he had experienced of late.

This child's presence called up both in Vronsky and in Anna a feeling akin to the feeling of a sailor who sees by the compass that the direction in which he is swiftly moving is far from the right one, but that to arrest his motion is not in his power, that every instant is carrying him further and further away, and that to admit to himself his deviation from the right direction is the same as admitting his certain ruin.

This child, with his innocent outlook upon life, was the compass that showed them the point to which they had departed from what they knew, but did not want to know.

This time Seryozha was not at home, and she was completely alone. She was sitting on the terrace waiting for the return of her son, who had gone out for his walk and been caught in the rain. She had sent a manservant and a maid out to look for him. Dressed in a white gown, deeply embroidered, she was sitting in a corner of the terrace behind some flowers, and did not hear him. Bending her curly black head, she pressed her forehead against a cool watering-pot that stood on the parapet, and both her lovely hands, with the rings he knew so well, clasped the pot. The beauty of her whole figure, her head, her neck, her hands, struck Vronsky every time as something new and unexpected. He stood still, gazing at her in ecstasy. But, directly he would have made a step to come nearer to her, she was aware of his presence, pushed away the watering-pot, and turned her flushed face towards him.

"What's the matter? You are ill?" he said to her in French, going up to her. He would have run to her, but remembering that there might be spectators, he looked round towards the balcony door, and reddened a little, as he always reddened, feeling that he had to be afraid and be on his guard.

"No. I'm quite well," she said, getting up and pressing his outstretched hand tightly. "I did not expect . . . thee."

"Mercy! what cold hands!" he said.

"You startled me," she said. "I'm alone, and expecting Seryozha; he's out for a walk; they'll come in from this side."

But, in spite of her efforts to be calm, her lips were quivering.

"Forgive me for coming, but I couldn't pass the day without seeing you," he went on, speaking French, as he always did to avoid using the stiff Russian plural form, so impossibly frigid between them, and the dangerously intimate singular.

"Forgive you? I'm so glad!"

"But you're ill or worried," he went on, not letting go her hands and bending over her. "What were you thinking of?"

"Always of the same thing," she said, with a smile.

She spoke the truth. If ever at any moment she had been asked what she was thinking of, she could have answered truly: of the same thing, of her happiness and her unhappiness. She was thinking, just when he came upon her, of this: why was it, she wondered, that to others, to Betsy (she knew of her secret connection with Tushkevitch) it was all easy, while to her it was such torture? To-day this thought gained special poignancy from certain other considerations. She asked him about the races. He answered her questions, and, seeing that she was agitated, trying to calm her, he began telling her in the simplest tone the details of his preparations for the races.

"Tell him or not tell him?" she thought, looking into his quiet, affectionate eyes. "He is so happy, so absorbed in his races that he won't understand as he ought, he won't understand all the gravity of this fact to us."

"But you haven't told me what you were thinking of when I came in," he said, interrupting his narrative; "please tell me!"

She did not answer, and, bending her head a little, she looked inquiringly at him from under her brows, her eyes shining under their long lashes. Her hand shook as it played with a leaf she had picked. He saw it, and his face expressed that utter subjection, that slavish devotion, which had done so much to win her.

"I see something has happened. Do you suppose I can be at peace, knowing you have a trouble I am not sharing? Tell me, for God's sake," he repeated imploringly.

"Yes, I shan't be able to forgive him if he does not realize all the gravity of it. Better not tell; why put him to the proof?" she thought, still staring at him in the same way, and feeling the hand that held the leaf was trembling more and more.

"For God's sake!" he repeated, taking her hand.

"Shall I tell you?"

"Yes, yes, yes . . ."

"I'm with child," she said, softly and deliberately. The leaf in her hand shook more violently, but she did not take her eyes off

him, watching how he would take it. He turned white, would have said something, but stopped; he dropped her hand, and his head sank on his breast. "Yes, he realizes all the gravity of it," she thought, and gratefully she pressed his hand.

But she was mistaken in thinking he realized the gravity of the fact as she, a woman, realized it. On hearing it, he felt come upon him with tenfold intensity that strange feeling of loathing of some one. But at the same time, he felt that the turning-point he had been longing for had come now; that it was impossible to go on concealing things from her husband, and it was inevitable in one way or another that they should soon put an end to their unnatural position. But, besides that, her emotion physically affected him, in the same way. He looked at her with a look of submissive tenderness, kissed her hand, got up, and, in silence, paced up and down the terrace.

"Yes," he said, going up to her resolutely. "Neither you nor I have looked on our relations as a passing amusement, and now our fate is sealed. It is absolutely necessary to put an end"—he looked round as he spoke—"to the deception in which we are living."

"Put an end? How put an end, Alexey?" she said softly.

She was calmer now, and her face lighted up with a tender smile.

"Leave your husband and make our life one."

"It is one as it is," she answered, scarcely audibly.

"Yes, but altogether; altogether."

"But how, Alexey, tell me how?" she said in melancholy mockery at the hopelessness of her own position. "Is there any way out of such a position? Am I not the wife of my husband?"

"There is a way out of every position. We must take our line," he said. "Anything's better than the position in which you're living. Of course, I see how you torture yourself over everything —the world and your son and your husband."

"Oh, not over my husband," she said, with a quiet smile. "I don't know him, I don't think of him. He doesn't exist."

"You're not speaking sincerely. I know you. You worry about him too."

"Oh, he doesn't even know," she said, and suddenly a hot flush came over her face; her cheeks, her brow, her neck crimsoned, and tears of shame came into her eyes. "But we won't talk of him."

CHAPTER XXIII

VRONSKY had several times already, though not so resolutely as now, tried to bring her to consider their position, and every time he had been confronted by the same superficiality and triviality with which she met his appeal now. It was as though there were something in this which she could not or would not face, as though directly she began to speak of this, she, the real Anna, retreated somehow into herself, and another strange and unaccountable woman came out, whom he did not love, and whom he feared, and who was in opposition to him. But to-day he was resolved to have it out.

"Whether he knows or not," said Vronsky, in his usual quiet and resolute tone, "that's nothing to do with us. We cannot . . . you cannot stay like this, especially now."

"What's to be done, according to you?" she asked with the same frivolous irony. She who had so feared he would take her condition too lightly was now vexed with him for deducing from it the necessity of taking some step.

"Tell him everything, and leave him."

"Very well, let us suppose I do that," she said. "Do you know what the result of that would be? I can tell you it all beforehand," and a wicked light gleamed in her eyes, that had been so soft a minute before. " 'Eh, you love another man, and have entered into criminal intrigues with him?' " (Mimicking her husband, she threw an emphasis on the word "criminal," as Alexey Alexandrovitch did.) " 'I warned you of the results in the religious, the civil, and the domestic relation. You have not listened to me. Now I cannot let you disgrace my name,—' " "and my son," she had meant to say, but about her son she could not jest,—" 'disgrace my name, and'—and more in the same style," she added. "In general terms, he'll say in his official manner, and with all distinctness and precision, that he cannot let me go, but will take all measures in his power to prevent scandal. And he will calmly and punctually act in accordance with his words. That's what will happen. He's not a man, but a machine, and a spiteful machine when he's angry," she added, recalling Alexey Alexandrovitch as she spoke, with all the peculiarities of his figure and manner of speaking, and reckoning against him every defect she could find in him, softening nothing for the great wrong she herself was doing him.

"But, Anna," said Vronsky, in a soft and persuasive voice, trying to soothe her, "we absolutely must, anyway, tell him, and then be guided by the line he takes."

"What, run away?"

"And why not run away? I don't see how we can keep on like this. And not for my sake—I see that you suffer."

"Yes, run away, and become your mistress," she said angrily.

"Anna," he said, with reproachful tenderness.

"Yes," she went on, "become your mistress, and complete the ruin of . . ."

Again she would have said "my son," but she could not utter that word.

Vronsky could not understand how she, with her strong and truthful nature, could endure this state of deceit, and not long to get out of it. But he did not suspect that the chief cause of it was the word—*son,* which she could not bring herself to pronounce. When she thought of her son, and his future attitude to his mother, who had abandoned his father, she felt such terror at what she had done, that she could not face it; but, like a woman, could only try to comfort herself with lying assurances that everything would remain as it always had been, and that it was possible to forget the fearful question of how it would be with her son.

"I beg you, I entreat you," she said suddenly, taking his hand, and speaking in quite a different tone, sincere and tender, "never speak to me of that!"

"But, Anna . . ."

"Never. Leave it to me. I know all the baseness, all the horror of my position; but it's not so easy to arrange as you think. And leave it to me, and do what I say. Never speak to me of it. Do you promise me? . . . No, no, promise! . . ."

"I promise everything, but I can't be at peace, especially after what you have told me. I can't be at peace, when you can't be at peace. . . ."

"I?" she repeated. "Yes, I am worried sometimes; but that will pass, if you will never talk about this. When you talk about it— it's only then it worries me."

"I don't understand," he said.

"I know," she interrupted him, "how hard it is for your truthful nature to lie, and I grieve for you. I often think that you have ruined your whole life for me."

"I was just thinking the very same thing," he said; "how could you sacrifice everything for my sake? I can't forgive myself that you're unhappy."

"I unhappy?" she said, coming closer to him, and looking at him with an ecstatic smile of love. "I am like a hungry man who has been given food. He may be cold, and dressed in rags, and ashamed, but he is not unhappy. I unhappy? No, this is my unhappiness. . . ."

She could hear the sound of her son's voice coming towards them, and glancing swiftly round the terrace, she got up impulsively. Her eyes glowed with the fire he knew so well; with a rapid movement she raised her lovely hands, covered with rings, took his head, looked a long look into his face, and, putting up her face with smiling, parted lips, swiftly kissed his mouth and both eyes, and pushed him away. She would have gone, but he held her back.

"When?" he murmured in a whisper, gazing in ecstasy at her.

"To-night, at one o'clock," she whispered, and, with a heavy sigh, she walked with her light, swift step to meet her son.

Seryozha had been caught by the rain in the big garden, and he and his nurse had taken shelter in an arbor.

"Well, *au revoir,*" she said to Vronsky. "I must soon be getting ready for the races. Betsy promised to fetch me."

Vronsky, looking at his watch, went away hurriedly.

CHAPTER XXIV

WHEN Vronsky looked at his watch on the Karenins' balcony, he was so greatly agitated and lost in his thoughts that he saw the figures on the watch's face, but could not take in what time it was. He came out on to the highroad and walked, picking his way carefully through the mud, to his carriage. He was so completely absorbed in his feeling for Anna, that he did not even think what o'clock it was, and whether he had time to go to Bryansky's. He had left him, as often happens, only the external faculty of memory, that points out each step one has to take, one after the other. He went up to his coachman, who was dozing on the box in the shadow, already lengthening, of a thick lime-tree; he admired the shifting clouds of midges circling over the hot horses, and, waking the coachman, he jumped into the carriage, and told him to drive to Bryansky's. It was only after driving nearly five miles that he had sufficiently recovered himself to look at his watch, and realize that it was half-past five, and he was late.

There were several races fixed for that day: the Mounted Guards' race, then the officers' mile-and-a-half race, then the three-mile race, and then the race for which he was entered. He could still be in time for his race, but if he went to Bryansky's he could only just be in time, and he would arrive when the whole of the court would be in their places. That would be a pity. But he had promised Bryansky to come, and so he decided to drive on, telling the coachman not to spare the horses.

He reached Bryansky's, spent five minutes there, and galloped back. This rapid drive calmed him. All that was painful in his relations with Anna, all the feeling of indefiniteness left by their conversation, had slipped out of his mind. He was thinking now with pleasure and excitement of the race, of his being anyhow, in time, and now and then the thought of the blissful interview awaiting him that night flashed across his imagination like a flaming light.

The excitement of the approaching race gained upon him as he drove further and further into the atmosphere of the races, overtaking carriages driving up from the summer villas or out of Petersburg.

At his quarters no one was left at home; all were at the races, and his valet was looking out for him at the gate. While he was changing his clothes, his valet told him that the second race had begun already, that a lot of gentlemen had been to ask for him, and a boy had twice run up from the stables. Dressing without hurry (he never hurried himself, and never lost his self-possession), Vronsky drove to the sheds. From the sheds he could see a perfect sea of carriages, and people on foot, soldiers surrounding the race-course, and pavilions swarming with people. The second race was apparently going on, for just as he went into the sheds he heard a bell ringing. Going towards the stable, he met the white-legged chestnut, Mahotin's Gladiator, being led to the race-course in a blue forage horsecloth, with what looked like huge ears edged with blue.

"Where's Cord?" he asked the stable-boy.

"In the stable, putting on the saddle."

In the open horse-box stood Frou-Frou, saddled ready. They were just going to lead her out.

"I'm not too late?"

"All right! All right!" said the Englishman; "don't upset yourself!"

Vronsky once more took in in one glance the exquisite lines of his favorite mare, who was quivering all over, and with an effort he tore himself from the sight of her, and went out of the stable. He went towards the pavilions at the most favorable moment for escaping attention. The mile-and-a-half race was just finishing, and all eyes were fixed on the horse-guard in front and the light hussar behind, urging their horses on with a last effort close to the winning-post. From the center and outside of the ring all were crowding to the winning-post, and a group of soldiers and officers of the horse-guards were shouting loudly their delight at the expected triumph of their officer and comrade. Vronsky moved into the middle of the crowd unnoticed, almost at the very moment when the bell rang at the finish of the race, and the tall, mud-spattered horse-guard who came in first, bending over the saddle, let go the reins of his panting gray horse that looked dark with sweat.

The horse, stiffening out its legs, with an effort stopped its rapid course, and the officer of the horse-guards looked round him like a man waking up from a heavy sleep, and just managed to smile. A crowd of friends and outsiders pressed round him.

Vronsky intentionally avoided that select crowd of the upper world, which was moving and talking with discreet freedom before the pavilions. He knew that Madame Karenina was there, and Betsy, and his brother's wife, and he purposely did not go near them for fear of something distracting his attention. But he was continually met and stopped by acquaintances, who told him about the previous races, and kept asking him why he was so late.

At the time when the racers had to go to the pavilion to receive the prizes, and all attention was directed to that point, Vronsky's elder brother, Alexander, a colonel with heavy fringed epaulets, came up to him. He was not tall, though as broadly built as Alexey, and handsomer and rosier than he; he had a red nose, and an open, drunken-looking face.

"Did you get my note?" he said. "There's never any finding you."

Alexander Vronsky, in spite of the dissolute life, and in especial the drunken habits, for which he was notorious, was quite one of the court circle.

Now, as he talked to his brother of a matter bound to be exceedingly disagreeable to him, knowing that the eyes of many people might be fixed upon him, he kept a smiling countenance, as though he were jesting with his brother about something of little moment.

"I got it, and I really can't make out what *you* are worrying yourself about," said Alexey.

"I'm worrying myself because the remark has just been made to me that you weren't here, and that you were seen in Peterhof on Monday."

"There are matters which only concern those directly interested in them, and the matter you are so worried about is . . ."

"Yes, but if so, you may as well cut the service. . . ."

"I beg you not to meddle, and that's all I have to say."

Alexey Vronsky's frowning face turned white, and his prominent lower jaw quivered, which happened rarely with him. Being a man of very warm heart, he was seldom angry; but when he was angry, and when his chin quivered, then, as Alexander Vronsky knew, he was dangerous. Alexander Vronsky smiled gaily.

"I only wanted to give you mother's letter. Answer it and don't worry about anything just before the race. *Bonne chance*," he added, smiling, and he moved away from him. But after him another friendly greeting brought Vronsky to a standstill.

"So you won't recognize your friends! How are you, *mon cher?*" said Stepan Arkadyevitch, as conspicuously brilliant in the midst of all the Petersburg brilliance as he was in Moscow, his face rosy, and his whiskers sleek and glossy. "I came up yesterday, and I'm delighted that I shall see your triumph. When shall we meet?"

"Come to-morrow to the mess-room," said Vronsky, and squeezing him by the sleeve of his coat, with apologies, he moved away to the center of the race-course, where the horses were being led for the great steeplechase.

The horses who had run in the last race were being led home, steaming and exhausted, by the stable-boys, and one after another the fresh horses for the coming race made their appearance, for the most part English racers, wearing horsecloths, and looking with their drawn-up bellies like strange, huge birds. On the right was led in Frou-Frou, lean and beautiful, lifting up her elastic, rather long pasterns, as though moved by springs. Not far from her they were taking the rug off the lop-eared Gladiator. The strong, exquisite, perfectly correct lines of the stallion, with his superb hind-quarters and excessively short pasterns almost over his hoofs, attracted Vronsky's attention in spite of himself. He would have gone up to his mare, but he was again detained by an acquaintance.

"Oh, there's Karenin!" said the acquaintance with whom he was chatting. "He's looking for his wife, and she's in the middle of the pavilion. Didn't you see her?"

"No," answered Vronsky, and without even glancing round towards the pavilion where his friend was pointing out Madame Karenina, he went up to his mare.

Vronsky had not had time to look at the saddle, about which he had to give some direction, when the competitors were summoned to the pavilion to receive their numbers and places in the row at starting. Seventeen officers, looking serious and severe, many with pale faces, met together in the pavilion and drew the numbers. Vronsky drew the number seven. The cry was heard: "Mount!"

Feeling that with the others riding in the race, he was the center upon which all eyes were fastened, Vronsky walked up to his mare in that state of nervous tension in which he usually became deliberate and composed in his movements. Cord, in honor of the races, had put on his best clothes, a black coat buttoned up, a stiffly starched collar, which propped up his cheeks, a round black hat, and top-boots. He was calm and dignified as ever, and was with his own hands holding Frou-Frou by both reins, standing straight in front of her. Frou-Frou was still trembling as though in a fever. Her eye, full of fire, glanced sideways at Vronsky. Vronsky slipped his finger under the saddle-girth. The mare glanced aslant at him, drew up her lip, and twitched her ear. The Englishman puckered up his lips, intending to indicate a smile that any one should verify his saddling.

"Get up; you won't feel so excited."

Vronsky looked round for the last time at his rivals. He knew that he would not see them during the race. Two were already riding forward to the point from which they were to start. Galtsin, a friend of Vronsky's and one of his more formidable rivals, was moving round a bay horse that would not let him mount. A little light hussar in tight riding-breeches rode off at a gallop, crouched up like a cat on the saddle, in imitation of English jockeys. Prince Kuzovlev sat with a white face on his thoroughbred mare from the Grabovsky stud, while an English groom led her by the bridle. Vronsky and all his comrades knew Kuzovlev and his peculiarity of "weak nerves" and terrible vanity. They knew that he was afraid of everything, afraid of riding a spirited horse. But now, just because it was terrible, because people broke their necks, and there was a doctor standing at each obstacle, and an ambulance with a cross on it, and a sister of mercy, he had made up his mind to take part in the race. Their eyes met, and Vronsky gave him a friendly and encouraging nod. Only one he did not see, his chief rival, Mahotin on Gladiator.

"Don't be in a hurry," said Cord to Vronsky, "and remember one thing: don't hold her in at the fences, and don't urge her on; let her go as she likes."

"All right, all right," said Vronsky, taking the reins.

"If you can, lead the race; but don't lose heart till the last minute, even if you're behind."

Before the mare had time to move, Vronsky stepped with an agile, vigorous movement into the steel-toothed stirrup, and lightly and firmly seated himself on the creaking leather of the saddle. Getting his right foot in the stirrup, he smoothed the double reins, as he always did, between his fingers, and Cord let go.

As though she did not know which foot to put first, Frou-Frou started, dragging at the reins with her long neck, and as though she were on springs, shaking her rider from side to side. Cord quickened his step, following him. The excited mare, trying to shake off her rider first on one side and then the other, pulled at the reins, and Vronsky tried in vain with voice and hand to soothe her.

They were just reaching the dammed-up stream on their way to the starting-point. Several of the riders were in front and several behind, when suddenly Vronsky heard the sound of a horse galloping in the mud behind him, and he was overtaken by Mahotin on his white-legged, lop-eared Gladiator. Mahotin smiled, showing his long teeth, but Vronsky looked angrily at him. He did not like him, and regarded him now as his most formidable rival. He was angry with him for galloping past and exciting his mare. Frou-Frou started into a gallop, her left foot forward, made two bounds, and fretting at the tightened reins, passed into a jolting trot, bumping her rider up and down. Cord, too, scowled, and followed Vronsky almost at a trot.

C H A P T E R   X X V

THERE were seventeen officers in all riding in this race. The race-course was a large three-mile ring of the form of an ellipse in front of the pavilion. On this course nine obstacles had been arranged: the stream, a big and solid barrier five feet high, just before the pavilion, a dry ditch, a ditch full of water, a precipitous slope, an Irish barricade (one of the most difficult obstacles, consisting of a mound fenced with brushwood, beyond which was a ditch out of sight for the horses, so that the horse had to clear both obstacles or might be killed); then two more ditches filled with water, and one dry one; and the end of the race was just facing the pavilion. But the race began not in the ring, but two hundred yards away from it, and in that part of the course was the first obstacle, a dammed-up stream, seven feet in breadth, which the racers could leap or wade through as they preferred.

Three times they were ranged ready to start, but each time some horse thrust itself out of line, and they had to begin again. The umpire who was starting them, Colonel Sestrin, was beginning to lose his temper, when at last for the fourth time he shouted "Away!" and the racers started.

Every eye, every opera-glass, was turned on the brightly colored group of riders at the moment they were in line to start.

"They're off! They're starting!" was heard on all sides after the hush of expectation.

And little groups and solitary figures among the public began running from place to place to get a better view. In the very first minute the close group of horsemen drew out, and it could be seen that they were approaching the stream in two's and three's and one behind another. To the spectators it seemed as though they had all started simultaneously, but to the racers there were seconds of difference that had great value to them.

235

Frou-Frou, excited and over-nervous, had lost the first moment, and several horses had started before her, but before reaching the stream, Vronsky, who was holding in the mare with all his force as she tugged at the bridle, easily overtook three, and there were left in front of him Mahotin's chestnut Gladiator, whose hind-quarters were moving lightly and rhythmically up and down exactly in front of Vronsky, and in front of all, the dainty mare Diana bearing Kuzovlev more dead than alive.

For the first instant Vronsky was not master either of himself or his mare. Up to the first obstacle, the stream, he could not guide the motions of his mare.

Gladiator and Diana came up to it together and almost at the same instant; simultaneously they rose above the stream and flew across to the other side; Frou-Frou darted after them, as if flying; but at the very moment when Vronsky felt himself in the air, he suddenly saw almost under his mare's hoofs Kuzovlev, who was floundering with Diana on the further side of the stream. (Kuzovlev had let go the reins as he took the leap, and the mare had sent him flying over her head.) Those details Vronsky learned later; at the moment all he saw was that just under him, where Frou-Frou must alight, Diana's legs or head might be in the way. But Frou-Frou drew up her legs and back in the very act of leaping, like a falling cat, and, clearing the other mare, alighted beyond her.

"O the darling!" thought Vronsky.

After crossing the stream Vronsky had complete control of his mare, and began holding her in, intending to cross the great barrier behind Mahotin, and to try to overtake him in the clear ground of about five hundred yards that followed it.

The great barrier stood just in front of the imperial pavilion. The Tsar and the whole court and crowds of people were all gazing at them—at him, and Mahotin a length ahead of him, as they drew near the "devil," as the solid barrier was called. Vronsky was aware of those eyes fastened upon him from all sides, but he saw nothing except the ears and neck of his own mare, the ground racing to meet him, and the back and white legs of Gladiator beating time swiftly before him, and keeping always the same distance ahead. Gladiator rose, with no sound of knocking

236

against anything. With a wave of his short tail he disappeared from Vronsky's sight.

"Bravo!" cried a voice.

At the same instant, under Vronsky's eyes, right before him flashed the palings of the barrier. Without the slightest change in her action his mare flew over it; the palings vanished, and he heard only a crash behind him. The mare, excited by Gladiator's keeping ahead, had risen too soon before the barrier, and grazed it with her hind hoofs. But her pace never changed, and Vronsky, feeling a spatter of mud in his face, realized that he was once more the same distance from Gladiator. Once more he perceived in front of him the same back and short tail, and again the same swiftly moving white legs that got no further away.

At the very moment when Vronsky thought that now was the time to overtake Mahotin, Frou-Frou herself, understanding his thoughts, without any incitement on his part, gained ground considerably, and began getting alongside of Mahotin on the most favorable side, close to the inner cord. Mahotin would not let her pass that side. Vronsky had hardly formed the thought that he could perhaps pass on the outer side, when Frou-Frou shifted her pace and began overtaking him on the other side. Frou-Frou's shoulder, beginning by now to be dark with sweat, was even with Gladiator's back. For a few lengths they moved evenly. But before the obstacle they were approaching, Vronsky began working at the reins, anxious to avoid having to take the outer circle, and swiftly passed Mahotin just upon the declivity. He caught a glimpse of his mud-stained face as he flashed by. He even fancied that he smiled. Vronsky passed Mahotin, but he was immediately aware of him close upon him, and he never ceased hearing the even-thudding hoofs and the rapid and still quite fresh breathing of Gladiator.

The next two obstacles, the water-course and the barrier, were easily crossed, but Vronsky began to hear the snorting and thud of Gladiator closer upon him. He urged on his mare, and to his delight felt that she easily quickened her pace, and the thud of Gladiator's hoofs was again heard at the same distance away.

Vronsky was at the head of the race, just as he wanted to be and as Cord had advised, and now he felt sure of being the winner. His excitement, his delight, and his tenderness for Frou-Frou grew keener and keener. He longed to look round again, but he did not dare do this, and tried to be cool and not to urge on his mare, so to keep the same reserve of force in her as he felt that Gladiator still kept. There remained only one obstacle, the most difficult; if he could cross it ahead of the others, he would come in first. He was flying towards the Irish barricade, Frou-Frou and he both together saw the barricade in the distance, and both the man and the mare had a moment's hesitation. He saw the uncertainty in the mare's ears and lifted the whip, but at the same time felt that his fears were groundless; the mare knew what was wanted. She quickened her pace and rose smoothly, just as he had fancied she would, and as she left the ground gave herself up to the force of her rush, which carried her far beyond the ditch; and with the same rhythm, without effort, with the same leg forward, Frou-Frou fell back into her pace again.

"Bravo, Vronsky!" he heard shouts from a knot of men—he knew they were his friends in the regiment—who were standing at the obstacle. He could not fail to recognize Yashvin's voice though he did not see him.

"O my sweet!" he said inwardly to Frou-Frou, as he listened for what was happening behind. "He's cleared it!" he thought, catching the thud of Gladiator's hoofs behind him. There remained only the last ditch, filled with water and five feet wide. Vronsky did not even look at it, but anxious to get in a long way first began sawing away at the reins, lifting the mare's head and letting it go in time with her paces. He felt that the mare was at her very last reserve of strength; not her neck and shoulders merely were wet, but the sweat was standing in drops on her mane, her head, her sharp ears, and her breath came in short, sharp gasps. But he knew that she had strength left more than enough for the remaining five hundred yards. It was only from feeling himself nearer the ground and from the peculiar smoothness of his motion that Vronsky knew how greatly the mare had quickened her pace. She flew over the ditch as though not noticing it. She flew over it like a bird; but at the same instant Vronsky, to his horror, felt that he had failed to keep up with the mare's pace, that he had, he did not know how, made a fearful, unpardonable mistake, in recovering his seat in the saddle. All at once his position had shifted and he knew that something awful had happened. He could not yet make out what had happened, when the white legs of a chestnut horse flashed by close to him, and Mahotin passed at a swift gallop. Vronsky was touching the ground with one foot, and his mare was sinking on that foot. He just had time to free his leg when she fell on one side, gasping painfully, and, making vain efforts to rise with her delicate, soaking neck, she fluttered on the ground at his feet like a shot bird. The clumsy movement made by Vronsky had broken her back. But that he only knew much later. At that moment he knew only that Mahotin had flown swiftly by, while he stood staggering alone on the muddy, motionless ground, and Frou-Frou lay gasping before him, bending her head back and gazing at him with her exquisite eyes. Still unable to realize what had happened, Vronsky tugged at his mare's reins. Again she struggled all over like a fish, and her shoulders setting the saddle heaving, she rose on her front legs but unable to lift her back, she quivered all over and again fell on her side. With a face hideous with passion, his lower jaw trembling, and his cheeks white, Vronsky kicked her with his heel in the stomach and again fell to tugging at the rein. She did not stir, but thrusting her nose into the ground, she simply gazed at her master with her speaking eyes.

"A—a—a!" groaned Vronsky, clutching at his head. "Ah! what have I done!" he cried. "The race lost! And my fault! shameful, unpardonable! And the poor darling, ruined mare! Ah! what have I done!"

A crowd of men, a doctor and his assistant, the officers of his regiment, ran up to him. To his misery he felt that he was whole and unhurt. The mare had broken her back, and it was decided to shoot her. Vronsky could not answer questions, could not speak to any one. He turned, and without picking up his cap that had fallen off, walked away from the race-course, not knowing where he was going. He felt utterly wretched. For the first time in his life he knew the bitterest sort of misfortune, misfortune beyond remedy, and caused by his own fault.

Yashvin overtook him with his cap, and led him home, and half an hour later Vronsky had regained his self-possession. But the memory of that race remained for long in his heart, the cruelest and bitterest memory of his life.

CHAPTER XXVI

THE external relations of Alexey Alexandrovitch and his wife had remained unchanged. The sole difference lay in the fact that he was more busily occupied than ever. As in former years, at the beginning of the spring he had gone to a foreign watering-place for the sake of his health, deranged by the winter's work that every year grew heavier. And just as always he returned in July and at once fell to work as usual with increased energy. As usual, too, his wife had moved for the summer to a villa out of town, while he remained in Petersburg. From the date of their conversation after the party at Princess Tverskaya's he had never spoken again to Anna of his suspicions and his jealousies, and that habitual tone of his of bantering mimicry was the most convenient tone possible for his present attitude to his wife. He was a little colder to his wife. He simply seemed to be slightly displeased with her for that first midnight conversation, which she had repelled. In his attitude to her there was a shade of vexation, but nothing more. "You would not be open with me," he seemed to say, mentally addressing her; "so much the worse for you. Now you may beg as you please, but I won't be open with you. So much the worse for you!" he said mentally, like a man who, after vainly attempting to extinguish a fire, should fly in a rage with his vain efforts and say, "Oh, very well then! you shall burn for this!" This man, so subtle and astute in official life, did not realize all the senselessness of such an attitude to his wife. He did not realize it, because it was too terrible to him to realize his actual position, and he shut down and locked and sealed up in his heart that secret place where lay hid his feelings towards his family, that is, his wife and son. He who had been such a careful father, had from the end of that winter become peculiarly frigid to his son, and adopted to him just the same bantering tone he used with his wife. "Aha, young man!" was the greeting with which he met him.

Alexey Alexandrovitch asserted and believed that he had never in any previous year had so much official business as that year. But he was not aware that he sought work for himself that year, that this was one of the means for keeping shut that secret place where lay hid his feelings towards his wife and son and his thoughts about them, which became more terrible the longer they lay there. If any one had had the right to ask Alexey Alexandrovitch what he thought of his wife's behavior, the mild and peaceable Alexey Alexandrovitch would have made no answer, but he would have been greatly angered with any man who should question him on that subject. For this reason there positively came into Alexey Alexandrovitch's face a look of haughtiness and severity whenever any one inquired after his wife's health. Alexey Alexandrovitch did not want to think at all about his wife's behavior, and he actually succeeded in not thinking about it at all.

Alexey Alexandrovitch's permanent summer villa was in Peterhof, and the Countess Lidia Ivanovna used as a rule to spend the summer there, close to Anna, and constantly seeing her. That year Countess Lidia Ivanovna declined to settle in Peterhof, was not once at Anna Arkadyevna's, and in conversation with Alexey Alexandrovitch hinted at the unsuitability of Anna's close intimacy with Betsy and Vronsky. Alexey Alexandrovitch sternly cut her short, roundly declaring his wife to be above suspicion, and from that time began to avoid Countess Lidia Ivanovna. He did not want to see, and did not see, that many people in society cast dubious glances on his wife; he did not want to understand, and did not understand, why his wife had so particularly insisted on staying at Tsarskoe, where Betsy was staying, and not far from the camp of Vronsky's regiment. He did not allow himself to think about it, and he did not think about it; but all the same though he never admitted it to himself, and had no proofs, not even suspicious evidence, in the bottom of his heart he knew beyond all doubt that he was a deceived husband, and he was profoundly miserable about it.

How often during those eight years of happy life with his wife Alexey Alexandrovitch had looked at other men's faithless wives and other deceived husbands and asked himself: "How can people descend to that? how is it they don't put an end to such a hideous position?" But now, when the misfortune had come upon himself, he was so far from thinking of putting an end to the position that he would not recognize it at all, would not recognize it just because it was too awful, too unnatural.

Since his return from abroad Alexey Alexandrovitch had twice been at their country villa. Once he dined there, another time he spent the evening there with a party of friends, but he had not once stayed the night there, as it had been his habit to do in previous years.

The day of the races had been a very busy day for Alexey Alexandrovitch; but when mentally sketching out the day in the morning, he made up his mind to go to their country house to see his wife immediately after dinner, and from there to the races, which all the Court were to witness, and at which he was bound to be present. He was going to see his wife, because he had determined to see her once a week to keep up appearances. And besides, on that day, as it was the fifteenth, he had to give his wife some money for her expenses, according to their usual arrangement.

With his habitual control over his thoughts, though he thought all this about his wife, he did not let his thoughts stray further in regard to her.

That morning was a very full one for Alexey Alexandrovitch. The evening before, Countess Lidia Ivanovna had sent him a pamphlet by a celebrated traveler in China, who was staying in Petersburg, and with it she enclosed a note begging him to see the traveler himself, as he was an extremely interesting person from various points of view, and likely to be useful. Alexey Alexandrovitch had not had time to read the pamphlet through in the evening, and finished it in the morning. Then people began arriving with petitions, and there came the reports, interviews, appointments, dismissals, apportionment of rewards, pensions, grants, notes, the workaday round, as Alexey Alexandrovitch called it, that always took up so much time. Then there was private business of his own, a visit from the doctor and the steward who managed his property. The steward did not take up much time. He simply gave Alexey Alexandrovitch the money he needed together with a brief statement of the position of his affairs, which was not altogether satisfactory, as it had happened that during that year, owing to increased expenses, more had been paid out than usual, and there was a deficit. But the doctor, a celebrated Petersburg doctor, who was an intimate acquaintance of Alexey Alexandrovitch, took up a great deal of time. Alexey Alexandrovitch had not expected him that day, and was surprised at his visit, and still more so when the doctor questioned him very carefully about his health, listened to his breathing, and tapped at his liver. Alexey Alexandrovitch did not know that his friend Lidia Ivanovna, noticing that he was not as well as usual that year, had begged the doctor to go and examine him. "Do this for my sake," the Countess Lidia Ivanovna had said to him.

"I will do it for the sake of Russia, countess," replied the doctor.

"A priceless man!" said the Countess Lidia Ivanovna.

The doctor was extremely dissatisfied with Alexey Alexandrovitch. He found the liver considerably enlarged, and the digestive powers weakened, while the course of mineral waters had been quite without effect. He prescribed more physical exercise as far as possible, and as far as possible less mental strain, and above all no worry—in other words, just what was as much out of Alexey Alexandrovitch's power as abstaining from breathing. Then he withdrew, leaving in Alexey Alexandrovitch an unpleasant sense that something was wrong with him, and that there was no chance of curing it.

As he was coming away, the doctor chanced to meet on the staircase an acquaintance of his, Sludin, who was secretary of Alexey Alexandrovitch's department. They had been comrades at the university, and though they rarely met, they thought highly of each other and were excellent friends, and so there was no one to whom the doctor would have given his opinion of a patient so freely as to Sludin.

"How glad I am you've been seeing him!" said Sludin. "He's not well, and I fancy . . . Well, what do you think of him?"

"I'll tell you," said the doctor, beckoning over Sludin's head to his coachman to bring the carriage round. "It's just this," said the doctor, taking a finger of his kid glove in his white hands and pulling it, "if you don't strain the strings, and then try to break them, you'll find it a difficult job; but strain a string to its very utmost, and the mere weight of one finger on the strained string will snap it. And with his close assiduity, his conscientious devotion to his work, he's strained to the utmost; and there's some outside burden weighing on him, and not a light one," concluded the doctor, raising his eyebrows significantly. "Will you be at the races?" he added, as he sank into his seat in the carriage.

"Yes, yes, to be sure; it does waste a lot of time," the doctor responded vaguely to some reply of Sludin's he had not caught.

Directly after the doctor, who had taken up so much time, came the celebrated traveler, and Alexey Alexandrovitch, by means of the pamphlet he had only just finished reading and his previous acquaintance with the subject, impressed the traveler by the depth of his knowledge of the subject and the breadth and enlightenment of his view of it.

At the same time as the traveler there was announced a provincial marshal of nobility on a visit to Petersburg, with whom Alexey Alexandrovitch had to have some conversation. After his departure, he had to finish the daily routine of business with his secretary, and then he still had to drive round to call on a certain great personage on a matter of grave and serious import. Alexey Alexandrovitch only just managed to be back by five o'clock, his dinner-hour, and after dining with his secretary, he invited him to drive with him to his country villa and to the races.

Though he did not acknowledge it to himself, Alexey Alexandrovitch always tried nowadays to secure the presence of a third person in his interviews with his wife.

ANNA was up-stairs, standing before the looking-glass, and, with Annushka's assistance, pinning the last ribbon on her gown when she heard carriage wheels crunching the gravel at the entrance.

"It's too early for Betsy," she thought, and glancing out of the window she caught sight of the carriage and the black hat of Alexey Alexandrovitch, and the ears that she knew so well sticking up each side of it. "How unlucky! Can he be going to stay the night?" she wondered, and the thought of all that might come of such a chance struck her as so awful and terrible that, without dwelling on it for a moment, she went down to meet him with a bright and radiant face; and conscious of the presence of that spirit of falsehood and deceit in herself that she had come to know of late, she abandoned herself to that spirit and began talking, hardly knowing what she was saying.

"Ah, how nice of you!" she said, giving her husband her hand, and greeting Sludin, who was like one of the family, with a smile. "You're staying the night, I hope?" was the first word the spirit of falsehood prompted her to utter; "and now we'll go together. Only it's a pity I've promised Betsy. She's coming for me."

Alexey Alexandrovitch knit his brows at Betsy's name.

"Oh, I'm not going to separate the inseparables," he said in his usual bantering tone. "I'm going with Mihail Vassilievitch. I'm ordered exercise by the doctors too. I'll walk, and fancy myself at the springs again."

"There's no hurry," said Anna. "Would you like tea?"

She rang.

"Bring in tea, and tell Seryozha that Alexey Alexandrovitch is here. Well, tell me, how have you been? Mihail Vassilievitch, you've not been to see me before. Look how lovely it is out on the terrace," she said, turning first to one and then to the other.

She spoke very simply and naturally, but too much and too fast. She was the more aware of this from noticing in the inquisitive look Mihail Vassilievitch turned on her that he was, as it were, keeping watch on her.

Mihail Vassilievitch promptly went out on the terrace.

She sat down beside her husband.

"You don't look quite well," she said.

"Yes," he said; "the doctor's been with me to-day and wasted an hour of my time. I feel that some one of our friends must have sent him: my health's so precious, it seems."

"No; what did he say?"

She questioned him about his health and what he had been doing, and tried to persuade him to take a rest and come out to her.

All this she said brightly, rapidly, and with a peculiar brilliance in her eyes. But Alexey Alexandrovitch did not now attach any special significance to this tone of hers. He heard only her words and gave them only the direct sense they bore. And he answered simply, though jestingly. There was nothing remarkable in all this conversation, but never after could Anna recall this brief scene without an agonizing pang of shame.

Seryozha came in preceded by his governess. If Alexey Alexandrovitch had allowed himself to observe he would have noticed the timid and bewildered eyes with which Seryozha glanced first at his father and then at his mother. But he would not see anything, and he did not see it.

"Ah, the young man! He's grown. Really, he's getting quite a man. How are you, young man?"

And he gave his hand to the scared child. Seryozha had been shy of his father before, and now, ever since Alexey Alexandrovitch had taken to calling him young man, and since that insoluble question had occurred to him whether Vronsky were a friend or a foe, he avoided his father. He looked round towards his mother as though seeking shelter. It was only with his mother that he was at ease. Meanwhile, Alexey Alexandrovitch was holding his son by the shoulder while he was speaking to the governess, and Seryozha was so miserably uncomfortable that Anna saw he was on the point of tears.

Anna, who had flushed a little the instant her son came in, noticing that Seryozha was uncomfortable, got up hurriedly, took Alexey Alexandrovitch's hand from her son's shoulder, and kissing the boy, led him out onto the terrace, and quickly came back.

"It's time to start, though," said she, glancing at her watch. "How is it Betsy doesn't come? . . ."

"Yes," said Alexey Alexandrovitch, and getting up, he folded his hands and cracked his fingers. "I've come to bring you some money, too, for nightingales, we know, can't live on fairy tales," he said. "You want it, I expect?"

"No, I don't . . . yes, I do," she said, not looking at him, and crimsoning to the roots of her hair. "But you'll come back here after the races, I suppose?"

"Oh, yes!" answered Alexey Alexandrovitch. "And here's the glory of Peterhof, Princess Tverskaya," he added, looking out of the window at the elegant English carriage with the tiny seats placed extremely high. "What elegance! Charming! Well, let us be starting too, then."

Princess Tverskaya did not get out of her carriage, but her groom, in high boots, a cape, and block hat, darted out at the entrance.

"I'm going; good-bye!" said Anna, and kissing her son, she went up to Alexey Alexandrovitch and held out her hand to him. "It was ever so nice of you to come."

Alexey Alexandrovitch kissed her hand.

"Well, *au revoir,* then! You'll come back for some tea; that's delightful!" she said, and went out, gay and radiant. But as soon as she no longer saw him, she was aware of the spot on her hand that his lips had touched, and she shuddered with repulsion.

CHAPTER XXVIII

WHEN Alexey Alexandrovitch reached the race-course, Anna was already sitting in the pavilion beside Betsy, in that pavilion where all the highest society had gathered. She caught sight of her husband in the distance. Two men, her husband and her lover, were the two centers of her existence, and unaided by her external senses she was aware of their nearness. She was aware of her husband approaching a long way off, and she could not help following him in the surging crowd in the midst of which he was moving. She watched his progress towards the pavilion, saw him now responding condescendingly to an ingratiating bow, now exchanging friendly, nonchalant greetings with his equals, now assiduously trying to catch the eye of some great one of this world, and taking off his big round hat that squeezed the tips of his ears. All these ways of his she knew, and all were hateful to her. "Nothing but ambition, nothing but the desire to get on, that's all there is in his soul," she thought; "as for these lofty ideals, love of culture, religion, they are only so many tools for getting on."

From his glances toward the ladies' pavilion (he was staring straight at her, but did not distinguish his wife in the sea of muslin, ribbons, feathers, parasols and flowers) she saw that he was looking for her, but she purposely avoided noticing him.

"Alexey Alexandrovitch!" Princess Betsy called to him; "I'm sure you don't see your wife: here she is."

He smiled his chilly smile.

"There's so much splendor here that one's eyes are dazzled," he said, and he went into the pavilion. He smiled to his wife as a man should smile on meeting his wife after only just parting from her, and greeted the princess and other acquaintances, giving to each what was due—that is to say, jesting with the ladies and dealing out friendly greetings among the men. Below, near the pavilion, was standing an adjutant-general of whom Alexey Alexandrovitch had a high opinion, noted for his intelligence and culture. Alexey Alexandrovitch entered into conversation with him.

There was an interval between the races, and so nothing hindered conversation. The adjutant-general expressed his disapproval of races. Alexey Alexandrovitch replied defending them. Anna heard his high, measured tones, not losing one word, and every word struck her as false, and stabbed her ears with pain.

When the three-mile steeplechase was beginning, she bent forward and gazed with fixed eyes at Vronsky as he went up to his horse and mounted, and at the same time she heard that loathsome, never-ceasing voice of her husband. She was in an agony of terror for Vronsky, but a still greater agony was the never-ceasing, as it seemed to her, stream of her husband's shrill voice with its familiar intonations.

"I'm a wicked woman, a lost woman," she thought; "but I

don't like lying, I can't endure falsehood, while as for *him* (her husband) it's the breath of his life—falsehood. He knows all about it, he sees it all; what does he care if he can talk so calmly? If he were to kill me, if he were to kill Vronsky, I might respect him. No, all he wants is falsehood and propriety," Anna said to herself, not considering exactly what it was she wanted of her husband, and how she would have liked to see him behave. She did not understand either that Alexey Alexandrovitch's peculiar loquacity that day, so exasperating to her, was merely the expression of his inward distress and uneasiness. As a child that has been hurt skips about, putting all his muscles into movement to drown the pain, in the same way Alexey Alexandrovitch needed mental exercise to drown the thoughts of his wife that in her presence and in Vronsky's, and with the continual iteration of his name, would force themselves on his attention. And it was as natural for him to talk well and cleverly, as it is natural for a child to skip about. He was saying:

"Danger in the races of officers, of cavalry men, is an essential element in the race. If England can point to the most brilliant feats of cavalry in military history, it is simply owing to the fact that she has historically developed this force both in beasts and in men. Sport has, in my opinion, a great value, and as is always the case, we see nothing but what is most superficial."

"It's not superficial," said Princess Tverskaya. "One of the officers, they say, has broken two ribs."

Alexey Alexandrovitch smiled his smile, which uncovered his teeth, but revealed nothing more.

"We'll admit, princess, that that's not superficial," he said, "but internal. But that's not the point," and he turned again to the general with whom he was talking seriously; "we mustn't forget that those who are taking part in the race are military men, who have chosen that career, and one must allow that every calling has its disagreeable side. It forms an integral part of the duties of an officer. Low sports, such as prize-fighting or Spanish bull-fights, are a sign of barbarity. But specialized trials of skill are a sign of development."

"No, I shan't come another time; it's too upsetting," said Princess Betsy. "Isn't it, Anna?"

"It is upsetting, but one can't tear oneself away," said another lady. "If I'd been a Roman woman I should never have missed a single circus."

Anna said nothing, and keeping her opera-glass up, gazed always at the same spot.

At that moment a tall general walked through the pavilion. Breaking off what he was saying, Alexey Alexandrovitch got up hurriedly, though with dignity, and bowed low to the general.

"You're not racing?" the officer asked, chaffing him.

"My race is a harder one," Alexey Alexandrovitch responded deferentially.

And though the answer meant nothing, the general looked as though he had heard a witty remark from a witty man, and fully relished *la pointe de la sauce.*

"There are two aspects," Alexey Alexandrovitch resumed: "those who take part and those who look on; and love for such spectacles is an unmistakable proof of a low degree of development in the spectator, I admit, but . . ."

"Princess, bets!" sounded Stepan Arkadyevitch's voice from below, addressing Betsy. "Who's your favorite?"

"Anna and I are for Kuzovlev," replied Betsy.

"I'm for Vronsky. A pair of gloves?"

"Done!"

"But it is a pretty sight, isn't it?"

Alexey Alexandrovitch paused while there was talking about him, but he began again directly.

"I admit that manly sports do not . . ." he was continuing.

But at that moment the racers started, and all conversation ceased. Alexey Alexandrovitch too was silent, and every one stood up and turned towards the stream. Alexey Alexandrovitch took no interest in the race, and so he did not watch the racers, but fell listlessly to scanning the spectators with his weary eyes. His eyes rested upon Anna.

Her face was white and set. She was obviously seeing nothing and no one but one man. Her hand had convulsively clutched her fan, and she held her breath. He looked at her and hastily turned away, scrutinizing other faces.

"But here's this lady too, and others very much moved as well; it's very natural," Alexey Alexandrovitch told himself. He tried not to look at her, but unconsciously his eyes were drawn to her.

He examined that face again, trying not to read what was so plainly written on it, and against his own will, with horror read on it what he did not want to know.

The first fall—Kuzovlev's, at the stream—agitated every one, but Alexey Alexandrovitch saw distinctly on Anna's pale, triumphant face that the man she was watching had not fallen. When, after Mahotin and Vronsky had cleared the worst barrier, the next officer had been thrown straight on his head at it and fatally injured, and a shudder of horror passed over the whole public, Alexey Alexandrovitch saw that Anna did not even notice it, and had some difficulty in realizing what they were talking of about her. But more and more often, and with greater persistence, he watched her. Anna, wholly engrossed as she was with the race, became aware of her husband's cold eyes fixed upon her from one side.

She glanced round for an instant, looked inquiringly at him, and with a slight frown turned away again.

"Ah, I don't care!" she seemed to say to him, and she did not once glance at him again.

The race was an unlucky one, and of the seventeen officers who rode in it more than half were thrown and hurt. Towards the end of the race every one was in a state of agitation, which was intensified by the fact that the Tsar was displeased.

CHAPTER XXIX

EVERY one was loudly expressing disapprobation, every one was repeating a phrase some one had uttered—"The lions and gladiators will be the next thing," and every one was feeling horrified; so that when Vronsky fell to the ground, and Anna moaned aloud, there was nothing very out of the way in it. But afterwards a change came over Anna's face which really was beyond decorum. She utterly lost her head. She began fluttering like a caged bird, at one moment would have got up and moved away, at the next turned to Betsy.

"Let us go, let us go!" she said.

But Betsy did not hear her. She was bending down, talking to a general who had come up to her.

Alexey Alexandrovitch went up to Anna and courteously of-fered her his arm.

"Let us go, if you like," he said in French, but Anna was listening to the general and did not notice her husband.

"He's broken his leg too, so they say," the general was saying. "This is beyond everything."

Without answering her husband, Anna lifted her opera-glass and gazed towards the place where Vronsky had fallen; but it was so far off, and there was such a crowd of people about it, that she could make out nothing. She laid down the opera-glass, and would have moved away, but at that moment an officer galloped up and made some announcement to the Tsar. Anna craned for-ward, listening.

"Stiva! Stiva!" she cried to her brother.

But her brother did not hear her. Again she would have moved away.

"Once more I offer you my arm if you want to be going," said Alexey Alexandrovitch, reaching towards her hand.

She drew back from him with aversion, and without looking in his face answered:

"No, no, let me be, I'll stay."

She saw now that from the place of Vronsky's accident an officer was running across the course towards the pavilion. Betsy waved her handkerchief to him. The officer brought the news that the rider was not killed, but the horse had broken its back.

On hearing this Anna sat down hurriedly, and hid her face in her fan. Alexey Alexandrovitch saw that she was weeping, and could not control her tears, nor even the sobs that were shaking her bosom. Alexey Alexandrovitch stood so as to screen her, giv-ing her time to recover herself.

"For the third time I offer you my arm," he said to her after a little time, turning to her. Anna gazed at him and did not know what to say. Princess Betsy came to her rescue.

"No, Alexey Alexandrovitch; I brought Anna and I promised to take her home," put in Betsy.

"Excuse me, princess," he said, smiling courteously but look-ing her very firmly in the face, "but I see that Anna's not very well, and I wish her to come home with me."

Anna looked about her in a frightened way, got up submissively, and laid her hand on her husband's arm.

"I'll send to him and find out, and let you know," Betsy whispered to her.

As they left the pavilion, Alexey Alexandrovitch, as always, talked to those he met, and Anna had, as always, to talk and answer; but she was utterly beside herself, and moved hanging on her husband's arm as though in a dream.

"Is he killed or not? Is it true? Will he come or not? Shall I see him to-day?" she was thinking.

She took her seat in her husband's carriage in silence, and in silence drove out of the crowd of carriages. In spite of all he had seen, Alexey Alexandrovitch still did not allow himself to consider his wife's real condition. He merely saw the outward symptoms. He saw that she was behaving unbecomingly, and considered it his duty to tell her so. But it was very difficult for him not to say more, to tell her nothing but that. He opened his mouth to tell her she had behaved unbecomingly, but he could not help saying something utterly different.

"What an inclination we all have, though, for these cruel spectacles!" he said. "I observe . . ."

"Eh? I don't understand," said Anna contemptuously.

He was offended, and at once began to say what he had meant to say.

"I am obliged to tell you," he began.

"So now we are to have it out," she thought, and she felt frightened.

"I am obliged to tell you that your behavior has been unbecoming to-day," he said to her in French.

"In what way has my behavior been unbecoming?" she said aloud, turning her head swiftly and looking him straight in the face, not with the bright expression that seemed covering something, but with a look of determination, under which she concealed with difficulty the dismay she was feeling.

"Mind," he said, pointing to the open window opposite the coachman.

He got up and pulled up the window.

"What did you consider unbecoming?" she repeated.

"The despair you were unable to conceal at the accident to one of the riders."

He waited for her to answer, but she was silent, looking straight before her.

"I have already begged you so to conduct yourself in society that even malicious tongues can find nothing to say against you. There was a time when I spoke of your inward attitude, but I am not speaking of that now. Now I speak only of your external attitude. You have behaved improperly, and I would wish it not to occur again."

She did not hear half of what he was saying; she felt panic-stricken before him, and was thinking whether it was true that Vronsky was not killed. Was it of him they were speaking when they said the rider was unhurt, but the horse had broken its back? She merely smiled with a pretense of irony when he finished, and made no reply, because she had not heard what he said. Alexey Alexandrovitch had begun to speak boldly, but as he realized plainly what he was speaking of, the dismay she was feeling infected him too. He saw the smile, and a strange misapprehension came over him.

"She is smiling at my suspicions. Yes, she will tell me directly what she told me before; that there is no foundation for my suspicions, that it's absurd."

At that moment, when the revelation of everything was hanging over him, there was nothing he expected so much as that she would answer mockingly as before that his suspicions were absurd and utterly groundless. So terrible to him was that he knew that now he was ready to believe anything. But the expression of her face, scared and gloomy, did not now promise even deception.

"Possibly I was mistaken," said he. "If so, I beg your pardon."

"No, you were not mistaken," she said deliberately, looking desperately into his cold face. "You were not mistaken. I was, and I could not help being in despair. I hear you, but I am thinking of him. I love him, I am his mistress; I can't bear you; I'm afraid of you, and I hate you. . . . You can do what you like to me."

And dropping back into the corner of the carriage, she broke into sobs, hiding her face in her hands. Alexey Alexandrovitch did not stir, and kept looking straight before him. But his whole face suddenly bore the solemn rigidity of the dead, and his expression did not change during the whole time of the drive home. On reaching the house he turned his head to her, still with the same expression.

"Very well! But I expect a strict observance of the external forms of propriety till such time"—his voice shook—"as I may take measures to secure my honor and communicate them to you."

He got out first and helped her to get out. Before the servants he pressed her hand, took his seat in the carriage, and drove back to Petersburg. Immediately afterwards a footman came from Princess Betsy and brought Anna a note.

"I sent to Alexey to find out how he is, and he writes me he is quite well and unhurt, but in despair."

"So *he* will be here," she thought. "What a good thing I told him all!"

She glanced at her watch. She had still three hours to wait, and the memories of their last meeting set her blood in flame.

"My God, how light it is! It's dreadful, but I do love to see his face, and I do love this fantastic light. . . . My husband! Oh! yes . . . Well, thank God! everything's over with him."

CHAPTER XXX

In the little German watering-place to which the Shtcherbatskys had betaken themselves, as in all places indeed where people are gathered together, the usual process, as it were, of the crystallization of society went on, assigning to each member of that society a definite and unalterable place. Just as the particle of water in frost, definitely and unalterably, takes the special form of the crystal of snow, so each new person that arrived at the springs was at once placed in his special place.

Fürst Shtcherbatsky, *sammt Gemahlin und Tochter,* by the apartments they took, and from their name and from the friends they made, were immediately crystallized into a definite place marked out for them.

There was visiting the watering-place that year a real German Fürstin, in consequence of which the crystallizing process went

255

on more vigorously than ever. Princess Shtcherbatskaya wished, above everything, to present her daughter to this German princess, and the day after their arrival she duly performed this rite. Kitty made a low and graceful curtsey in the *very simple,* that is to say, very elegant frock that had been ordered her from Paris. The German princess said, "I hope the roses will soon come back to this pretty little face," and for the Shtcherbatskys certain definite lines of existence were at once laid down from which there was no departing. The Shtcherbatskys made the acquaintance too of the family of an English Lady Somebody, and of a German countess and her son, wounded in the last war, and of a learned Swede, and of M. Canut and his sister. But yet inevitably the Shtcherbatskys were thrown most into the society of a Moscow lady, Marya Yevgenyevna Rtishtcheva and her daughter, whom Kitty disliked, because she had fallen ill, like herself, over a love affair, and a Moscow colonel, whom Kitty had known from childhood, and always seen in uniform and epaulets, and who now, with his little eyes and his open neck and flowered cravat, was uncommonly ridiculous and tedious, because there was no getting rid of him. When all this was so firmly established, Kitty began to be very much bored, especially as the prince went away to Carlsbad and she was left alone with her mother. She took no interest in the people she knew, feeling that nothing fresh would come of them. Her chief mental interest in the watering-place consisted in watching and making theories about the people she did not know. It was characteristic of Kitty that she always imagined everything in people in the most favorable light possible, especially so in those she did not know. And now as she made surmises as to who people were, what were their relations to one another, and what they were like, Kitty endowed them with the most marvelous and noble characters, and found confirmation of her idea in her observations.

Of these people the one that attracted her most was a Russian girl who had come to the watering-place with an invalid Russian lady, Madame Stahl, as every one called her. Madame Stahl belonged to the highest society, but she was so ill that she could not walk, and only on exceptionally fine days made her appearance at the springs in an invalid carriage. But it was not so much from ill-health as from pride—so Princess Shtcherbatskaya interpreted it—that Madame Stahl had not made the acquaintance of any one among the Russians there. The Russian girl looked after Madame Stahl, and besides that, she was, as Kitty observed, on friendly terms with all the invalids who were seriously ill, and there were many of them at the springs, and looked after them in the most natural way. This Russian girl was not, as Kitty gathered, related to Madame Stahl, nor was she a paid attendant. Madame Stahl called her Varenka, and other people called her "Mademoiselle Varenka." Apart from the interest Kitty took in this girl's relations with Madame Stahl and with other unknown persons, Kitty, as often happened, felt an inexplicable attraction to Mademoiselle Varenka, and was aware when their eyes met that she too liked her.

Of Mademoiselle Varenka one would not say that she had passed her first youth, but she was, as it were, a creature without youth; she might have been taken for nineteen or for thirty. If her features were criticized separately, she was handsome rather than plain, in spite of the sickly hue of her face. She would have been a good figure, too, if it had not been for her extreme thinness and the size of her head, which was too large for her medium height. But she was not likely to be attractive to men. She was like a fine flower, already past its bloom and without fragrance, though the petals were still unwithered. Moreover, she would have been unattractive to men also from the lack of just what Kitty had too much of—of the suppressed fire of vitality, and the consciousness of her own attractiveness.

She always seemed absorbed in work about which there could be no doubt, and so it seemed she could not take interest in anything outside it. It was just this contrast with her own position that was for Kitty the great attraction of Mademoiselle Varenka. Kitty felt that in her, in her manner of life, she would find an example of what she was now so painfully seeking: interest in life, a dignity in life—apart from the worldly relations of girls with men, which so revolted Kitty, and appeared to her now as a shameful hawking about of goods in search of a purchaser. The more attentively Kitty watched her unknown friend, the more convinced she was this girl was the perfect creature she fancied her, and the more eagerly she wished to make her acquaintance.

The two girls used to meet several times a day, and every time they met, Kitty's eyes said: "Who are you? What are you? Are you really the exquisite creature I imagine you to be? But for goodness' sake don't suppose," her eyes added, "that I would force my acquaintance on you, I simply admire you and like you." "I like you too, and you're very, very sweet. And I should like you better still, if I had time," answered the eyes of the unknown girl. Kitty saw indeed, that she was always busy. Either she was taking the children of a Russian family home from the springs, or fetching a shawl for a sick lady, and wrapping her up in it, or trying to interest an irritable invalid, or selecting and buying cakes for tea for some one.

Soon after the arrival of the Shtcherbatskys there appeared in the morning crowd at the springs two persons who attracted universal and unfavorable attention. These were a tall man with a stooping figure, and huge hands, in an old coat too short for him, with black, simple, and yet terrible, eyes, and a pockmarked, kind-looking woman, very badly and tastelessly dressed. Recognizing these persons as Russians, Kitty had already in her imagination begun constructing a delightful and touching romance about them. But the princess, having ascertained from the visitors' list that this was Nikolay Levin and Marya Nikolaevna, explained to Kitty what a bad man this Levin was, and all her fancies about these two people vanished. Not so much from what her mother told her, as from the fact that it was Konstantin's brother, this pair suddenly seemed to Kitty intensely unpleasant. This Levin, with his continual twitching of his head, aroused in her now an irrepressible feeling of disgust.

It seemed to her that his big, terrible eyes, which persistently pursued her, expressed a feeling of hatred and contempt, and she tried to avoid meeting him.

CHAPTER XXXI

It was a wet day; it had been raining all the morning, and the invalids, with their parasols, had flocked into the arcades.

Kitty was walking there with her mother and the Moscow colonel, smart and jaunty in his European coat, bought ready-made at Frankfort. They were walking on one side of the arcade, trying to avoid Levin, who was walking on the other side. Varenka, in her dark dress, in a black hat with a turndown brim, was walking up and down the whole length of the arcade with a blind Frenchwoman, and, every time she met Kitty, they exchanged friendly glances.

"Mamma, couldn't I speak to her?" said Kitty, watching her unknown friend, and noticing that she was going up to the spring, and that they might come there together.

"Oh, if you want to so much, I'll find out about her first and make her acquaintance myself," answered her mother. "What do you see in her out of the way? A companion, she must be. If you like, I'll make acquaintance with Madame Stahl; I used to know her *belle-sœur*," added the princess, lifting her head haughtily.

Kitty knew that the princess was offended that Madame Stahl had seemed to avoid making her acquaintance. Kitty did not insist.

"How wonderfully sweet she is!" she said, gazing at Varenka just as she handed a glass to the Frenchwoman. "Look how natural and sweet it all is."

"It's so funny to see your *engouements*," said the princess. "No, we'd better go back," she added, noticing Levin coming towards them with his companion and a German doctor, to whom he was talking very noisily and angrily.

They turned to go back, when suddenly they heard, not noisy talk, but shouting. Levin, stopping short, was shouting at the doctor, and the doctor, too, was excited. A crowd gathered about them. The princess and Kitty beat a hasty retreat, while the colonel joined the crowd to find out what was the matter.

A few minutes later the colonel overtook them.

"What was it?" inquired the princess.

"Scandalous and disgraceful!" answered the colonel. "The one thing to be dreaded is meeting Russians abroad. That tall gentleman was abusing the doctor, flinging all sorts of insults at him because he wasn't treating him quite as he liked, and he began waving his stick at him. It's simply a scandal!"

"Oh, how unpleasant!" said the princess. "Well, and how did it end?"

"Luckily at that point that . . . the one in the mushroom

hat . . . intervened. A Russian lady, I think she is," said the colonel.

"Mademoiselle Varenka?" asked Kitty.

"Yes, yes. She came to the rescue before any one; she took the man by the arm and led him away."

"There, mamma," said Kitty; "you wonder that I'm enthusiastic about her."

The next day, as she watched her unknown friend, Kitty noticed that Mademoiselle Varenka was already on the same terms with Levin and his companion as with her other protégés. She went up to them, entered into conversation with them, and served as interpreter for the woman, who could not speak any foreign language.

Kitty began to entreat her mother still more urgently to let her make friends with Varenka. And, disagreeable as it was to the princess to seem to take the first step in wishing to make the acquaintance of Madame Stahl, who thought fit to give herself airs, she made inquiries about Varenka, and, having ascertained particulars about her tending to prove that there could be no harm though little good in the acquaintance, she herself approached Varenka and made acquaintance with her.

Choosing a time when her daughter had gone to the spring, while Varenka had stopped outside the baker's, the princess went up to her.

"Allow me to make your acquaintance," she said, with her dignified smile. "My daughter has lost her heart to you," she said. "Possibly you do not know me. I am . . ."

"That feeling is more than reciprocal, princess," Varenka answered hurriedly.

"What a good deed you did yesterday to our poor compatriot!" said the princess.

Varenka flushed a little. "I don't remember. I don't think I did anything," she said.

"Why, you saved that Levin from disagreeable consequences."

"Yes, *sa compagne* called me, and I tried to pacify him; he's very ill, and was dissatisfied with the doctor. I'm used to looking after such invalids."

"Yes, I've heard you live at Mentone with your aunt—I think —Madame Stahl: I used to know her *belle-sœur*."

"No, she's not my aunt. I call her mamma, but I am not related to her; I was brought up by her," answered Varenka, flushing a little again.

This was so simply said, and so sweet was the truthful and candid expression of her face, that the princess saw why Kitty had taken such a fancy to Varenka.

"Well, and what's this Levin going to do?" asked the princess.

"He's going away," answered Varenka.

At that instant Kitty came up from the spring beaming with delight that her mother had become acquainted with her unknown friend.

"Well, see, Kitty, your intense desire to make friends with Mademoiselle . . ."

"Varenka," Varenka put in smiling, "that's what every one calls me."

Kitty blushed with pleasure, and slowly, without speaking, pressed her new friend's hand, which did not respond to her pressure, but lay motionless in her hand. The hand did not respond to her pressure, but the face of Mademoiselle Varenka glowed with a soft, glad, though rather mournful, smile, that showed large but handsome teeth.

"I have long wished for this too," she said.

"But you are so busy."

"Oh, no, I'm not at all busy," answered Varenka, but at that moment she had to leave her new friends because two little Russian girls, children of an invalid, ran up to her.

"Varenka, mamma's calling!" they cried.

And Varenka went after them.

CHAPTER XXXII

The particulars which the princess had learned in regard to Varenka's past and her relations with Madame Stahl were as follows:

Madame Stahl, of whom some people said that she had worried her husband out of his life, while others said it was he who had made her wretched by his immoral behavior, had always been a woman of weak health and enthusiastic temperament. When after her separation from her husband, she gave birth to her only child, the child had died almost immediately, and the family of Madame Stahl, knowing her sensibility, and fearing the news would kill her, had substituted another child, a baby born the same night and in the same house in Petersburg, the daughter of the chief cook of the Imperial Household. This was Varenka. Madame Stahl learned later on that Varenka was not her own child, but she went on bringing her up, especially as very soon afterwards Varenka had not a relation of her own living. Madame Stahl had now been living more than ten years continuously abroad, in the south, never leaving her couch. And some people said that Madame Stahl had made her social position as a philanthropic, highly religious woman; other people said she really was at heart the highly ethical being, living for nothing but the good of her fellow-creatures, which she represented herself to be. No one knew what her faith was—Catholic, Protestant or Orthodox. But one fact was indubitable—she was in amicable relations with the highest dignitaries of all the churches and sects.

Varenka lived with her all the while abroad, and every one

who knew Madame Stahl knew and liked Mademoiselle Varenka, as every one called her.

Having learned all these facts, the princess found nothing to object to in her daughter's intimacy with Varenka, more especially as Varenka's breeding and education were of the best—she spoke French and English extremely well—and what was of the most weight, brought a message from Madame Stahl expressing her regret that she was prevented by her ill-health from making the acquaintance of the princess.

After getting to know Varenka, Kitty became more and more fascinated by her friend, and every day she discovered new virtues in her.

The princess, hearing that Varenka had a good voice, asked her to come and sing to them in the evening.

"Kitty plays, and we have a piano; not a good one, it's true, but you will give us so much pleasure," said the princess with her affected smile, which Kitty disliked particularly just then, because she noticed that Varenka had no inclination to sing. Varenka came, however, in the evening and brought a roll of music with her. The princess had invited Marya Yevgenyevna and her daughter and the colonel.

Varenka seemed quite unaffected by there being persons present she did not know, and she went directly to the piano. She could not accompany herself, but she could sing music at sight very well. Kitty, who played well, accompanied her.

"You have an extraordinary talent," the princess said to her after Varenka had sung the first song extremely well.

Marya Yevgenyevna and her daughter expressed their thanks and admiration.

"Look," said the colonel, looking out of the window, "what an audience has collected to listen to you." There actually was quite a considerable crowd under the windows.

"I am very glad it gives you pleasure," Varenka answered simply.

Kitty looked with pride at her friend. She was enchanted by her talent, and her voice and her face, but most of all by her manner, by the way Varenka obviously thought nothing of her singing and was quite unmoved by their praises. She seemed only to be asking: "Am I to sing again, or is that enough?"

"If it had been I," thought Kitty, "how proud I should have been! How delighted I should have been to see that crowd under the windows! But she's utterly unmoved by it. Her only motive is to avoid refusing and to please mamma. What is there in her? What is it gives her the power to look down on everything, to be calm independently of everything? How I should like to know it and to learn it of her!" thought Kitty, gazing into her serene face. The princess asked Varenka to sing again, and Varenka sang another song, also smoothly, distinctly, and well, standing erect at the piano and beating time on it with her thin, dark-skinned hand.

The next song in the book was an Italian one. Kitty played the opening bars, and looked round at Varenka.

"Let's skip that," said Varenka, flushing a little. Kitty let her eyes rest on Varenka's face, with a look of dismay and inquiry.

"Very well, the next one," she said hurriedly, turning over the pages, and at once feeling that there was something connected with the song.

"No," answered Varenka with a smile, laying her hand on the music, "no, let's have that one." And she sang it just as quietly, as coolly, and as well as the others.

When she had finished, they all thanked her again, and went off to tea. Kitty and Varenka went out into the little garden that adjoined the house.

"Am I right, that you have some reminiscences connected with that song?" said Kitty. "Don't tell me," she added hastily, "only say if I'm right."

"No, why not? I'll tell you simply," said Varenka, and, without waiting for a reply, she went on: "Yes, it brings up memories, once painful ones. I cared for some one once, and I used to sing him that song."

Kitty with big, wide-open eyes gazed silently, sympathetically at Varenka.

"I cared for him, and he cared for me; but his mother did not wish it, and he married another girl. He's living now not far from us, and I see him sometimes. You didn't think I had a love-story too," she said, and there was a faint gleam in her handsome face of that fire which Kitty felt must once have glowed all over her.

"I didn't think so? Why, if I were a man, I could never care for any one else after knowing you. Only I can't understand how he could, to please his mother, forget you and make you unhappy; he had no heart."

"Oh, no, he's a very good man, and I'm not unhappy; quite the contrary, I'm very happy. Well, so we shan't be singing any more now," she added, turning towards the house.

"How good you are! how good you are!" cried Kitty, and stopping her, she kissed her. "If I could only be even a little like you!"

"Why should you be like any one? You're nice as you are," said Varenka, smiling her gentle, weary smile.

"No, I'm not nice at all. Come, tell me . . . Stop a minute, let's sit down," said Kitty, making her sit down again beside her. "Tell me, isn't it humiliating to think that a man has disdained your love, that he hasn't cared for it? . . ."

"But he didn't disdain it; I believe he cared for me, but he was a dutiful son . . ."

"Yes, but if it hadn't been on account of his mother, if it had been his own doing? . . ." said Kitty, feeling she was giving away her secret, and that her face, burning with the flush of shame, had betrayed her already.

"In that case he would have done wrong, and I should not have regretted him," answered Varenka, evidently realizing that they were now talking not of her, but of Kitty.

"But the humiliation," said Kitty, "the humiliation one can never forget, can never forget," she said, remembering her look at the last ball during the pause in the music.

"Where is the humiliation? Why, you did nothing wrong?"

"Worse than wrong—shameful."

Varenka shook her head and laid her hand on Kitty's hand.

"Why, what is there shameful?" she said. "You didn't tell a man, who didn't care for you, that you loved him, did you?"

"Of course not; I never said a word, but he knew it. No, no, there are looks, there are ways; I can't forget it, if I live a hundred years."

"Why so? I don't understand. The whole point is whether you love him now or not," said Varenka, who called everything by its name.

"I hate him; I can't forgive myself."

"Why, what for?"

"The shame, the humiliation!"

"Oh! if every one were as sensitive as you are!" said Varenka. "There isn't a girl who hasn't been through the same. And it's all so unimportant."

"Why, what is important?" said Kitty, looking into her face with inquisitive wonder.

"Oh, there's so much that's important," said Varenka, smiling.

"Why, what?"

"Oh, so much that's more important," answered Varenka, not knowing what to say. But at that instant they heard the princess's voice from the window. "Kitty, it's cold! Either get a shawl, or come indoors."

"It really is time to go in!" said Varenka, getting up. "I have to go on to Madame Berthe's; she asked me to."

Kitty held her by the hand, and with passionate curiosity and entreaty her eyes asked her: "What is it, what is this of such importance that gives you such tranquillity? You know, tell me!" But Varenka did not even know what Kitty's eyes were asking her. She merely thought that she had to go to see Madame Berthe too that evening, and to make haste home in time for *maman's* tea at twelve o'clock. She went indoors, collected her music, and saying good-bye to every one, was about to go.

"Allow me to see you home," said the colonel.

"Yes, how can you go alone at night like this?" chimed in the princess. "Anyway, I'll send Parasha."

Kitty saw that Varenka could hardly restrain a smile at the idea that she needed an escort.

"No, I always go about alone and nothing ever happens to me," she said, taking her hat. And kissing Kitty once more, without saying what was important, she stepped out courageously with the music under her arm and vanished into the twilight of the summer night, bearing away with her her secret of what was important and what gave her the calm and dignity so much to be envied.

KITTY made the acquaintance of Madame Stahl too, and this acquaintance, together with her friendship with Varenka, did not merely exercise a great influence on her, it also comforted her in her mental distress. She found this comfort through a completely new world being opened to her by means of this acquaintance, a world having nothing in common with her past, an exalted, noble world, from the height of which she could contemplate her past calmly. It was revealed to her that besides the instinctive life to which Kitty had given herself up hitherto there was a spiritual life. This life was disclosed in religion, but a religion having nothing in common with that one which Kitty had known from childhood, and which found expression in litanies and all-night services at the Widow's Home, where one might meet one's friends, and in learning by heart Slavonic texts with the priest. This was a lofty, mysterious religion connected with a whole series of noble thoughts and feelings, which one could do more than merely believe because one was told to, which one could love.

Kitty found all this out not from words. Madame Stahl talked to Kitty as to a charming child that one looks on with pleasure as on the memory of one's youth, and only once she said in passing that in all human sorrows nothing gives comfort but love and faith, and that in the sight of Christ's compassion for us no sorrow is trifling—and immediately talked of other things. But in every gesture of Madame Stahl, in every word, in every heavenly —as Kitty called it—look, and above all in the whole story of her life, which she heard from Varenka, Kitty recognized that something "that was important," of which, till then, she had known nothing.

Yet, elevated as Madame Stahl's character was, touching as was her story, and exalted and moving as was her speech, Kitty could not help detecting in her some traits which perplexed her. She noticed that when questioning her about her family, Madame Stahl had smiled contemptuously, which was not in accord with Christian meekness. She noticed, too, that when she had found a Catholic priest with her, Madame Stahl had studiously kept her face in the shadow of the lamp-shade and had smiled in a peculiar way. Trivial as these two observations were, they perplexed her, and she had her doubts as to Madame Stahl. But on the other hand Varenka, alone in the world, without friends or relations, with a melancholy disappointment in the past, desiring nothing, regretting nothing, was just that perfection of which Kitty dared hardly dream. In Varenka she realized that one has but to forget oneself and love others, and one will be calm, happy, and noble. And that was what Kitty longed to be. Seeing now clearly what was *the most important,* Kitty was not satisfied with being enthusiastic over it; she at once gave herself up with her whole soul to the new life that was opening to her. From Varenka's accounts of the doings of Madame Stahl and other people whom she mentioned, Kitty had already constructed the plan of her own future life. She would, like Madame Stahl's niece, Aline, of whom Varenka had talked to her a great deal, seek out those who were in trouble, wherever she might be living, help them as far as she could, give them the Gospel, read the Gospel to the sick, the criminals, to the dying. The idea of reading the Gospel to criminals, as Aline did, particularly fascinated Kitty. But all these were secret dreams, of which Kitty did not talk either to her mother or to Varenka.

While awaiting the time for carrying out her plans on a large scale, however, Kitty, even then at the springs, where there were so many people ill and unhappy, readily found a chance for practicing her new principles in imitation of Varenka.

At first the princess noticed nothing but that Kitty was much under the influence of her *engouement,* as she called it, for Madame Stahl, and still more for Varenka. She saw that Kitty did not merely imitate Varenka in her conduct, but unconsciously imitated her in her manner of walking, of talking, of blinking her eyes. But later on the princess noticed that, apart from this adoration, some kind of serious spiritual change was taking place in her daughter.

The princess saw that in the evenings Kitty read a French testament that Madame Stahl had given her—a thing she had never done before; that she avoided society acquaintances and associated with the sick people who were under Varenka's protection, and especially one poor family, that of a sick painter, Petrov. Kitty was unmistakably proud of playing the part of a sister of mercy in that family. All this was well enough, and the princess had nothing to say against it, especially as Petrov's wife was a perfectly nice sort of woman, and that the German princess, noticing Kitty's devotion, praised her, calling her an angel of consolation. All this would have been very well, if there had been no exaggeration. But the princess saw that her daughter was rushing into extremes, and so indeed she told her.

"Il ne faut jamais rien outrer," she said to her.

Her daughter made her no reply, only in her heart she thought that one could not talk about exaggeration where Christianity was concerned. What exaggeration could there be in the practice of a doctrine wherein one was bidden to turn the other cheek when one was smitten, and give one's cloak if one's coat were taken? But the princess disliked this exaggeration, and disliked even more the fact that she felt her daughter did not care to show her all her heart. Kitty did in fact conceal her new views and feelings from her mother. She concealed them not because she did not respect or did not love her mother, but simply because she was her mother. She would have revealed them to any one sooner than to her mother.

"How is it Anna Pavlovna's not been to see us for so long?" the princess said one day of Madame Petrova. "I've asked her, but she seems put out about something."

"No, I've not noticed it, maman," said Kitty, flushing hotly.

"Is it long since you went to see them?"

"We're meaning to make an expedition to the mountains to-morrow," answered Kitty.

"Well, you can go," answered the princess, gazing at her daughter's embarrassed face and trying to guess the cause of her embarrassment.

That day Varenka came to dinner and told them that Anna Pavlovna had changed her mind and given up the expedition for the morrow. And the princess noticed again that Kitty reddened.

"Kitty, haven't you had some misunderstanding with the Petrovs?" said the princess, when they were left alone. "Why has she given up sending the children and coming to see us?"

Kitty answered that nothing had happened between them, and

269

that she could not tell why Anna Pavlovna seemed displeased with her. Kitty answered perfectly truly. She did not know the reason Anna Pavlovna had changed to her, but she guessed it. She guessed at something which she could not tell her mother, which she did not put into words to herself. It was one of those things which one knows but which one can never speak of even to oneself so terrible and shameful would it be to be mistaken.

Again and again she went over in her memory all her relations with the family. She remembered the simple delight expressed on the round, good-humored face of Anna Pavlovna at their meetings; she remembered their secret confabulations about the invalid, their plots to draw him away from the work which was forbidden him, and to get him out-of-doors; the devotion of the youngest boy, who used to call her "my Kitty," and would not go to bed without her. How nice it all was! Then she recalled the thin, terribly thin figure of Petrov, with his long neck, in his brown coat, his scant, curly hair, his questioning blue eyes that were so terrible to Kitty at first, and his painful attempts to seem hearty and lively in her presence. She recalled the efforts she had made at first to overcome the repugnance she felt for him, as for all consumptive people, and the pains it had cost her to think of things to say to him. She recalled the timid, softened look with which he gazed at her, and the strange feeling of compassion and awkwardness, and later of a sense of her own goodness, which she had felt at it. How nice it all was! But all that was at first. Now, a few days ago, everything was suddenly spoiled. Anna Pavlovna had met Kitty with affected cordiality, and had kept continual watch on her and on her husband.

Could that touching pleasure he showed when she came near be the cause of Anna Pavlovna's coolness?

"Yes," she mused, "there was something unnatural about Anna Pavlovna, and utterly unlike her good nature, when she said angrily the day before yesterday: 'There, he will keep waiting for you; he wouldn't drink his coffee without you, though he's grown so dreadfully weak.'"

"Yes, perhaps, too, she didn't like it when I gave him the rug. It was all so simple, but he took it so awkwardly, and was so long thanking me, that I felt awkward too. And then that portrait of me he did so well. And most of all that look of confusion and tenderness! Yes, yes, that's it!" Kitty repeated to herself with horror. "No, it can't be, it oughtn't to be! He's so much to be pitied!" she said to herself directly after.

This doubt poisoned the charm of her new life.

CHAPTER XXXIV

BEFORE the end of the course of drinking the waters, Prince Shtcherbatsky, who had gone on from Carlsbad to Baden and Kissingen to Russian friends—to get a breath of Russian air, as he said—came back to his wife and daughter.

The views of the prince and of the princess on life abroad were completely opposed. The princess thought everything delightful, and in spite of her established position in Russian society, she tried abroad to be like a European fashionable lady, which she was not—for the simple reason that she was a typical Russian gentlewoman; and so she was affected, which did not altogether suit her. The prince, on the contrary, thought everything foreign detestable, got sick of European life, kept to his Russian habits, and purposely tried to show himself abroad less European than he was in reality.

The prince returned thinner, with the skin hanging in loose bags on his cheeks, but in the most cheerful frame of mind. His good-humor was even greater when he saw Kitty completely recovered. The news of Kitty's friendship with Madame Stahl and Varenka, and the reports the princess gave him of some kind of change she had noticed in Kitty, troubled the prince and aroused his habitual feeling of jealousy of everything that drew his daughter away from him, and a dread that his daughter might have got out of the reach of his influence into regions inaccessible to him. But there unpleasant matters were all drowned in the sea of kindliness and good-humor which was always within him, and more so than ever since his course of Carlsbad waters.

The day after his arrival the prince, in his long overcoat, with his Russian wrinkles and baggy cheeks propped up by a starched collar, set off with his daughter to the spring in the greatest good-humor.

It was a lovely morning: the bright, cheerful houses with their little gardens, the sight of the red-faced, red-armed, beer-drinking German waitresses, working away merrily, did the heart good. But the nearer they got to the springs the oftener they met sick people; and their appearance seemed more pitiable than ever among the every-day conditions of prosperous German life. Kitty was no longer struck by this contrast. The bright sun, the brilliant green of the foliage, the strains of the music were for her the natural setting of all these familiar faces, with their changes to greater emaciation or to convalescence, for which she watched. But to the prince the brightness and gaiety of the June morning, and the sound of the orchestra playing a gay waltz then in fashion, and above all, the appearance of the healthy attendants, seemed something unseemly and monstrous, in conjunction with these slowly moving, dying figures gathered together from all parts of Europe. In spite of his feeling of pride and, as it were, of the return of youth, with his favorite daughter on his arm, he felt awkward, and almost ashamed of his vigorous step and his sturdy, stout limbs. He felt almost like a man not dressed in a crowd.

"Present me to your new friends," he said to his daughter, squeezing her hand with his elbow. "I like even your horrid Soden for making you so well again. Only it's melancholy, very melancholy here. Who's that?"

Kitty mentioned the names of all the people they met, with some of whom she was acquainted and some not. At the entrance of the garden they met the blind lady, Madame Berthe, with her guide, and the prince was delighted to see the old Frenchwoman's face light up when she heard Kitty's voice. She at once began talking to him with French exaggerated politeness, applauding him for having such a delightful daughter, extolling Kitty to the skies before her face, and calling her a treasure, a pearl, and a consoling angel.

"Well, she's the second angel, then," said the prince, smiling. "She calls Mademoiselle Varenka angel number one."

"Oh! Mademoiselle Varenka, she's a real angel, allez," Madame Berthe assented.

In the arcade they met Varenka herself. She was walking rapidly towards them carrying an elegant red bag.

"Here is papa come," Kitty said to her.

Varenka made—simply and naturally as she did everything—a movement between a bow and curtsey, and immediately began talking to the prince, without shyness, naturally, as she talked to every one.

"Of course I know you; I know you very well," the prince said to her with a smile, in which Kitty detected with joy that her father liked her friend. "Where are you off to in such haste?"

"Maman's here," she said, turning to Kitty. "She has not slept all night, and the doctor advised her to go out. I'm taking her her work."

"So that's angel number one?" said the prince when Varenka had gone on.

Kitty saw that her father had meant to make fun of Varenka, but that he could not do it because he liked her.

"Come, so we shall see all your friends," he went on, "even Madame Stahl, if she deigns to recognize me."

"Why, did you know her, papa?" Kitty asked apprehensively, catching the gleam of irony that kindled in the prince's eyes at the mention of Madame Stahl.

"I used to know her husband, and her too a little, before she'd joined the Pietists."

"What is a Pietist, papa?" asked Kitty, dismayed to find that what she prized so highly in Madame Stahl had a name.

"I don't quite know myself. I only know that she thanks God for everything, for every misfortune, and thanks God too that her husband died. And that's rather droll, as they didn't get on together.

"Who's that? What a piteous face!" he asked, noticing a sick man of medium height sitting on a bench, wearing a brown overcoat and white trousers that fell in strange folds about his long, fleshless legs. This man lifted his straw hat, showed his scanty curly hair and high forehead, painfully reddened by the pressure of the hat.

"That's Petrov, an artist," answered Kitty, blushing. "And that's his wife," she added, indicating Anna Pavlovna, who, as though on purpose, at the very instant they approached walked away after a child that had run off along a path.

"Poor fellow! and what a nice face he has!" said the prince. "Why don't you go up to him? He wanted to speak to you."

"Well, let us go, then," said Kitty, turning round resolutely. "How are you feeling to-day?" she asked Petrov.

Petrov got up, leaning on his stick, and looked shyly at the prince.

"This is my daughter," said the prince. "Let me introduce myself."

The painter bowed and smiled, showing his strangely dazzling white teeth.

"We expected you yesterday, princess," he said to Kitty. He staggered as he said this, and then repeated the motion, trying to make it seem as if it had been intentional.

"I meant to come, but Varenka said that Anna Pavlovna sent word you were not going."

"Not going!" said Petrov, blushing, and immediately beginning to cough, and his eyes sought his wife. "Anita! Anita!" he said loudly, and the swollen veins stood out like cords on his thin white neck.

Anna Pavlovna came up.

"So you sent word to the princess that we weren't going!" he whispered to her angrily, losing his voice.

"Good-morning, princess," said Anna Pavlovna, with an assumed smile utterly unlike her former manner. "Very glad to make your acquaintance," she said to the prince. "You've long been expected, prince."

"What did you send word to the princess that we weren't going for?" the artist whispered hoarsely once more, still more angrily, obviously exasperated that his voice failed him so that he could not give his words the expression he would have liked to.

"Oh, mercy on us! I thought we weren't going," his wife answered crossly.

"What, when . . ." He coughed and waved his hand. The prince took off his hat and moved away with his daughter.

"Ah! ah!" he sighed deeply. "Oh, poor things!"

"Yes, papa," answered Kitty. "And you must know they've three children, no servant, and scarcely any means. He gets something from the Academy," she went on briskly, trying to drown the distress that the queer change in Anna Pavlovna's manner to her had aroused in her.

"Oh, here's Madame Stahl," said Kitty, indicating an invalid carriage, where, propped on pillows, something in gray and blue was lying under a sunshade. This was Madame Stahl. Behind her stood the gloomy, healthy-looking German workman who pushed the carriage. Close by was standing a flaxen-headed Swedish count, whom Kitty knew by name. Several invalids were lingering near the low carriage, staring at the lady as though she were some curiosity.

The prince went up to her, and Kitty detected that disconcerting gleam of irony in his eyes. He went up to Madame Stahl, and addressed her with extreme courtesy and affability in that excellent French that so few speak nowadays.

"I don't know if you remember me, but I must recall myself to thank you for your kindness to my daughter," he said, taking off his hat and not putting it on again.

"Prince Alexander Shtcherbatsky," said Madame Stahl, lifting upon him her heavenly eyes, in which Kitty discerned a look of annoyance. "Delighted! I have taken a great fancy to your daughter."

"You are still in weak health?"

"Yes; I'm used to it," said Madame Stahl, and she introduced the prince to the Swedish count.

"You are scarcely changed at all," the prince said to her. "It's ten or eleven years since I had the honor of seeing you."

"Yes; God sends the cross and sends the strength to bear it. Often one wonders what is the goal of this life? . . . The other side!" she said angrily to Varenka, who had rearranged the rug over her feet not to her satisfaction.

"To do good, probably," said the prince with a twinkle in his eye.

"That is not for us to judge," said Madame Stahl, perceiving the shade of expression on the prince's face. "So you will send me that book, dear count? I'm very grateful to you," she said to the young Swede.

"Ah!" cried the prince, catching sight of the Moscow colonel standing near, and with a bow to Madame Stahl he walked away with his daughter and the Moscow colonel, who joined them.

"That's our aristocracy, prince!" the Moscow colonel said with ironical intention. He cherished a grudge against Madame Stahl for not making his acquaintance.

"She's just the same," replied the prince.

"Did you know her before her illness, prince—that's to say before she took to her bed?"

"Yes. She took to her bed before my eyes," said the prince.

"They say it's ten years since she has stood on her feet."

"She doesn't stand up because her legs are too short. She's a very bad figure."

"Papa, it's not possible!" cried Kitty.

"That's what wicked tongues say, my darling. And your Varenka catches it too," he added. "Oh, these invalid ladies!"

"Oh, no, papa!" Kitty objected warmly. "Varenka worships her. And then she does so much good! Ask any one! Every one knows her and Aline Stahl."

"Perhaps so," said the prince, squeezing her hand with his elbow; "but it's better when one does good so that you may ask every one and no one knows."

Kitty did not answer, not because she had nothing to say, but because she did not care to reveal her secret thoughts even to her father. But, strange to say, although she had so made up her mind not to be influenced by her father's views, not to let him into her inmost sanctuary, she felt that the heavenly image of Madame Stahl, which she had carried for a whole month in her heart, had vanished, never to return, just as the fantastic figure made up of some clothes thrown down at random vanishes when one sees that it is only some garment lying there. All that was left was a woman with short legs, who lay down because she has a bad figure, and worried patient Varenka for not arranging her rug to her liking. And by no effort of the imagination could Kitty bring back the former Madame Stahl.

CHAPTER XXXV

The prince communicated his good-humor to his own family and his friends, and even to the German landlord in whose rooms the Shtcherbatskys were staying.

On coming back with Kitty from the springs, the prince, who had asked the colonel, and Marya Yevgenyevna, and Varenka all to come and have coffee with them, gave orders for a table and chairs to be taken into the garden under the chestnut-tree, and lunch to be laid there. The landlord and the servants, too, grew brisker under the influence of his good spirits. They knew his open-handedness; and half an hour later the invalid doctor from Hamburg, who lived on the top floor, looked enviously out of the window at the merry party of healthy Russians assembled under the chestnut-tree. In the trembling circles of shadow cast by the leaves, at a table, covered with a white cloth, and set with coffee-pot, bread-and-butter, cheese, and cold game, sat the princess in a high cap with lilac ribbons, distributing cups and bread-and-butter. At the other end sat the prince, eating heartily, and talking loudly and merrily. The prince had spread out near him his purchases, carved boxes, and knick-knacks, paper-knives of all sorts, of which he bought a heap at every watering-place, and be-stowed them upon every one, including Lieschen, the servant girl, and the landlord, with whom he jested in his comically bad German, assuring him that it was not the water had cured Kitty, but his splendid cookery, especially his plum-soup. The princess laughed at her husband for his Russian ways, but she was more lively and good-humored than she had been all the while she had been at the waters. The colonel smiled, as he always did, at the prince's jokes, but as far as regards Europe, of which he believed himself to be making a careful study, he took the princess's side. The simple-hearted Marya Yevgenyevna simply roared with laughter at everything absurd the prince said, and his jokes made Varenka helpless with feeble but infectious laughter, which was something Kitty had never seen before.

Kitty was glad of all this, but she could not be light-hearted. She could not solve the problem her father had unconsciously set her by his good-humored view of her friends, and of the life that had so attracted her. To this doubt there was joined the change in her relations with the Petrovs, which had been so conspicuously and unpleasantly marked that morning. Every one was good-humored, but Kitty could not feel good-humored, and this increased her distress. She felt a feeling such as she had known in childhood, when she had been shut in her room as a punishment, and had heard her sisters' merry laughter outside.

"Well, but what did you buy this mass of things for?" said the princess, smiling, and handing her husband a cup of coffee.

"One goes for a walk, one looks in a shop, and they ask you to buy. *'Erlaucht, Durchlaucht?'* Directly they say *'Durchlaucht,'* I can't hold out. I lose ten thalers."

"It's simply from boredom," said the princess.

"Of course it is. Such boredom, my dear, that one doesn't know what to do with oneself."

"How can you be bored, prince? There's so much that's interesting now in Germany," said Marya Yevgenyevna.

"But I know everything that's interesting: the plum-soup I know, and the pea-sausages I know. I know everything."

"No, you may say what you like, prince, there's the interest of their institutions," said the colonel.

"But what is there interesting about it? They're all as pleased as brass halfpence. They've conquered everybody, and why am I to be pleased at that? I haven't conquered any one; and I'm obliged to take off my own boots, yes, and put them away too; in the morning, get up and dress at once, and go to the dining-room to drink bad tea! How different it is at home! You get up in no haste, you get cross, grumble a little, and come round again. You've time to think things over, and no hurry."

"But time's money, you forget that," said the colonel.

"Time, indeed, that depends! Why, there's time one would give a month of for sixpence, and time you wouldn't give half an hour of for any money. Isn't that so, Katinka? What is it? why are you so depressed?"

"I'm not depressed."

"Where are you off to? Stay a little longer," he said to Varenka.

"I must be going home," said Varenka, getting up, and again she went off into a giggle. When she had recovered, she said good-bye, and went into the house to get her hat.

Kitty followed her. Even Varenka struck her as different. She was not worse, but different from what she had fancied her before.

"Oh, dear! it's a long while since I've laughed so much!" said Varenka, gathering up her parasol and her bag. "How nice he is, your father!"

Kitty did not speak.

"When shall I see you again?" asked Varenka.

"Mamma meant to go and see the Petrovs. Won't you be there?" said Kitty, to try Varenka.

"Yes," answered Varenka. "They're getting ready to go away, so I promised to help them pack."

"Well, I'll come too, then."

"No, why should you?"

"Why not? why not? why not?" said Kitty, opening her eyes wide, and clutching at Varenka's parasol, so as not to let her go. "No, wait a minute; why not?"

"Oh, nothing; your father has come, and besides, they will feel awkward at your helping."

"No, tell me why you don't want me to be often at the Petrovs. You don't want me to—why not?"

"I didn't say that," said Varenka quietly.

"No, please tell me!"

"Tell you everything?" asked Varenka.

"Everything, everything!" Kitty assented.

"Well, there's really nothing of any consequence; only that Mihail Alexeyevitch" (that was the artist's name) "had meant to leave earlier, and now he doesn't want to go away," said Varenka, smiling.

"Well, well!" Kitty urged impatiently, looking darkly at Varenka.

"Well, and for some reason Anna Pavlovna told him that he didn't want to go because you are here. Of course, that was nonsense; but there was a dispute over it—over you. You know how irritable these sick people are."

Kitty, scowling more than ever, kept silent, and Varenka went on speaking alone, trying to soften or soothe her, and seeing a storm coming—she did not know whether of tears or of words.

"So you'd better not go. . . . You understand; you won't be offended? . . ."

"And it serves me right! And it serves me right!" Kitty cried quickly, snatching the parasol out of Varenka's hand, and looking past her friend's face.

Varenka felt inclined to smile, looking at her childish fury, but she was afraid of wounding her.

"How does it serve you right? I don't understand," she said.

"It serves me right, because it was all sham; because it was all done on purpose, and not from the heart. What business had I to interfere with outsiders? And so it's come about that I'm a cause of quarrel, and that I've done what nobody asked me to do. Because it was all a sham! a sham! a sham! . . ."

"A sham! with what object?" said Varenka gently.

"Oh, it's so idiotic! so hateful! There was no need whatever for me. . . . Nothing but sham!" she said, opening and shutting the parasol.

"But with what object?"

"To seem better to people, to myself, to God; to deceive every one. No! now I won't descend to that. I'll be bad; but anyway not a liar, a cheat."

"But who is a cheat?" said Varenka reproachfully. "You speak as if . . ."

But Kitty was in one of her gusts of fury, and she would not let her finish.

"I don't talk about you, not about you at all. You're perfection. Yes, yes, I know you're all perfection; but what am I to do if I'm bad? This would never have been if I weren't bad. So let me be what I am. I won't be a sham. What have I to do with Anna Pavlovna? Let them go their way, and me go mine. I can't be different. . . . And yet it's not that, it's not that."

"What is not that?" asked Varenka in bewilderment.

"Everything. I can't act except from the heart, and you act from principle. I liked you simply, but you most likely only wanted to save me, to improve me."

"You are unjust," said Varenka.

"But I'm not speaking of other people, I'm speaking of myself."

"Kitty," they heard her mother's voice, "come here, show papa your necklace."

Kitty, with a haughty air, without making peace with her friend, took the necklace in a little box from the table and went to her mother.

"What's the matter? Why are you so red?" her mother and father said to her with one voice.

"Nothing," she answered. "I'll be back directly," and she ran back.

"She's still here," she thought. "What am I to say to her? Oh, dear! what have I done, what have I said? Why was I rude to her? What am I to do? What am I to say to her?" thought Kitty, and she stopped in the doorway.

Varenka in her hat and with the parasol in her hands was sitting at the table examining the spring which Kitty had broken. She lifted her head.

"Varenka, forgive me, do forgive me," whispered Kitty, going up to her. "I don't remember what I said. I . . . ."

"I really didn't mean to hurt you," said Varenka, smiling.

Peace was made. But with her father's coming all the world in which she had been living was transformed for Kitty. She did not give up everything she had learned, but she became aware that she had deceived herself in supposing she could be what she wanted to be. Her eyes were, it seemed, opened; she felt all the difficulty of maintaining herself without hypocrisy and self-conceit on the pinnacle to which she had wished to mount. Moreover, she became aware of all the dreariness of the world of sorrow, of sick and dying people, in which she had been living. The efforts she had made to like it seemed to her intolerable, and she felt a longing to get back quickly into the fresh air, to Russia, to Ergushovo, where, as she knew from letters, her sister Dolly had already gone with her children.

But her affection for Varenka did not wane. As she said good-bye, Kitty begged her to come to them in Russia.

"I'll come when you get married," said Varenka.

"I shall never marry."

"Well, then, I shall never come."

"Well, then, I shall be married simply for that. Mind now, remember your promise," said Kitty.

The doctor's prediction was fulfilled. Kitty returned home to Russia cured. She was not so gay and thoughtless as before, but she was serene. Her Moscow troubles had become a memory to her.

Part Three

CHAPTER I

SERGEY IVANOVITCH KOZNISHEV wanted a rest from mental work, and instead of going abroad as he usually did, he came towards the end of May to stay in the country with his brother. In his judgment the best sort of life was a country life. He had come now to enjoy such a life at his brother's. Konstantin Levin was very glad to have him, especially as he did not expect his brother Nikolay that summer. But in spite of his affection and respect for Sergey Ivanovitch, Konstantin Levin was uncomfortable with his brother in the country. It made him uncomfortable, and it positively annoyed him to see his brother's attitude to the country. To Konstantin Levin the country was the background of life, that is of pleasures, endeavors, labor. To Sergey Ivanovitch the country meant on one hand rest from work, on the other a valuable antidote to the corrupt influences of town, which he took with satisfaction and a sense of its utility. To Konstantin Levin the country was good first because it afforded a field for labor, of the usefulness of which there could be no doubt. To Sergey Ivanovitch the country was particularly good, because there it was possible and fitting to do nothing. Moreover, Sergey Ivanovitch's attitude to the peasants rather piqued Konstantin. Sergey Ivanovitch used to say that he knew and liked the peasantry, and he often talked to the peasants, which he knew how to do without affectation or condescension, and from every such conversation he would deduce general conclusions in favor of the peasantry and in confirmation of his knowing them. Konstantin Levin did not like such an attitude to the peasants. To Konstantin the peasant was simply the chief partner in their common labor, and in spite of all the respect and the love, almost like that of kinship, he had for the peasant—sucked in probably, as he said himself, with the milk of his peasant nurse—still as a fellow-worker with him, while sometimes enthusiastic over the vigor, gentleness, and justice of these men, he was very often, when their common labors called for other qualities, exasperated with the peasant for his carelessness, lack of method, drunkenness, and lying. If he had been asked whether he liked or didn't like the peasants, Konstantin Levin would have been absolutely at a loss what to reply. He liked and did not like the peasants, just as he liked and did not like men in general. Of course, being a good-hearted man, he liked men rather than he disliked them, and so too with the peasants. But like or dislike "the people" as something apart he could not, not only because he lived with "the people," and all his interests were bound up with theirs, but also because he regarded himself as a part of "the people," did not see any special qualities or failings distinguishing himself and "the people," and could not contrast himself with them. Moreover, although he had lived so long in the closest relations with the peasants, as farmer and arbitrator, and what was more, as adviser (the peasants trusted him, and for thirty miles round they would come to ask his advice), he had not definite views of "the people," and would have been as much at a loss to answer the question whether he knew "the people" as the question whether he liked them. For him to say he knew the peasantry would have been the same as to say he knew men. He was continually watching and getting to know people of all sorts, and among them peasants, whom he regarded as good and interesting people, and he was continually observing new points in them, altering his former views of them and forming new ones. With Sergey Ivanovitch it was quite the contrary. Just as he liked and praised a country life in comparison with the life he did not like, so too he liked the peasantry in contradistinction to the class of men he did not like, and so too he knew the peasantry as something distinct from and opposed to men generally. In his methodical brain there were distinctly formulated certain aspects of peasant life, deduced partly from that life itself, but chiefly from contrast with other modes of life. He never changed his opinion of the peasantry and his sympathetic attitude towards them.

In the discussions that arose between the brothers on their views of the peasantry, Sergey Ivanovitch always got the better of his brother, precisely because Sergey Ivanovitch had definite ideas about the peasant—his character, his qualities, and his tastes. Konstantin Levin had no definite and unalterable idea on the subject, and so in their arguments Konstantin was readily convicted of contradicting himself.

In Sergey Ivanovitch's eyes his younger brother was a capital fellow, *with his heart in the right place* (as he expressed it in French), but with a mind which, though fairly quick, was too much influenced by the impressions of the moment, and consequently filled with contradictions. With all the condescension of an elder brother he sometimes explained to him the true import of things, but he derived little satisfaction from arguing with him because he got the better of him too easily.

Konstantin Levin regarded his brother as a man of immense intellect and culture, as generous in the highest sense of the word, and possessed of a special faculty for working for the public good. But in the depths of his heart, the older he became, and the more intimately he knew his brother, the more and more frequently the thought struck him that this faculty of working for the public good, of which he felt himself utterly devoid, was possibly not so much a quality as a lack of something—not a lack of good, honest, noble desires and tastes, but a lack of vital force, of what is called heart, of that impulse which drives a man to choose some one out of the innumerable paths of life, and to care only for that one. The better he knew his brother, the more he noticed that Sergey Ivanovitch, and many other people who worked for the public welfare, were not led by an impulse of the heart to care for the public good, but reasoned from intellectual considerations that it was a right thing to take interest in public affairs, and consequently took interest in them. Levin was confirmed in this generalization by observing that his brother did not take questions affecting the public welfare or the question of the immortality of the soul a bit more to heart than he did chess problems, or the ingenious construction of a new machine.

Besides this, Konstantin Levin was not at his ease with his brother, because in summer in the country Levin was continually busy with work on the land, and the long summer day was not long enough for him to get through all he had to do, while Sergey Ivanovitch was taking a holiday. But though he was taking a holiday now, that is to say, he was doing no writing, he was so used to intellectual activity that he liked to put into concise and eloquent shape the ideas that occurred to him, and liked to have some one to listen to him. His most usual and natural listener was his brother. And so in spite of the friendliness and directness of their relations, Konstantin felt an awkwardness in leaving him alone. Sergey Ivanovitch liked to stretch himself on the grass in the sun, and to lie so, basking and chatting lazily.

"You wouldn't believe," he would say to his brother, "what a pleasure this rural laziness is to me. Not an idea in one's brain, as empty as a drum!"

But Konstantin Levin found it dull sitting and listening to him, especially when he knew that while he was away they would be carting dung onto the fields not ploughed ready for it, and heaping it all up anyhow; and would not screw the shares in the ploughs, but would let them come off and then say that the new ploughs were a silly invention, and there was nothing like the old Andreevna plough, and so on.

"Come, you've done enough trudging about in the heat," Sergey Ivanovitch would say to him.

"No, I must just run round to the counting-house for a minute," Levin would answer, and he would run off to the fields.

CHAPTER II

EARLY in June it happened that Agafea Mihalovna, the old nurse and housekeeper, in carrying to the cellar a jar of mushrooms she had just pickled, slipped, fell, and sprained her wrist. The district doctor, a talkative young medical student, who had just finished his studies, came to see her. He examined the wrist, said it was not broken, was delighted at a chance of talking to the celebrated Sergey Ivanovitch Koznishev, and to show his advanced views of things told him all the scandal of the district, complaining of the poor state into which the district council had fallen. Sergey Ivanovitch listened attentively, asked him questions, and, roused by a new listener, he talked fluently, uttered a few keen and weighty observations, respectfully appreciated by the young doctor, and was soon in that eager frame of mind his brother knew so well, which always, with him, followed a brilliant and eager conversation. After the departure of the doctor,

he wanted to go with a fishing-rod to the river. Sergey Ivanovitch was fond of angling, and was, it seemed, proud of being able to care for such a stupid occupation.

Konstantin Levin, whose presence was needed in the plough-land and the meadows, had come to take his brother in the trap.

It was that time of the year, the turning-point of summer, when the crops of the present year are a certainty, when one begins to think of the sowing for next year, and the mowing is at hand; when the rye is all in ear, though its ears are still light, not yet full, and it waves in gray-green billows in the wind; when the green oats, with tufts of yellow grass scattered here and there among it, droop irregularly over the late-sown fields; when the early buckwheat is already out and hiding the ground; when the fallow-lands, trodden hard as stone by the cattle, are half-ploughed over, with paths left untouched by the plough; when from the dry dung-heaps carted onto the fields there comes at sunset a smell of manure mixed with meadow-sweet, and on the low-lying lands the riverside meadows are a thick sea of grass waiting for the mowing, with blackened heaps of the stalks of sorrel among it.

It was the time when there comes a brief pause in the toil of the fields before the beginning of the labors of harvest—every year recurring, every year straining every nerve of the peasants. The crop was a splendid one, and bright, hot summer days had set in with short, dewy nights.

The brothers had to drive through the woods to reach the meadows. Sergey Ivanovitch was all the while admiring the beauty of the woods, which were a tangled mass of leaves, pointing out to his brother now an old lime-tree on the point of flowering, dark on the shady side, and brightly spotted with yellow stipules, now the young shoots of this year's saplings brilliant with emerald. Konstantin Levin did not like talking and hearing about the beauty of nature. Words for him took away the beauty of what he saw. He assented to what his brother said, but he could not help beginning to think of other things. When they came out of the woods, all his attention was engrossed by the view of the fallow-land on the upland, in parts yellow with grass, in parts trampled and checkered with furrows, in parts dotted with ridges of dung, and in parts even ploughed. A string of carts was moving across it. Levin counted the carts, and was pleased that all that were wanted had been brought, and at the sight of the meadows his thoughts passed to the mowing. He always felt something special moving him to the quick at the hay-making. On reaching the meadow Levin stopped the horse.

The morning dew was still lying on the thick undergrowth of the grass, and that he might not get his feet wet, Sergey Ivanovitch asked his brother to drive him in the trap up to the willow-tree from which the carp was caught. Sorry as Konstantin Levin was to crush down his mowing-grass, he drove him into the meadow. The high grass softly turned about the wheels and the horse's legs, leaving its seeds clinging to the wet axles and spokes of the wheels. His brother seated himself under a bush, arranging his tackle, while Levin led the horse away, fastened him up, and walked into the vast gray-green sea of grass unstirred by the wind. The silky grass with its ripe seeds came almost to his waist in the dampest spots.

Crossing the meadow, Konstantin Levin came out onto the road, and met an old man with a swollen eye, carrying a skep on his shoulder.

"What? taken a stray swarm, Fomitch?" he asked.

"No, indeed, Konstantin Dmitritch! All we can do to keep our own! This is the second swarm that has flown away. . . . Luckily the lads caught them. They were ploughing your field. They unyoked the horses and galloped after them."

"Well, what do you say, Fomitch—start mowing or wait a bit?"

"Eh, well. Our way's to wait till St. Peter's Day. But you always mow sooner. Well, to be sure, please God, the hay's good. There'll be plenty for the beasts."

"What do you think about the weather?"

"That's in God's hands. Maybe it will be fine."

Levin went up to his brother.

Sergey Ivanovitch had caught nothing, but he was not bored, and seemed in the most cheerful frame of mind. Levin saw that, stimulated by his conversation with the doctor, he wanted to talk. Levin, on the other hand, would have liked to get home as soon as possible to give orders about getting together the mowers for next day, and to set at rest his doubts about the mowing, which greatly absorbed him.

"Well, let's be going," he said.

"Why be in such a hurry? Let's stay a little. But how wet you are! Even though one catches nothing, it's nice. That's the best thing about every part of sport, that one has to do with nature. How exquisite this steely water is!" said Sergey Ivanovitch. "These riverside banks always remind me of the riddle—do you know it? 'The grass says to the water: we quiver and we quiver.' "

"I don't know the riddle," answered Levin wearily.

CHAPTER III

"Do you know I've been thinking about you," said Sergey Ivanovitch. "It's beyond everything what's being done in the district, according to what this doctor tells me. He's a very intelligent fellow. And as I've told you before, I tell you again: it's not right for you not to go to the meetings, and altogether to keep out of the district business. If decent people won't go into it, of course it's bound to go all wrong. We pay the money, and it all goes in salaries, and there are no schools, nor district nurses, nor midwives, nor drug-stores—nothing."

"Well, I did try, you know," Levin said slowly and unwillingly. "I can't! and so there's no help for it."

"But why can't you? I must own I can't make it out. Indifference, incapacity—I won't admit; surely it's not simply laziness?"

"None of those things. I've tried, and I see I can do nothing," said Levin.

He had hardly grasped what his brother was saying. Looking towards the plough-land across the river, he made out something black, but he could not distinguish whether it was a horse or the bailiff on horseback.

"Why is it you can do nothing? You made an attempt and didn't succeed, as you think, and you give in. How can you have so little self-respect?"

"Self-respect!" said Levin, stung to the quick by his brother's words; "I don't understand. If they'd told me at college that other people understood the integral calculus, and I didn't, then pride would have come in. But in this case one wants first to be convinced that one has certain qualifications for this sort of business, and especially that all this business is of great importance."

"What! do you mean to say it's not of importance?" said Sergey Ivanovitch, stung to the quick too at his brother's considering anything of no importance that interested him, and still more at his obviously paying little attention to what he was saying.

"I don't think it important; it does not take hold of me, I can't help it," answered Levin, making out that what he saw was the bailiff, and that the bailiff seemed to be letting the peasants go off the ploughed land. They were turning the plough over. "Can they have finished ploughing?" he wondered.

"Come, really though," said the elder brother, with a frown on his handsome, clever face, "there's a limit to everything. It's very well to be original and genuine, and to dislike everything conventional—I know all about that; but really, what you're saying either has no meaning, or it has a very wrong meaning. How can you think it a matter of no importance whether the peasant, whom you love as you assert . . ."

"I never did assert it," thought Konstantin Levin.

—"dies without help? The ignorant peasant-women starve the children, and the people stagnate in darkness, and are helpless in the hands of every village clerk, while you have at your disposal a means of helping them, and don't help them because to your mind it's of no importance."

And Sergey Ivanovitch put before him the alternative: either you are so undeveloped that you can't see all that you can do, or you won't sacrifice your ease, your vanity, or whatever it is, to do it.

Konstantin Levin felt that there was no course open to him but to submit, or to confess to a lack of zeal for the public good. And this mortified him and hurt his feelings.

"It's both," he said resolutely; "I don't see that it was possible . . ."

"What! was it impossible, if the money were properly laid out, to provide medical aid?"

"Impossible, as it seems to me. . . . For the three thousand square miles of our district, what with our thaws, and the storms, and the work in the fields, I don't see how it is possible to provide medical aid all over. And besides, I don't believe in medicine."

"Oh, well, that's unfair. . . . I can quote to you thousands of instances. . . . But the schools, anyway."

"Why have schools?"

"What do you mean? Can there be two opinions of the advantage of education? If it's a good thing for you, it's a good thing for every one."

Konstantin Levin felt himself morally pinned against a wall, and so he got hot, and unconsciously blurted out the chief cause of his indifference to public business.

"Perhaps it may all be very good; but why should I worry myself about establishing dispensaries which I shall never make use of, and schools to which I shall never send my children, to which even the peasants don't want to send their children, and to which I've no very firm faith that they ought to send them?" said he.

Sergey Ivanovitch was for a minute surprised at this unexpected view of the subject; but he promptly made a new plan of attack. He was silent for a little, drew out a hook, threw it in again, and turned to his brother smiling.

"Come, now. . . . In the first place, the dispensary is needed. We ourselves sent for the district doctor for Agafea Mihalovna."

"Oh, well, but I fancy her wrist will never be straight again."

"That remains to be proved. . . . Next, the peasant who can read and write is as a workman of more use and value to you."

"No; you can ask any one you like," Konstantin Levin answered with decision, "the man that can read and write is much inferior as a workman. And mending the highroads is an impossibility; and as soon as they put up bridges they're stolen."

"Still, that's not the point," said Sergey Ivanovitch, frowning. He disliked contradiction, and still more, arguments that were continually skipping from one thing to another, introducing new and disconnected points, so that there was no knowing to which to reply. "Do you admit that education is a benefit for the people?"

"Yes, I admit it," said Levin without thinking, and he was conscious immediately that he had said what he did not think. He felt that if he admitted that, it would be proved that he had been talking meaningless rubbish. How it would be proved he could not tell, but he knew that this would inevitably be logically proved to him, and he awaited the proofs.

The argument turned out to be far simpler than he had expected.

"If you admit that it is a benefit," said Sergey Ivanovitch, "then, as an honest man, you cannot help caring about it and sympathizing with the movement, and so wishing to work for it."

"But I still do not admit this movement to be just," said Konstantin Levin, reddening a little.

"What! But you said just now . . ."

"That's to say, I don't admit it's being either good or possible."

"That you can't tell without making the trial."

"Well, supposing that's so," said Levin, though he did not suppose so at all, "supposing that is so, still I don't see, all the same, what I'm to worry myself about it for."

"How so?"

"No; since we are talking, explain it to me from the philosophical point of view," said Levin.

"I can't see where philosophy comes in," said Sergey Ivanovitch, in a tone, Levin fancied, as though he did not admit his brother's right to talk about philosophy. And that irritated Levin.

"I'll tell you, then," he said with heat, "I imagine the mainspring of all our actions is, after all, self-interest. Now in the local institutions I, as a nobleman, see nothing that could conduce to my prosperity, and the roads are not better and could not be better; my horses carry me well enough over bad ones. Doctors and dispensaries are no use to me. An arbitrator of disputes is no use to me. I never appeal to him, and never shall appeal to him. The schools are no good to me, but positively harmful, as I told you. For me the district institutions simply mean the liability to pay fourpence halfpenny for every three acres, to drive into the town, sleep with bugs, and listen to all sorts of idiocy and loathsomeness, and self-interest offers me no inducement."

"Excuse me," Sergey Ivanovitch interposed with a smile, "self-interest did not induce us to work for the emancipation of the serfs, but we did work for it."

"No!" Konstantin Levin broke in with still greater heat; "the emancipation of the serfs was a different matter. There self-interest did come in. One longed to throw off that yoke that crushed us, all decent people among us. But to be a town-councilor and discuss how many dustmen are needed, and how chimneys shall be constructed in the town in which I don't live—to serve on a jury and try a peasant who's stolen a flitch of bacon, and listen for six hours at a stretch to all sorts of jabber from the counsel for the defense and the prosecution, and the president cross-examining my old half-witted Alioshka, 'Do you admit, prisoner in the dock, the fact of the removal of the bacon?' 'Eh?'"

Konstantin Levin had warmed to his subject, and began mimicking the president and the half-witted Alioshka: it seemed to him that it was all to the point.

But Sergey Ivanovitch shrugged his shoulders.

"Well, what do you mean to say, then?"

"I simply mean to say that those rights that touch me . . . my interest, I shall always defend to the best of my ability; that when they made raids on us students, and the police read our letters, I was ready to defend those rights to the utmost, to defend my rights to education and freedom. I can understand compulsory military service, which affects my children, my brothers, and myself, I am ready to deliberate on what concerns me; but deliberating on how to spend forty thousand roubles of district council money, or judging the half-witted Alioshka—I don't understand, and I can't do it."

Konstantin Levin spoke as though the floodgates of his speech had burst open. Sergey Ivanovitch smiled.

"But to-morrow it'll be your turn to be tried; would it have suited your tastes better to be tried in the old criminal tribunal?"

"I'm not going to be tried. I shan't murder anybody, and I've no need of it. Well, I tell you what," he went on, flying off again to a subject quite beside the point, "our district self-government and all the rest of it—it's just like the birch-branches we stick in the ground on Trinity Day, for instance, to look like a copse which has grown up of itself in Europe, and I can't gush over these birch-branches and believe in them."

Sergey Ivanovitch merely shrugged his shoulders, as though to express his wonder how the birch-branches had come into their argument at that point, though he did really understand at once what his brother meant.

"Excuse me, but you know one really can't argue in that way," he observed.

But Konstantin Levin wanted to justify himself for the failing, of which he was conscious, of lack of zeal for the public welfare, and he went on.

"I imagine," he said, "that no sort of activity is likely to be lasting if it is not founded on self-interest, that's a universal principle, a philosophical principle," he said, repeating the word "philosophical" with determination, as though wishing to show that he had as much right as any one else to talk of philosophy.

Sergey Ivanovitch smiled. "He too has a philosophy of his own at the service of his natural tendencies," he thought.

"Come, you'd better let philosophy alone," he said. "The chief problem of the philosophy of all ages consists just in finding the indispensable connection which exists between individual and social interests. But that's not to the point; what is to the point is a correction I must make in your comparison. The birches are not simply stuck in, but some are sown and some are planted, and one must deal carefully with them. It's only those peoples that have an intuitive sense of what's of importance and significance in their institutions, and know how to value them, that have a future before them—it's only those peoples that one can truly call historical."

And Sergey Ivanovitch carried the subject into the regions of philosophical history where Konstantin Levin could not follow him, and showed him all the incorrectness of his view.

"As for your dislike of it, excuse my saying so, that's simply our Russian sloth and old serf-owner's ways, and I'm convinced that in you it's a temporary error and will pass."

Konstantin was silent. He felt himself vanquished on all sides, but he felt at the same time that what he wanted to say was unintelligible to his brother. Only he could not make up his mind whether it was unintelligible because he was not capable of expressing his meaning clearly, or because his brother would not or could not understand him. But he did not pursue the speculation, and without replying, he fell to musing on a quite different and personal matter.

Sergey Ivanovitch wound up the last line, untied the horse, and they drove off.

CHAPTER IV

THE personal matter that absorbed Levin during his conversation with his brother was this. Once in a previous year he had gone to look at the mowing, and being made very angry by the bailiff he had recourse to his favorite means for regaining his temper,—he took a scythe from a peasant and began mowing.

He liked the work so much that he had several times tried his hand at mowing since. He had cut the whole of the meadow in front of his house, and this year ever since the early spring he had cherished a plan for mowing for whole days together with the peasants. Ever since his brother's arrival, he had been in doubt whether to mow or not. He was loth to leave his brother alone all day long, and he was afraid his brother would laugh at him about it. But as he drove into the meadow, and recalled the sensations of mowing, he came near deciding that he would go mowing. After the irritating discussion with his brother, he pondered over this intention again.

297

"I must have physical exercise, or my temper'll certainly be ruined," he thought, and he determined he would go mowing, however awkward he might feel about it with his brother or the peasants.

Towards evening Konstantin Levin went to his counting-house, gave directions as to the work to be done, and sent about the village to summon the mowers for the morrow, to cut the hay in Kalinov meadow, the largest and best of his grass lands.

"And send my scythe, please, to Tit, for him to set it, and bring it round to-morrow. I shall maybe do some mowing myself too," he said trying not to be embarrassed.

The bailiff smiled and said: "Yes, sir."

At tea the same evening Levin said to his brother:

"I fancy the fine weather will last," said he. "To-morrow I shall start mowing."

"I'm so fond of that form of field labor," said Sergey Ivanovitch.

"I'm awfully fond of it. I sometimes mow myself with the peasants, and to-morrow I want to try mowing the whole day."

Sergey Ivanovitch lifted his head, and looked with interest at his brother.

"How do you mean? Just like one of the peasants, all day long?"

"Yes, it's very pleasant," said Levin.

"It's splendid as exercise, only you'll hardly be able to stand it," said Sergey Ivanovitch, without a shade of irony.

"I've tried it. It's hard work at first, but you get into it. I dare say I shall manage to keep it up. . . ."

"Really! what an idea! But tell me, how do the peasants look at it? I suppose they laugh in their sleeves at their master's being such a queer fish?"

"No, I don't think so; but it's so delightful, and at the same time such hard work, that one has no time to think about it."

"But how will you do about dining with them? To send you a bottle of Lafitte and roast turkey out there would be a little awkward."

"No, I'll simply come home at the time of their noonday rest."

Next morning Konstantin Levin got up earlier than usual, but he was detained giving directions on the farm, and when he reached the mowing-grass the mowers were already at their second row.

From the uplands he could get a view of the shaded cut part of the meadow below, with its grayish ridges of cut grass, and the black heaps of coats, taken off by the mowers at the place from which they had started cutting.

Gradually, as he rode towards the meadow, the peasants came into sight, some in coats, some in their shirts mowing, one behind another in a long string, swinging their scythes differently. He counted forty-two of them.

They were mowing slowly over the uneven, low-lying parts of the meadow, where there had been an old dam. Levin recognized some of his own men. Here was old Yermil in a very long white smock, bending forward to swing a scythe; there was a young fellow, Vaska, who had been a coachman of Levin's, taking every row with a wide sweep. Here, too, was Tit, Levin's preceptor in the art of mowing, a thin little peasant. He was in front of all, and cut his wide row without bending, as though playing with the scythe.

Levin got off his mare, and fastening her up by the roadside went to meet Tit, who took a second scythe out of a bush and gave it to him.

"It's ready, sir; it's like a razor, cuts of itself," said Tit, taking off his cap with a smile and giving him the scythe.

Levin took the scythe, and began trying it. As they finished their rows, the mowers, hot and good-humored, came out into the road one after another, and, laughing a little, greeted the master. They all stared at him, but no one made any remark, till a tall old man, with a wrinkled, beardless face, wearing a short sheepskin jacket, came out into the road and accosted him.

"Look'ee now, master, once take hold of the rope there's no letting it go!" he said, and Levin heard smothered laughter among the mowers.

"I'll try not to let it go," he said, taking his stand behind Tit, and waiting for the time to begin.

"Mind'ee," repeated the old man.

Tit made room, and Levin started behind him. The grass was short close to the road, and Levin, who had not done any mowing for a long while, and was disconcerted by the eyes fastened upon him, cut badly for the first moments, though he swung his scythe vigorously. Behind him he heard voices:

"It's not set right; handle's too high; see how he has to stoop to it," said one.

"Press more on the heel," said another.

"Never mind, he'll get on all right," the old man resumed.

"He's made a start. . . . You swing it too wide, you'll tire yourself out. . . . The master, sure, does his best for himself! But see the grass missed out! For such work us fellows would catch it!"

The grass became softer, and Levin, listening without answering, followed Tit, trying to do the best he could. They moved a hundred paces. Tit kept moving on, without stopping, not showing the slightest weariness, but Levin was already beginning to be afraid he would not be able to keep it up: he was so tired.

He felt as he swung his scythe that he was at the very end of his strength, and was making up his mind to ask Tit to stop. But at that very moment Tit stopped of his own accord, and stooping down picked up some grass, rubbed his scythe, and began whetting it. Levin straightened himself, and drawing a deep breath looked round. Behind him came a peasant, and he too was evidently tired, for he stopped at once without waiting to mow up to Levin, and began whetting his scythe. Tit sharpened his scythe and Levin's, and they went on. The next time it was just the same. Tit moved on with sweep after sweep of his scythe, not stopping or showing signs of weariness. Levin followed him, trying not to get left behind, and he found it harder and harder: the moment came when he felt he had no strength left, but at that very moment Tit stopped and whetted the scythes.

So they mowed the first row. And this long row seemed particularly hard work to Levin; but when the end was reached and Tit, shouldering his scythe, began with deliberate stride returning on the tracks left by his heels in the cut grass, and Levin walked back in the same way over the space he had cut, in spite of the sweat that ran in streams over his face and fell in drops down his nose, and drenched his back as though he had been soaked in water, he felt very happy. What delighted him particularly was that now he knew he would be able to hold out.

His pleasure was only disturbed by his row not being well cut.

"I will swing less with my arm and more with my whole body," he thought, comparing Tit's row, which looked as if it had been cut with a line, with his own unevenly and irregularly lying grass.

The first row, as Levin noticed, Tit had mowed specially quickly, probably wishing to put his master to the test, and the row happened to be a long one. The next rows were easier, but still Levin had to strain every nerve not to drop behind the peasants.

He thought of nothing, wished for nothing, but not to be left behind the peasants, and to do his work as well as possible. He heard nothing but the swish of scythes, and saw before him Tit's upright figure mowing away, the crescent-shaped curve of the cut grass, the grass and flower heads slowly and rhythmically falling before the blade of his scythe, and ahead of him the end of the row, where would come the rest.

Suddenly, in the midst of his toil, without understanding what it was or whence it came, he felt a pleasant sensation of chill on his hot, moist shoulders. He glanced at the sky in the interval for whetting the scythes. A heavy, lowering storm-cloud had blown up, and big raindrops were falling. Some of the peasants went to their coats and put them on; others—just like Levin himself—merely shrugged their shoulders, enjoying the pleasant coolness of it.

Another row, and yet another row, followed—long rows and short rows, with good grass and with poor grass. Levin lost all sense of time, and could not have told whether it was late or early now. A change began to come over his work, which gave him immense satisfaction. In the midst of his toil there were moments during which he forgot what he was doing, and it came all easy to him, and at those same moments his row was almost as smooth and well cut as Tit's. But so soon as he recollected what he was doing, and began trying to do better, he was at once conscious of all the difficulty of his task, and the row was badly mown.

On finishing yet another row he would have gone back to the top of the meadow again to begin the next, but Tit stopped, and going up to the old man said something in a low voice to him. They both looked at the sun. "What are they talking about, and why doesn't he go back?" thought Levin, not guessing that the peasants had been mowing no less than four hours without stopping, and it was time for their lunch.

"Lunch, sir," said the old man.

"Is it really time? That's right; lunch, then."

Levin gave his scythe to Tit, and together with the peasants, who were crossing the long stretch of mown grass, slightly sprinkled with rain, to get their bread from the heap of coats, he went towards his house. Only then he suddenly awoke to the fact that he had been wrong about the weather and the rain was drenching his hay.

"The hay will be spoiled," he said.

"Not a bit of it, sir; mow in the rain, and you'll rake in fine weather!" said the old man.

Levin untied his horse and rode home to his coffee. Sergey Ivanovitch was only just getting up. When he had drunk his coffee, Levin rode back again to the mowing before Sergey Ivanovitch had had time to dress and come down to the dining-room.

CHAPTER V

AFTER lunch Levin was not in the same place in the string of mowers as before, but stood between the old man who had accosted him jocosely, and now invited him to be his neighbor, and a young peasant, who had only been married in the autumn, and who was mowing this summer for the first time.

The old man, holding himself erect, moved in front, with his feet turned out, taking long, regular strides, and with a precise and regular action which seemed to cost him no more effort than swinging one's arms in walking, as though it were in play, he laid down the high, even row of grass. It was as though it were not he but the sharp scythe of itself swishing through the juicy grass.

Behind Levin came the lad Mishka. His pretty, boyish face, with a twist of fresh grass bound round his hair, was all working with effort; but whenever any one looked at him he smiled. He would clearly have died sooner than own it was hard work for him.

Levin kept between them. In the very heat of the day the mowing did not seem such hard work to him. The perspiration with which he was drenched cooled him, while the sun, that burned his back, his head, and his arms, bare to the elbow, gave a vigor and dogged energy to his labor; and more and more often now came those moments of unconsciousness, when it was possible not to think what one was doing. The scythe cut of itself. These were happy moments. Still more delightful were the moments when they reached the stream where the rows ended, and the old man rubbed his scythe with the wet, thick grass, rinsed its blade in the fresh water of the stream, ladled out a little in a tin dipper, and offered Levin a drink.

"What do you say to my home-brew, eh? Good, eh?" said he, winking.

And truly Levin had never drunk any liquor so good as this warm water with green bits floating in it, and a taste of rust from the tin dipper. And immediately after this came the delicious, slow saunter, with his hand on the scythe, during which he could wipe away the streaming sweat, take deep breaths of air, and look about at the long string of mowers and at what was happening around in the forest and the country.

The longer Levin mowed, the oftener he felt the moments of unconsciousness in which it seemed not his hands that swung the scythe, but the scythe mowing of itself, a body full of life and consciousness of its own, and as though by magic, without thinking of it, the work turned out regular and well-finished of itself. These were the most blissful moments.

It was only hard work when he had to break off the motion, which had become unconscious, and to think; when he had to mow round a hillock or a tuft of sorrel. The old man did this easily. When a hillock came he changed his action, and at one time with the heel, and at another with the tip of his scythe, clipped the hillock round both sides with short strokes. And while he did this he kept looking about and watching what came into his view: at one moment he picked a wild berry and ate it or offered it to Levin, then he flung away a twig with the blade of the scythe, then he looked at a quail's nest, from which the bird flew just under the scythe, or caught a snake that crossed his path, and lifting it on the scythe as though on a fork showed it to Levin and threw it away.

For both Levin and the young peasant behind him, such changes of position were difficult. Both of them, repeating over and over again the same strained movement, were in a perfect frenzy of toil, and were incapable of shifting their position and at the same time watching what was before them.

Levin did not notice how time was passing. If he had been asked how long he had been working he would have said half an hour—and it was getting on for dinner-time. As they were walking back over the cut grass, the old man called Levin's attention to the little girls and boys who were coming from different directions, hardly visible through the long grass, and along the road towards the mowers, carrying sacks of bread dragging at their little hands and pitchers of the sour rye-beer, with cloths wrapped round them.

"Look'ee, the little emmets crawling!" he said, pointing to them, and he shaded his eyes with his hand to look at the sun. They mowed two more rows; the old man stopped.

"Come, master, dinner-time!" he said briskly. And on reaching the stream the mowers moved off across the lines of cut grass towards their pile of coats, where the children who had brought their dinners were sitting waiting for them. The peasants gathered into groups—those further away under a cart, those nearer under a willow bush.

Levin sat down by them; he felt disinclined to go away.

All constraint with the master had disappeared long ago. The peasants got ready for dinner. Some washed, the young lads bathed in the stream, others made a place comfortable for a rest, untied their sacks of bread, and uncovered the pitchers of rye-beer. The old man crumbled up some bread in a cup, stirred it with the handle of a spoon, poured water on it from the dipper, broke up some more bread, and having seasoned it with salt, he turned to the east to say his prayer.

"Come, master, taste my sop," said he, kneeling down before the cup.

The sop was so good that Levin gave up the idea of going

home. He dined with the old man, and talked to him about his family affairs, taking the keenest interest in them, and told him about his own affairs and all the circumstances that could be of interest to the old man. He felt much nearer to him than to his brother, and could not help smiling at the affection he felt for this man. When the old man got up again, said his prayer, and lay down under a bush, putting some grass under his head for a pillow, Levin did the same, and in spite of the clinging flies that were so persistent in the sunshine, and the midges that tickled his hot face and body, he fell asleep at once and only waked when the sun had passed to the other side of the bush and reached him. The old man had been awake a long while, and was sitting up whetting the scythes of the younger lads.

Levin looked about him and hardly recognized the place, everything was so changed. The immense stretch of meadow had been mown and was sparkling with a peculiar fresh brilliance, with its lines of already sweet-smelling grass in the slanting rays of the evening sun. And the bushes about the river had been cut down, and the river itself, not visible before, now gleaming like steel in its bends, and the moving, ascending peasants, and the sharp wall of grass of the unmown part of the meadow, and the hawks hovering over the stripped meadow—all was perfectly new. Raising himself, Levin began considering how much had been cut and how much more could still be done that day.

The work done was exceptionally much for forty-two men. They had cut the whole of the big meadow, which had, in the years of serf labor, taken thirty scythes

305

two days to mow. Only the corners remained to do, where the rows were short. But Levin felt a longing to get as much mowing done that day as possible, and was vexed with the sun sinking so quickly in the sky. He felt no weariness; all he wanted was to get his work done more and more quickly and as much done as possible.

"Could you cut Mashkin Upland too?—what do you think?" he said to the old man.

"As God wills, the sun's not high. A little vodka for the lads?"

At the afternoon rest, when they were sitting down again, and those who smoked had lighted their pipes, the old man told the men that Mashkin Upland's to be cut—"there'll be some vodka."

"Why not cut it? Come on, Tit! We'll look sharp! We can eat at night. Come on!" cried voices, and eating up their bread, the mowers went back to work.

"Come, lads, keep it up!" said Tit, and ran on ahead almost at a trot.

"Get along, get along!" said the old man, hurrying after him and easily overtaking him, "I'll mow you down, look out!"

And young and old mowed away, as though they were racing with one another. But however fast they worked, they did not spoil the grass, and the rows were laid just as neatly and exactly. The little piece left uncut in the corner was mown in five minutes. The last of the mowers were just ending their rows while the foremost snatched up their coats onto their shoulders, and crossed the road towards Mashkin Upland.

The sun was already sinking into the trees when they went with their jingling dippers into the wooded ravine of Mashkin Upland. The grass was up to their waists in the middle of the hollow, soft, tender, and feathery, spotted here and there among the trees with wild heart's-ease.

After a brief consultation—whether to take the rows lengthwise or diagonally—Prohor Yermilin, also a renowned mower, a huge, black-haired peasant, went on ahead. He went up to the top, turned back again and started mowing, and they all proceeded to form in line behind him, going downhill through the hollow and uphill right up to the edge of the forest. The sun sank behind the forest. The dew was falling by now; the mowers were in the sun only on the hillside, but below, where a mist was rising, and on the opposite side, they mowed into the fresh, dewy shade. The work went rapidly. The grass cut with a juicy sound, and was at once laid in high, fragrant rows. The mowers from all sides, brought closer together in the short row, kept urging one another on to the sound of jingling dipper and clanging scythes, and the hiss of the whetstones sharpening them, and good-humored shouts.

Levin still kept between the young peasant and the old man. The old man, who had put on his short sheepskin jacket, was just as good-humored, jocose, and free in his movements. Among the trees they were continually cutting with their scythes the so-called "birch mushrooms," swollen fat in the succulent grass. But the old man bent down every time he came across a mushroom, picked it up and put it in his bosom. "Another present for my old woman," he said as he did so.

Easy as it was to mow the wet, soft grass, it was hard work going up and down the steep sides of the ravine. But this did not trouble the old man. Swinging his scythe just as ever, and moving his feet in their big, plaited shoes with firm, little steps, he climbed slowly up the steep place, and though his breeches hanging out below his smock, and his whole frame trembled with effort, he did not miss one blade of grass or one mushroom on his way, and kept making jokes with the peasants and Levin. Levin walked after him and often thought he must fall, as he climbed with a scythe up a steep cliff where it would have been hard work to clamber without anything. But he climbed up and did what he had to do. He felt as though some external force were moving him.

CHAPTER VI

Mashkin Upland was mown, the last row finished, the peasants had put on their coats and were gaily trudging home. Levin got on his horse, and parting regretfully from the peasants, rode homewards. On the hillside he looked back; he could not see them in the mist that had risen from the valley; he could only hear rough, good-humored voices, laughter, and the sound of clanking scythes.

Sergey Ivanovitch had long ago finished dinner, and was drinking iced lemon and water in his own room, looking through the reviews and papers, which he had only just received by post, when Levin rushed into the room, talking merrily, with his wet and matted hair sticking to his forehead, and his back and chest grimed and moist.

"We mowed the whole meadow! Oh, it is nice, delicious! And how have you been getting on?" said Levin, completely forgetting the disagreeable conversation of the previous day.

"Mercy! what do you look like!" said Sergey Ivanovitch, for the first moment looking round with some dissatisfaction. "And the door, do shut the door!" he cried. "You must have let in a dozen at least."

Sergey Ivanovitch could not endure flies, and in his own room he never opened the window except at night, and carefully kept the door shut.

"Not one, on my honor. But if I have, I'll catch them. You wouldn't believe what a pleasure it is! How have you spent the day?"

"Very well. But have you really been mowing the whole day? I expect you're as hungry as a wolf. Kouzma has got everything ready for you."

"No, I don't feel hungry even. I had something to eat there. But I'll go and wash."

"Yes, go along, go along, and I'll come to you directly," said Sergey Ivanovitch, shaking his head as he looked at his brother. "Go along, make haste," he added smiling, and gathering up his books, he prepared to go too. He, too, felt suddenly good-humored and disinclined to leave his brother's side. "But what did you do while it was raining?"

"Rain? Why, there was scarcely a drop. I'll come directly. So you had a nice day too? That's first-rate." And Levin went off to change his clothes.

Five minutes later the brothers met in the dining-room. Although it seemed to Levin that he was not hungry, and he sat down to dinner simply so as not to hurt Kouzma's feelings, yet when he began to eat the dinner struck him as extraordinarily good. Sergey Ivanovitch watched him with a smile.

"Oh, by the way, there's a letter for you," said he. "Kouzma, bring it down, please. And mind you shut the doors."

The letter was from Oblonsky. Levin read it aloud. Oblonsky wrote to him from Petersburg: "I have had a letter from Dolly; she's at Ergushovo, and everything seems going wrong there. Do ride over and see her, please; help her with advice; you know all about it. She will be so glad to see you. She's quite alone, poor thing. My mother-in-law and all of them are still abroad."

"That's capital! I will certainly ride over to her," said Levin. "Or we'll go together. She's such a splendid woman, isn't she?"

"They're not far from here, then?"

"Twenty-five miles. Or perhaps it is thirty. But a capital road. Capital, we'll drive over."

"I shall be delighted," said Sergey Ivanovitch, still smiling. The sight of his younger brother's appearance had immediately put him in a good humor.

"Well, you have an appetite!" he said, looking at his dark-red, sunburnt face and neck bent over the plate.

"Splendid! You can't imagine what an effectual remedy it is for every sort of foolishness. I want to enrich medicine with a new word: *Arbeitskur*."

"Well, but you don't need it, I should fancy."

"No, but for all sorts of nervous invalids."

"Yes, it ought to be tried. I had meant to come to the mowing to look at you, but it was so unbearably hot that I got no further than the forest. I sat there a little, and went on by the forest to the village, met your old nurse, and sounded her as to the peasants' view of you. As far as I can make out, they don't approve of this. She said: 'It's not a gentleman's work.' Altogether, I fancy that in the people's ideas there are very clear and definite notions of certain, as they call it, 'gentlemanly' lines of action. And they don't sanction the gentry's moving outside bounds clearly laid down in their ideas."

"Maybe so; but anyway it's a pleasure such as I have never known in my life. And there's no harm in it, you know. Is there?" answered Levin. "I can't help it if they don't like it. Though I do believe it's all right. Eh?"

"Altogether," pursued Sergey Ivanovitch, "you're satisfied with your day?"

"Quite satisfied. We cut the whole meadow. And such a splendid old man I made friends with there! You can't fancy how delightful he was!"

"Well, so you're content with your day. And so am I. First, I solved two chess problems, and one a very pretty one—a pawn opening. I'll show it you. And then—I thought over our conversation yesterday."

"Eh! our conversation yesterday?" said Levin, blissfully dropping his eyelids and drawing deep breaths after finishing his dinner, and absolutely incapable of recalling what their conversation yesterday was about.

"I think you are partly right. Our difference of opinion amounts to this, that you make the mainspring self-interest, while I suppose that interest in the common weal is bound to exist in every man of a certain degree of advancement. Possibly you are right too, that action founded on material interest would be more desirable. You are altogether, as the French say, too *primesautière* a nature; you must have intense, energetic action, or nothing."

Levin listened to his brother and did not understand a single word, and did not want to understand. He was only afraid his brother might ask him some question which would make it evident he had not heard.

"So that's what I think it is, my dear boy," said Sergey Ivanovitch, touching him on the shoulder.

"Yes, of course. But, do you know? I won't stand up for my view," answered Levin, with a guilty, childlike smile. "Whatever was it I was disputing about?" he wondered. "Of course, I'm right, and he's right, and it's all first-rate. Only I must go round to the counting-house and see to things." He got up, stretching and smiling. Sergey Ivanovitch smiled too.

"If you want to go out, let's go together," he said, disinclined to be parted from his brother, who seemed positively breathing out freshness and energy. "Come, we'll go to the counting-house, if you have to go there."

"Oh, heavens!" shouted Levin, so loudly that Sergey Ivanovitch was quite frightened.

"What, what is the matter?"

"How's Agafea Mihalovna's hand?" said Levin, slapping himself on the head. "I'd positively forgotten her even."

"It's much better."

"Well, anyway I'll run down to her. Before you've time to get your hat on, I'll be back."

And he ran down-stairs, clattering with his heels like a spring-rattle.

CHAPTER VII

STEPAN ARKADYEVITCH had gone to Petersburg to perform the most natural and essential official duty—so familiar to every one in the government service, though incomprehensible to outsiders—that duty, but for which one could hardly be in government service, of reminding the ministry of his existence—and having, for the due performance of this rite, taken all the available cash from home, was gaily and agreeably spending his days at the races and in the summer villas. Meanwhile Dolly and the children had moved into the country, to cut down expenses as much as possible. She had gone to Ergushovo, the estate that had been her dowry, and the one where in spring the forest had been sold. It was nearly forty miles from Levin's Pokrovskoe. The big, old house at Ergushovo had been pulled down long ago, and the old prince had had the lodge done up and built on to. Twenty years before, when Dolly was a child, the lodge had been roomy and comfortable, though, like all lodges, it stood sideways to the entrance avenue, and faced the south. But by now this lodge was old and dilapidated. When Stepan Arkadyevitch had gone down in the spring to sell the forest, Dolly had begged him to look over the house and order what repairs might be needed. Stepan Arkadyevitch, like all unfaithful husbands indeed, was very solicitous for his wife's comfort, and he had himself looked over the house, and given instructions about everything that he considered necessary. What he considered necessary was to cover all the furniture with cretonne, to put up curtains, to weed the garden, to make a little bridge on the pond, and to plant flowers. But he forgot many other essential matters, the want of which greatly distressed Darya Alexandrovna later on.

In spite of Stepan Arkadyevitch's efforts to be an attentive father and husband, he never could keep in his mind that he had a wife and children. He had bachelor tastes, and it was in accordance with them that he shaped his life. On his return to Moscow he informed his wife with pride that everything was ready, that the house would be a little paradise, and that he advised her most certainly to go. His wife's staying away in the country was very agreeable to Stepan Arkadyevitch from every point of view: it did the children good, it decreased expenses, and it left him more at liberty. Darya Alexandrovna regarded staying in the country for the summer as essential for the children, especially for the little girl, who had not succeeded in regaining her strength after the scarlatina, and also as a means of escaping the petty humiliations, the little bills owing to the wood-merchant, the fishmonger, the shoemaker, which made her miserable. Besides this, she was pleased to go away to the country because she was dreaming of getting her sister Kitty to stay with her there. Kitty was to be back from abroad in the middle of the summer, and bathing had been prescribed for her. Kitty wrote that no prospect was so alluring as to spend the summer with Dolly at Ergushovo, full of childish associations for both of them.

The first days of her existence in the country were very hard for Dolly. She used to stay in the country as a child, and the impression she had retained of it was that the country was a refuge from all the unpleasantness of the town, that life there, though not luxurious—Dolly could easily make up her mind to that—was cheap and comfortable; that there was plenty of everything, everything was cheap, everything could be got, and children were happy. But now coming to the country as the head of a family, she perceived that it was all utterly unlike what she had fancied.

The day after their arrival there was a heavy fall of rain and in the night the water came through in the corridor and in the nursery, so that the beds had to be carried into the drawing-room. There was no kitchenmaid to be found; of the nine cows, it appeared from the words of the cowherd-woman that some were about to calve, others had just calved, others were old, and others again hard-uddered; there was not butter nor milk enough even for the children. There were no eggs. They could get no fowls; old, purplish, stringy cocks were all they had for roasting and boiling. Impossible to get women to scrub the floors—all were potato-hoeing. Driving was out of the question, because one of the horses was restive, and bolted in the shafts. There was no place where they could bathe; the whole of the river-bank was trampled by the cattle and open to the road; even walks were impossible, for the cattle strayed into the garden through a gap in the hedge, and there was one terrible bull, who bellowed, and therefore might be expected to gore somebody. There were no proper cupboards for their clothes; what cupboards there were either would not close at all, or burst open whenever any one passed by them. There were no pots and pans; there was no copper in the wash-house, nor even an ironing-board in the maids' room.

Finding instead of peace and rest all these, from her point of view, fearful calamities, Darya Alexandrovna was at first in despair. She exerted herself to the utmost, felt the hopelessness of the position, and was every instant suppressing the tears that started into her eyes. The bailiff, a retired quartermaster, whom Stepan Arkadyevitch had taken a fancy to and had appointed bailiff on account of his handsome and respectful appearance as a hall-porter, showed no sympathy for Darya Alexandrovna's woes. He said respectfully, "nothing can be done, the peasants are such a wretched lot," and did nothing to help her.

The position seemed hopeless. But in the Oblonskys' household, as in all families indeed, there was one inconspicuous but most valuable and useful person, Marya Philimonovna. She soothed her mistress, assured her that everything would *come round* (it was her expression, and Matvey had borrowed it from her), and without fuss or hurry proceeded to set to work herself. She had immediately made friends with the bailiff's wife, and on the very first day she drank tea with her and the bailiff under the acacias, and reviewed all the circumstances of the position. Very soon Marya Philimonovna had established her club, so to say, under the acacias, and there it was, in this club, consisting of the bailiff's wife, the village elder, and the counting-house clerk, that the difficulties of existence were gradually smoothed away, and in a week's time everything actually had come round. The roof was mended, a kitchenmaid was found—a crony of the village elder's—hens were bought, the cows began giving milk, the garden hedge was stopped up with stakes, the carpenter made a mangle, hooks were put in the cupboards, and they ceased to burst open spontaneously, and an ironing-board covered with army cloth was placed across from the arm of a chair to the chest of drawers, and there was a smell of flatirons in the maids' room.

"Just see, now, and you were quite in despair," said Marya Philimonovna, pointing to the ironing-board. They even rigged up a bathing-shed of straw hurdles. Lily began to bathe, and Darya Alexandrovna began to realize, if only in part, her expectations, if not of a peaceful, at least of a comfortable, life in the country. Peaceful with six children Darya Alexandrovna could not be. One would fall ill, another might easily become so, a third would be without something necessary, a fourth would show symptoms of a bad disposition, and so on. Rare indeed were the brief periods of peace. But these cares and anxieties were for Darya Alexandrovna the sole happiness possible. Had it not been for them, she would have been left alone to brood over her husband who did not love her. And besides, hard though it was for the mother to bear the dread of illness, the illnesses themselves, and the grief of seeing signs of evil propensities in her children —the children themselves were even now repaying her in small joys for her sufferings. Those joys were so small that they passed unnoticed, like gold in sand, and at bad moments she could see nothing but the pain, nothing but sand; but there were good moments too when she saw nothing but the joy, nothing but gold.

Now in the solitude of the country, she began to be more and more frequently aware of those joys. Often, looking at them, she would make every possible effort to persuade herself that she was mistaken, that she as a mother was partial to her children. All the same, she could not help saying to herself that she had charming children, all six of them in different ways, but a set of children such as is not often to be met with, and she was happy in them, and proud of them.

TOWARDS the end of May, when everything had been more or less satisfactorily arranged, she received her husband's answer to her complaints of the disorganized state of things in the country. He wrote begging her forgiveness for not having thought of everything before, and promised to come down at the first chance. This chance did not present itself, and till the beginning of June Darya Alexandrovna stayed alone in the country.

On the Sunday in St. Peter's week Darya Alexandrovna drove to mass for all her children to take the sacrament. Darya Alexandrovna in her intimate, philosophical talks with her sister, her mother, and her friends very often astonished them by the freedom of her views in regard to religion. She had a strange religion of transmigration of souls all her own, in which she had firm faith, troubling herself little about the dogmas of the Church. But in her family she was strict in carrying out all that was required by the Church—and not merely in order to set an example, but with all her heart in it. The fact that the children had not been at the sacrament for nearly a year worried her extremely, and with the full approval and sympathy of Marya Philimonovna she decided that this should take place now in the summer.

For several days before, Darya Alexandrovna was busily deliberating on how to dress all the children. Frocks were made or altered and washed, seams and flounces were let out, buttons were sewn on, and ribbons got ready. One dress, Tanya's, which the English governess had undertaken, cost Darya Alexandrovna much loss of temper. The English governess in altering it had made the seams in the wrong place, had taken up the sleeves too much, and altogether spoilt the dress. It was so narrow on Tanya's shoulders that it was quite painful to look at her. But Marya Philimonovna had the happy thought of putting in gussets, and adding a little shoulder-cape. The dress was set right, but there was nearly a quarrel with the English governess. On the morning, however, all was happily arranged, and towards ten o'clock —the time at which they had asked the priest to wait for them for the mass—the children in their new dresses, with beaming faces stood on the step before the carriage waiting for their mother.

To the carriage, instead of the restive Raven, they had harnessed, thanks to the representations of Marya Philimonovna, the bailiff's horse, Brownie, and Darya Alexandrovna, delayed by anxiety over her own attire, came out and got in, dressed in a white muslin gown.

Darya Alexandrovna had done her hair, and dressed with care and excitement. In the old days she had dressed for her own sake to look pretty and be admired. Later on, as she got older, dress became more and more distasteful to her. She saw that she was losing her good looks. But now she began to feel pleasure and interest in dress again. Now she did not dress for her own sake, not for the sake of her own beauty, but simply that as the mother of those exquisite creatures she might not spoil the general effect. And looking at herself for the last time in the looking-glass she was satisfied with herself. She looked nice. Not nice as she would have wished to look nice in old days at a ball, but nice for the object which she now had in view.

In the church there was no one but the peasants, the servants and their women-folk. But Darya Alexandrovna saw, or fancied she saw, the sensation produced by her children and her. The children were not only beautiful to look at in their smart little dresses, but they were charming in the way they behaved. Aliosha, it is true, did not stand quite correctly; he kept turning round, trying to look at his little jacket from behind; but all the same he was wonderfully sweet. Tanya behaved like a grown-up person, and looked after the little ones. And the smallest, Lily, was bewitching in her naïve astonishment at everything, and it was difficult not to smile when, after taking the sacrament, she said in English, "Please, some more."

On the way home the children felt that something solemn had happened, and were very sedate.

Everything went happily at home too; but at lunch Grisha began whistling, and, what was worse, was disobedient to the English governess, and was forbidden to have any tart. Darya Alexandrovna would not have let things go so far on such a day had she been present; but she had to support the English governess's authority, and she upheld her decision that Grisha should have no tart. This rather spoiled the general good-humor. Grisha cried, declaring that Nikolinka had whistled too, and he was not punished, and that he wasn't crying for the tart—he didn't care—but at being unjustly treated. This was really too tragic, and Darya Alexandrovna made up her mind to persuade the English governess to forgive Grisha, and she went to speak to her. But on the way, as she passed the drawing-room, she beheld a scene, filling her heart with such pleasure that the tears came into her eyes, and she forgave the delinquent herself.

The culprit was sitting at the window in the corner of the drawing-room; beside him was standing Tanya with a plate. On the pretext of wanting to give some dinner to her dolls, she had asked the governess's permission to take her share of tart to the nursery, and had taken it instead to her brother. While still weeping over the injustice of his punishment, he was eating the tart, and kept saying through his sobs, "Eat yourself; let's eat it together . . . together."

Tanya had at first been under the influence of her pity for Grisha, then of a sense of her noble action, and tears were standing in her eyes too; but she did not refuse, and ate her share.

On catching sight of their mother they were dismayed, but, looking into her face, they saw they were not doing wrong. They burst out laughing, and, with their mouths full of tart, they began wiping their smiling lips with their hands, and smearing their radiant faces all over with tears and jam.

"Mercy! Your new white frock; Tanya! Grisha!" said their mother, trying to save the frock, but with tears in her eyes, smiling a blissful, rapturous smile.

The new frocks were taken off, and orders were given for the little girls to have their blouses put on, and the boys their old jackets, and the wagonette to be harnessed; with Brownie, to the bailiff's annoyance, again in the shafts, to drive out for mushroom-picking and bathing. A roar of delighted shrieks arose in the nursery, and never ceased till they had set off for the bathing-place.

They gathered a whole basketful of mushrooms; even Lily found a birch mushroom. It had always happened before that Miss Hoole found them and pointed them out to her; but this

time she found a big one quite of herself, and there was a general scream of delight, "Lily has found a mushroom!"

Then they reached the river, put the horses under the birch-trees, and went to the bathing-place. The coachman, Terenty fastened the horses, who kept whisking away the flies, to a tree and, treading down the grass, lay down in the shade of a birch and smoked his shag, while the never-ceasing shrieks of delight of the children floated across to him from the bathing-place.

Though it was hard work to look after all the children and restrain their wild pranks, though it was difficult too to keep in one's head and not mix up all the stockings, little breeches, and shoes for the different legs, and to undo and to do up again all the tapes and buttons, Darya Alexandrovna, who had always liked bathing herself, and believed it to be very good for the children, enjoyed nothing so much as bathing with all the children. To go over all those fat little legs, pulling on their stockings, to take in her arms and dip those little naked bodies and to hear their screams of delight and alarm, to see the breathless faces with wide-open, scared, and happy eyes of all her splashing cherubs, was a great pleasure to her.

When half the children had been dressed, some peasant women in holiday dress, out picking herbs, came up to the bathing-shed and stopped shyly. Marya Philimonovna called one of them and handed her a sheet and a shirt that had dropped into the water for her to dry them, and Darya Alexandrovna began to talk to the women. At first they laughed behind their hands and did not understand her questions, but soon they grew bolder and began to talk, winning Darya Alexandrovna's heart at once by the genuine admiration of the children that they showed.

"My, what a beauty! as white as sugar," said one, admiring Tanitchka, and shaking her head; "but thin . . ."

"Yes, she has been ill."

"And so they've been bathing you too," said another to the baby.

"No; he's only three months old," answered Darya Alexandrovna with pride.

"You don't say so!"

"And have you any children?"

"I've had four; I've two living—a boy and a girl. I weaned her last carnival."

"How old is she?"

"Why, two years old."

"Why did you nurse her so long?"

"It's our custom; for three fasts. . . ."

And the conversation became most interesting to Darya Alexandrovna. What sort of time did she have? What was the matter with the boy? Where was her husband? Did it often happen?

Darya Alexandrovna felt disinclined to leave the peasant women, so interesting to her was their conversation, so completely identical were all their interests. What pleased her most of all was that she saw clearly what all the women admired more than anything was her having so many children, and such fine ones. The peasant women even made Darya Alexandrovna laugh, and offended the English governess, because she was the cause of the laughter she did not understand. One of the younger women kept staring at the Englishwoman, who was dressing after all the rest, and when she put on her third petticoat she could not refrain from the remark, "My, she keeps putting on and putting on, and she'll never have done!" she said, and they all went off into roars.

CHAPTER IX

On the drive home, as Darya Alexandrovna, with all her children round her, their heads still wet from their bath, and a kerchief tied over her own head, was getting near the house, the coachman said, "There's some gentleman coming: the master of Pokrovskoe, I do believe."

Darya Alexandrovna peeped out in front, and was delighted when she recognized in the gray hat and gray coat the familiar figure of Levin walking to meet them. She was glad to see him at any time, but at this moment she was specially glad he should see her in all her glory. No one was better able to appreciate her grandeur than Levin.

Seeing her, he found himself face to face with one of the pictures of his day-dream of family life.

"You're like a hen with your chickens, Darya Alexandrovna."

"Ah, how glad I am to see you!" she said, holding out her hand to him.

"Glad to see me, but you didn't let me know. My brother's staying with me. I got a note from Stiva that you were here."

"From Stiva?" Darya Alexandrovna asked with surprise.

"Yes; he writes that you are here, and that he thinks you might allow me to be of use to you," said Levin, and as he said it he became suddenly embarrassed, and, stopping abruptly, he walked on in silence by the wagonette, snapping off the buds of the lime-trees and nibbling them. He was embarrassed through a sense that Darya Alexandrovna would be annoyed by receiving from an outsider help that should by rights have come from her own husband. Darya Alexandrovna certainly did not like this little way of Stepan Arkadyevitch's of foisting his domestic duties on others. And she was at once aware that Levin was aware of this. It was just for this fineness of perception, for this delicacy, that Darya Alexandrovna liked Levin.

"I know, of course," said Levin, "that that simply means that you would like to see me, and I'm exceedingly glad. Though I can fancy that, used to town housekeeping as you are, you must feel in the wilds here, and if there's anything wanted, I'm altogether at your disposal."

"Oh, no!" said Dolly. "At first things were rather uncomfortable, but now we've settled everything capitally—thanks to my old nurse," she said, indicating Marya Philimonovna, who, seeing that they were speaking of her, smiled brightly and cordially to Levin. She knew him, and knew that he would be a good match for her young lady, and was very keen to see the matter settled.

"Won't you get in, sir, we'll make room this side!" she said to him.

"No, I'll walk. Children, who'd like to race the horses with me?"

The children knew Levin very little, and could not remember when they had seen him, but they experienced in regard to him none of that strange feeling of shyness and hostility which children so often experience towards hypocritical, grown-up people, and for which they are so often and miserably punished. Hypocrisy in anything whatever may deceive the cleverest and most penetrating man, but the least wide-awake of children recognizes it, and is revolted by it, however ingeniously it may be disguised. Whatever faults Levin had, there was not a trace of hypocrisy in him, and so the children showed him the same friendliness that they saw in their mother's face. On his invitation, the two elder ones at once jumped out to him and ran with him as simply as they would have done with their nurse or Miss Hoole or their mother. Lily, too, began begging to go to him, and her mother handed her to him; he sat her on his shoulder and ran along with her.

"Don't be afraid, don't be afraid, Darya Alexandrovna!" he said, smiling good-humoredly to the mother; "there's no chance of my hurting or dropping her."

And, looking at his strong, agile, assiduously careful and needlessly wary movements, the mother felt her mind at rest, and smiled gaily and approvingly as she watched him.

Here, in the country, with children, and with Darya Alexandrovna, with whom he was in sympathy, Levin was in a mood not infrequent with him, of childlike light-heartedness that he particularly liked in him. As he ran with the children, he taught them gymnastic feats, set Miss Hoole laughing with his queer English accent, and talked to Darya Alexandrovna of his pursuits in the country.

After dinner, Darya Alexandrovna, sitting alone with him on the balcony, began to speak of Kitty.

321

"You know, Kitty's coming here, and is going to spend the summer with me."

"Really," he said, flushing, and at once, to change the conversation, he said: "Then I'll send you two cows, shall I? If you insist on a bill you shall pay me five roubles a month; but it's really too bad of you."

"No, thank you. We can manage very well now."

"Oh, well, then, I'll have a look at your cows, and if you'll allow me, I'll give directions about their food. Everything depends on their food."

And Levin, to turn the conversation, explained to Darya Alexandrovna the theory of cow-keeping, based on the principle that the cow is simply a machine for the transformation of food into milk, and so on.

He talked of this, and passionately longed to hear more of Kitty, and, at the same time, was afraid of hearing it. He dreaded the breaking up of the inward peace he had gained with such effort.

"Yes, but still all this has to be looked after, and who is there to look after it?" Darya Alexandrovna responded, without interest.

She had by now got her household matters so satisfactorily arranged, thanks to Marya Philimonovna, that she was disinclined to make any change in them; besides, she had no faith in Levin's knowledge of farming. General principles, as to the cow being a machine for the production of milk, she looked on with suspicion. It seemed to her that such principles could only be a hindrance in farm management. It all seemed to her a far simpler matter: all that was needed, as Marya Philimonovna had explained, was to give Brindle and Whitebreast more food and drink, and not to let the cook carry all the kitchen slops to the laundry-maid's cow. That was clear. But general propositions as to feeding on meal and on grass were doubtful and obscure. And, what was most important, she wanted to talk about Kitty.

"KITTY writes to me that there's nothing she longs for so much as quiet and solitude," Dolly said after the silence that had followed.

"And how is she—better?" Levin asked in agitation.

"Thank God, she's quite well again. I never believed her lungs were affected."

"Oh, I'm very glad!" said Levin, and Dolly fancied she saw something touching, helpless, in his face as he said this and looked silently into her face.

"Let me ask you, Konstantin Dmitrievitch," said Darya Alexandrovna, smiling her kindly and rather mocking smile, "why is it you are angry with Kitty?"

"I? I'm not angry with her," said Levin.

"Yes, you are angry. Why was it you did not come to see us nor them when you were in Moscow?"

"Darya Alexandrovna," he said, blushing up to the roots of his hair, "I wonder really that with your kind heart you don't feel this. How it is you feel no pity for me, if nothing else, when you know . . ."

"What do I know?"

"You know I made an offer and that I was refused," said Levin, and all the tenderness he had been feeling for Kitty a minute before was replaced by a feeling of anger for the slight he had suffered.

"What makes you suppose I know?"

"Because everybody knows it . . ."

"That's just where you are mistaken; I did not know it, though I had guessed it was so."

"Well, now you know it."

"All I knew was that something had happened that made her dreadfully miserable, and that she begged me never to speak of it. And if she would not tell me, she would certainly not speak of it to any one else. But what did pass between you? Tell me."

"I have told you."

"When was it?"

"When I was at their house the last time."

"Do you know that," said Darya Alexandrovna, "I am awfully, awfully sorry for her. You suffer only from pride. . . ."

"Perhaps so," said Levin, "but . . ."

She interrupted him.

"But she, poor girl . . . I am awfully, awfully sorry for her. Now I see it all."

"Well, Darya Alexandrovna, you must excuse me," he said, getting up. "Good-bye, Darya Alexandrovna, till we meet again."

"No, wait a minute," she said, clutching him by the sleeve. "Wait a minute, sit down."

"Please, please, don't let us talk of this," he said, sitting down, and at the same time feeling rise up and stir within his heart a hope he had believed to be buried.

"If I did not like you," she said, and tears came into her eyes; "if I did not know you, as I do know you . . ."

The feeling that had seemed dead revived more and more, rose up and took possession of Levin's heart.

"Yes, I understand it all now," said Darya Alexandrovna. "You can't understand it; for you men, who are free and make your own choice, it's always clear whom you love. But a girl's in a position of suspense, with all a woman's or maiden's modesty, a girl who sees you men from afar, who takes everything on trust,—a girl may have, and often has, such a feeling that she cannot tell what to say."

"Yes, if the heart does not speak . . ."

"No, the heart does speak; but just consider: you men have views about a girl, you come to the house, you make friends, you criticize, you wait to see if you have found what you love, and then, when you are sure you love her, you make an offer. . . ."

"Well, that's not quite it."

"Anyway you make an offer, when your love is ripe or when the balance has completely turned between the two you are choosing from. But a girl is not asked. She is expected to make her choice, and yet she cannot choose, she can only answer 'yes' or 'no.'"

"Yes, to choose between me and Vronsky," thought Levin, and the dead thing that had come to life within him died again, and only weighed on his heart and set it aching.

"Darya Alexandrovna," he said, "that's how one chooses a new dress, or some purchase or other, not love. The choice has been made, and so much the better. . . . And there can be no repeating it."

"Ah, pride, pride!" said Darya Alexandrovna, as though despising him for the baseness of this feeling in comparison with that other feeling which only women know. "At the time when you made Kitty an offer she was just in a position in which she could not answer. She was in doubt. Doubt between you and Vronsky. Him she was seeing every day, and you she had not seen for a long while. Supposing she had been older . . . I, for instance, in her place could have felt no doubt. I always disliked him, and so it has turned out."

Levin recalled Kitty's answer. She had said: *"No, that cannot be. . . ."*

"Darya Alexandrovna," he said dryly, "I appreciate your confidence in me; I believe you are making a mistake. But whether I am right or wrong, that pride you so despise makes any thought of Katerina Alexandrovna out of the question for me,—you understand, utterly out of the question."

"I will only say one thing more: you know that I am speaking of my sister, whom I love as I love my own children. I don't say she cared for you, all I meant to say is that her refusal at that moment proves nothing."

"I don't know!" said Levin, jumping up. "If you only knew how you are hurting me. It's just as if a child of yours were dead, and they were to say to you: He would have been like this and like that, and he might have lived, and how happy you would have been in him. But he's dead, dead, dead! . . ."

"How absurd you are!" said Darya Alexandrovna, looking with mournful tenderness at Levin's excitement. "Yes, I see it all more and more clearly," she went on musingly. "So you won't come to see us, then, when Kitty's here?"

"No, I shan't come. Of course I won't avoid meeting Katerina Alexandrovna, but as far as I can, I will try to save her the annoyance of my presence."

"You are very, very absurd," repeated Darya Alexandrovna, looking with tenderness into his face. "Very well then, let it be as though we had not spoken of this. What have you come for,

325

Tanya?" she said in French to the little girl who had come in.

"Where's my spade, mamma?"

"I speak French, and you must too."

The little girl tried to say it in French, but could not remember the French for spade; the mother prompted her, and then told her in French where to look for the spade. And this made a disagreeable impression on Levin.

Everything in Darya Alexandrovna's house and children struck him now as by no means so charming as a little while before. "And what does she talk French with the children for?" he thought; "how unnatural and false it is! And the children feel it so: Learning French and unlearning sincerity," he thought to himself, unaware that Darya Alexandrovna had thought all that over twenty times already, and yet, even at the cost of some loss of sincerity, believed it necessary to teach her children French in that way.

"But why are you going? Do stay a little."

Levin stayed to tea; but his good-humor had vanished, and he felt ill at ease.

After tea he went out into the hall to order his horses to be put in, and, when he came back, he found Darya Alexandrovna greatly disturbed, with a troubled face, and tears in her eyes. While Levin had been outside, an incident had occurred which had utterly shattered all the happiness she had been feeling that day, and her pride in her children. Grisha and Tanya had been fighting over a ball. Darya Alexandrovna, hearing a scream in the nursery, ran in and saw a terrible sight. Tanya was pulling Grisha's hair, while he, with a face hideous with rage, was beating her with his fists wherever he could get at her. Something snapped in Darya Alexandrovna's heart when she saw this. It was as if darkness had swooped down upon her life; she felt that these children of hers, that she was so proud of, were not merely most ordinary, but positively bad, ill-bred children, with coarse, brutal propensities—wicked children.

She could not talk or think of anything else, and she could not speak to Levin of her misery.

Levin saw she was unhappy and tried to comfort her, saying that it showed nothing bad, that all children fight; but, even as he said it, he was thinking in his heart: "No, I won't be artificial and talk French with my children; but my children won't be like that. All one has to do is not spoil children, not to distort their nature, and they'll be delightful. No, my children won't be like that."

He said good-bye and drove away, and she did not try to keep him.

CHAPTER XI

IN THE middle of July the elder of the village on Levin's sister's estate, about fifteen miles from Pokrovskoe, came to Levin to report on how things were going there and on the hay. The chief source of income on his sister's estate was from the riverside meadows. In former years the hay had been bought by the peasants for twenty roubles the three acres. When Levin took over the management of the estate, he thought on examining the grass-lands that they were worth more, and he fixed the price at twenty-five roubles the three acres. The peasants would not give that price, and, as Levin suspected, kept off other purchasers. Then Levin had driven over himself, and arranged to have the grass cut, partly by hired labor, partly at a payment of a certain proportion of the crop. His own peasants put every hindrance they could in the way of this new arrangement, but it was carried out, and the first year the meadows had yielded a profit almost double. The previous year—which was the third year—the peasants had maintained the same opposition to the arrangement, and the hay had been cut on the same system. This year the peasants were doing all the mowing for a third of the hay crop, and the village elder had come now to announce that the hay had been cut, and that, fearing rain, they had invited the counting-house clerk over, had divided the crop in his presence, and had raked together eleven stacks as the owner's share. From the vague answers to his question how much hay had been cut on the principal meadow, from the hurry of the village elder who had made the division, not asking leave, from the whole tone of the peasant, Levin perceived that there was something wrong in the division of the hay, and made up his mind to drive over himself to look into the matter.

Arriving to dinner at the village, and leaving his horse at the cottage of an old friend of his, the husband of his brother's wet-nurse, Levin went to see the old man in his bee-house, wanting to find out from him the truth about the hay. Parmenitch, a talk-ative, comely old man, gave Levin a very warm welcome, showed him all he was doing, told him everything about his bees and the swarms of that year; but gave vague and unwilling answers to Levin's inquiries about the mowing. This confirmed Levin still more in his suspicions. He went to the hay-fields and examined the stacks. The haystacks could not possibly contain fifty wagon-loads each, and to convict the peasants Levin ordered the wagons that had carried the hay to be brought up directly, to lift one stack, and carry it into the barn. There turned out to be only thirty-two loads in the stack. In spite of the village elder's asser-tions about the compressibility of hay, and its having settled down in the stacks, and his swearing that everything had been done in the fear of God, Levin stuck to his point that the hay had been divided without his orders, and that, therefore, he would not accept that hay as fifty loads to a stack. After a prolonged dispute the matter was decided by the peasants taking these eleven stacks, reckoning them as fifty loads each. The arguments and the division of the haycocks lasted the whole afternoon. When the last of the hay had been divided, Levin, intrusting the superintendence of the rest to the counting-house clerk, sat down on a haycock marked off by a stake of willow, and looked admiringly at the meadow swarming with peasants.

In front of him, in the bend of the river beyond the marsh, moved a bright-colored line of peasant women, and the scattered hay was being rapidly formed into gray winding rows over the pale green stubble. After the women came the men with pitch-forks, and from the gray rows there were growing up broad, high, soft haycocks. To the left, carts were rumbling over the meadow that had been already cleared, and one after another the haycocks vanished, flung up in huge forkfuls, and in their place there were rising heavy cartloads of fragrant hay hanging over the horses' hind-quarters.

"What weather for haying! What hay it'll be!" said an old man, squatting down beside Levin. "It's tea, not hay! It's like scattering grain to the ducks, the way they pick it up!" he added,

pointing to the growing haycocks. "Since dinner-time they've carried a good half of it."

"The last load, eh?" he shouted to a young peasant, who drove by, standing in the front of an empty cart, shaking the cord reins.

"The last, dad!" the lad shouted back, pulling in the horse, and, smiling, he looked round at a bright, rosy-cheeked peasant girl who sat in the cart smiling too, and drove on.

"Who's that? Your son?" asked Levin.

"My baby," said the old man with a tender smile.

"What a fine fellow!"

"The lad's all right."

"Married already?"

"Yes, it's two years last St. Philip's day."

"Any children?"

"Children indeed! Why, for over a year he was innocent as a babe himself, and bashful too," answered the old man. "Well, the hay! It's as fragrant as tea!" he repeated, wishing to change the subject.

Levin looked more attentively at Ivan Parmenov and his wife. They were loading a haycock onto the cart not far from him. Ivan Parmenov was standing on the cart, taking, laying in place, and stamping down the huge bundles of hay, which his pretty young wife deftly handed up to him, at first in armfuls, and then on the pitchfork. The young wife worked easily, merrily, and dexterously. The close-packed hay did not once break away off her fork. First she gathered it together, stuck the fork into it, then with a rapid, supple movement leaned the whole weight of her body on it, and at once with a bend of her back under the red belt she drew herself up, and arching her full bosom under the white smock, with a smart turn swung the fork in her arms, and flung the bundle of hay high onto the cart. Ivan, obviously doing his best to save her every minute of unnecessary labor, made haste, opening wide his arms to clutch the bundle and lay it in the cart. As she raked together what was left of the hay, the young wife shook off the bits of hay that had fallen on her neck, and straightening the red kerchief that had dropped forward over her white brow, not browned like her face by the sun, she crept under the cart to tie up the load. Ivan directed her how to fasten the cord to the cross-piece, and at something she said he laughed aloud. In the expressions of both faces was to be seen vigorous, young, freshly awakened love.

CHAPTER XII

THE load was tied on. Ivan jumped down and took the quiet, sleek horse by the bridle. The young wife flung the rake up on the load, and with a bold step, swinging her arms, she went to join the women, who were forming a ring for the haymakers' dance. Ivan drove off to the road and fell into line with the other loaded carts. The peasant women, with their rakes on their shoulders, gay with bright flowers, and chattering with ringing, merry voices, walked behind the hay-cart. One wild untrained female voice broke into a song, and sang it alone through a verse, and then the same verse was taken up and repeated by half a hundred strong healthy voices, of all sorts, coarse and fine, singing in unison.

The women, all singing, began to come close to Levin, and he felt as though a storm were swooping down upon him with a thunder of merriment. The storm swooped down, enveloped him and the haycock on which he was lying, and the other haycocks, and the wagon-loads, and the whole meadow and distant fields all seemed to be shaking and singing to the measures of this wild merry song with its shouts and whistles and clapping. Levin felt envious of this health and mirthfulness; he longed to take part in the expression of this joy of life. But he could do nothing, and had to lie and look on and listen. When the peasants, with their singing, had vanished out of sight and hearing, a weary feeling of despondency at his own isolation, his physical inactivity, his alienation from this world, came over Levin.

Some of the very peasants who had been most active in wrangling with him over the hay, some whom he had treated with contumely, and who had tried to cheat him, those very peasants had greeted him good-humoredly, and evidently had not, were incapable of having any feeling of rancor against him, any regret, any recollection even of having tried to deceive him. All that was drowned in a sea of merry common labor. God gave the day, God gave the strength. And the day and the strength were consecrated to labor, and that labor was its own reward. For whom the labor? What would be its fruits? These were idle considerations—beside the point.

Often Levin had admired this life, often he had a sense of envy of the men who led this life; but to-day for the first time, especially under the influence of what he had seen in the attitude of Ivan Parmenov to his young wife, the idea presented itself definitely to his mind that it was in his power to exchange the dreary, artificial, idle, and individualistic life he was leading for this laborious, pure, and social delightful life.

The old man who had been sitting beside him had long ago gone home; the people had all separated. Those who lived near had gone home, while those who came from far were gathered into a group for supper, and to spend the night in the meadow. Levin, unobserved by the peasants, still lay on the haycock, and

still looked on and listened and mused. The peasants who remained for the night in the meadow scarcely slept all the short
summer night. At first there was the sound of merry talk and
laughing all together over the supper, then singing again and
laughter.

All the long day of toil had left no trace in them but lightness
of heart. Before the early dawn all was hushed. Nothing was to
be heard but the night sounds of the frogs that never ceased in
the marsh, and the horses snorting in the mist that rose over the
meadow before the morning. Rousing himself, Levin got up
from the haycock, and looking at the stars, he saw that the night
was over.

"Well, what am I going to do? How am I to set about it?" he
said to himself, trying to express to himself all the thoughts and
feelings he had passed through in that brief night. All the
thoughts and feelings he had passed through fell into three separate trains of thought. One was the renunciation of his old life,
of his utterly useless education. This renunciation gave him
satisfaction, and was easy and simple. Another series of thoughts
and mental images related to the life he longed to live now. The
simplicity, the purity, the sanity of this life he felt clearly, and
he was convinced he would find in it the content, the peace, and
the dignity, of the lack of which he was so miserably conscious.
But a third series of ideas turned upon the question how to effect
this transition from the old life to the new. And there nothing
took clear shape for him. "Have a wife? Have work and the necessity of work? Leave Pokrovskoe? Buy land? Become a member of a peasant community? Marry a peasant girl? How am I to
set about it?" he asked himself again, and could not find an
answer. "I haven't slept all night, though, and I can't think it
out clearly," he said to himself. "I'll work it out later. One thing's
certain, this night has decided my fate. All my old dreams of
home-life were absurd, not the real thing," he told himself. "It's
all ever so much simpler and better. . . ."

"How beautiful!" he thought, looking at the strange, as it
were, mother-of-pearl shell of white fleecy cloudlets resting right
over his head in the middle of the sky. "How exquisite it all is
in this exquisite night! And when was there time for that cloud-
shell to form? Just now I looked at the sky, and there was noth-

ing in it—only two white streaks. Yes, and so imperceptibly too my views of life changed!"

He went out of the meadow and walked along the highroad towards the village. A slight wind arose, and the sky looked gray and sullen. The gloomy moment had come that usually precedes the dawn, the full triumph of light over darkness.

Shrinking from the cold, Levin walked rapidly, looking at the ground. "What's that? Some one coming," he thought, catching the tinkle of bells, and lifting his head. Forty paces from him a carriage with four horses harnessed abreast was driving towards him along the grassy highroad on which he was walking. The shaft-horses were tilted against the shafts by the ruts, but the dexterous driver sitting on the box held the shaft over the ruts, so that the wheels ran on the smooth part of the road.

This was all Levin noticed, and without wondering who it could be, he gazed absently at the coach.

In the coach was an old lady dozing in one corner, and at the window, evidently only just awake, sat a young girl holding in both hands the ribbons of a white cap. With a face full of light and thought, full of a subtle, complex inner life, that was remote from Levin, she was gazing beyond him at the glow of the sunrise.

At the very instant when this apparition was vanishing, the truthful eyes glanced at him. She recognized him, and her face lighted up with wondering delight.

He could not be mistaken. There were no other eyes like those in the world. There was only one creature in the world that could concentrate for him all the brightness and meaning of life. It was she. It was Kitty. He understood that she was driving to Ergushovo from the railway station. And everything that had been stirring Levin during that sleepless night, all the resolutions he had made, all vanished at once. He recalled with horror his dreams of marrying a peasant girl. There only, in the carriage that had crossed over to the other side of the road, and was rapidly disappearing, there only could he find the solution of the riddle of his life, which had weighed so agonizingly upon him of late.

She did not look out again. The sound of the carriage-springs was no longer audible, the bells could scarcely be heard. The barking of dogs showed the carriage had reached the village, and all that was left was the empty fields all round, the village in front, and he himself isolated and apart from it all, wandering lonely along the deserted highroad.

He glanced at the sky, expecting to find there the cloud-shell he had been admiring and taking as the symbol of the ideas and feelings of that night. There was nothing in the sky in the least like a shell. There, in the remote heights above, a mysterious change had been accomplished. There was no trace of shell, and there was stretched over fully half the sky an even cover of tiny and ever tinier cloudlets. The sky had grown blue and bright; and with the same softness, but with the same remoteness, it met his questioning gaze.

"No," he said to himself, "however good that life of simplicity and toil may be, I cannot go back to it. I love *her*."

CHAPTER XIII

NONE but those who were most intimate with Alexey Alexandrovitch knew that, while on the surface the coldest and most reasonable of men, he had one weakness quite opposed to the general trend of his character. Alexey Alexandrovitch could not hear or see a child or woman crying without being moved. The sight of tears threw him into a state of nervous agitation, and he utterly lost all power of reflection. The chief secretary of his department and his private secretary were aware of this, and used to warn women who came with petitions on no account to give way to tears, if they did not want to ruin their chances. "He will get angry, and will not listen to you," they used to say. And as a fact, in such cases the emotional disturbance set up in Alexey Alexandrovitch by the sight of tears found expression in hasty anger. "I can do nothing. Kindly leave the room!" he would commonly cry in such cases.

When returning from the races Anna had informed him of her relations with Vronsky, and immediately afterwards had burst into tears, hiding her face in her hands, Alexey Alexandrovitch, for all the fury aroused in him against her, was aware at the same time of a rush of that emotional disturbance always produced in him by tears. Conscious of it, and conscious that any expression of his feelings at that minute would be out of keeping with the position, he tried to suppress every manifestation of life in himself, and so neither stirred nor looked at her. This was what had caused that strange expression of deathlike rigidity in his face which had so impressed Anna.

When they reached the house he helped her to get out of the carriage, and making an effort to master himself, took leave of her with his usual urbanity, and uttered that phrase that bound him to nothing; he said that to-morrow he would let her know his decision.

His wife's words, confirming his worst suspicions, had sent a cruel pang to the heart of Alexey Alexandrovitch. That pang was intensified by the strange feeling of physical pity for her set up by her tears. But when he was all alone in the carriage Alexey Alexandrovitch, to his surprise and delight, felt complete relief both from this pity and from the doubts and agonies of jealousy.

He experienced the sensations of a man who has had a tooth out after suffering long from toothache. After a fearful agony and a sense of something huge, bigger than the head itself, being torn out of his jaw, the sufferer, hardly able to believe in his own good luck, feels all at once that what has so long poisoned his existence and enchained his attention, exists no longer, and that he can live and think again, and take interest in other things besides his tooth. This feeling Alexey Alexandrovitch was experiencing. The agony had been strange and terrible, but now it was over; he felt that he could live again and think of something other than his wife.

"No honor, no heart, no religion; a corrupt woman. I always knew it and always saw it, though I tried to deceive myself to spare her," he said to himself. And it actually seemed to him that he always had seen it: he recalled incidents of their past life, in which he had never seen anything wrong before—now these incidents proved clearly that she had always been a corrupt woman. "I made a mistake in linking my life to hers; but there was nothing wrong in my mistake, and so I cannot be unhappy. It's not I that am to blame," he told himself, "but she. But I have nothing to do with her. She does not exist for me. . . ."

Everything relating to her and her son, towards whom his sentiments were as much changed as towards her, ceased to interest him. The only thing that interested him now was the question of in what way he could best, with most propriety and comfort for himself, and thus with most justice, extricate himself from the mud with which she had spattered him in her fall, and then proceed along his path of active, honorable, and useful existence.

"I cannot be made unhappy by the fact that a contemptible woman has committed a crime. I have only to find the best way out of the difficult position in which she has placed me. And I shall find it," he said to himself, frowning more and more. "I'm not the first nor the last." And to say nothing of historical instances dating from the "Fair Helen" of Menelaus, recently revived in the memory of all, a whole list of contemporary examples of husbands with unfaithful wives in the highest society rose before Alexey Alexandrovitch's imagination. "Daryalov, Poltavsky, Prince Karibanov, Count Paskudin, Dram . . . Yes, even Dram, such an honest, capable fellow. . . . Semyonov, Tchagin, Sigonin," Alexey Alexandrovitch remembered. "Admitting that a certain quite irrational *ridicule* falls to the lot of these men, yet I never saw anything but a misfortune in it, and always felt sympathy for it," Alexey Alexandrovitch said to himself, though indeed this was not the fact, and he had never felt sympathy for misfortunes of that kind, but the more frequently he had heard of instances of unfaithful wives betraying their husbands, the more highly he had thought of himself. "It is a misfortune which may befall any one. And this misfortune has befallen me. The only thing to be done is to make the best of the position."

And he began passing in review the methods of proceeding of men who had been in the same position that he was in.

"Daryalov fought a duel. . . ."

The duel had particularly fascinated the thoughts of Alexey Alexandrovitch in his youth, just because he was physically a coward, and was himself well aware of the fact. Alexey Alexandrovitch could not without horror contemplate the idea of a pistol aimed at himself, and never made use of any weapon in his life. This horror had in his youth set him pondering on dueling, and picturing himself in a position in which he would have to expose his life to danger. Having attained success and an established position in the world, he had long ago forgotten this feeling; but the habitual bent of feeling reasserted itself, and dread of his own cowardice proved even now so strong that Alexey Alexandrovitch spent a long while thinking over the question of dueling in all its aspects, and hugging the idea of a duel, though he was fully aware beforehand that he would never under any circumstances fight one.

"There's no doubt our society is still so barbarous (it's not the same in England) that very many"—and among these were those whose opinion Alexey Alexandrovitch particularly valued —"look favorably on the duel; but what result is attained by it? Suppose I call him out," Alexey Alexandrovitch went on to himself, and vividly picturing the night he would spend after the challenge, and the pistol aimed at him, he shuddered, and knew that he never would do it—"suppose I call him out. Suppose I am taught," he went on musing, "to shoot; I press the trigger," he said to himself, closing his eyes, "and it turns out I have killed him," Alexey Alexandrovitch said to himself, and he shook his head as though to dispel such silly ideas. "What sense is there in murdering a man in order to define one's relation to a guilty wife and son? I should still just as much have to decide what I ought to do with her. But what is more probable and what would doubtless occur—I should be killed or wounded. I, the innocent person, should be the victim—killed or wounded. It's even more senseless. But apart from that, a challenge to fight would be an act hardly honest on my side. Don't I know perfectly well that my friends would never allow me to fight a duel—would never allow the life of a statesman, needed by Russia, to be exposed to danger? Knowing perfectly well beforehand that the matter would never come to real danger, it would amount to my simply trying to gain a certain sham reputation by such a challenge. That would be dishonest, that would be false, that would be deceiving myself and others. A duel is quite irrational, and no one expects it of me. My aim is simply to safeguard my reputation, which is essential for the uninterrupted pursuit of my public duties." Official duties, which had always been of great consequence in Alexey Alexandrovitch's eyes, seemed of special importance to his mind at this moment. Considering and rejecting the duel, Alexey Alexandrovitch turned to divorce—another solution selected by several of the husbands he remembered. Passing in mental review all the instances he knew of divorces (there were plenty of them in the very highest society with which he was very familiar), Alexey Alexandrovitch could not find a single example in which the object of divorce was that which he had in view. In all these instances the husband had practically ceded or sold his unfaithful wife, and the very party which, being in fault, had not the right to contract a fresh marriage, had formed counterfeit, pseudo-matrimonial ties with a self-styled husband. In his own case, Alexey Alexandrovitch saw that a legal divorce, that is to say, one in which only the guilty wife would be repudiated, was impossible of attainment. He saw that the complex conditions of the life they led made the coarse proofs of his wife's guilt, required by the law, out of the question; he saw that a certain refinement in that life would not admit of such proofs being brought forward, even if he had them, and that to bring forward such proofs would damage him in the public estimation more than it would her.

An attempt at divorce could lead to nothing but a public scandal, which would be a perfect godsend to his enemies for calumny and attacks on his high position in society. His chief object, to define the position with the least amount of disturbance possible, would not be attained by divorce either. Moreover, in the event of divorce, or even of an attempt to obtain a divorce, it was obvious that the wife broke off all relations with the husband and threw in her lot with the lover. And in spite of the complete, as he supposed, contempt and indifference he now felt for his wife, at the bottom of his heart, Alexey Alexandrovitch still had one feeling left in regard to her—a disinclination to see her free to throw in her lot with Vronsky, so that her crime would be to her advantage. The mere notion of this so exasperated Alexey Alexandrovitch, that directly it rose to his mind he groaned with inward agony, and got up and changed his place in the carriage, and for a long while after, he sat with scowling brows, wrapping his numbed and bony legs in the fleecy rug.

"Apart from formal divorce, one might still do like Karibanov, Paskudin, and that good fellow Dram—that is, separate from one's wife," he went on thinking, when he had regained his composure. But this step too presented the same drawback of public scandal as a divorce, and what was more, a separation, quite as much as a regular divorce, flung his wife into the arms of Vronsky. "No, it's out of the question, out of the question!" he said again, twisting his rug about him again. "I cannot be unhappy, but neither she nor he ought to be happy."

The feeling of jealousy, which had tortured him during the period of uncertainty, had passed away at the instant when the tooth had been with agony extracted by his wife's words. But that feeling had been replaced by another, the desire, not merely that she should not be triumphant, but that she should get due punishment for her crime. He did not acknowledge this feeling, but at the bottom of his heart he longed for her to suffer for having destroyed his peace of mind—his honor. And going once again over the conditions inseparable from a duel, a divorce, a separation, and once again rejecting them, Alexey Alexandrovitch felt convinced that there was only one solution,—to keep her with him, concealing what had happened from the world, and using every measure in his power to break off the intrigue, and still more—though this he did not admit to himself—to punish her. "I must inform her of my conclusion, that thinking over the terrible position in which she has placed her family, all other solutions will be worse for both sides than an external *status quo,* and that such I agree to retain, on the strict condition of obedience on her part to my wishes, that is to say, cessation of all intercourse with her lover." When this decision had been

339

finally adopted, another weighty consideration occurred to Alexey Alexandrovitch in support of it. "By such a course only shall I be acting in accordance with the dictates of religion," he told himself. "In adopting this course, I am not casting off a guilty wife, but giving her a chance of amendment; and, indeed, difficult as the task will be to me, I shall devote part of my energies to her reformation and salvation."

Though Alexey Alexandrovitch was perfectly aware that he could not exert any moral influence over his wife, that such an attempt at reformation could lead to nothing but falsity; though in passing through these difficult moments he had not once thought of seeking guidance in religion, yet now, when his conclusion corresponded, as it seemed to him, with the requirements of religion, this religious sanction to his decision gave him complete satisfaction, and to some extent restored his peace of mind. He was pleased to think that, even in such an important crisis in life, no one would be able to say that he had not acted in accordance with the principles of that religion whose banner he had always held aloft amid the general coolness and indifference. As he pondered over subsequent developments, Alexey Alexandrovitch did not see, indeed, why his relations with his wife should not remain practically the same as before. No doubt, she could never regain his esteem, but there was not, and there could not be, any sort of reason that his existence should be troubled, and that he should suffer because she was a bad and faithless wife. "Yes, time will pass; time, which arranges all things, and the old relations will be reëstablished," Alexey Alexandrovitch told himself; "so far reëstablished, that is, that I shall not be sensible of a break in the continuity of my life. She is bound to be unhappy, but I am not to blame, and so I cannot be unhappy."

CHAPTER XIV

As HE neared Petersburg, Alexey Alexandrovitch not only adhered entirely to his decision, but was even composing in his head the letter he would write to his wife. Going into the porter's room, Alexey Alexandrovitch glanced at the letters and papers brought from his office, and directed that they should be brought to him in his study.

"The horses can be taken out and I will see no one," he said in answer to the porter, with a certain pleasure, indicative of his agreeable frame of mind, emphasizing the words, "see no one."

In his study Alexey Alexandrovitch walked up and down twice, and stopped at an immense writing-table, on which six candles had already been lighted by the valet who had preceded him. He cracked his knuckles, and sat down, sorting out his writing appurtenances. Putting his elbows on the table, he bent his head on one side, thought a minute, and began to write, without pausing for a second. He wrote without using any form of address to her, and wrote in French, making use of the plural *"vous,"* which has not the same note of coldness as the corresponding Russian form.

"At our last conversation, I notified you of my intention to communicate to you my decision in regard to the subject of that conversation. Having carefully considered everything, I am writing now with the object of fulfilling that promise. My decision is as follows. Whatever your conduct may have been, I do not consider myself justified in breaking the ties in which we are bound by a Higher Power. The family cannot be broken up by a whim, a caprice, or even by the sin of one of the partners in the marriage, and our life must go on as it has done in the past. This is essential for me, for you, and for our son. I am fully persuaded that you have repented and do repent of what has called forth the present letter, and that you will coöperate with me in eradicating the cause of our estrangement, and forgetting the past. In the contrary event, you can conjecture what awaits you and your son. All this I hope to discuss more in detail in a personal interview. As the season is drawing to a close, I would beg you to return to Petersburg as quickly as possible, not later than Tuesday. All necessary preparations shall be made for your arrival here. I beg you to note that I attach particular significance to compliance with this request.

A. Karenin

"P.S.—I enclose the money which may be needed for your expenses."

341

He read the letter through and felt pleased with it, and especially that he had remembered to enclose money: there was not a harsh word, not a reproach in it, nor was there undue indulgence. Most of all, it was a golden bridge for return. Folding the letter and smoothing it with a massive ivory knife, and putting it in an envelope with the money, he rang the bell with the gratification it always afforded him to use the well-arranged appointments of his writing-table.

"Give this to the courier to be delivered to Anna Arkadyevna to-morrow at the summer villa," he said, getting up.

"Certainly, your excellency; tea to be served in the study?"

Alexey Alexandrovitch ordered tea to be brought to the study, and playing with the massive paper-knife, he moved to his easy-chair, near which there had been placed ready for him a lamp and the French work on Egyptian hieroglyphics that he had begun. Over the easy-chair there hung in a gold frame an oval portrait of Anna, a fine painting by a celebrated artist. Alexey Alexandrovitch glanced at it. The unfathomable eyes gazed ironically and insolently at him. Insufferably insolent and challenging was the effect in Alexey Alexandrovitch's eyes of the black lace about the head, admirably touched in by the painter, the black hair and handsome white hand with one finger lifted, covered with rings. After looking at the portrait for a minute, Alexey Alexandrovitch shuddered so that his lips quivered and he uttered the sound "brrr," and turned away. He made haste to sit down in his easy-chair and opened the book. He tried to read, but he could not revive the very vivid interest he had felt before in Egyptian hieroglyphics. He looked at the book and thought of something else. He thought not of his wife, but of a complication that had arisen in his official life, which at the time constituted the chief interest of it. He felt that he had penetrated more deeply than ever before into this intricate affair, and that he had originated a leading idea—he could say it without self-flattery—calculated to clear up the whole business, to strengthen him in his official career, to discomfit his enemies, and thereby to be of the greatest benefit to the government. Directly the servant had set the tea and left the room, Alexey Alexandrovitch got up and went to the writing-table. Moving into the middle of the table a portfolio of papers, with a scarcely perceptible smile of self-satisfaction, he took a pencil from a rack and plunged into the perusal of a complex report relating to the present complication. The complication was of this nature: Alexey Alexandrovitch's characteristic quality as a politician, that special individual qualification that every rising functionary possesses, the qualification that with his unflagging ambition, his reserve, his honesty, and his self-confidence had made his career, was his contempt for red tape, his cutting down of correspondence, his direct contact, wherever possible, with the living fact, and his economy. It happened that the famous Commission of the 2nd of June had set on foot an inquiry into the irrigation of lands in the Zaraisky province, which fell under Alexey Alexandrovitch's department, and was a glaring example of fruitless expenditure and paper reforms. Alexey Alexandrovitch was aware of the truth of this. The irrigation of these lands in the Zaraisky province had been initiated by the predecessor of Alexey Alexandrovitch's predecessor. And vast sums of money had actually been spent and were still being spent on this business, and utterly unproductively, and the whole business could obviously lead to nothing whatever. Alexey Alexandrovitch had perceived this at once on entering office, and would have liked to lay hands on the Board of Irrigation. But at first, when he did not yet feel secure in his position, he knew it would affect too many interests, and would be injudicious. Later on he had been engrossed in other questions, and had simply forgotten the Board of Irrigation. It went of itself, like all such boards, by the mere force of inertia. (Many people gained their livelihood by the Board of Irrigation, especially one highly conscientious and musical family: all the daughters played on stringed instruments, and Alexey Alexandrovitch knew the family and had stood godfather to one of the elder daughters.) The raising of this question by a hostile department was in Alexey Alexandrovitch's opinion a dishonorable proceeding, seeing that in every department there were things similar and worse, which no one inquired into, for well-known reasons of official etiquette. However, now that the glove had been thrown down to him, he had boldly picked it up and demanded the appointment of a special commission to investigate and verify the working of the Board of Irrigation of the lands in the Zaraisky province. But in compensation he gave no quarter to the enemy either. He demanded the appointment of another special commission to inquire into the question of the Native Tribes Organization Committee. The question of the Native Tribes had been brought up incidentally in the Commission of the 2nd of June, and had been pressed forward actively by Alexey Alexandrovitch as one admitting of no delay on account of the deplorable condition of the native tribes. In the commission this question had been a ground of contention between several departments. The department hostile to Alexey Alexandrovitch proved that the condition of the native tribes was exceedingly flourishing, that the proposed reconstruction might be the ruin of their prosperity, and that if there were anything wrong, it arose mainly from the failure on the part of Alexey Alexandrovitch's department to carry out the measures prescribed by law. Now Alexey Alexandrovitch intended to demand: First, that a new commission should be formed which should be empowered to investigate the condition of the native tribes on the spot; secondly, if it should appear that the condition of the native tribes actually was such as it appeared to be from the official documents in the hands of the committee, that another new scientific commission should be appointed to investigate the deplorable condition of the native tribes from the—(1) political, (2) administrative, (3) economic, (4) ethnographical, (5) material, and (6) religious points of view; thirdly, that evidence should be required from the rival department of the measures that had been taken during the last ten years by that department for averting the disastrous conditions in which the native tribes were now placed; and fourthly and finally, that that department be asked to explain why it had, as appeared from the evidence before the committee, from No. 17,015 and 18,308, from December 5, 1863, and June 7, 1864, acted in direct contravention of the intention of the law T . . . Act 18, and the note to Act 36. A flash of eagerness suffused the face of Alexey Alexandrovitch as he rapidly wrote out a synopsis of these ideas for his own benefit. Having filled a sheet of paper, he got up, rang, and sent a note to the chief secretary of his department to look up certain necessary facts for him. Getting up and walking about the room, he glanced again at the portrait, frowned and smiled contemptuously. After reading a little more of the book on Egyptian hieroglyphics, and renewing his interest in it, Alexey Alexandrovitch went to bed at eleven o'clock, and recollecting as he lay in bed the incident with his wife, he saw it now in by no means such a gloomy light.

CHAPTER XV

THOUGH Anna had obstinately and with exasperation contradicted Vronsky when he told her their position was impossible, at the bottom of her heart she regarded her own position as false and dishonorable, and she longed with her whole soul to change it. On the way home from the races she had told her husband the truth in a moment of excitement, and in spite of the agony she had suffered in doing so, she was glad of it. After her husband had left her, she told herself that she was glad, that now everything was made clear, and at least there would be no more lying and deception. It seemed to her beyond doubt that her position was now made clear forever. It might be bad, this new position, but it would be clear; there would be no indefiniteness or falsehood about it. The pain she had caused herself and her husband in uttering those words would be rewarded now by everything being made clear, she thought. That evening she saw Vronsky, but she did not tell him of what had passed between her and her husband, though, to make the position definite, it was necessary to tell him.

When she woke up next morning the first thing that rose to her mind was what she had said to her husband, and those words seemed to her so awful that she could not conceive now how she could have brought herself to utter those strange, coarse words, and could not imagine what would come of it. But the words were spoken, and Alexey Alexandrovitch had gone away without saying anything. "I saw Vronsky and did not tell him. At the very instant he was going away I would have turned him back and told him, but I changed my mind, because it was strange that I had not told him the first minute. Why was it I wanted to tell him and did not tell him?" And in answer to this question a burning blush of shame spread over her face. She knew what had kept her from it, she knew that she had been ashamed. Her position, which had seemed to her simplified the night before, suddenly struck her now as not only not simple, but as absolutely hopeless. She felt terrified at the disgrace, of which she had not ever thought before. Directly she thought of what her husband would do, the most terrible ideas came to her mind. She had a vision of being turned out of the house, of her shame being proclaimed to all the world. She asked herself where she should go when she was turned out of the house, and she could not find an answer.

When she thought of Vronsky, it seemed to her that he did not love her, that he was already beginning to be tired of her, that she could not offer herself to him, and she felt bitter against him for it. It seemed to her that the words that she had spoken to her husband, and had continually repeated in her imagination, she had said to every one, and every one had heard them. She could not bring herself to look those of her own household in the face. She could not bring herself to call her maid, and still less go down-stairs and see her son and his governess.

The maid, who had been listening at her door for a long while, came into her room of her own accord. Anna glanced inquiringly into her face, and blushed with a scared look. The maid begged her pardon for coming in, saying that she had fancied the bell rang. She brought her clothes and a note. The note was from Betsy. Betsy reminded her that Liza Merkalova and Baroness Shtoltz were coming to play croquet with her that morning with their adorers, Kaluzhsky and old Stremov. "Come, if only as a study in morals. I shall expect you," she finished.

Anna read the note and heaved a deep sigh.

"Nothing, I need nothing," she said to Annushka, who was rearranging the bottles and brushes on the dressing-table. "You can go. I'll dress at once and come down. I need nothing."

Annushka went out, but Anna did not begin dressing, and sat in the same position, her head and hands hanging listlessly, and every now and then she shivered all over, seemed as though she would make some gesture, utter some word, and sank back into lifelessness again. She repeated continually, "My God! my God!" But neither "God" nor "my" had any meaning to her. The idea of seeking help in her difficulty in religion was as remote from her as seeking help from Alexey Alexandrovitch himself, although she had never had doubts of the faith in which she had been brought up. She knew that the support of religion was possible only upon condition of renouncing what made up for her the whole meaning of life. She was not simply miserable, she began to feel alarm at the new spiritual condition, never experienced before, in which she found herself. She felt as though everything were beginning to be double in her soul, just as objects sometimes appear double to over-tired eyes. She hardly knew at times what it was she feared, and what she hoped for. Whether she feared or desired what had happened, or what was going to happen, and exactly what she longed for, she could not have said.

"Ah, what am I doing!" she said to herself, feeling a sudden thrill of pain in both sides of her head. When she came to herself, she saw that she was holding her hair in both hands, each side of her temples, and pulling it. She jumped up, and began walking about.

"The coffee is ready, and mademoiselle and Seryozha are waiting," said Annushka, coming back again and finding Anna in the same position.

"Seryozha? What about Seryozha?" Anna asked, with sudden eagerness, recollecting her son's existence for the first time that morning.

"He's been naughty, I think," answered Annushka with a smile.

"In what way?"

"Some peaches were lying on the table in the corner room. I think he slipped in and ate one of them on the sly."

The recollection of her son suddenly roused Anna from the helpless condition in which she found herself. She recalled the partly sincere, though greatly exaggerated, rôle of the mother living for her child, which she had taken up of late years, and she felt with joy that in the plight in which she found herself she had a support, quite apart from her relation to her husband or to Vronsky. This support was her son. In whatever position she might be placed, she could not lose her son. Her husband might put her to shame and turn her out, Vronsky might grow cold to her and go on living his own life apart (she thought of him again with bitterness and reproach) ; she could not leave her son. She had an aim in life. And she must act; act to secure this relation to her son, so that he might not be taken from her. Quickly indeed, as quickly as possible, she must take action before he was taken from her. She must take her son and go away. Here was the one thing she had to do now. She needed consolation. She must be calm, and get out of this insufferable position. The thought of immediate action binding her to her son, of going away somewhere with him, gave her this consolation.

She dressed quickly, went down-stairs, and with resolute steps walked into the drawing-room, where she found, as usual, waiting for her, the coffee, Seryozha, and his governess. Seryozha, all in white, with his back and head bent, was standing at a table under a looking-glass, and with an expression of intense concentration which she knew well, and in which he resembled his father, he was doing something to the flowers he carried.

The governess had a particularly severe expression. Seryozha screamed shrilly, as he often did, "Ah, mamma!" and stopped, hesitating whether to go to greet his mother and put down the flowers, or to finish making the wreath and go with the flowers.

The governess, after saying good-morning, began a long and detailed account of Seryozha's naughtiness, but Anna did not hear her; she was considering whether she would take her with her or not. "No, I won't take her," she decided. "I'll go alone with my child."

"Yes, it's very wrong," said Anna, and taking her son by the shoulder she looked at him, not severely, but with a timid glance that bewildered and delighted the boy, and she kissed him. "Leave him to me," she said to the astonished governess, and not letting go of her son, she sat down at the table, where coffee was set ready for her.

"Mamma! I . . . I . . . didn't . . ." he said, trying to make out from her expression what was in store for him in regard to the peaches.

"Seryozha," she said, as soon as the governess had left the room, "that was wrong, but you'll never do it again, will you? . . . You love me?"

She felt that the tears were coming into her eyes. "Can I help loving him?" she said to herself, looking deeply into his scared and at the same time delighted eyes. "And can he ever join his father in punishing me? Is it possible he will not feel for me?" Tears were already flowing down her face, and to hide them she got up abruptly and almost ran out on to the terrace.

After the thunder-showers of the last few days, cold, bright weather had set in. The air was cold in the bright sun that filtered through the freshly washed leaves.

She shivered, both from the cold and from the inward horror which had clutched her with fresh force in the open air.

"Run along, run along to Mariette," she said to Seryozha, who had followed her out, and she began walking up and down on the straw matting of the terrace. "Can it be that they won't forgive me, won't understand how it all couldn't be helped?" she said to herself.

Standing still, and looking at the tops of the aspen-trees waving in the wind, with their freshly washed, brightly shining leaves in the cold sunshine, she knew that they would not forgive her, that every one and everything would be merciless to her now as was that sky, that green. And again she felt that everything was split in two in her soul. "I mustn't, mustn't think," she said to herself. "I must get ready. To go where? When? Whom to take with me? Yes, to Moscow by the evening train. Annushka and Seryozha, and only the most necessary things. But first I must write to them both." She went quickly indoors into her boudoir, sat down at the table, and wrote to her husband:— "After what has happened, I cannot remain any longer in your house. I am going away, and taking my son with me. I don't know the law, and so I don't know with which of the parents the son should remain; but I take him with me because I cannot live without him. Be generous, leave him me."

Up to this point she wrote rapidly and naturally, but the appeal to his generosity, a quality she did not recognize in him, and the necessity of winding up the letter with something touching, pulled her up. "Of my fault and my remorse I cannot speak, because . . ."

She stopped again, finding no connection in her ideas. "No," she said to herself, "there's no need of anything," and tearing up the letter, she wrote it again, leaving out the allusion to generosity, and sealed it up.

Another letter had to be written to Vronsky. "I have told my husband," she wrote, and she sat a long while unable to write more. It was so coarse, so unfeminine. "And what more am I to write him?" she said to herself. Again a flush of shame spread over her face; she recalled his composure, and a feeling of anger against him impelled her to tear the sheet with the phrase she had written into tiny bits. "No need of anything," she said to herself, and closing her blotting-case she went up-stairs, told the governess and the servants that she was going that day to Moscow, and at once set to work to pack up her things.

CHAPTER XVI

ALL the rooms of the summer villa were full of porters, gardeners, and footmen going to and fro carrying out things. Cupboards and chests were open; twice they had sent to the shop for cord; pieces of newspaper were tossing about on the floor. Two trunks, some bags and strapped-up rugs, had been carried down into the hall. The carriage and two hired cabs were waiting at the steps. Anna, forgetting her inward agitation in the work of packing, was standing at a table in her boudoir, packing her traveling-bag, when Annushka called her attention to the rattle of some carriage driving up. Anna looked out of the window and saw Alexey Alexandrovitch's courier on the steps, ringing at the front door bell.

"Run and find out what it is," she said, and with a calm sense of being prepared for anything, she sat down in a low chair, folding her hands on her knees. A footman brought in a thick packet directed in Alexey Alexandrovitch's hand.

"The courier had orders to wait for an answer," he said.

"Very well," she said, and as soon as he had left the room she tore open the letter with trembling fingers. A roll of unfolded notes done up in a wrapper fell out of it. She disengaged the letter and began reading it at the end. "Preparations shall be made for your arrival here. . . . I attach particular significance to compliance . . ." she read. She ran on, then back, read it all through, and once more read the letter all through again from the beginning. When she had finished, she felt that she was cold all over, and that a fearful calamity, such as she had not expected, had burst upon her.

In the morning she had regretted that she had spoken to her husband, and wished for nothing so much as that those words could be unspoken. And here this letter regarded them as unspoken, and gave her what she had wanted. But now this letter seemed to her more awful than anything she had been able to conceive.

"He's right!" she said; "of course, he's always right; he's a Christian, he's generous! Yes, vile, base creature! And no one understands it except me, and no one ever will; and I can't explain it. They say he's so religious, so high-principled, so upright, so clever; but they don't see what I've seen. They don't know how he has crushed my life for eight years, crushed everything that was living in me—he has not once even thought that I'm a live woman who must have love. They don't know how at every step he's humiliated me, and been just as pleased with himself. Haven't I striven, striven with all my strength, to find something to give meaning to my life? Haven't I struggled to love him, to love my son when I could not love my husband? But the time came when I knew that I couldn't cheat myself any longer, that I was alive, that I was not to blame, that God has made me so that I must love and live. And now what does he do? If he'd killed me, if he'd killed him, I could have borne anything, I could have forgiven anything; but, no, he . . . How was it I didn't guess what he would do? He's doing just what's characteristic of his mean character. He'll keep himself in the right, while me, in my ruin, he'll drive still lower to worse ruin yet. . . ."

She recalled the words from the letter. "You can conjecture what awaits you and your son. . . ." "That's a threat to take away my child, and most likely by their stupid law he can. But I know very well why he says it. He doesn't believe even in my love for my child, or he despises it (just as he always used to ridicule it). He despises that feeling in me, but he knows that I won't abandon my child, that I can't abandon my child, that there could be no life for me without my child, even with him whom I love; but that if I abandoned my child and ran away from him, I should be acting like the most infamous, basest of

351

women. He knows that, and knows that I am incapable of doing that."

She recalled another sentence in the letter. "Our life must go on as it has done in the past. . . ." "That life was miserable enough in old days; it has been awful of late. What will it be now? And he knows all that; he knows that I can't repent that I breathe, that I love; he knows that it can lead to nothing but lying and deceit; but he wants to go on torturing me. I know him; I know that he's at home and is happy in deceit, like a fish swimming in the water. No, I won't give him that happiness. I'll break through the spiderweb of lies in which he wants to catch me, come what may. Anything's better than lying and deceit.

"But how? My God! my God! Was ever a woman so miserable as I am? . . .

"No; I will break through it, I will break through it!" she cried, jumping up and keeping back her tears. And she went to the writing-table to write him another letter. But at the bottom of her heart she felt that she was not strong enough to break through anything, that she was not strong enough to get out of her old position, however false and dishonorable it might be.

She sat down at the writing-table, but instead of writing she clasped her hands on the table, and, laying her head on them, burst into tears, with sobs and heaving breast like a child crying. She was weeping that her dream of her position being made clear and definite had been annihilated forever. She knew beforehand that everything would go on in the old way, and far worse, indeed, than in the old way. She felt that the position in the world that she enjoyed, and that had seemed to her of so little consequence in the morning, that this position was precious to

her, that she would not have the strength to exchange it for the shameful position of a woman who has abandoned husband and child to join her lover; that however much she might struggle, she could not be stronger than herself. She would never know freedom in love, but would remain forever a guilty wife, with the menace of detection hanging over her at every instant; deceiving her husband for the sake of a shameful connection with a man living apart and away from her, whose life she could never share. She knew that this was how it would be, and at the same time it was so awful that she could not even conceive what it would end in. And she cried without restraint, as children cry when they are punished.

The sound of the footman's steps forced her to rouse herself, and hiding her face from him, she pretended to be writing.

"The courier asks if there's an answer," the footman announced.

"An answer? Yes," said Anna. "Let him wait. I'll ring."

"What can I write?" she thought. "What can I decide upon alone? What do I know? What do I want? What is there I care for?" Again she felt that her soul was beginning to be split in two. She was terrified again at this feeling, and clutched at the first pretext for doing something which might divert her thoughts from herself. "I ought to see Alexey" (so she called Vronsky in her thoughts); "no one but he can tell me what I ought to do. I'll go to Betsy's, perhaps I shall see him there," she said to herself, completely forgetting that when she had told him the day before that she was not going to Princess Tverskaya's, he had said that in that case he should not go either. She went up to the table, wrote to her husband, "I have received your letter.— A."; and, ringing the bell, gave it to the footman.

"We are not going," she said to Annushka, as she came in.

"Not going at all?"

"No; don't unpack till to-morrow, and let the carriage wait. I'm going to the princess's."

"Which dress am I to get ready?"

THE croquet party to which the Princess Tverskaya had invited Anna was to consist of two ladies and their adorers. These two ladies were the chief representatives of a select new Petersburg circle, nicknamed, in imitation of some imitation, *les sept merveilles du monde.* These ladies belonged to a circle which, though of the highest society, was utterly hostile to that in which Anna moved. Moreover, Stremov, one of the most influential people in Petersburg, and the elderly admirer of Liza Merkalova, was Alexey Alexandrovitch's enemy in the political world. From all these considerations Anna had not meant to go, and the hints in Princess Tverskaya's note referred to her refusal. But now Anna was eager to go, in the hope of seeing Vronsky.

Anna arrived at Princess Tverskaya's earlier than the other guests.

At the same moment as she entered, Vronsky's footman, with side-whiskers combed out like a *Kammerjunker,* went in too. He stopped at the door, and, taking off his cap, let her pass. Anna recognized him, and only then recalled that Vronsky had told her the day before that he would not come. Most likely he was sending a note to say so.

As she took off her outer garment in the hall, she heard the footman, pronouncing his *"r's"* even like a *Kammerjunker,* say, "From the count for the princess," and hand the note.

She longed to question him as to where his master was. She longed to turn back and send him a letter to come and see her, or to go herself to see him. But neither the first nor the second nor the third course was possible. Already she heard bells ringing to announce her arrival ahead of her, and Princess Tverskaya's footman was standing at the open door waiting for her to go forward into the inner rooms.

"The princess is in the garden; they will inform her immediately. Would you be pleased to walk into the garden?" announced another footman in another room.

The position of uncertainty, of indecision, was still the same as at home—worse, in fact, since it was impossible to take any step, impossible to see Vronsky, and she had to remain here among outsiders, in company so uncongenial to her present mood. But she was wearing a dress that she knew suited her. She was not alone; all around was that luxurious setting of idleness that she was used to, and she felt less wretched than at home. She was not forced to think what she was to do. Everything would be done of itself. On meeting Betsy coming towards her in a white gown that struck her by its elegance, Anna smiled to her just as she always did. Princess Tverskaya was walking with Tushkevitch and a young lady, a relation, who, to the great joy of her parents in the provinces, was spending the summer with the fashionable princess.

There was probably something unusual about Anna, for Betsy noticed it at once.

"I slept badly," answered Anna, looking intently at the footman who came to meet them, and, as she supposed, brought Vronsky's note.

"How glad I am you've come!" said Betsy. "I'm tired, and was just longing to have some tea before they come. You might go" —she turned to Tushkevitch—"with Masha, and try the croquet-ground over there where they've been cutting it. We shall have time to talk a little over tea; we'll have a cozy chat, eh?" she said in English to Anna, with a smile, pressing the hand with which she held a parasol.

"Yes, especially as I can't stay very long with you. I'm forced to go on to old Madame Vrede. I've been promising to go for a century," said Anna, to whom lying, alien as it was to her nature, had become not merely simple and natural in society, but a positive source of satisfaction. Why she said this, which she had not thought of a second before, she could not have explained. She had said it simply from the reflection that as Vronsky would not be here, she had better secure her own freedom, and try to see him somehow. But why she had spoken of old Madame Vrede, whom she had to go and see, as she had to see many other people, she could not have explained; and yet, as it afterwards turned out, had she contrived the most cunning devices to meet Vronsky, she could have thought of nothing better.

"No. I'm not going to let you go for anything," answered Betsy, looking intently into Anna's face. "Really, if I were not fond of you, I should feel offended. One would think you were afraid my society would compromise you. Tea in the little dining-room, please," she said, half closing her eyes, as she always did when addressing the footman.

Taking the note from him, she read it.

"Alexey's playing us false," she said in French; "he writes that he can't come," she added in a tone as simple and natural as though it could never enter her head that Vronsky could mean anything more to Anna than a game of croquet. Anna knew that Betsy knew everything, but, hearing how she spoke of Vronsky before her, she almost felt persuaded for a minute that she knew nothing.

"Ah!" said Anna indifferently, as though not greatly interested in the matter, and she went on smiling: "How can you or your friends compromise any one?"

This playing with words, this hiding of a secret, had a great fascination for Anna, as, indeed, it has for all women. And it was not the necessity of concealment, not the aim with which the concealment was contrived, but the process of concealment itself attracted her.

"I can't be more Catholic than the Pope," she said. "Stremov and Liza Merkalova, why, they're the cream of the cream of society. Besides, they're received everywhere, and *I*"—she laid special stress on the I—"have never been strict and intolerant. It's simply that I haven't the time.

"No; you don't care, perhaps, to meet Stremov? Let him and Alexey Alexandrovitch tilt at each other in the committee—that's no affair of ours. But in the world, he's the most amiable man I know, and a devoted croquet-player. You shall see. And, in spite of his absurd position as Liza's lovesick swain at his age, you ought to see how he carries off the absurd position. He's very nice. Sappho Shtoltz you don't know? Oh, that's a new type, quite new."

Betsy said all this, and, at the same time, from her good-humored, shrewd glance, Anna felt that she partly guessed her plight, and was hatching something for her benefit. They were in the little boudoir.

"I must write to Alexey though," and Betsy sat down to the table, scribbled a few lines, and put the note in an envelope.

"I'm telling him to come to dinner. I've one lady extra to dinner with me, and no man to take her in. Look what I've said, will that persuade him? Excuse me, I must leave you for a minute. Would you seal it up, please, and send it off?" she said from the door; "I have to give some directions."

Without a moment's thought, Anna sat down to the table with Betsy's letter, and, without reading it, wrote below: "It's essential for me to see you. Come to the Vrede garden. I shall be there at six o'clock." She sealed it up, and, Betsy coming back, in her presence handed the note to be taken.

At tea, which was brought them on a little tea-table in the cool little drawing-room, the cozy chat promised by Princess Tverskaya before the arrival of her visitors really did come off between the two women. They criticized the people they were expecting, and the conversation fell upon Liza Merkalova.

"She's very sweet, and I always liked her," said Anna.

"You ought to like her. She raves about you. Yesterday she came up to me after the races and was in despair at not finding you. She says you're a real heroine of romance, and that if she were a man she would do all sorts of mad things for your sake. Stremov says she does that as it is."

"But do tell me, please, I never could make it out," said Anna, after being silent for some time, speaking in a tone that showed she was not asking an idle question, but that what she was asking was of more importance to her than it should have been; "do tell me, please, what are her relations with Prince Kaluzhsky, Mishka, as he's called? I've met them so little. What does it mean?"

Betsy smiled with her eyes, and looked intently at Anna.

"It's a new manner," she said. "They've all adopted that manner. They've flung their caps over the windmills. But there are ways and ways of flinging them."

"Yes, but what are her relations precisely with Kaluzhsky?"

Betsy broke into unexpectedly mirthful and irrepressible laughter, a thing which rarely happened with her.

"You're encroaching on Princess Myakaya's special domain now. That's the question of an *enfant terrible*," and Betsy obviously tried to restrain herself, but could not, and went off into peals of that infectious laughter that people laugh who do not laugh often. "You'd better ask them," she brought out, between tears of laughter.

"No; you laugh," said Anna, laughing too in spite of herself, "but I never could understand it. I can't understand the husband's rôle in it."

"The husband? Liza Merkalova's husband carries her shawl, and is always ready to be of use. But anything more than that in reality, no one cares to inquire. You know in decent society one doesn't talk or think even of certain details of the toilet. That's how it is with this."

"Will you be at Madame Rolandak's fête?" asked Anna, to change the conversation.

"I don't think so," answered Betsy, and, without looking at her friend, she began filling the little transparent cups with fragrant tea. Putting a cup before Anna, she took out a cigarette, and, fitting it into a silver holder, she lighted it.

"It's like this, you see: I'm in a fortunate position," she began, quite serious now, as she took up her cup. "I understand you, and I understand Liza. Liza now is one of those naïve natures that, like children, don't know what's good and what's bad. Anyway, she didn't comprehend it when she was very young. And now she's aware that the lack of comprehension suits her. Now, perhaps, she doesn't know on purpose," said Betsy, with a subtle smile. "But, anyway, it suits her. The very same thing, don't you see, may be looked at tragically, and turned into a misery, or it may be looked at simply and even humorously. Possibly you are inclined to look at things too tragically."

"How I should like to know other people just as I know myself!" said Anna, seriously and dreamily. "Am I worse than other people, or better? I think I'm worse."

"*Enfant terrible, enfant terrible!*" repeated Betsy. "But here they are."

CHAPTER XVIII

THEY heard the sound of steps and a man's voice, then a woman's voice and laughter, and immediately thereafter there walked in the expected guests: Sappho Shtoltz, and a young man beaming with excess of health, the so-called Vaska. It was evident that ample supplies of beefsteak, truffles, and Burgundy never failed to reach him at the fitting hour. Vaska bowed to the two ladies, and glanced at them, but only for one second. He walked after Sappho into the drawing-room, and followed her about as though he were chained to her, keeping his sparkling eyes fixed on her as though he wanted to eat her. Sappho Shtoltz was a blonde beauty with black eyes. She walked with smart little steps in high-heeled shoes, and shook hands with the ladies vigorously like a man.

Anna had never met this new star of fashion, and was struck by her beauty, the exaggerated extreme to which her dress was carried, and the boldness of her manners. On her head there was such a superstructure of soft, golden hair—her own and false mixed—that her head was equal in size to the elegantly rounded bust, of which so much was exposed in front. The impulsive abruptness of her movements was such that at every step the lines of her knees and the upper part of her legs were distinctly marked under her dress, and the question involuntarily rose to the mind where in the undulating, piled-up mountain of material at the back the real body of the woman, so small and slender, so naked in front, and so hidden behind and below, really came to an end.

Betsy made haste to introduce her to Anna.

"Only fancy, we all but ran over two soldiers," she began telling them at once, using her eyes, smiling and twitching away her tail, which she flung back at one stroke all on one side. "I drove here with Vaska. . . . Ah, to be sure, you don't know each other." And mentioning his surname she introduced the young man, and reddening a little, broke into a ringing laugh at her mistake—that is at her having called him Vaska to a stranger. Vaska bowed once more to Anna, but he said nothing to her. He addressed Sappho: "You've lost your bet. We got here first. Pay up," said he, smiling.

Sappho laughed still more festively.

"Not just now," said she.

"Oh, all right, I'll have it later."

"Very well, very well. Oh, yes." She turned suddenly to Princess Betsy: "I am a nice person . . . I positively forgot it

. . . I've brought you a visitor. And here he comes." The unexpected young visitor, whom Sappho had invited, and whom she had forgotten, was, however, a personage of such consequence that, in spite of his youth, both the ladies rose on his entrance.

He was a new admirer of Sappho's. He now dogged her footsteps, like Vaska.

Soon after Prince Kaluzhsky arrived, and Liza Merkalova with Stremov. Liza Merkalova was a thin brunette, with an Oriental, languid type of face, and—as every one used to say—exquisite enigmatic eyes. The tone of her dark dress (Anna immediately observed and appreciated the fact) was in perfect harmony with her style of beauty. Liza was as soft and enervated as Sappho was smart and abrupt.

But to Anna's taste Liza was far more attractive. Betsy had said to Anna that she had adopted the pose of an innocent child, but when Anna saw her, she felt that this was not the truth. She really was both innocent and corrupt, but a sweet and passive woman. It is true that her tone was the same as Sappho's; that like Sappho, she had two men, one young and one old, tacked onto her, and devouring her with their eyes. But there was something in her higher than what surrounded her. There was in her the glow of the real diamond among glass imitations. This glow shone out in her exquisite, truly enigmatic eyes. The weary, and at the same time passionate, glance of those eyes, encircled by dark rings, impressed one by its perfect sincerity. Every one looking into those eyes fancied he knew her wholly, and knowing her, could not but love her. At the sight of Anna, her whole face lighted up at once with a smile of delight.

"Ah, how glad I am to see you!" she said, going up to her. "Yesterday at the races all I wanted was to get to you, but you'd gone away. I did so want to see you, yesterday especially. Wasn't it awful?" she said, looking at Anna with eyes that seemed to lay bare all her soul.

"Yes; I had no idea it would be so thrilling," said Anna, blushing.

The company got up at this moment to go into the garden.

"I'm not going," said Liza, smiling and settling herself close to Anna. "You won't go either, will you? Who wants to play croquet?"

"Oh, I like it," said Anna.

"There, how do you manage never to be bored by things? It's delightful to look at you. You're alive, but I'm bored."

"How can you be bored? Why, you live in the liveliest set in Petersburg," said Anna.

"Possibly the people who are not of our set are even more bored; but we—I certainly—are not happy, but awfully, awfully bored."

Sappho smoking a cigarette went off into the garden with the two young men. Betsy and Stremov remained at the tea-table.

"What, bored!" said Betsy. "Sappho says they did enjoy themselves tremendously at your house last night."

"Ah, how dreary it all was!" said Liza Merkalova. "We all drove back to my place after the races. And always the same people, always all the same. Always the same thing. We lounged about on sofas all the evening. What is there to enjoy in that? No; do tell me how you manage never to be bored?" she said, addressing Anna again. "One has but to look at you and one sees, here's a woman who may be happy or unhappy, but isn't bored. Tell me how you do it?"

"I do nothing," answered Anna, blushing at these searching questions.

"That's the best way," Stremov put it. Stremov was a man of fifty, partly gray, but still vigorous-looking, very ugly, but with a characteristic and intelligent face. Liza Merkalova was his wife's niece, and he spent all his leisure hours with her. On meeting Anna Karenina, as he was Alexey Alexandrovitch's enemy in the government, he tried, like a shrewd man and a man of the world, to be particularly cordial with her, the wife of his enemy.

" 'Nothing,' " he put in with a subtle smile, "that's the very best way. I told you long ago," he said, turning to Liza Merkalova, "that if you don't want to be bored, you mustn't think you're going to be bored. It's just as you mustn't be afraid of not being able to fall asleep, if you're afraid of sleeplessness. That's just what Anna Arkadyevna has just said."

"I should be very glad if I had said it, for it's not only clever but true," said Anna, smiling.

"No, do tell me why it is one can't go to sleep, and one can't help being bored?"

"To sleep well one ought to work, and to enjoy oneself one ought to work too."

"What am I to work for when my work is no use to anybody? And I can't and won't knowingly make a pretense about it."

"You're incorrigible," said Stremov, not looking at her, and he spoke again to Anna. As he rarely met Anna, he could say nothing but commonplaces to her, but he said those commonplaces as to when she was returning to Petersburg, and how fond Countess Lidia Ivanovna was of her, with an expression which suggested that he longed with his whole soul to please her and show his regard for her and even more than that.

Tushkevitch came in, announcing that the party were awaiting the other players to begin croquet.

"No, don't go away, please don't," pleaded Liza Merkalova, hearing that Anna was going. Stremov joined in her entreaties.

"It's too violent a transition," he said, "to go from such company to old Madame Vrede. And besides, you will only give her a chance for talking scandal, while here you arouse none but such different feelings of the highest and most opposite kind," he said to her.

Anna pondered for an instant in uncertainty. This shrewd man's flattering words, the naïve, childlike affection shown her by Liza Merkalova, and all the social atmosphere she was used to, —it was all so easy, and what was in store for her was so difficult, that she was for a minute in uncertainty whether to remain, whether to put off a little longer the painful moment of explanation. But remembering what was in store for her alone at home, if she did not come to some decision, remembering that gesture —terrible even in memory—when she had clutched her hair in both hands—she said good-bye and went away.

<h2 style="text-align:center">C H A P T E R   X I X</h2>

IN SPITE of Vronsky's apparently frivolous life in society, he was a man who hated irregularity. In early youth in the Corps of Pages, he had experienced the humiliation of a refusal, when he had tried, being in difficulties, to borrow money, and since then he had never once put himself in the same position again.

In order to keep his affairs in some sort of order, he used about five times a year (more or less frequently, according to circumstances) to shut himself up alone and put all his affairs into definite shape. This he used to call his day of reckoning or *faire la lessive*.

On waking up the day after the races, Vronsky put on a white linen coat, and without shaving or taking his bath, he distributed about the table moneys, bills, and letters, and set to work. Petritsky, who knew he was ill-tempered on such occasions, on waking up and seeing his comrade at the writing-table, quietly dressed and went out without getting in his way.

Every man who knows to the minutest details all the complexity of the conditions surrounding him, cannot help imagining that the complexity of these conditions, and the difficulty of making them clear, is something exceptional and personal, peculiar to himself, and never supposes that others are surrounded by just as complicated an array of personal affairs as he is. So indeed it seemed to Vronsky. And not without inward pride, and not without reason, he thought that any other man would long ago have been in difficulties, and would have been forced to some dishonorable course, if he had found himself in such a difficult position. But Vronsky felt that now especially it was essential for him to clear up and define his position if he were to avoid getting into difficulties.

What Vronsky attacked first as being the easiest was his pecuniary position. Writing out on note-paper in his minute hand all that he owed, he added up the amount and found that his debts amounted to seventeen thousand and some odd hundreds, which he left out for the sake of clearness. Reckoning up his money and his bank-book, he found that he had left one thousand eight hundred roubles, and nothing coming in before the New Year. Reckoning over again his list of debts, Vronsky copied it, dividing it into three classes. In the first class he put the debts which he would have to pay at once, or for which he must in any case have the money ready so that on demand for payment there could not be a moment's delay in paying. Such debts amounted to about four thousand: one thousand five hundred for a horse, and two thousand five hundred as surety for a young comrade, Venovsky, who had lost that sum to a cardsharper in Vronsky's presence. Vronsky had wanted to pay the money at the time (he had that amount then), but Venovsky and Yashvin had insisted that they would pay and not Vronsky, who had not played. That was so far well, but Vronsky knew that in this dirty business, though his only share in it was undertaking by word of mouth to be surety for Venovsky, it was absolutely necessary for him to have the two thousand five hundred roubles so as to be able to fling it at the swindler, and have no more words with him. And so for this first and most important division he must have four thousand roubles. The second class—eight thousand roubles—consisted of less important debts. These were principally accounts owing in connection with his race-horses, to the purveyor of oats and hay, the English saddler, and so on. He would have to pay some two thousand roubles on these debts too, in order to be quite free from anxiety. The last class of debts—to shops, to hotels, to his tailor—were such as need not be considered. So that he needed at least six thousand roubles for current expenses, and he only had one thousand eight hundred. For a man with one hundred thousand roubles of revenue, which was what every one fixed as Vronsky's income, such debts, one would suppose, could hardly be embarrassing; but the fact was that he was far from having one hundred thousand. His father's immense property, which alone yielded a yearly income of two hundred thousand, was left undivided between the brothers. At the time when the elder brother, with a mass of debts, married Princess Varya Tchirkova, the daughter of a Decembrist without any fortune whatever, Alexey had given up to his elder brother almost the whole income from his father's estate, reserving for himself only twenty-five thousand a year from it. Alexey had said at the time to his brother that that sum would be sufficient for him until he married, which he probably never would do. And his brother, who was in command of one of the most expensive regiments, and was only just married, could not decline the gift. His mother, who had her own separate property, had allowed Alexey every year twenty thousand in addition to the twenty-five thousand he had reserved, and Alexey had spent it all. Of late his mother, incensed with him on account of his love-affair and his leaving Moscow, had given up sending him the money. And in consequence of this, Vronsky, who had been in the habit of living on the scale of forty-five thousand a year, having only received twenty thousand that year, found himself now in difficulties. To get out of these difficulties, he could not apply to his mother for money. Her last letter, which he had received the day before, had particularly exasperated him by the hints in it that she was quite ready to help him to succeed in the world and in the army, but not to lead a life which was a scandal to all good society. His mother's attempt to buy him stung him to the quick and made him feel colder than ever to her. But he could not draw back from the generous word when it was once uttered, even though he felt now, vaguely foreseeing certain eventualities in his intrigue with Madame Karenina, that this generous word had been spoken thoughtlessly, and that even though he were not married he might need all the hundred thousand of income. But it was impossible to draw back. He had only to recall his brother's wife, to remember how that sweet, delightful Varya sought, at every convenient opportunity, to remind him that she remembered his generosity and appreciated it, to grasp the impossibility of taking back his gift. It was as impossible as beating a woman, stealing, or lying. One thing only could and ought to be done, and Vronsky determined upon it without an instant's hesitation: to borrow money from a money-lender, ten thousand roubles, a proceeding which presented no difficulty, to cut down his expenses generally, and to sell his race-horses. Resolving on this, he promptly wrote a note to Rolandak, who had more than once sent to him with offers to buy horses from him. Then he sent for the Englishman and the money-lender, and divided what money he had according to the accounts he intended to pay. Having finished this business, he wrote a cold and cutting answer to his mother. Then he took out of his note-book three notes of Anna's, read them again, burned them, and remembering their conversation on the previous day, he sank into meditation.

CHAPTER XX

VRONSKY's life was particularly happy in that he had a code of principles, which defined with unfailing certitude what he ought and what he ought not to do. This code of principles covered only a very small circle of contingencies, but then the principles were never doubtful, and Vronsky, as he never went outside that circle, had never had a moment's hesitation about doing what he ought to do. These principles laid down as invariable rules: that one must pay a cardsharper, but need not pay a tailor; that one must never tell a lie to a man, but one may to a woman; that one must never cheat any one, but one may a husband; that one must never pardon an insult, but one may give one and so on. These principles were possibly not reasonable and not good, but they were of unfailing certainty, and so long as he adhered to them, Vronsky felt that his heart was at peace and he could hold his head up. Only quite lately in regard to his relations with Anna, Vronsky had begun to feel that his code of principles did not fully cover all possible contingencies, and to foresee in the future difficulties and perplexities for which he could find no guiding clue.

His present relation to Anna and to her husband was to his mind clear and simple. It was clearly and precisely defined in the code of principles by which he was guided.

She was an honorable woman who had bestowed her love upon him, and he loved her, and therefore she was in his eyes a woman who had a right to the same, or even more, respect than a lawful wife. He would have had his hand chopped off before he would have allowed himself by a word, by a hint, to humiliate her, or even to fall short of the fullest respect a woman could look for.

His attitude to society, too, was clear. Every one might know, might suspect it, but no one might dare to speak of it. If any did so, he was ready to force all who might speak to be silent and to respect the non-existent honor of the woman he loved.

His attitude to the husband was the clearest of all. From the moment that Anna loved Vronsky, he had regarded his own right over her as the one thing unassailable. Her husband was simply a superfluous and tiresome person. No doubt he was in a pitiable position, but how could that be helped? The one thing the husband had a right to was to demand satisfaction with a weapon in his hand, and Vronsky was prepared for this at any minute.

But of late new inner relations had arisen between him and her, which frightened Vronsky by their indefiniteness. Only the

day before she had told him that she was with child. And he felt
that this fact and what she expected of him called for something
not fully defined in that code of principles by which he had
hitherto steered his course in life. And he had been indeed caught
unawares, and at the first moment when she spoke to him of her
position, his heart had prompted him to beg her to leave her
husband. He had said that, but now thinking things over he saw
clearly that it would be better to manage to avoid that; and at the
same time, as he told himself so, he was afraid whether it was
not wrong.

"If I told her to leave her husband, that must mean uniting
her life with mine; am I prepared for that? How can I take her
away now, when I have no money? Supposing I could arrange
. . . But how can I take her away while I'm in the service? If I
say that—I ought to be prepared to do it, that is, I ought to have
the money and to retire from the army."

And he grew thoughtful. The question whether to retire from
the service or not brought him to the other and perhaps the chief
though hidden interest of his life, of which none knew but he.

Ambition was the old dream of his youth and childhood, a
dream which he did not confess even to himself, though it was
so strong that now this passion was even doing battle with his
love. His first steps in the world and in the service had been
successful, but two years before he had made a great mistake.
Anxious to show his independence and to advance, he had refused
a post that had been offered him, hoping that this refusal would
heighten his value; but it turned out that he had been too bold,
and he was passed over. And having, whether he liked or not,
taken up for himself the position of an independent man, he
carried it off with great tact and good sense, behaving as though
he bore no grudge against any one, did not regard himself as
injured in any way, and cared for nothing but to be left alone
since he was enjoying himself. In reality he had ceased to enjoy
himself as long ago as the year before, when he went away to
Moscow. He felt that this independent attitude of a man who
might have done anything, but cared to do nothing was already
beginning to pall, that many people were beginning to fancy
that he was not really capable of anything but being a straight-
forward, good-natured fellow. His connection with Madame

Karenina, by creating so much sensation and attracting general attention, had given him a fresh distinction which soothed his gnawing worm of ambition for a while, but a week before that worm had been roused up again with fresh force. The friend of his childhood, a man of the same set, of the same coterie, his comrade in the Corps of Pages, Serpuhovskoy, who had left school with him and had been his rival in class, in gymnastics, in their scrapes and their dreams of glory, had come back a few days before from Central Asia, where he had gained two steps up in rank, and an order rarely bestowed upon generals so young.

As soon as he arrived in Petersburg, people began to talk about him as a newly risen star of the first magnitude. A schoolfellow of Vronsky's and of the same age, he was a general and was expecting a command, which might have influence on the course of political events; while Vronsky, independent and brilliant and beloved by a charming woman though he was, was simply a cavalry captain who was readily allowed to be as independent as ever he liked. "Of course I don't envy Serpuhovskoy and never could envy him; but his advancement shows me that one has only to watch one's opportunity, and the career of a man like me may be very rapidly made. Three years ago he was in just the same position as I am. If I retire, I burn my ships. If I remain in the army, I lose nothing. She said herself she did not wish to change her position. And with her love I cannot feel envious of Serpuhovskoy." And slowly twirling his mustaches, he got up from the table and walked about the room. His eyes shone particularly brightly, and he felt in that confident, calm, and happy frame of mind which always came after he had thoroughly faced his position. Everything was straight and clear, just as after former days of reckoning. He shaved, took a cold bath, dressed and went out.

CHAPTER XXI

"I've come to fetch you. Your *lessive* lasted a good time to-day," said Petritsky. "Well, is it over?"

"It is over," answered Vronsky, smiling with his eyes only, and twirling the tips of his mustaches as circumspectly as though after the perfect order into which his affairs had been brought any over-bold or rapid movement might disturb it.

"You're always just as if you'd come out of a bath after it," said Petritsky. "I've come from Gritsky's" (that was what they called the colonel); "they're expecting you."

Vronsky, without answering, looked at his comrade, thinking of something else.

"Yes; is that music at his place?" he said, listening to the familiar sounds of polkas and waltzes floating across to him. "What's the fête?"

"Serpuhovskoy's come."

"Aha!" said Vronsky, "why, I didn't know."

The smile in his eyes gleamed more brightly than ever.

Having once made up his mind that he was happy in his love, that he sacrificed his ambition to it—having anyway taken up this position, Vronsky was incapable of feeling either envious of Serpuhovskoy or hurt with him for not coming first to him when he came to the regiment. Serpuhovskoy was a good friend, and he was delighted he had come.

"Ah, I'm very glad!"

The colonel, Demin, had taken a large country house. The whole party were in the wide lower balcony. In the courtyard the first objects that met Vronsky's eyes were a band of singers in white linen coats, standing near a barrel of vodka, and the robust, good-humored figure of the colonel surrounded by officers. He had gone out as far as the first step of the balcony and was loudly shouting across the band that played Offenbach's quadrille, waving his arms and giving some orders to a few soldiers standing on one side. A group of soldiers, a quartermaster, and several subalterns came up to the balcony with Vronsky. The colonel returned to the table, went out again onto the steps with a tumbler in his hand, and proposed the toast, "To the health of our former comrade, the gallant general, Prince Serpuhovskoy. Hurrah!"

The colonel was followed by Serpuhovskoy, who came out onto the steps smiling, with a glass in his hand.

"You always get younger, Bondarenko," he said to the rosy-cheeked, smart-looking quartermaster standing just before him, still youngish-looking though doing his second term of service.

It was three years since Vronsky had seen Serpuhovskoy. He looked more robust, had let his whiskers grow, but was still the same graceful creature, whose face and figure were even more striking from their softness and nobility than their beauty. The only change Vronsky detected in him was that subdued, continual radiance of beaming content which settles on the faces of men who are successful and are sure of the recognition of their success by every one. Vronsky knew that radiant air, and immediately observed it in Serpuhovskoy.

As Serpuhovskoy came down the steps he saw Vronsky. A smile of pleasure lighted up his face. He tossed his head upwards and waved the glass in his hand, greeting Vronsky, and showing him by the gesture that he could not come to him before the quartermaster, who stood craning forward his lips ready to be kissed.

"Here he is!" shouted the colonel. "Yashvin told me you were in one of your gloomy tempers."

Serpuhovskoy kissed the moist, fresh lips of the gallant-looking quartermaster, and wiping his mouth with his handkerchief, went up to Vronsky.

"How glad I am!" he said, squeezing his hand and drawing him on one side.

"You look after him," the colonel shouted to Yashvin, pointing to Vronsky; and he went down below to the soldiers.

"Why weren't you at the races yesterday? I expected to see you there," said Vronsky, scrutinizing Serpuhovskoy.

"I did go, but late. I beg your pardon," he added, and he turned to the adjutant: "Please have this divided from me, each man as much as it runs to." And he hurriedly took notes for three hundred roubles from his pocketbook, blushing a little.

"Vronsky! Have anything to eat or drink?" asked Yashvin. "Hi, something for the count to eat! Ah, here it is: have a glass!"

The fête at the colonel's lasted a long while. There was a great deal of drinking. They tossed Serpuhovskoy in the air and caught him again several times. Then they did the same to the colonel. Then, to the accompaniment of the band, the colonel himself danced with Petritsky. Then the colonel, who began to

show signs of feebleness, sat down on a bench in the courtyard
and began demonstrating to Yashvin the superiority of Russia
over Poland, especially in cavalry attack, and there was a lull
in the revelry for a moment. Serpuhovskoy went into the house
to the bathroom to wash his hands and found Vronsky there;

Vronsky was drenching his head with water. He had taken off
his coat and put his sunburnt, hairy neck under the tap, and was
rubbing it and his head with his hands. When he had finished,
Vronsky sat down by Serpuhovskoy. They both sat down in the
bathroom on a lounge, and a conversation began which was very
interesting to both of them.

"I've always been hearing about you through my wife," said
Serpuhovskoy. "I'm glad you've been seeing her pretty often."

"She's friendly with Varya, and they're the only women in
Petersburg I care about seeing," answered Vronsky, smiling. He

smiled because he foresaw the topic the conversation would turn on, and he was glad of it.

"The only ones?" Serpuhovskoy queried, smiling.

"Yes; and I heard news of you, but not only through your wife," said Vronsky, checking his hint by a stern expression of face. "I was greatly delighted to hear of your success, but not a bit surprised. I expected even more."

Serpuhovskoy smiled. Such an opinion of him was obviously agreeable to him, and he did not think it necessary to conceal it.

"Well, I on the contrary expected less—I'll own frankly. But I'm glad, very glad. I'm ambitious; that's my weakness, and I confess to it."

"Perhaps you wouldn't confess to it if you hadn't been success-ful," said Vronsky.

"I don't suppose so," said Serpuhovskoy, smiling again. "I won't say life wouldn't be worth living without it, but it would be dull. Of course I may be mistaken, but I fancy I have a certain capacity for the line I've chosen, and that power of any sort in my hands, if it is to be, will be better than in the hands of a good many people I know," said Serpuhovskoy, with beaming con-sciousness of success; "and so the nearer I get to it, the better pleased I am."

"Perhaps that is true for you, but not for every one. I used to think so too, but here I live and think life worth living not only for that."

"There it's out! here it comes!" said Serpuhovskoy, laughing. "Ever since I heard about you, about your refusal, I began . . . Of course, I approved of what you did. But there are ways of doing everything. And I think your action was good in itself, but you didn't do it quite in the way you ought to have done."

"What's done can't be undone, and you know I never go back on what I've done. And besides, I'm very well off."

"Very well off—for the time. But you're not satisfied with that. I wouldn't say this to your brother. He's a nice child, like our host here. There he goes!" he added, listening to the roar of "hurrah!"—"and he's happy, that does not satisfy you."

"I didn't say it did satisfy me."

"Yes, but that's not the only thing. Such men as you are wanted."

"By whom?"

"By whom? By society, by Russia. Russia needs men; she needs a party, or else everything goes and will go to the dogs."

"How do you mean? Bertenev's party against the Russian communists?"

"No," said Serpuhovskoy, frowning with vexation at being suspected of such an absurdity. *"Tout ça est une blague.* That's always been and always will be. There are no communists. But intriguing people have to invent a noxious, dangerous party. It's an old trick. No, what's wanted is a powerful party of independent men like you and me."

"But why so?" Vronsky mentioned a few men who were in power. "Why aren't they independent men?"

"Simply because they have not, or have not had from birth, an independent fortune; they've not had a name, they've not been close to the sun and center as we have. They can be bought either by money or by favor. And they have to find a support for themselves in inventing a policy. And they bring forward some notion, some policy that they don't believe in, that does harm; and the whole policy is really only a means to a government house and so much income. *Cela n'est pas plus fin que ça,* when you get a peep at their cards. I may be inferior to them, stupider perhaps, though I don't see why I should be inferior to them. But you and I have one important advantage over them for certain, in being more difficult to buy. And such men are more needed than ever."

Vronsky listened attentively, but he was not so much interested by the meaning of the words as by the attitude of Serpuhovskoy who was already contemplating a struggle with the existing powers, and already had his likes and dislikes in that higher world, while his own interest in the governing world did not go beyond the interests of his regiment. Vronsky felt, too, how powerful Serpuhovskoy might become through his unmistakable faculty for thinking things out and for taking things in, through his intelligence and gift of words, so rarely met with in the world in which he moved. And, ashamed as he was of the feeling, he felt envious.

"Still I haven't the one thing of most importance for that," he answered; "I haven't the desire for power. I had it once, but it's gone."

"Excuse me, that's not true," said Serpuhovskoy, smiling.

"Yes, it is true, it is true . . . now!" Vronsky added, to be truthful.

"Yes, it's true now, that's another thing; but that *now* won't last forever."

"Perhaps," answered Vronsky.

"You say *perhaps*," Serpuhovskoy went on, as though guessing his thoughts, "but I say *for certain*. And that's what I wanted to see you for. Your action was just what it should have been. I see that, but you ought not to keep it up. I only ask you to give me *carte blanche*. I'm not going to offer you my protection . . . though, indeed, why shouldn't I protect you?—you've protected me often enough! I should hope our friendship rises above all that sort of thing. Yes," he said, smiling to him as tenderly as a woman, "give me *carte blanche,* retire from the regiment, and I'll draw you upwards imperceptibly."

"But you must understand that I want nothing," said Vronsky, "except that all should be as it is."

Serpuhovskoy got up and stood facing him.

"You say that all should be as it is. I understand what that means. But listen: we're the same age, you've known a greater number of women perhaps than I have." Serpuhovskoy's smile and gestures told Vronsky that he mustn't be afraid, that he would be tender and careful in touching the sore place. "But I'm married, and believe me, in getting to know thoroughly one's wife, if one loves her, as some one has said, one gets to know all women better than if one knew thousands of them."

"We're coming directly!" Vronsky shouted to an officer, who looked into the room and called them to the colonel.

Vronsky was longing now to hear to the end and know what Serpuhovskoy would say to him.

"And here's my opinion for you. Women are the chief stumbling-block in a man's career. It's hard to love a woman and do anything. There's only one way of having love conveniently without its being a hindrance—that's marriage. How, how am I to tell you what I mean?" said Serpuhovskoy, who liked similes. "Wait a minute, wait a minute! Yes, just as you can only carry a *fardeau* and do something with your hands, when the *fardeau* is tied on your back, and that's marriage. And that's what I felt when I was married. My hands were suddenly set free. But to drag that *fardeau* about with you without marriage, your hands will always be so full that you can do nothing. Look at Mazankov, at Krupov. They've ruined their careers for the sake of women."

"What women!" said Vronsky, recalling the Frenchwoman and the actress with whom the two men he had mentioned were connected.

"The firmer the woman's footing in society, the worse it is. That's much the same as—not merely carrying the *fardeau* in your arms—but tearing it away from some one else."

"You have never loved," Vronsky said softly, looking straight before him and thinking of Anna.

"Perhaps. But you remember what I've said to you. And another thing, women are all more materialistic than men. We make something immense out of love, but they are always *terre-à-terre.*"

"Directly, directly!" he cried to a footman who came in. But the footman had not come to call them again, as he supposed. The footman brought Vronsky a note.

"A man brought it from Princess Tverskaya."

Vronsky opened the letter, and flushed crimson.

"My head's begun to ache; I'm going home," he said to Serpu-hovskoy.

"Oh, good-bye then. You give me *carte blanche!*"

"We'll talk about it later on; I'll look you up in Petersburg."

CHAPTER XXII

It was six o'clock already, and so, in order to be there quickly, and at the same time not to drive with his own horses, known to every one, Vronsky got into Yashvin's hired fly, and told the driver to drive as quickly as possible. It was a roomy, old-fashioned fly, with seats for four. He sat in one corner, stretched his legs out on the front seat, and sank into meditation.

A vague sense of the order into which his affairs had been brought, a vague recollection of the friendliness and flattery of

Serpuhovskoy, who had considered him a man that was needed, and most of all, the anticipation of the interview before him—all blended into a general, joyous sense of life. This feeling was so strong that he could not help smiling. He dropped his legs, crossed one leg over the other knee, and taking it in his hand, felt the springy muscle of the calf, where it had been grazed the day before by his fall, and leaning back he drew several deep breaths.

"I'm happy, very happy!" he said to himself. He had often before had this sense of physical joy in his own body, but he had never felt so fond of himself, of his own body, as at that moment. He enjoyed the slight ache in his strong leg, he enjoyed the muscular sensation of movement in his chest as he breathed. The bright, cold August day, which had made Anna feel so hopeless, seemed to him keenly stimulating, and refreshed his face and neck that still tingled from the cold water. The scent of brilliantine on his whiskers struck him as particularly pleasant in the fresh air. Everything he saw from the carriage-window, everything in that cold pure air, in the pale light of the sunset, was as fresh, and gay, and strong as he was himself: the roofs of the houses shining in the rays of the setting sun, the sharp outlines of fences and angles of buildings, the figures of passers-by, the carriages that met him now and then, the motionless green of the trees and grass, the fields with evenly drawn furrows of potatoes, and the slanting shadows that fell from the houses, and trees, and bushes, and even from the rows of potatoes—everything was bright like a pretty landscape just finished and freshly varnished.

"Get on, get on!" he said to the driver, putting his head out of the window, and pulling a three-rouble note out of his pocket he handed it to the man as he looked round. The driver's hand fumbled with something at the lamp, the whip cracked, and the carriage rolled rapidly along the smooth highroad.

"I want nothing, nothing but this happiness," he thought, staring at the bone button of the bell in the space between the windows, and picturing to himself Anna just as he had seen her last time. "And as I go on, I love her more and more. Here's the garden of the Vrede Villa. Whereabouts will she be? Where? How? Why did she fix on this place to meet me, and why does she write in Betsy's letter?" he thought, wondering now for the first time at it. But there was now no time for wonder. He called to the driver to stop before reaching the avenue, and opening the door, jumped out of the carriage as it was moving, and went into the avenue that led up to the house. There was no one in the avenue; but looking round to the right he caught sight of her. Her face was hidden by a veil, but he drank in with glad eyes the special movement in walking, peculiar to her alone, the slope of the shoulders, and the setting of the head, and at once a sort of electric shock ran all over him. With fresh force, he felt conscious of himself from the springy motions of his legs to the movements of his lungs as he breathed, and something set his lips twitching.

Joining him, she pressed his hand tightly.

"You're not angry that I sent for you? I absolutely had to see you," she said; and the serious and set line of her lips, which he saw under the veil, transformed his mood at once.

"I angry! But how have you come, where from?"

"Never mind," she said, laying her hand on his, "come along, I must talk to you."

He saw that something had happened, and that the interview would not be a joyous one. In her presence he had no will of his own: without knowing the grounds of her distress, he already felt the same distress unconsciously passing over him.

"What is it? what?" he asked her, squeezing her hand with his elbow, and trying to read her thoughts in her face.

She walked on a few steps in silence, gathering up her courage; then suddenly she stopped.

"I did not tell you yesterday," she began, breathing quickly and painfully, "that coming home with Alexey Alexandrovitch I told him everything . . . told him I could not be his wife, that . . . and told him everything."

He heard her, unconsciously bending his whole figure down to her as though hoping in this way to soften the hardness of her position for her. But directly she had said this he suddenly drew himself up, and a proud and hard expression came over his face.

"Yes, yes, that's better, a thousand times better! I know how painful it was," he said. But she was not listening to his words, she was reading his thoughts from the expression of his face. She could not guess that that expression arose from the first idea that presented itself to Vronsky—that a duel was now inevitable.

The idea of a duel had never crossed her mind, and so she put a different interpretation on this passing expression of hardness.

When she got her husband's letter, she knew then at the bottom of her heart that everything would go on in the old way, that she would not have the strength of will to forego her position, to abandon her son, and to join her lover. The morning spent at Princess Tverskaya's had confirmed her still more in this. But this interview was still of the utmost gravity for her. She hoped that this interview would transform her position, and save her. If on hearing this news he were to say to her resolutely, passionately, without an instant's wavering: "Throw up everything and come with me!" she would give up her son and go away with him. But this news had not produced what she had expected in him; he simply seemed as though he were resenting some affront.

"It was not in the least painful to me. It happened of itself," she said irritably; "and see . . ." She pulled her husband's letter out of her glove.

"I understand, I understand," he interrupted her, taking the letter, but not reading it, and trying to soothe her. "The one thing I longed for, the one thing I prayed for, was to cut short this position, so as to devote my life to your happiness."

"Why do you tell me that?" she said. "Do you suppose I can doubt it? If I doubted . . ."

"Who's that coming?" said Vronsky suddenly, pointing to two ladies walking towards them. "Perhaps they know us!" and he hurriedly turned off, drawing her after him into a side path.

"Oh, I don't care!" she said. Her lips were quivering. And he fancied that her eyes looked with strange fury at him from under the veil. "I tell you that's not the point—I can't doubt that; but see what he writes to me. Read it." She stood still again.

Again, just as at the first moment of hearing of her rupture with her husband, Vronsky, on reading the letter, was unconsciously carried away by the natural sensation aroused in him by his own relation to the betrayed husband. Now while he held his letter in his hands, he could not help picturing the challenge, which he would most likely find at home to-day or to-morrow, and the duel itself in which, with the same cold and haughty expression that his face was assuming at this moment he would

await the injured husband's shot, after having himself fired into the air. And at that instant there flashed across his mind the thought of what Serpuhovskoy had just said to him, and what he had himself been thinking in the morning—that it was better not to bind himself—and he knew that this thought he could not tell her.

Having read the letter, he raised his eyes to her, and there was no determination in them. She saw at once that he had been thinking about it before by himself. She knew that whatever he might say to her, he would not say all he thought. And she knew that her last hope had failed her. This was not what she had been reckoning on.

"You see the sort of man he is," she said, with a shaking voice; "he . . ."

"Forgive me, but I rejoice at it," Vronsky interrupted. "For God's sake, let me finish!" he added, his eyes imploring her to give him time to explain his words. "I rejoice, because things cannot, cannot possibly remain as he supposes."

"Why can't they?" Anna said, restraining her tears, and obviously attaching no sort of consequence to what he said. She felt that her fate was sealed.

Vronsky meant that after the duel—inevitable, he thought—things could not go on as before, but he said something different.

"It can't go on. I hope that now you will leave him. I hope"—he was confused, and reddened—"that you will let me arrange and plan our life. To-morrow . . ." he was beginning.

She did not let him go on.

"But my child!" she shrieked. "You see what he writes! I should have to leave him, and I can't and won't do that."

"But, for God's sake, which is better?—leave your child, or keep up this degrading position?"

"To whom is it degrading?"

"To all, and most of all to you."

"You say degrading . . . don't say that. Those words have no meaning for me," she said in a shaking voice. She did not want him now to say what was untrue. She had nothing left her but his love, and she wanted to love him. "Don't you understand that from the day I loved you everything has changed for me? For me there is one thing, and one thing only—your love.

If that's mine, I feel so exalted, so strong, that nothing can be humiliating to me. I am proud of my position, because . . . proud of being . . . proud . . ." She could not say what she was proud of. Tears of shame and despair choked her utterance. She stood still and sobbed.

He felt, too, something swelling in his throat and twitching in his nose, and for the first time in his life he felt on the point of weeping. He could not have said exactly what it was touched him so. He felt sorry for her, and he felt he could not help her, and with that he knew that he was to blame for her wretchedness, and that he had done something wrong.

"Is not a divorce possible?" he said feebly. She shook her head, not answering. "Couldn't you take your son, and still leave him?"

"Yes; but it all depends on him. Now I must go to him," she said shortly. Her presentiment that all would again go on in the old way had not deceived her.

"On Tuesday I shall be in Petersburg, and everything can be settled."

"Yes," she said. "But don't let us talk any more of it."

Anna's carriage, which she had sent away, and ordered to come back to the little gate of the Vrede garden, drove up. Anna said good-bye to Vronsky, and drove home.

CHAPTER XXIII

ON MONDAY there was the usual sitting of the Commission of the 2nd of June. Alexey Alexandrovitch walked into the hall where the sitting was held, greeted the members and the president, as usual, and sat down in his place, putting his hand on the papers laid ready before him. Among these papers lay the necessary evidence and a rough outline of the speech he intended to make. But he did not really need these documents. He remembered every point, and did not think it necessary to go over in his memory what he would say. He knew that when the time came, and when he saw his enemy facing him, and studiously endeavoring to assume an expression of indifference, his speech would flow of itself better than he could prepare it now. He felt that the import of his speech was of such magnitude that every word of it would have weight. Meantime, as he listened to the usual report, he had the most innocent and inoffensive air. No one, looking at his white hands, with their swollen veins and long fingers, so softly stroking the edges of the white paper that lay before him, and at the air of weariness with which his head drooped on one side, would have suspected that in a few minutes a torrent of words would flow from his lips that would arouse a fearful storm, set the members shouting and attacking one another, and force the president to call for order. When the report was over, Alexey Alexandrovitch announced in his subdued, delicate voice that he had several points to bring before the meeting in regard to the Commission for the Reorganization of the Native Tribes. All attention was turned upon him. Alexey Alexandrovitch cleared his throat, and not looking at his opponent, but selecting, as he always did while he was delivering his speeches, the first person sitting opposite him, an inoffensive little old man, who never had an opinion of any sort in the Commission, began to expound his views. When he reached the point about the fundamental and radical law, his opponent jumped up and began to protest. Stremov, who was also a member of the Commission, and also stung to the quick, began defending himself, and altogether a stormy sitting followed; but Alexey Alexandrovitch triumphed, and his motion was carried, three new commissions were appointed, and the next day in a certain Petersburg circle nothing else was talked of but this sitting. Alexey Alexandrovitch's success had been even greater than he had anticipated.

Next morning, Tuesday, Alexey Alexandrovitch, on waking up, recollected with pleasure his triumph of the previous day, and he could not help smiling, though he tried to appear indifferent, when the chief secretary of his department, anxious to flatter him, informed him of the rumors that had reached him concerning what had happened in the Commission.

Absorbed in business with the chief secretary, Alexey Alexandrovitch had completely forgotten that it was Tuesday, the day fixed by him for the return of Anna Arkadyevna, and he was surprised and received a shock of annoyance when a servant came in to inform him of her arrival.

Anna had arrived in Petersburg early in the morning; the

carriage had been sent to meet her in accordance with her telegram, and so Alexey Alexandrovitch might have known of her
arrival. But when she arrived, he did not meet her. She was told
that he had not yet gone out, but was busy with his secretary.
She sent word to her husband that she had come, went to her own
room, and occupied herself in sorting out her things, expecting
he would come to her. But an hour passed; he did not come. She
went into the dining-room on the pretext of giving some directions, and spoke loudly on purpose, expecting him to come out
there; but he did not come, though she heard him go to the door
of his study as he parted from the chief secretary. She knew that
he usually went out quickly to his office, and she wanted to see
him before that, so that their attitude to one another might be
defined.

She walked across the drawing-room and went resolutely to
him. When she went into his study he was in official uniform,
obviously ready to go out, sitting at a little table on which he
rested his elbows, looking dejectedly before him. She saw him
before he saw her, and she saw that he was thinking of her.

On seeing her, he would have risen, but changed his mind,
then his face flushed hotly—a thing Anna had never seen before,
and he got up quickly and went to meet her, looking not at her
eyes, but above them at her forehead and hair. He went up to her,
took her by the hand, and asked her to sit down.

"I am very glad you have come," he said, sitting down beside
her, and obviously wishing to say something, he stuttered. Several times he tried to begin to speak, but stopped. In spite of the
fact that, preparing herself for meeting him, she had schooled
herself to despise and reproach him, she did not know what to
say to him, and she felt sorry for him. And so the silence lasted
for some time. "Is Seryozha quite well?" he said, and not waiting
for an answer, he added: "I shan't be dining at home to-day, and
I have got to go out directly."

"I had thought of going to Moscow," she said.

"No, you did quite, quite right to come," he said, and was silent again.

Seeing that he was powerless to begin the conversation, she
began herself.

"Alexey Alexandrovitch," she said, looking at him and not

dropping her eyes under his persistent gaze at her hair, "I'm a guilty woman, I'm a bad woman, but I am the same as I was, as I told you then, and I have come to tell you that I can change nothing."

"I have asked you no question about that," he said, all at once, resolutely and with hatred looking her straight in the face; "that was as I had supposed." Under the influence of anger he apparently regained complete possession of all his faculties. "But as I told you then, and have written to you," he said in a thin, shrill voice, "I repeat now, that I am not bound to know this. I ignore it. Not all wives are so kind as you, to be in such a hurry to communicate such agreeable news to their husbands." He laid special emphasis on the word "agreeable." "I shall ignore it so long as the world knows nothing of it, so long as my name is not disgraced. And so I simply inform you that our relations must be just as they have always been, and that only in the event of your compromising me I shall be obliged to take steps to secure my honor."

"But our relations cannot be the same as always," Anna began in a timid voice, looking at him with dismay.

When she saw once more those composed gestures, heard that shrill, childish, and sarcastic voice, her aversion for him extinguished her pity for him, and she felt only afraid, but at all costs she wanted to make clear her position.

"I cannot be your wife while I . . ." she began.

He laughed a cold and malignant laugh.

"The manner of life you have chosen is reflected, I suppose, in your ideas. I have too much respect or contempt, or both . . . I respect your past and despise your present . . . that I was far from the interpretation you put on my words."

Anna sighed and bowed her head.

"Though indeed I fail to comprehend how, with the independence you show," he went on, getting hot, "—announcing your infidelity to your husband and seeing nothing reprehensible in it, apparently—you can see anything reprehensible in performing a wife's duties in relation to your husband."

"Alexey Alexandrovitch! What is it you want of me?"

"I want you not to meet that man here, and to conduct yourself so that neither the world nor the servants can reproach you

. . . not to see him. That's not much, I think. And in return you will enjoy all the privileges of a faithful wife without fulfilling her duties. That's all I have to say to you. Now it's time for me to go. I'm not dining at home." He got up and moved towards the door.

Anna got up too. Bowing in silence, he let her pass before him.

THE night spent by Levin on the haycock did not pass without result for him. The way in which he had been managing his land revolted him and had lost all attraction for him. In spite of the magnificent harvest, never had there been, or, at least, never it seemed to him, had there been so many hindrances and so many quarrels between him and the peasants as that year, and the origin of these failures and this hostility was now perfectly comprehensible to him. The delight he had experienced in the work itself, and the consequent greater intimacy with the peasants, the envy he felt of them, of their life, the desire to adopt that life, which had been to him that night not a dream but an intention, the execution of which he had thought out in detail—all this had so transformed his view of the farming of the land as he had managed it, that he could not take his former interest in it, and could not help seeing that unpleasant relation between him and the workspeople which was the foundation of it all. The herd of improved cows such as Pava, the whole land ploughed over and enriched, the nine level fields surrounded with hedges, the two hundred and forty acres heavily manured, the seed sown in drills, and all the rest of it—it was all splendid if only the work had been done for themselves, or for themselves and comrades—people in sympathy with them. But he saw clearly now (his work on a book of agriculture, in which the chief element in husbandry was to have been the laborer, greatly assisted him in this) that the sort of farming he was carrying on was nothing but a cruel and stubborn struggle between him and the laborers, in which there was on one side—his side—a continual intense effort to change everything to a pattern he considered better; on the other side, the natural order of things. And in this struggle he saw that with immense expenditure of force on his side, and with no effort or even intention on the other side, all that was attained was that the work did not go to the liking of either side, and that splendid tools, splendid cattle and land were spoiled with no good to any one. Worst of all, the energy expended on this work was not simply wasted. He could not help feeling now, since the meaning of this system had become clear to him, that the aim of his energy was a most unworthy one. In reality, what was the struggle about? He was struggling for every farthing of his share (and he could not help it, for he had only to relax his efforts, and he would not have had the money to pay his laborers' wages), while they were only struggling to be able to do their work easily and agreeably, that is to say, as they were used to doing it. It was for his interests that every laborer should work as hard as possible, and that while doing so he should keep his wits about him, so as to try not to break the winnowing-machines, the horse-rakes, the thrashing-machines, that he should attend to what he was doing. What the laborer wanted was to work as pleasantly as possible, with rests, and above all, carelessly and heedlessly, without thinking. That summer Levin saw this at every step. He sent the men to mow some clover for hay, picking out the worst patches where the clover was overgrown with grass and weeds and of no use for seed; again and again they mowed the best acres of clover, justifying themselves by the pretense that the bailiff had told them to, and trying to pacify him with the assurance that it would be splendid hay; but he knew that it was owing to those acres being so much easier to mow. He sent out a hay machine for pitching the hay—it was broken at the first row because it was dull work for a peasant to sit on the seat in front with the great wings waving above him. And he was told, "Don't trouble, your honor, sure, the women-folks will pitch it quick enough." The ploughs were practically useless, because it never occurred to the laborer to raise the share when he turned the plough, and forcing it round, he strained the horses and tore up the ground, and Levin was begged not to mind about it. The horses were allowed to stray into the wheat because not a single laborer would consent to be night-watchman, and in spite of orders to the contrary, the laborers insisted on taking turns for night duty, and Ivan, after working all day long, fell asleep, and was very penitent for his fault, saying, "Do what you will to me, your honor."

They killed three of the best calves by letting them into the clover aftermath without care as to their drinking, and nothing would make the men believe that they had been blown out by the clover, but they told him, by way of consolation, that one of his neighbors had lost a hundred and twelve head of cattle in three days. All this happened, not because anyone felt ill-will to Levin or his farm; on the contrary, he knew that they liked him, thought him a simple gentleman (their highest praise); but it happened simply because all they wanted was to work merrily and carelessly, and his interests were not only remote and incomprehensible to them, but fatally opposed to their most just claims. Long before, Levin had felt dissatisfaction with his own position in regard to the land. He saw where his boat leaked, but he did not look for the leak, perhaps purposely deceiving himself. (Nothing would be left him if he lost faith in it.) But now he could deceive himself no longer. The farming of the land, as he was managing it, had become not merely unattractive but revolting to him, and he could take no further interest in it.

To this now was joined the presence, only twenty-five miles off, of Kitty Shtcherbatskaya, whom he longed to see and could not see. Darya Alexandrovna Oblonskaya had invited him, when he was over there, to come; to come with the object of renewing his offer to her sister, who would, so she gave him to understand, accept him now. Levin himself had felt on seeing Kitty Shtcherbatskaya that he had never ceased to love her; but he could not go over to the Oblonskys', knowing she was there. The fact that he had made her an offer, and she had refused him, had placed an insuperable barrier between her and him. "I can't ask her to be my wife merely because she can't be the wife of the man she wanted to marry," he said to himself. The thought of this made him cold and hostile to her. "I should not be able to speak to her without a feeling of reproach; I could not look at her without resentment; and she will only hate me all the more, as she's bound to. And besides, how can I now, after what Darya Alexandrovna told me, go to see them? Can I help showing that I know what she told me? And me to go magnanimously to forgive her, and have pity on her! Me go through a performance before her of forgiving, and deigning to bestow my love on her! . . . What induced Darya Alexandrovna to tell me that? By chance I might have seen her, then everything would have happened of itself; but, as it is, it's out of the question, out of the question!"

Darya Alexandrovna sent him a letter, asking him for a side-saddle for Kitty's use. "I'm told you have a side-saddle," she wrote to him; "I hope you will bring it over yourself."

This was more than he could stand. How could a woman of any intelligence, of any delicacy, put her sister in such a humiliating position! He wrote ten notes, and tore them all up, and sent the saddle without any reply. To write that he would go was impossible, because he could not go; to write that he could not come because something prevented him, or that he would be away, that was still worse. He sent the saddle without an answer, and with a sense of having done something shameful; he handed over all the now revolting business of the estate to the bailiff, and set off next day to a remote district to see his friend Sviazhsky, who had splendid marshes for grouse in his neighborhood, and had lately written to ask him to keep a long-standing promise to stay with him. The grouse-marsh, in the Surovsky district, had long tempted Levin, but he had continually put off this visit on account of his work on the estate. Now he was glad to get away from the neighborhood of the Shtcherbatskys, and still more from his farm-work, especially on a shooting expedition, which always in trouble served as the best consolation.

CHAPTER XXV

IN THE Surovsky district there was no railway nor service of post-horses, and Levin drove there with his own horses in his big, old-fashioned carriage.

He stopped half-way at a well-to-do peasant's to feed his horses. A bald, well-preserved old man, with a broad, red beard, gray on his cheeks, opened the gate, squeezing against the gate-post to let the three horses pass. Directing the coachman to a place under the shed in the big, clean, tidy yard, with charred, old-fashioned ploughs in it, the old man asked Levin to come into the parlor. A cleanly dressed young woman, with clogs on her bare feet, was scrubbing the floor in the new outer room. She was frightened of the dog, that ran in after Levin, and uttered a shriek, but began laughing at her own fright at once when she was told the dog would not hurt her. Pointing Levin with her bare arm to the door into the parlor, she bent down again, hiding her handsome face, and went on scrubbing.

"Would you like the samovar?" she asked.

"Yes, please."

The parlor was a big room, with a Dutch stove, and a screen dividing it into two. Under the holy pictures stood a table painted in patterns, a bench, and two chairs. Near the entrance was a dresser full of crockery. The shutters were closed, there were few flies, and it was so clean that Levin was anxious that Laska, who had been running along the road and bathing in puddles, should not muddy the floor, and ordered her to a place in the corner by the door. After looking round the parlor, Levin went out in the back yard. The good-looking young woman in clogs, swinging the empty pails on the yoke ran on before him to the well for water.

"Look sharp, my girl!" the old man shouted after her, good-humoredly, and he went up to Levin. "Well, sir, are you going to Nikolay Ivanovitch Sviazhsky? His honor comes to us too," he began, chatting, leaning his elbows on the railing of the steps. In the middle of the old man's account of his acquaintance with Sviazhsky, the gates creaked again, and laborers came into the yard from the fields, with wooden ploughs and harrows. The horses harnessed to the ploughs and harrows were sleek and fat. The laborers were obviously of the household: two were young men in cotton shirts and caps, the two others were hired laborers in homespun shirts, one an old man, the other a young fellow. Moving off from the steps, the old man went up to the horses and began unharnessing them.

"What have they been ploughing?" asked Levin.

"Ploughing up the potatoes. We rent a bit of land too. Fedot, don't let out the gelding, but take it to the trough, and we'll put the other in harness."

"Oh, father, the ploughshares I ordered, has he brought them along?" asked the big, healthy-looking fellow, obviously the old man's son.

"There . . . in the outer room," answered the old man, bundling together the harness he had taken off, and flinging it on the ground. "You can put them on, while they have dinner."

The good-looking young woman came into the outer room with the full pails dragging at her shoulders. More women came on the scene from somewhere, young and handsome, middle-aged, old and ugly, with children and without children.

The samovar was beginning to sing; the laborers and the family, having disposed of the horses, came in to dinner. Levin, getting his provisions out of his carriage, invited the old man to take tea with him.

"Well, I have had some to-day already," said the old man, obviously accepting the invitation with pleasure. "But just a glass for company."

Over their tea Levin heard all about the old man's farming. Ten years before, the old man had rented three hundred acres from the lady who owned them, and a year ago he had bought them and rented another three hundred from a neighboring landowner. A small part of the land—the worst part—he let out for rent, while a hundred acres of arable land he cultivated himself with his family and two hired laborers. The old man complained that things were doing badly. But Levin saw that he simply did so from a feeling of propriety, and that his farm was in a flourishing condition. If it had been unsuccessful he would not have bought land at thirty-five roubles the acre, he would not have married his three sons and a nephew, he would not have rebuilt twice after fires, and each time on a larger scale. In spite of the old man's complaints, it was evident that he was proud, and justly proud, of his prosperity, proud of his sons, his nephew, his sons' wives, his horses and his cows, and especially of the fact that he was keeping all this farming going. From his conversation with the old man, Levin thought he was not averse to new methods either. He had planted a great many potatoes, and his potatoes, as Levin had seen driving past, were already past flowering and beginning to die down, while Levin's were only just coming into flower. He earthed up his potatoes with a modern plough borrowed from a neighboring landowner. He sowed wheat. The trifling fact that, thinning out his rye, the old man used the rye he thinned out for his horses, specially struck Levin.

How many times had Levin seen this splendid fodder wasted, and tried to get it saved; but always it had turned out to be impossible. The peasant got this done, and he could not say enough in praise of it as food for the beasts.

"What have the wenches to do? They carry it out in bundles to the roadside, and the cart brings it away."

"Well, we landowners can't manage well with our laborers," said Levin, handing him a glass of tea.

"Thank you," said the old man, and he took the glass, but refused sugar, pointing to a lump he had left. "They're simple destruction," said he. "Look at Sviazhsky's, for instance. We know what the land's like—first-rate, yet there's not much of a crop to boast of. It's not looked after enough—that's all it is!"

"But you work your land with hired laborers?"

"We're all peasants together. We go into everything ourselves. If a man's no use, he can go, and we can manage by ourselves."

"Father, Finogen wants some tar," said the young woman in the clogs, coming in.

"Yes, yes, that's how it is, sir!" said the old man, getting up, and crossing himself deliberately, he thanked Levin and went out.

When Levin went into the kitchen to call his coachman he saw the whole family at dinner. The women were standing up waiting on them. The young, sturdy-looking son was telling something funny with his mouth full of pudding, and they were all laughing, the woman in the clogs, who was pouring cabbage-soup into a bowl, laughing most merrily of all.

Very probably the good-looking face of the young woman in the clogs had a good deal to do with the impression of well-being this peasant household made upon Levin, but the impression was so strong that Levin could never get rid of it. And all the way from the old peasant's to Sviazhsky's he kept recalling this peasant farm as though there were something in this impression that demanded his special attention.

CHAPTER XXVI

Sviazhsky was the marshal of his district. He was five years older than Levin, and had long been married. His sister-in-law, a young girl Levin liked very much, lived in his house; and Levin knew that Sviazhsky and his wife would have greatly liked to marry the girl to him. He knew this with certainty, as so-called eligible young men always know it, though he could never have brought himself to speak of it to any one; and he knew too that, although he wanted to get married, and although by every token this very attractive girl would make an excellent wife, he could no more have married her, even if he had not been in love with Kitty Shtcherbatskaya, than he could have flown up to the sky. And this knowledge poisoned the pleasure he had hoped to find in the visit to Sviazhsky.

On getting Sviazhsky's letter with the invitation for shooting, Levin had immediately thought of this; but in spite of it he had made up his mind that Sviazhsky's having such views for him was simply his own groundless supposition, and so he would go, all the same. Besides, at the bottom of his heart he had a desire to try himself, put himself to the test in regard to this girl. The Sviazhskys' home-life was exceedingly pleasant, and Sviazhsky himself, the best type of man taking part in local affairs that Levin knew, was very interesting to him.

Sviazhsky was one of those people, always a source of wonder to Levin, whose convictions, very logical though never original, go one way by themselves, while their life, exceedingly definite and firm in its direction, goes its way quite apart and almost always in direct contradiction to their convictions. Sviazhsky was an extremely advanced man. He despised the nobility, and believed the mass of the nobility to be secretly in favor of serfdom, and only concealing their views from cowardice. He regarded Russia as a ruined country, rather after the style of Turkey, and the government of Russia as so bad that he never permitted himself to criticize its doings seriously, and yet he was a functionary of that government and a model marshal of nobility, and when he drove about he always wore the cockade of office

and the cap with the red band.
He considered human life tolerable only abroad, and went abroad to stay at every opportunity, and at the same time he carried on a complex and improved system of agriculture in Russia, and with extreme interest followed everything and knew everything that was being done in Russia. He considered the Russian peasant as occupying a stage of development intermediate between the ape and the man, and at the same time in the local assemblies no one was readier to shake hands with the peasants and listen to their opinion. He believed neither in God nor the devil, but was much concerned about the question of the improvement of the clergy and the maintenance of their revenues, and took special trouble to keep up the church in his village.

On the woman question he was on the side of the extreme advocates of complete liberty for women, and especially their right to labor. But he lived with his wife on such terms that their affectionate childless home-life was the admiration of every one, and arranged his wife's life so that she did nothing and could do nothing but share her husband's efforts that her time should pass as happily and as agreeably as possible.

If it had not been a characteristic of Levin's to put the most favorable interpretation on people, Sviazhsky's character would have presented no doubt or difficulty to him: he would have said to himself, "a fool or a knave," and everything would have seemed clear. But he could not say "a fool," because Sviazhsky was unmistakably clever, and moreover, a highly cultivated man, who was exceptionally modest over his culture. There was not a subject he knew nothing of. But he did not display his knowledge except when he was compelled to do so. Still less could Levin say that he was a knave, as Sviazhsky was unmistakably an honest, good-hearted, sensible man, who worked good-humoredly, keenly, and perseveringly at his work; he was held in high honor by every one about him, and certainly he had never consciously done, and was indeed incapable of doing, anything base.

Levin tried to understand him, and could not understand him, and looked at him and his life as at a living enigma.

Levin and he were very friendly, and so Levin used to venture to sound Sviazhsky, to try to get at the very foundation of his view of life; but it was always in vain. Every time Levin tried to penetrate beyond the outer chambers of Sviazhsky's mind, which were hospitably open to all, he noticed that Sviazhsky was slightly disconcerted; faint signs of alarm were visible in his eyes, as though he were afraid Levin would understand him, and he would give him a kindly, good-humored repulse.

Just now, since his disenchantment with farming, Levin was particularly glad to stay with Sviazhsky. Apart from the fact that the sight of this happy and affectionate couple, so pleased with themselves and every one else, and their well-ordered home had always a cheering effect on Levin, he felt a longing, now that he was so dissatisfied with his own life, to get at that secret in Sviazhsky that gave him such clearness, definiteness, and good courage in life. Moreover, Levin knew that at Sviazhsky's he should meet the landowners of the neighborhood, and it was particularly interesting for him just now to hear and take part in those rural conversations concerning crops, laborers' wages, and so on, which, he was aware, are conventionally regarded as something very low, but which seemed to him just now to constitute the one subject of importance. "It was not, perhaps, of importance in the days of serfdom, and it may not be of importance in England. In both cases the conditions of agriculture are firmly established; but among us now, when everything has been turned upside down and is only just taking shape, the question what form these conditions will take is the one question of importance in Russia," thought Levin.

The shooting turned out to be worse than Levin had expected. The marsh was dry and there were no grouse at all. He walked about the whole day and only brought back three birds, but to make up for that—he brought back, as he always did from shooting, an excellent appetite, excellent spirits, and that keen, intellectual mood which with him always accompanied violent physical exertion. And while out shooting, when he seemed to be thinking of nothing at all, suddenly the old man and his family kept coming back to his mind, and the impression of them seemed to claim not merely his attention, but the solution of some question connected with them.

In the evening at tea, two landowners who had come about some business connected with a wardship were of the party, and the interesting conversation Levin had been looking forward to sprang up.

Levin was sitting beside his hostess at the tea-table, and was obliged to keep up a conversation with her and her sister, who was sitting opposite him. Madame Sviazhskaya was a round-faced, fair-haired, rather short woman, all smiles and dimples. Levin tried through her to get a solution of the weighty enigma her husband presented to his mind; but he had not complete freedom of ideas, because he was in an agony of embarrassment. This agony of embarrassment was due to the fact that the sister-in-law was sitting opposite to him, in a dress, specially put on, as he fancied, for his benefit, cut particularly open, in the shape of a trapeze, on her white bosom. This quadrangular opening, in spite of the bosom's being very white, or just because it was very white, deprived Levin of the full use of his faculties. He imagined, probably mistakenly, that this low-necked bodice had been made on his account, and felt that he had no right to look at it, and tried not to look at it; but he felt that he was to blame for the very fact of the low-necked bodice having been made. It seemed to Levin that he had deceived some one, that he ought to explain something, but that to explain it was impossible, and for that reason he was continually blushing, was ill at ease and awkward. His awkwardness infected the pretty sister-in-law too.

But their hostess appeared not to observe this, and kept purposely drawing her into the conversation.

"You say," she said, pursuing the subject that had been started, "that my husband cannot be interested in what's Russian. It's quite the contrary; he is always in cheerful spirits abroad, but not as he is here. Here, he feels in his proper place. He has so much to do, and he has the faculty of interesting himself in everything. Oh, you've not been to see our school, have you?"

"I've seen it. . . . The little house covered with ivy, isn't it?"

"Yes; that's Nastia's work," she said, indicating her sister.

"You teach in it yourself?" asked Levin, trying to look above the open neck, but feeling that wherever he looked in that direction he should see it.

"Yes; I used to teach in it myself, and do teach still, but we have a first-rate schoolmistress now. And we've started gymnastic exercises."

"No, thank you, I won't have any more tea," said Levin, and conscious of doing a rude thing, but incapable of continuing the conversation, he got up, blushing. "I hear a very interesting conversation," he added, and walked to the other end of the table, where Sviazhsky was sitting with the two gentlemen of the neighborhood. Sviazhsky was sitting sideways, with one elbow on the table, and a cup in one hand, while with the other hand he gathered up his beard, held it to his nose and let it drop again, as though he were smelling it. His brilliant black eyes were looking straight at the excited country gentleman with gray whiskers, and apparently he derived amusement from his remarks. The gentleman was complaining of the peasants. It was evident to Levin that Sviazhsky knew an answer to this gentleman's complaints, which would at once demolish his whole contention, but that in his position he could not give utterance to this answer, and listened, not without pleasure, to the landowner's comic speeches.

The gentleman with the gray whiskers was obviously an inveterate adherent of serfdom and a devoted agriculturist, who had lived all his life in the country. Levin saw proofs of this in his dress, in the old-fashioned threadbare coat, obviously not his every-day attire, in his shrewd, deep-set eyes, in his idiomatic, fluent Russian, in the imperious tone that had become habitual from long use, and in the resolute gestures of his large, red, sunburnt hands, with an old betrothal-ring on the little finger.

C H A P T E R   X X V I I

"If I'd only the heart to throw up what's been set going . . . such a lot of trouble wasted . . . I'd turn my back on the whole business, sell up, go off like Nikolay Ivanovitch . . . to hear *La Belle Hélène*," said the landowner, a pleasant smile lighting up his shrewd old face.

"But you see you don't throw it up," said Nikolay Ivanovitch Sviazhsky; "so there must be something gained."

"The only gain is that I live in my own house, neither bought nor hired. Besides, one keeps hoping the people will learn sense. Though, instead of that, you'd never believe it—the drunkenness, the immorality! They keep chopping and changing their bits of land. Not a sight of a horse or a cow. The peasant's dying of hunger, but just go and take him on as a laborer, he'll do his best to do you a mischief, and then bring you up before the justice of the peace."

"But then you make complaints to the justice too," said Sviazhsky.

"I lodge complaints? Not for anything in the world! Such a talking, and such a to-do, that one would have cause to regret it. At the works, for instance, they pocketed the advance-money and made off. What did the justice do? Why, acquitted them. Nothing keeps them in order but their own communal court and their village elder. He'll flog them in the good old style! But for that there'd be nothing for it but to give it all up and run away."

Obviously the landowner was chaffing Sviazhsky, who, far from resenting it, was apparently amused by it.

"But you see we manage our land without such extreme measures," said he, smiling: "Levin and I and this gentleman."

He indicated the other landowner.

"Yes, the thing's done at Mihail Petrovitch's, but ask him how it's done. Do you call that a rational system?" said the landowner, obviously rather proud of the word "rational."

396

"My system's very simple," said Mihail Petrovitch, "thank God. All my management rests on getting the money ready for the autumn taxes, and the peasants come to me, 'Father, master, help us!' Well, the peasants are all one's neighbors; one feels for them. So one advances them a third, but one says: 'Remember, lads, I have helped you, and you must help me when I need it—whether it's the sowing of the oats, or the hay-cutting, or the harvest'; and well, one agrees, so much for each taxpayer—though there are dishonest ones among them too, it's true."

Levin, who had long been familiar with these patriarchal methods, exchanged glances with Sviazhsky and interrupted Mihail Petrovitch, turning again to the gentleman with the gray whiskers.

"Then what do you think?" he asked; "what system is one to adopt nowadays?"

"Why, manage like Mihail Petrovitch, or let the land for half the crop or for rent to the peasants; that one can do—only that's just how the general prosperity of the country is being ruined. Where the land with serf-labor and good management gave a yield of nine to one, on the half-crop system it yields three to one. Russia has been ruined by the emancipation!"

Sviazhsky looked with smiling eyes at Levin, and even made a faint gesture of irony to him; but Levin did not think the landowner's words absurd, he understood them better than he did Sviazhsky. A great deal more of what the gentleman with the gray whiskers said to show in what way Russia was ruined by the emancipation struck him indeed as very true, new to him, and quite incontestable. The landowner unmistakably spoke his own individual thought—a thing that very rarely happens—and a thought to which he had been brought not by a desire of finding some exercise for an idle brain, but a thought which had grown up out of the conditions of his life, which he had brooded over in the solitude of his village, and had considered in every aspect.

"The point is, don't you see, that progress of every sort is only made by the use of authority," he said, evidently wishing to show he was not without culture. "Take the reforms of Peter, of Catherine, of Alexander. Take European history. And progress in agriculture more than anything else—the potato, for instance, that was introduced among us by force. The wooden plough too wasn't always used. It was introduced maybe in the days before the Empire, but it was probably brought in by force. Now, in our own day, we landowners in the serf times used various improvements in our husbandry: drying machines and thrashing-machines, and carting manure and all the modern implements—all that we brought into use by our authority, and the peasants opposed it at first, and ended by imitating us. Now by the abolition of serfdom we have been deprived of our authority; and so our husbandry, where it had been raised to a high level, is bound to sink to the most savage primitive condition. That's how I see it."

"But why so? If it's rational, you'll be able to keep up the same system with hired labor," said Sviazhsky.

"We've no power over them. With whom am I going to work the system, allow me to ask?"

"There it is—the labor force—the chief element in agriculture," thought Levin.

"With laborers."

"The laborers won't work well, and won't work with good implements. Our laborer can do nothing but get drunk like a pig, and when he's drunk he ruins everything you give him. He makes the horses ill with too much water, cuts good harness, barters the tires of the wheels for drink, drops bits of iron into the thrashing-machine, so as to break it. He loathes the sight of anything that's not after his fashion. And that's how it is the whole level of husbandry has fallen. Lands gone out of cultivation, overgrown with weeds, or divided among the peasants, and where millions of bushels were raised you get a hundred thousand; the wealth of the country has decreased. If the same thing had been done, but with care that . . ."

And he proceeded to unfold his own scheme of emancipation by means of which these drawbacks might have been avoided.

This did not interest Levin, but when he had finished, Levin went back to his first position, and, addressing Sviazhsky, and trying to draw him into expressing his serious opinion:—

"That the standard of culture is falling, and that with our present relations to the peasants there is no possibility of farming on a rational system to yield a profit—that's perfectly true," said he.

"I don't believe it," Sviazhsky replied quite seriously; "all I see is that we don't know how to cultivate the land, and that our system of agriculture in the serf-days was by no means too high, but too low. We have no machines, no good stock, no efficient supervision; we don't even know how to keep accounts. Ask any landowner; he won't be able to tell you what crop's profitable, and what's not."

"Italian bookkeeping," said the gentleman of the gray whiskers ironically. "You may keep your books as you like, but if they spoil everything for you, there won't be any profit."

"Why do they spoil things? A poor thrashing-machine, or your Russian presser, they will break, but my steam-press they don't break. A wretched Russian nag they'll ruin, but keep good dray-horses—they won't ruin them. And so it is all round. We must raise our farming to a higher level."

"Oh, if one only had the means to do it, Nikolay Ivanovitch! It's all very well for you; but for me, with a son to keep at the university, lads to be educated at the high school—how am I going to buy these dray-horses?"

"Well, that's what the land banks are for."

"To get what's left me sold by auction? No, thank you."

"I don't agree that it's necessary or possible to raise the level of agriculture still higher," said Levin. "I devote myself to it, and I have means, but I can do nothing. As to the banks, I don't know to whom they're any good. For my part, anyway, whatever I've spent money on in the way of husbandry, it has been a loss: stock—a loss, machinery—a loss."

"That's true enough," the gentleman with the gray whiskers chimed in, positively laughing with satisfaction.

"And I'm not the only one," pursued Levin. "I mix with all the neighboring landowners, who are cultivating their land on a rational system; they all, with rare exceptions, are doing so at a loss. Come, tell us how does your land do—does it pay?" said Levin, and at once in Sviazhsky's eyes he detected that fleeting expression of alarm which he had noticed whenever he had tried to penetrate beyond the outer chambers of Sviazhsky's mind.

Moreover, this question on Levin's part was not quite in good faith. Madame Sviazhskaya had just told him at tea that they had that summer invited a German expert in bookkeeping from

Moscow, who for a consideration of five hundred roubles had investigated the management of their property, and found that it was costing them a loss of three thousand odd roubles. She did not remember the precise sum, but it appeared that the German had worked it out to the fraction of a farthing.

The gray-whiskered landowner smiled at the mention of the profits of Sviazhsky's farming, obviously aware how much gain his neighbor and marshal was likely to be making.

"Possibly it does not pay," answered Sviazhsky. "That merely proves either that I'm a bad manager, or that I've sunk my capital for the increase of my rents."

"Oh, rent!" Levin cried with horror. "Rent there may be in Europe, where land has been improved by the labor put into it; but with us all the land is deteriorating from the labor put into it—in other words, they're working it out; so there's no question of rent."

"How no rent? It's a law."

"Then we're outside the law; rent explains nothing for us, but simply muddles us. No, tell me how there can be a theory of rent? . . ."

"Will you have some junket? Masha, pass us some junket or raspberries." He turned to his wife. "Extraordinarily late the raspberries are lasting this year."

And in the happiest frame of mind Sviazhsky got up and walked off, apparently supposing the conversation to have ended at the very point when to Levin it seemed that it was only just beginning.

Having lost his antagonist, Levin continued the conversation with the gray-whiskered landowner, trying to prove to him that all the difficulty arises from the fact that we don't find out the peculiarities and habits of our laborer; but the landowner, like all men who think independently and in isolation, was slow in taking in any other person's idea, and particularly partial to his own. He stuck to it that the Russian peasant is a swine and likes swinishness, and that to get him out of his swinishness one must have authority, and there is none; one must have the stick, and we have become so liberal that we have all of a sudden replaced the stick that served us for a thousand years by lawyers and model prisons, where the worthless, stinking peasant is fed on good soup and has a fixed allowance of cubic feet of air.

"What makes you think," said Levin, trying to get back to the question, "that it's impossible to find some relation to the laborer in which the labor would become productive?"

"That never could be so with the Russian peasantry; we've no power over them," answered the landowner.

"How can new conditions be found?" said Sviazhsky. Having eaten some junket and lighted a cigarette, he came back to the discussion. "All possible relations to the labor force have been defined and studied," he said. "The relic of barbarism, the primitive commune with each guarantee for all, will disappear of itself; serfdom has been abolished—there remains nothing but free labor, and its forms are fixed and ready made, and must be adopted. Permanent hands, day-laborers, farmers—you can't get out of those forms."

"But Europe is dissatisfied with these forms."

"Dissatisfied, and seeking new ones. And will find them, in all probability."

"That's just what I was meaning," answered Levin. "Why shouldn't we seek them for ourselves?"

"Because it would be just like inventing afresh the means for constructing railways. They are ready, invented."

"But if they don't do for us, if they're stupid?" said Levin.

And again he detected the expression of alarm in the eyes of Sviazhsky.

"Oh, yes; we'll bury the world under our caps! We've found the secret Europe was seeking for! I've heard all that; but, excuse me, do you know all that's been done in Europe on the question of the organization of labor?"

"No, very little."

"That question is now absorbing the best minds in Europe. The Schulze-Delitsch movement. . . . And then all this enormous literature of the labor question, the most liberal Lassalle movement . . . the Mulhausen experiment? That's a fact by now, as you're probably aware."

"I have some idea of it, but very vague."

"No, you only say that; no doubt you know all about it as well as I do. I'm not a professor of sociology, of course, but it interested me, and really, if it interests you, you ought to study it."

"But what conclusion have they come to?"

"Excuse me . . ."

The two neighbors had risen, and Sviazhsky, once more checking Levin in his inconvenient habit of peeping into what was beyond the outer chambers of his mind, went to see his guests out.

C H A P T E R   X X V I I I

Levin was insufferably bored that evening with the ladies; he was stirred as he had never been before by the idea that the dissatisfaction he was feeling with his system of managing his land was not an exceptional case, but the general condition of things in Russia; that the organization of some relation of the laborers to the soil in which they would work, as with the peasant he had met half-way to the Sviazhskys' was not a dream, but a problem which must be solved. And it seemed to him that the problem could be solved, and that he ought to try and solve it.

After saying good-night to the ladies, and promising to stay the whole of the next day, so as to make an expedition on horseback with them to see an interesting ruin in the crown forest, Levin went, before going to bed, into his host's study to get the books on the labor question that Sviazhsky had offered him. Sviazhsky's study was a huge room, surrounded by bookcases and with two tables in it—one a massive writing-table, standing in the middle of the room, and the other a round table, covered with recent numbers of reviews and journals in different languages, ranged like the rays of a star round the lamp. On the writing-table was a stand of drawers marked with gold lettering, and full of papers of various sorts.

Sviazhsky took out the books, and sat down in a rocking-chair.

"What are you looking at there?" he said to Levin, who was standing at the round table looking through the reviews.

"Oh, yes, there's a very interesting article here," said Sviazhsky of the review Levin was holding in his hand. "It appears," he went on, with eager interest, "that Friedrich was not, after all, the person chiefly responsible for the partition of Poland. It is proved . . ."

And with his characteristic clearness, he summed up those new, very important, and interesting revelations. Although Levin was engrossed at the moment by his ideas about the problem of the land, he wondered, as he heard Sviazhsky: "What is there inside of him? And why, why is he interested in the partition of Poland?" When Sviazhsky had finished, Levin could not help asking: "Well, and what then?" But there was nothing to follow. It was simply interesting that it had been proved to be so and so. But Sviazhsky did not explain, and saw no need to explain why it was interesting to him.

"Yes, but I was very much interested by your irritable neighbor," said Levin, sighing. "He's a clever fellow, and said a lot that was true."

"Oh, get along with you! An inveterate supporter of serfdom at heart, like all of them!" said Sviazhsky.

"Whose marshal you are."

"Yes, only I marshal them in the other direction," said Sviazhsky, laughing.

"I'll tell you what interests me very much," said Levin. "He's right that our system, that's to say of rational farming, doesn't answer, that the only thing that answers is the money-lender system, like that meek-looking gentleman's, or else the very simplest . . . Whose fault is it?"

"Our own, of course. Besides, it's not true that it doesn't answer. It answers with Vassiltchikov."

"A factory . . ."

"But I really don't know what it is you are surprised at. The people are at such a low stage of rational and moral development, that it's obvious they're bound to oppose everything that's strange to them. In Europe, a rational system answers because the people are educated; it follows that we must educate the people—that's all."

"But how are we to educate the people?"

"To educate the people three things are needed: schools, and schools, and schools."

"But you said yourself the people are at such a low stage of material development: what help are schools for that?"

"Do you know, you remind me of the story of the advice given to the sick man—You should try purgative medicine. Taken: worse. Try leeches. Tried them: worse. Well, then, there's nothing left but to pray to God. Tried it: worse. That's just how it is with us. I say political economy; you say—worse. I say socialism: worse. Education: worse."

"But how do schools help matters?"

"They give the peasant fresh wants."

"Well, that's a thing I've never understood," Levin replied with heat. "In what way are schools going to help the people to improve their material position? You say schools, education, will give them fresh wants. So much the worse, since they won't be capable of satisfying them. And in what way a knowledge of addition and subtraction and the catechism is going to improve their material condition, I never could make out. The day before yesterday, I met a peasant woman in the evening with a little baby, and asked her where she was going. She said she was going to the wise woman; her boy had screaming fits, so she was taking him to be doctored. I asked, 'Why, how does the wise woman cure screaming fits?' 'She puts the child on the hen-roost and repeats some charm. . . .'"

"Well, you're saying it yourself! What's wanted to prevent her taking her child to the hen-roost to cure it of screaming fits is just . . ." Sviazhsky said, smiling good-humoredly.

"Oh, no!" said Levin with annoyance; "that method of doctoring I merely meant as a simile for doctoring the people with schools. The people are poor and ignorant—that we see as surely as the peasant woman sees the baby is ill because it screams. But in what way this trouble of poverty and ignorance is to be cured by schools is as incomprehensible as how the hen-roost affects the screaming. What has to be cured is what makes him poor."

"Well, in that, at least, you're in agreement with Spencer, whom you dislike so much. He says, too, that education may be the consequence of greater prosperity and comfort, of more frequent washing, as he says, but not of being able to read and write. . . ."

"Well, then, I'm very glad—or the contrary, very sorry, that I'm in agreement with Spencer; only I've known it a long while. Schools can do no good; what will do good is an economic organization in which the people will become richer, will have more leisure—and then there will be schools."

"Still, all over Europe now schools are obligatory."

"And how far do you agree with Spencer yourself about it?" asked Levin.

But there was a gleam of alarm in Sviazhsky's eyes, and he said smiling:

"No; that screaming story is positively capital! Did you really hear it yourself?"

Levin saw that he was not to discover the connection between this man's life and his thoughts. Obviously he did not care in the least what his reasoning led him to; all he wanted was the process of reasoning. And he did not like it when the process of reasoning brought him into a blind alley. That was the only thing he disliked, and avoided by changing the conversation to something agreeable and amusing.

All the impressions of the day, beginning with the impression made by the old peasant, which served, as it were, as the fundamental basis of all the conceptions and ideas of the day, threw Levin into violent excitement. This dear good Sviazhsky, keeping a stock of ideas simply for social purposes, and obviously having some other principles hidden from Levin, while with the crowd, whose name is legion, he guided public opinion by ideas he did not share; that irascible country gentleman, perfectly correct in the conclusions that he had been worried into by life, but wrong in his exasperation against a whole class, and that the best class in Russia; his own dissatisfaction with the work he had been doing, and the vague hope of finding a remedy for all this —all was blended in a sense of inward turmoil, and anticipation of some solution near at hand.

Left alone in the room assigned him, lying on a spring mattress that yielded unexpectedly at every movement of his arm or his leg, Levin did not fall asleep for a long while. Not one conversation with Sviazhsky, though he had said a great deal that was clever, had interested Levin; but the conclusions of the irascible landowner required consideration. Levin could not help recalling every word he had said, and in imagination amending his own replies.

"Yes, I ought to have said to him: You say that our husbandry does not answer because the peasant hates improvements, and that they must be forced on him by authority. If no system of husbandry answered at all without these improvements, you. would be quite right. But the only system that does answer is when the laborer is working in accordance with his habits, just as on the old peasant's land half-way here. Your and our general dissatisfaction with the system shows that either we are to blame or the laborers. We have gone our way—the European way—a long while, without asking ourselves about the qualities of our labor force. Let us try to look upon the labor force not as an abstract force, but as the *Russian peasant* with his instincts, and we shall arrange our system of culture in accordance with that. Imagine, I ought to have said to him, that you have the same system as the old peasant has, that you have found means of making your laborers take an interest in the success of the work, and have found the happy mean in the way of improvements which they will admit, and you will, without exhausting the soil, get twice or three times the yield you got before. Divide it in halves, give half as the share of labor, the surplus left you will be greater, and the share of labor will be greater too. And to do this one must lower the standard of husbandry and interest the laborers in its success. How to do this?—that's a matter of detail; but undoubtedly it can be done."

This idea threw Levin into a great excitement. He did not sleep half the night, thinking over in detail the putting of his idea into practice. He had not intended to go away next day, but he now determined to go home early in the morning. Besides, the sister-in-law with her low-necked bodice aroused in him a feeling akin to shame and remorse for some utterly base action. Most important of all—he must get back without delay: he would have to make haste to put his new project to the peasants before the sowing of the winter wheat, so that the sowing might be undertaken on a new basis. He had made up his mind to revolutionize his whole system.

CHAPTER XXIX

The carrying out of Levin's plan presented many difficulties; but he struggled on, doing his utmost, and attained a result which, though not what he desired, was enough to enable him, without self-deception, to believe that the attempt was worth the trouble. One of the chief difficulties was that the process of cultivating the land was in full swing, that it was impossible to stop everything and begin it all again from the beginning, and the machine had to be mended while in motion.

When on the evening that he arrived home he informed the bailiff of his plans, the latter with visible pleasure agreed with what he said so long as he was pointing out that all that had been done up to that time was stupid and useless. The bailiff said that he had said so a long while ago, but no heed had been paid him. But as for the proposal made by Levin—to take a part as shareholder with his laborers in each agricultural undertaking—at this the bailiff simply expressed a profound despondency, and offered no definite opinion, but began immediately talking of the urgent necessity of carrying the remaining sheaves of rye the next day, and of sending the men out for the second ploughing, so that Levin felt that this was not the time for discussing it.

On beginning to talk to the peasants about it, and making a proposition to cede them the land on new terms, he came into collision with the same great difficulty that they were so much absorbed by the current work of the day, that they had not time to consider the advantages and disadvantages of the proposed scheme.

The simple-hearted Ivan, the cowherd, seemed completely to grasp Levin's proposal—that he should with his family take a share of the profits of the cattle-yard—and he was in complete sympathy with the plan. But when Levin hinted at the future advantages, Ivan's face expressed alarm and regret that he could not hear all he had to say, and he made haste to find himself some task that would admit of no delay: he either snatched up the fork to pitch the hay out of the pens, or ran to get water or to clear out the dung.

Another difficulty lay in the invincible disbelief of the peasant that a landowner's object could be anything else than a desire to squeeze all he could out of them. They were firmly convinced that his real aim (whatever he might say to them) would always be in what he did not say to them. And they themselves, in giving their opinion, said a great deal but never said what was their real object. Moreover (Levin felt that the irascible landowner had been right) the peasants made their first and unalterable condition of any agreement whatever that they should not be forced to any new methods of tillage of any kind, nor to use new implements. They agreed that the modern plough ploughed better, that the scarifier did the work more quickly, but they found thousands of reasons that made it out of the question for them to use either of them; and though he had accepted the conviction that he would have to lower the standard of cultivation, he felt sorry to give up improved methods, the advantages of which were so obvious. But in spite of all these difficulties he got his way, and by autumn the system was working, or at least so it seemed to him.

At first Levin had thought of giving up the whole farming of the land just as it was to the peasants, the laborers, and the bailiff on new conditions of partnership; but he was very soon convinced that this was impossible, and determined to divide it up. The cattle-yard, the garden, hay-fields, and arable land, divided into several parts, had to be made into separate lots. The simple-hearted cowherd, Ivan, who, Levin fancied, understood the matter better than any of them, collecting together a gang of workers to help him, principally of his own family, became a partner in the cattle-yard. A distant part of the estate, a tract of waste land that had lain fallow for eight years, was with the help of the clever carpenter, Fyodor Ryezunov, taken by six families of peasants on new conditions of partnership, and the peasant Shuraev took the management of all the vegetable gardens on the same terms. The remainder of the land was still worked on the old system, but these three associated partnerships were the first step to a new organization of the whole, and they completely took up Levin's time.

It is true that in the cattle-yard things went no better than before, and Ivan strenuously opposed warm housing for the cows and butter made of fresh cream, affirming that cows require less food if kept cold, and that butter is more profitable made from sour cream, and he asked for wages just as under the old system, and took not the slightest interest in the fact that the money he received was not wages but an advance out of his future share in the profits.

It is true that Fyodor Ryezunov's company did not plough over the ground twice before sowing, as had been agreed, justifying themselves on the plea that the time was too short. It is true that the peasants of the same company, though they had agreed to work the land on new conditions, always spoke of the land, not as held in partnership, but as rented for half the crop, and more than once the peasants and Ryezunov himself said to Levin, "If you would take a rent for the land, it would save you trouble, and we should be more free." Moreover the same peasants kept putting off, on various excuses, the building of a cattle-yard and barn on the land as agreed upon, and delayed doing it till the winter.

It is true that Shuraev would have liked to let out the kitchen gardens he had undertaken in small lots to the peasants. He evidently quite misunderstood, and apparently intentionally misunderstood, the conditions upon which the land had been given to him.

Often, too, talking to the peasants and explaining to them all the advantages of the plan, Levin felt that the peasants heard nothing but the sound of his voice, and were firmly resolved, whatever he might say, not to let themselves be taken in. He felt this especially when he talked to the cleverest of the peasants, Ryezunov, and detected the gleam in Ryezunov's eyes which showed so plainly both ironical amusement at Levin, and the firm conviction that, if any one were to be taken in, it would not be he, Ryezunov. But in spite of all this Levin thought the system worked, and that by keeping accounts strictly and insisting on his own way, he would prove to them in the future the advantages of the arrangement, and then the system would go of itself.

These matters, together with the management of the land still left on his hands, and the indoor work over his book, so engrossed Levin the whole summer that he scarcely ever went out shooting.

At the end of August he heard that the Oblonskys had gone away to Moscow, from their servant who brought back the side-saddle. He felt that in not answering Darya Alexandrovna's letter he had by his rudeness, of which he could not think without a flush of shame, burned his ships, and that he would never go and see them again. He had been just as rude with the Sviazhskys, leaving them without saying good-bye. But he would never go to see them again either. He did not care about that now. The business of reorganizing the farming of his land absorbed him as completely as though there would never be anything else in his life. He read the books lent him by Sviazhsky, and copying out what he had not got, he read both the economic and socialistic books on the subject, but, as he had anticipated, found nothing bearing on the scheme he had undertaken. In the books on political economy—in Mill, for instance, whom he studied first with great ardor, hoping every minute to find an answer to the questions that were engrossing him—he found laws deduced from the condition of land culture in Europe; but he did not see why these laws, which did not apply in Russia, must be general. He saw just the same thing in the socialistic books: either they were the beautiful but impracticable fantasies which had fascinated him when he was a student, or they were attempts at improving, rectifying the economic position in which Europe was placed, with which the system of land tenure in Russia had nothing in common. Political economy told him that the laws by which the wealth of Europe had been developed, and was developing, were universal and unvarying. Socialism told him that development along these lines leads to ruin. And neither of them gave an answer, or even a hint, in reply to the question what he, Levin, and all the Russian peasants and landowners, were to do with their millions of hands and millions of acres, to make them as productive as possible for the common weal.

Having once taken the subject up, he read conscientiously everything bearing on it, and intended in the autumn to go abroad to study land systems on the spot, in order that he might not on this question be confronted with what so often met him on various subjects. Often, just as he was beginning to understand the idea in the mind of any one he was talking to, and was beginning to explain his own, he would suddenly be told: "But

Kauffmann, but Jones, but Dubois, but Michelli? You haven't read them: they've thrashed that question out thoroughly."

He saw now distinctly that Kauffmann and Michelli had nothing to tell him. He knew what he wanted. He saw that Russia has splendid land, splendid laborers, and that in certain cases, as at the peasant's on the way to Sviazhsky's, the produce raised by the laborers and the land is great—in the majority of cases when capital is applied in the European way the produce is small, and that this simply arises from the fact that the laborers want to work and work well only in their own peculiar way, and that this antagonism is not incidental but invariable, and has its roots in the national spirit. He thought that the Russian people whose task it was to colonize and cultivate vast tracts of unoccupied land, consciously adhered, till all their land was occupied, to the methods suitable to their purpose, and that their methods were by no means so bad as was generally supposed. And he wanted to prove this theoretically in his book and practically on his land.

CHAPTER XXX

AT THE end of September the timber had been carted for building the cattle-yard on the land that had been allotted to the association of peasants, and the butter from the cows was sold and the profits divided. In practice the system worked capitally, or, at least, so it seemed to Levin. In order to work out the whole subject theoretically and to complete his book, which, in Levin's day-dreams, was not merely to effect a revolution in political economy, but to annihilate that science entirely and to lay the foundation of a new science of the relation of the people to the soil, all that was left to do was to make a tour abroad, and to study on the spot all that had been done in the same direction, and to collect conclusive evidence that all that had been done there was not what was wanted. Levin was only waiting for the delivery of his wheat to receive the money for it and go abroad. But the rains began, preventing the harvesting of the corn and potatoes left in the fields, and putting a stop to all work, even to the delivery of the wheat.

The mud was impassable along the roads; two mills were carried away, and the weather got worse and worse.

On the 30th of September the sun came out in the morning, and hoping for fine weather, Levin began making final preparations for his journey. He gave orders for the wheat to be delivered, sent the bailiff to the merchant to get the money owing him, and went out himself to give some final directions on the estate before setting off.

Having finished all his business, soaked through with the streams of water which kept running down the leather behind his neck and his gaiters, but in the keenest and most confident temper, Levin returned homewards in the evening. The weather had become worse than ever towards evening; the hail lashed the drenched mare so cruelly that she went along sideways, shaking her head and ears; but Levin was all right under his hood, and he looked cheerfully about him at the muddy streams running under the wheels, at the drops hanging on every bare twig, at the whiteness of the patch of unmelted hailstones on the planks of the bridge, at the thick layer of still juicy, fleshy leaves that lay heaped up about the stripped elm-tree. In spite of the gloominess of nature around him, he felt peculiarly eager. The talks he had been having with the peasants in the further village had shown that they were beginning to get used to their new position. The old servant to whose hut he had gone to get dry evidently approved of Levin's plan, and of his own accord proposed to enter the partnership by the purchase of cattle.

"I have only to go stubbornly on towards my aim, and I shall attain my end," thought Levin; "and it's something to work and take trouble for. This is not a matter of myself individually, the question of the public welfare comes into it. The whole system of culture, the chief element in the condition of the people, must be completely transformed. Instead of poverty, general prosperity and content; instead of hostility, harmony and unity of interests. In short, a bloodless revolution, but a revolution of the greatest magnitude, beginning in the little circle of our district, then the province, then Russia, the whole world. Because a just idea cannot but be fruitful. Yes, it's an aim worth working for. And it's being me, Kostya Levin, who went to a ball in a black tie, and was refused by the Shtcherbatskaya girl, and who was intrinsically such a pitiful, worthless creature—that proves nothing; I feel sure Franklin felt just as worthless, and he too had no faith in himself, thinking of himself as a whole. That means nothing. And he too, most likely, had an Agafea Mihalovna to whom he confided his secrets."

Musing on such thoughts Levin reached home in the darkness.

The bailiff, who had been to the merchant, had come back and brought part of the money for the wheat. An agreement had been made with the old servant, and on the road the bailiff had learned that everywhere the corn was still standing in the fields, so that his one hundred and sixty shocks that had not been carried were nothing in comparison with the losses of others.

After dinner Levin was sitting, as he usually did, in an easy-chair with a book, and as he read he went on thinking of the journey before him in connection with his book. To-day all the significance of his book rose before him with special distinctness, and whole periods ranged themselves in his mind in illustration of his theories. "I must write that down," he thought. "That ought to form a brief introduction, which I thought unnecessary before." He got up to go to his writing-table, and Laska, lying at his feet, got up too, stretching and looking at him as though to inquire where to go. But he had not time to write it down, for the head peasants had come round, and Levin went out into the hall to them.

After his levee, that is to say, giving directions about the labors of the next day, and seeing all the peasants who had business with him, Levin went back to his study and sat down to work.

Laska lay under the table; Agafea Mihalovna settled herself in her place with her stocking.

After writing for a little while, Levin suddenly thought with exceptional vividness of Kitty, her refusal, and their last meeting. He got up and began walking about the room.

"What's the use of being dreary?" said Agafea Mihalovna. "Come, why do you stay on at home? You ought to go to some warm springs, especially now you're ready for the journey."

"Well, I am going away the day after to-morrow, Agafea Mihalovna; I must finish my work."

"There, there, your work, you say! As if you hadn't done enough for the peasants! Why, as 'tis, they're saying, 'Your master will be getting some honor from the Tsar for it.' Indeed and it is a strange thing; why need you worry about the peasants?"

"I'm not worrying about them; I'm doing it for my own good."

Agafea Mihalovna knew every detail of Levin's plans for his land. Levin often put his views before her in all their complexity, and not uncommonly he argued with her and did not agree with her comments. But on this occasion she entirely misinterpreted what he had said.

"Of one's soul's salvation we all know and must think before all else," she said with a sigh. "Parfen Denisitch now, for all he was no scholar, he died a death that God grant every one of us the like," she said, referring to a servant who had died recently. "Took the sacrament and all."

"That's not what I mean," said he. "I mean that I'm acting for my own advantage. It's all the better for me if the peasants do their work better."

"Well, whatever you do, if he's a lazy good-for-nought, everything'll be at sixes and sevens. If he has a conscience, he'll work, and if not, there's no doing anything."

"Oh, come, you say yourself Ivan has begun looking after the cattle better."

"All I say is," answered Agafea Mihalovna, evidently not

speaking at random, but in strict sequence of idea, "that you ought to get married, that's what I say."

Agafea Mihalovna's allusion to the very subject he had only just been thinking about, hurt and stung him. Levin scowled, and without answering her, he sat down again to his work, repeating to himself all that he had been thinking of the real significance of that work. Only at intervals he listened in the stillness to the click of Agafea Mihalovna's needles, and recollecting what he did not want to remember, he frowned again.

At nine o'clock they heard the bell and the faint vibration of a carriage over the mud.

"Well, here's visitors come to us, and you won't be dull," said Agafea Mihalovna, getting up and going to the door. But Levin overtook her. His work was not going well now, and he was glad of a visitor, whoever it might be.

CHAPTER XXXI

RUNNING half-way down the staircase, Levin caught a sound he knew, a familiar cough in the hall. But he heard it indistinctly through the sound of his own footsteps, and hoped he was mistaken. Then he caught sight of a long, bony, familiar figure, and now it seemed there was no possibility of mistake; and yet he still went on hoping that this tall man taking off his fur cloak and coughing was not his brother Nikolay.

Levin loved his brother, but being with him was always a torture. Just now, when Levin, under the influence of the thoughts that had come to him, and Agafea Mihalovna's hint, was in a troubled and uncertain humor, the meeting with his brother that he had to face seemed particularly difficult. Instead of a lively, healthy visitor, some outsider who would, he hoped, cheer him up in his uncertain humor, he had to see his brother, who knew him through and through, who would call forth all the thoughts nearest his heart, would force him to show himself fully. And that he was not disposed to do.

Angry with himself for so base a feeling, Levin ran into the hall; as soon as he had seen his brother close, this feeling of selfish disappointment vanished instantly and was replaced by pity. Terrible as his brother Nikolay had been before in his emaciation and sickliness, now he looked still more emaciated, still more wasted. He was a skeleton covered with skin.

He stood in the hall, jerking his long thin neck, and pulling the scarf off it, and smiled a strange and pitiful smile. When he saw that smile, submissive and humble, Levin felt something clutching at his throat.

"You see, I've come to you," said Nikolay in a thick voice, never for one second taking his eyes off his brother's face. "I've been meaning to a long while, but I've been unwell all the time. Now I'm ever so much better," he said, rubbing his beard with his big thin hands.

"Yes, yes!" answered Levin. And he felt still more frightened when, kissing him, he felt with his lips the dryness of his brother's skin and saw close to him his big eyes, full of a strange light.

A few weeks before, Konstantin Levin had written to his brother that through the sale of the small part of the property, that had remained undivided, there was a sum of about two thousand roubles to come to him as his share.

Nikolay said that he had come now to take this money and, what was more important, to stay a while in the old nest, to get in touch with the earth, so as to renew his strength like the heroes of old for the work that lay before him. In spite of his exaggerated stoop, and the emaciation that was so striking from his height, his movements were as rapid and abrupt as ever. Levin led him into his study.

His brother, dressed with particular care—a thing he never used to do—combed his scanty, lank hair, and, smiling, went upstairs.

He was in the most affectionate and good-humored mood, just as Levin often remembered him in childhood. He even referred to Sergey Ivanovitch without rancor. When he saw Agafea Mihalovna, he made jokes with her and asked after the old servants. The news of the death of Parfen Denisitch made a painful impression on him. A look of fear crossed his face, but he regained his serenity immediately.

"Of course he was quite old," he said, and changed the subject. "Well, I'll spend a month or two with you, and then I'm off to

Moscow. Do you know, Myakov has promised me a place there, and I'm going into the service. Now I'm going to arrange my life quite differently," he went on. "You know I got rid of that woman."

"Marya Nikolaevna? Why, what for?"

"Oh, she was a horrid woman! She caused me all sorts of worries." But he did not say what the annoyances were. He could not say that he had cast off Marya Nikolaevna because the tea was weak, and, above all, because she would look after him, as though he were an invalid.

"Besides, I want to turn over a new leaf completely now. I've done silly things, of course, like every one else, but money's the last consideration; I don't regret it. So long as there's health, and my health, thank God, is quite restored."

Levin listened and racked his brains, but could think of nothing to say. Nikolay probably felt the same; he began questioning his brother about his affairs; and Levin was glad to talk about himself, because then he could speak without hypocrisy. He told his brother of his plans and his doings.

His brother listened, but evidently he was not interested by it.

These two men were so akin, so near each other, that the slightest gesture, the tone of voice, told both more than could be said in words.

Both of them now had only one thought—the illness of Nikolay and the nearness of his death—which stifled all else. But neither of them dared to speak of it, and so whatever they said—not uttering the one thought that filled their minds—was all falsehood. Never had Levin been so glad when the evening was over and it was time to go to bed. Never with any outside person, never on any official visit had he been so unnatural and false as he was that evening. And the consciousness of this unnaturalness, and the remorse he felt at it, made him even more unnatural. He wanted to weep over his dying, dearly loved brother, and he had to listen and keep on talking of how he meant to live.

As the house was damp, and only one bedroom had been kept heated, Levin put his brother to sleep in his own bedroom behind a screen.

His brother got into bed, and whether he slept or did not sleep, tossed about like a sick man, coughed, and when he could not get his throat clear, mumbled something. Sometimes when his breathing was painful, he said, "Oh, my God!" Sometimes when he was choking he muttered angrily, "Ah, the devil!" Levin could not sleep for a long while, hearing him. His thoughts were of the most various, but the end of all his thoughts was the same —death. Death, the inevitable end of all, for the first time presented itself to him with irresistible force. And death, which was here in this loved brother, groaning half asleep and from habit calling without distinction on God and the devil, was not so remote as it had hitherto seemed to him. It was in himself too, he felt that. If not to-day, to-morrow, if not to-morrow, in thirty years, wasn't it all the same! And what was this inevitable death —he did not know, had never thought about it, and what was more, had not the power, had not the courage to think about it.

"I work, I want to do something, but I had forgotten it must all end; I had forgotten—death."

He sat on his bed in the darkness, crouched up, hugging his knees, and holding his breath from the strain of thought, he pondered. But the more intensely he thought, the clearer it became to him that it was indubitably so, that in reality, looking

upon life, he had forgotten one little fact—that death will come, and all ends; that nothing was even worth beginning, and that there was no helping it anyway. Yes, it was awful, but it was so.

"But I am alive still. Now what's to be done? what's to be done?" he said in despair. He lighted a candle, got up cautiously and went to the looking-glass, and began looking at his face and hair. Yes, there were gray hairs about his temples. He opened his mouth. His back teeth were beginning to decay. He bared his muscular arms. Yes, there was strength in them. But Nikolay, who lay there breathing with what was left of lungs, had had a strong, healthy body too. And suddenly he recalled how they used to go to bed together as children, and how they only waited till Fyodor Bogdanitch was out of the room to fling pillows at each other and laugh, laugh irrepressibly, so that even their awe of Fyodor Bogdanitch could not check the effervescing, over-brimming sense of life and happiness. "And now that bent, hollow chest . . . and I, not knowing what will become of me, or wherefore . . ."

"K . . . ha! K . . . ha! Damnation! Why do you keep fidgeting, why don't you go to sleep?" his brother's voice called to him.

"Oh, I don't know; I'm not sleepy."

"I have had a good sleep, I'm not in a sweat now. Just see, feel my shirt; it's all wet, is it?"

Levin felt, withdrew behind the screen, and put out the candle, but for a long while he could not sleep. The question how to live had hardly begun to grow a little clearer to him, when a new, insoluble question presented itself—death.

"Why, he's dying—yes, he'll die in the spring, and how help him? What can I say to him? What do I know about it? I'd even forgotten that it was at all."

CHAPTER XXXII

LEVIN had long before made the observation that when one is uncomfortable with people from their being excessively amenable and meek, one is apt very soon after to find things intolerable from their touchiness and irritability. He felt that this was how it would be with his brother. And his brother Nikolay's gentleness did in fact not last out for long. The very next morning he began to be irritable, and seemed doing his best to find fault with his brother, attacking him on his tenderest points.

Levin felt himself to blame, and could not set things right. He felt that if they had both not kept up appearances, but had spoken, as it is called, from the heart—that is to say, had said only just what they were thinking and feeling—they would simply have looked into each other's faces, and Konstantin could only have said, "You're dying, you're dying," and Nikolay could only have answered, "I know I'm dying, but I'm afraid, I'm afraid, I'm afraid!" And they could have said nothing more, if they had said only what was in their hearts. But life like that was impossible, and so Konstantin tried to do what he had been trying to do all his life, and never could learn to do, though, as far as he could observe, many people knew so well how to do it, and without it there was no living at all. He tried to say what he was not thinking, but he felt continually that it had a ring of falsehood, that his brother detected him in it, and was exasperated at it.

The third day Nikolay induced his brother to explain his plan to him again, and began not merely attacking it, but intentionally confounding it with communism.

"You've simply borrowed an idea that's not your own, but you've distorted it, and are trying to apply it where it's not applicable."

"But I tell you it's nothing to do with it. They deny the justice of property, of capital, of inheritance, while I do not deny this chief stimulus." (Levin felt disgusted himself at using such expressions, but ever since he had been engrossed by his work, he had unconsciously come more and more frequently to use words not Russian.) "All I want is to regulate labor."

"Which means, you've borrowed an idea, stripped it of all that gave it its force, and want to make believe that it's something new," said Nikolay, angrily tugging at his necktie.

"But my idea has nothing in common . . ."

"That, anyway," said Nikolay Levin, with an ironical smile, his eyes flashing malignantly, "has the charm of—what's one to call it?—geometrical symmetry, of clearness, of definiteness.

It may be a Utopia. But if once one allows the possibility of making of all the past a *tabula rasa*—no property, no family—then labor would organize itself. But you gain nothing . . ."

"Why do you mix things up? I've never been a communist."

"But I have, and I consider it's premature, but rational, and it has a future, just like Christianity in its first ages."

"All that I maintain is that the labor force ought to be investigated from the point of view of natural science; that is to say, it ought to be studied, its qualities ascertained . . ."

"But that's utter waste of time. That force finds a certain form of activity of itself, according to the stage of its development. There have been slaves first everywhere, then metayers; and we have the half-crop system, rent, and day-laborers. What are you trying to find?"

Levin suddenly lost his temper at these words, because at the bottom of his heart he was afraid that it was true—true that he was trying to hold the balance even between communism and the familiar forms, and that this was hardly possible.

"I am trying to find means of working productively for myself and for the laborers. I want to organize . . ." he answered hotly.

"You don't want to organize anything; it's simply just as you've been all your life, that you want to be original to pose as not exploiting the peasants simply, but with some idea in view."

"Oh, all right, that's what you think—and let me alone!" answered Levin, feeling the muscles of his left cheek twitching uncontrollably.

"You've never had, and never have, convictions; all you want is to please your vanity."

"Oh, very well; then let me alone!"

"And I will let you alone! and it's high time I did, and go to the devil with you! and I'm very sorry I ever came!"

In spite of all Levin's efforts to soothe his brother afterwards, Nikolay would listen to nothing he said, declaring that it was better to part, and Konstantin saw that it simply was that life was unbearable to him.

Nikolay was just getting ready to go, when Konstantin went in to him again and begged him, rather unnaturally, to forgive him if he had hurt his feelings in any way.

"Ah, generosity!" said Nikolay, and he smiled. "If you want to be right, I can give you that satisfaction. You're in the right; but I'm going all the same."

It was only just at parting that Nikolay kissed him, and said, looking with sudden strangeness and seriousness at his brother:

"Anyway, don't remember evil against me, Kostya!" and his voice quivered. These were the only words that had been spoken sincerely between them. Levin knew that those words meant, "You see, and you know, that I'm in a bad way, and maybe we shall not see each other again." Levin knew this, and the tears gushed from his eyes. He kissed his brother once more, but he could not speak, and knew not what to say.

Three days after his brother's departure, Levin too set off for his foreign tour. Happening to meet Shtcherbatsky, Kitty's cousin, in the railway train, Levin greatly astonished him by his depression.

"What's the matter with you?" Shtcherbatsky asked him.

"Oh, nothing; there's not much happiness in life."

"Not much? You come with me to Paris instead of to Mulhausen. You shall see how to be happy."

"No, I've done with it all. It's time I was dead."

"Well, that's a good one!" said Shtcherbatsky, laughing; "why, I'm only just getting ready to begin."

"Yes, I thought the same not long ago, but now I know I shall soon be dead."

Levin said what he had genuinely been thinking of late. He saw nothing but death or the advance towards death in everything. But his cherished scheme only engrossed him the more. Life had to be got through somehow till death did come. Darkness had fallen upon everything for him; but just because of this darkness he felt that the one guiding clue in the darkness was his work, and he clutched it and clung to it with all his strength.

Part Four

CHAPTER I

THE Karenins, husband and wife, continued living in the same house, met every day, but were complete strangers to one another. Alexey Alexandrovitch made it a rule to see his wife every day, so that the servants might have no grounds for suppositions, but avoided dining at home. Vronsky was never at Alexey Alexandrovitch's house, but Anna saw him away from home, and her husband was aware of it.

The position was one of misery for all three; and not one of them would have been equal to enduring this position for a single day, if it had not been for the expectation that it would change, that it was merely a temporary painful ordeal which would pass over. Alexey Alexandrovitch hoped that this passion would pass, as everything does pass, that every one would forget about it, and his name would remain unsullied. Anna, on whom the position depended, and for whom it was more miserable than for any one, endured it because she not merely hoped, but firmly believed, that it would all very soon be settled and come right. She had not the least idea what would settle the position, but she firmly believed that something would very soon turn up now. Vronsky, against his own will or wishes, followed her lead, hoped too that something, apart from his own action, would be sure to solve all difficulties.

In the middle of the winter Vronsky spent a very tiresome week. A foreign prince, who had come on a visit to Petersburg, was put under his charge, and he had to show him the sights worth seeing. Vronsky was of distinguished appearance; he possessed, moreover, the art of behaving with respectful dignity, and was used to having to do with such grand personages—that was how he came to be put in charge of the prince. But he felt his duties very irksome. The prince was anxious to miss nothing of which he would be asked at home, had he seen that in Russia?

And on his own account he was anxious to enjoy to the utmost all Russian forms of amusement. Vronsky was obliged to be his guide in satisfying both these inclinations. The mornings they spent driving to look at places of interest; the evenings they passed enjoying the national entertainments. The prince rejoiced in health exceptional even among princes. By gymnastics and careful attention to his health he had brought himself to such a point that in spite of his excess in pleasure he looked as fresh as a big glossy green Dutch cucumber. The prince had traveled a great deal, and considered one of the chief advantages of modern facilities of communication was the accessibility of the pleasures of all nations.

He had been in Spain, and there had indulged in serenades and had made friends with a Spanish girl who played the mandolin. In Switzerland he had killed chamois. In England he had galloped in a red coat over hedges and killed two hundred pheasants for a bet. In Turkey he had got into a harem; in India he had hunted on an elephant, and now in Russia he wished to taste all the specially Russian forms of pleasure.

Vronsky, who was, as it were, chief master of the ceremonies to him, was at great pains to arrange all the Russian amusements suggested by various persons to the prince. They had race-horses, and Russian pancakes and bear-hunts and three horse sledges, and gypsies and drinking feasts, with the Russian accompaniment of broken crockery. And the prince with surprising ease fell in with the Russian spirit, smashed trays full of crockery, sat with a gypsy girl on his knee, and seemed to be asking— what more, and does the whole Russian spirit consist in just this?

In reality, of all the Russian entertainments the prince liked best French actresses and ballet-dancers and white-seal champagne. Vronsky was used to princes, but, either because he had himself changed of late, or that he was in too close proximity to the prince, that week seemed fearfully wearisome to him. The whole of that week he experienced a sensation such as a man might have set in charge of a dangerous madman, afraid of the madman, and at the same time, from being with him, fearing for his own reason. Vronsky was continually conscious of the necessity of never for a second relaxing the tone of stern official respectfulness, that he might not himself be insulted. The prince's manner of treating the very people who, to Vronsky's surprise, were ready to descend to any depths to provide him with Russian amusements, was contemptuous. His criticisms of Russian women, whom he wished to study, more than once made Vronsky crimson with indignation. The chief reason why the prince was so particularly disagreeable to Vronsky was that he could not help seeing himself in him. And what he saw in this mirror did not gratify his self-esteem. He was a very stupid and very self-satisfied and very healthy and very well-washed man, and nothing else. He was a gentleman—that was true, and Vronsky could not deny it. He was equable and not cringing with his superiors, was free and ingratiating in his behavior with his equals, and was contemptuously indulgent with his inferiors. Vronsky was himself the same, and regarded it as a great merit to be so. But for this prince he was an inferior, and his contemptuous and indulgent attitude to him revolted him.

"Brainless beef! can I be like that?" he thought.

Be that as it might, when, on the seventh day, he parted from the prince, who was starting for Moscow, and received his thanks, he was happy to be rid of his uncomfortable position and the unpleasant reflection of himself. He said good-bye to him at the station on their return from a bear-hunt, at which they had had a display of Russian prowess kept up all night.

CHAPTER II

WHEN he got home, Vronsky found there a note from Anna. She wrote, "I am ill and unhappy. I cannot come out, but cannot go on longer without seeing you. Come in this evening. Alexey Alexandrovitch goes to the council at seven and will be there till ten." Thinking for an instant of the strangeness of her bidding him come straight to her, in spite of her husband's insisting on her not receiving him, he decided to go.

Vronsky had that winter got his promotion, was now a colonel, had left the regimental quarters, and was living alone. After having some lunch, he lay down on the sofa immediately, and in five minutes memories of the hideous scenes he had witnessed during the last few days were confused together and joined on to a mental image of Anna and of the peasant who had played an important part in the bear-hunt, and Vronsky fell asleep. He waked up in the dark, trembling with horror, and made haste to light a candle. "What was it? What? What was the dreadful thing I dreamed? Yes, yes; I think a little dirty man with a disheveled beard was stooping down doing something, and all of a sudden he began saying some strange words in French. Yes, there was nothing else in the dream," he said to himself. "But why was it so awful?" He vividly recalled the peasant again and those incomprehensible French words the peasant had uttered, and a chill of horror ran down his spine.

"What nonsense!" thought Vronsky, and glanced at his watch.

It was half-past eight already. He rang up his servant, dressed in haste, and went out onto the steps, completely forgetting the dream and only worried at being late. As he drove up to

the Karenins' entrance he looked at his watch and saw it was ten minutes to nine. A high, narrow carriage with a pair of grays was standing at the entrance. He recognized Anna's carriage. "She is coming to me," thought Vronsky, "and better she should. I don't like going into that house. But no matter; I can't hide myself," he thought, and with that manner peculiar to him from childhood, as of a man who has nothing to be ashamed of, Vronsky got out of his sledge and went to the door. The door opened, and the hall-porter with a rug on his arm called the carriage. Vronsky, though he did not usually notice details, noticed at this moment the amazed expression with which the porter glanced at him. In the very doorway Vronsky almost ran up against Alexey Alexandrovitch. The gas jet threw its full light on the bloodless, sunken face under the black hat and on the white cravat, brilliant against the beaver of the coat. Karenin's fixed, dull eyes were fastened upon Vronsky's face. Vronsky bowed, and Alexey Alexandrovitch, chewing his lips, lifted his hand to his hat and went on. Vronsky saw him without looking round get into the carriage, pick up the rug and the opera-glass at the window and disappear. Vronsky went into the hall. His brows were scowling, and his eyes gleamed with a proud and angry light in them.

"What a position!" he thought. "If he would fight, would stand up for his honor, I could act, could express my feelings; but this weakness or baseness . . . He puts me in the position of playing false, which I never meant and never mean to do."

Vronsky's ideas had changed since the day of his conversation with Anna in the Vrede garden. Unconsciously yielding to the weakness of Anna—who had surrendered herself up to him utterly, and simply looked to him to decide her fate, ready to submit to anything—he had long ceased to think that their tie might end as he had thought then. His ambitious plans had retreated into the background again, and feeling that he had got out of that circle of activity in which everything was definite, he had given himself entirely to his passion, and that passion was binding him more and more closely to her.

He was still in the hall when he caught the sound of her retreating footsteps. He knew she had been expecting him, had listened for him, and was now going back to the drawing-room.

"No," she cried, on seeing him, and at the first sound of her voice the tears came into her eyes. "No; if things are to go on like this, the end will come much, much too soon."

"What is it, dear one?"

"What? I've been waiting in agony for an hour, two hours. . . . No, I won't . . . I can't quarrel with you. Of course you couldn't come. No, I won't." She laid her two hands on his shoulders, and looked a long while at him with a profound, passionate, and at the same time searching look. She was studying his face to make up for the time she had not seen him. She was, every time she saw him, making the picture of him in her imagination (incomparably superior, impossible in reality) fit with him as he really was.

CHAPTER III

"You met him?" she asked, when they had sat down at the table in the lamplight. "You're punished, you see, for being late."

"Yes; but how was it? Wasn't he to be at the council?"

"He had been and come back, and was going out somewhere again. But that's no matter. Don't talk about it. Where have you been? With the prince still?"

She knew every detail of his existence. He was going to say that he had been up all night and had dropped asleep, but looking at her thrilled and rapturous face, he was ashamed. And he said he had had to go to report on the prince's departure.

"But it's over now? He is gone!"

"Thank God it's over! You wouldn't believe how insufferable it's been for me."

"Why so? Isn't it the life all of you, all young men, always lead?" she said, knitting her brows; and taking up the crochet-work that was lying on the table, she began drawing the hook out of it, without looking at Vronsky.

"I gave that life up long ago," said he, wondering at the change in her face, and trying to divine its meaning. "And I confess," he said, with a smile, showing his thick, white teeth, "this week I've been, as it were, looking at myself in a glass, seeing that life, and I didn't like it."

She held the work in her hands, but did not crochet, and looked at him with strange, shining, and hostile eyes.

"This morning Liza came to see me—they're not afraid to call on me, in spite of the Countess Lidia Ivanovna," she put in—"and she told me about your Athenian evening. How loathsome!"

"I was just going to say . . ."

She interrupted him.

"It was that Thérèse you used to know?"

"I was just saying . . ."

"How disgusting you are, you men! How is it you can't understand that a woman can never forget that," she said, getting more and more angry, and so letting him see the cause of her irritation, "especially a woman who cannot know your life? What do I know? What have I ever known?" she said; "what you tell me. And how do I know whether you tell me the truth? . . ."

"Anna, you hurt me. Don't you trust me? Haven't I told you that I haven't a thought I wouldn't lay bare to you?"

"Yes, yes," she said, evidently trying to suppress her jealous thoughts. "But if only you knew how wretched I am! I believe you, I believe you. . . . What were you saying?"

But he could not at once recall what he had been going to say. These fits of jealousy, which of late had been more and more frequent with her, horrified him, and however much he tried to disguise the fact, made him feel cold to her, although he knew the cause of her jealousy was her love for him. How often he had told himself that her love was happiness; and now she loved him as a woman can love when love has outweighed for her all the good things of life—and he was much further from happiness than when he had followed her from Moscow. Then he had thought himself unhappy, but happiness was before him; now he felt that the best happiness was already left behind. She was utterly unlike what she had been when he first saw her. Both morally and physically she had changed for the worse. She had broadened out all over, and in her face at the time when she was speaking of the actress there was an evil expression of hatred that distorted it. He looked at her as a man looks at a faded flower

431

he has gathered, with difficulty recognizing in it the beauty for which he picked and ruined it. And in spite of this he felt that then, when his love was stronger, he could, if he had greatly wished it, have torn that love out of his heart; but now, when as at that moment it seemed to him he felt no love for her, he knew that what bound him to her could not be broken.

"Well, well, what was it you were going to say about the prince? I have driven away the fiend," she added. The fiend was the name they had given her jealousy. "What did you begin to tell me about the prince? Why did you find it so tiresome?"

"Oh, it was intolerable!" he said, trying to pick up the thread of his interrupted thought. "He does not improve on closer acquaintance. If you want him defined, here he is: a prime, well-fed beast such as takes medals at the cattle-shows, and nothing more," he said, with a tone of vexation that interested her.

"No; how so?" she replied. "He's seen a great deal, anyway; he's cultured?"

"It's an utterly different culture—their culture. He's cultivated, one sees, simply to be able to despise culture, as they despise everything but animal pleasures."

"But don't you all care for these animal pleasures?" she said, and again he noticed a dark look in her eyes that avoided him.

"How is it you're defending him?" he said, smiling.

"I'm not defending him, it's nothing to me; but I imagine, if you had not cared for those pleasures yourself, you might have got out of them. But if it affords you satisfaction to gaze at Thérèse in the attire of Eve . . ."

"Again, the devil again," Vronsky said, taking the hand she had laid on the table and kissing it.

"Yes; but I can't help it. You don't know what I have suffered waiting for you. I believe I'm not jealous. I'm not jealous: I believe you when you're here; but when you're away somewhere leading your life, so incomprehensible to me . . ."

She turned away from him, pulled the hook at last out of the crochet-work, and rapidly, with the help of her forefinger, began working loop after loop of the wool that was dazzling white in the lamplight, while the slender wrist moved swiftly, nervously in the embroidered cuff.

"How was it, then? Where did you meet Alexey Alexandrovitch?" Her voice sounded in an unnatural and jarring tone.

"We ran up against each other in the doorway."

"And he bowed to you like this?"

She drew a long face, and half-closing her eyes, quickly transformed her expression, folded her hands, and Vronsky suddenly saw in her beautiful face the very expression with which Alexey Alexandrovitch had bowed to him. He smiled, while she laughed gaily, with that sweet, deep laugh, which was one of her greatest charms.

"I don't understand him in the least," said Vronsky. "If after your avowal to him at your country house he had broken with you, if he had called me out—but this I can't understand. How can he put up with such a position? He feels it, that's evident."

"He?" she said sneeringly. "He's perfectly satisfied."

"What are we all miserable for, when everything might be so happy?"

"Only not he. Don't I know him, the falsity in which he's utterly steeped? . . . Could one, with any feeling, live as he is living with me? He understands nothing, and feels nothing. Could a man of any feeling live in the same house with his unfaithful wife? Could he talk to her, call her 'my dear'?"

And again she could not help mimicking him: " 'Anna, *ma chère;* Anna, dear'!"

"He's not a man, not a human being—he's a doll! No one knows him; but I know him. Oh, if I'd been in his place, I'd long ago have killed, have torn to pieces a wife like me. I wouldn't have said, 'Anna, *ma chère'!* He's not a man, he's an official machine. He doesn't understand that I'm your wife, that he's outside, that he's superfluous. . . . Don't let's talk of him! . . ."

"You're unfair, very unfair, dearest," said Vronsky, trying to soothe her. "But never mind, don't let's talk of him. Tell me what you've been doing? What is the matter? What has been wrong with you, and what did the doctor say?"

She looked at him with mocking amusement. Evidently she had hit on other absurd and grotesque aspects in her husband and was awaiting the moment to give expression to them.

But he went on:

"I imagine that it's not illness, but your condition. When will it be?"

The ironical light died away in her eyes, but a different smile, a consciousness of something, he did not know what, and of quiet melancholy, came over her face.

"Soon, soon. You say that our position is miserable, that we must put an end to it. If you knew how terrible it is to me, what I would give to be able to love you freely and boldly! I should not torture myself and torture you with my jealousy. . . . And it will come soon but not as we expect."

And at the thought of how it would come, she seemed so pitiable to herself that tears came into her eyes, and she could not go on. She laid her hand on his sleeve, dazzling and white with its rings in the lamplight.

"It won't come as we suppose. I didn't mean to say this to you, but you've made me. Soon, soon, all will be over, and we shall all, all be at peace, and suffer no more."

"I don't understand," he said, understanding her.

"You asked when? Soon. And I shan't live through it. Don't interrupt me!" and she made haste to speak. "I know it; I know for certain. I shall die; and I'm very glad I shall die, and release myself and you."

Tears dropped from her eyes; he bent down over her hand and began kissing it, trying to hide his emotion, which, he knew, had no sort of grounds, though he could not control it.

"Yes, it's better so," she said, tightly gripping his hand. "That's the only way, the only way left us."

He had recovered himself, and lifted his head.

"How absurd! What absurd nonsense you are talking!"

"No, it's the truth."

"What, what's the truth?"

"That I shall die. I have had a dream."

"A dream?" repeated Vronsky, and instantly he recalled the peasant of his dream.

"Yes, a dream," she said. "It's a long while since I dreamed it. I dreamed that I ran into my bedroom, that I had to get something there, to find out something; you know how it is in dreams," she said, her eyes wide with horror; "and in the bedroom, in the corner, stood something."

"Oh, what nonsense! How can you believe . . ."

But she would not let him interrupt her. What she was saying was too important to her.

"And the something turned round, and I saw it was a peasant with a disheveled beard, little, and dreadful-looking. I wanted to run away, but he bent down over a sack, and was fumbling there with his hands. . . ."

She showed how he had moved his hands. There was terror in her face. And Vronsky, remembering his dream, felt the same terror filling his soul.

"He was fumbling and kept talking quickly, quickly in French, you know: *Il faut le battre, le fer, le broyer, le pétrir.* . . . And in my horror I tried to wake up, and woke up . . . but woke up in the dream. And I began asking myself what it meant. And Korney said to me: 'In childbirth you'll die, ma'am, you'll die. . . .' And I woke up."

"What nonsense, what nonsense!" said Vronsky; but he felt himself that there was no conviction in his voice.

"But don't let's talk of it. Ring the bell, I'll have tea. And stay a little, now; it's not long I shall . . ."

But all at once she stopped. The expression of her face instantaneously changed. Horror and excitement were suddenly replaced by a look of soft, solemn, blissful attention. He could not comprehend the meaning of the change. She was listening to the stirring of the new life within her.

CHAPTER IV

ALEXEY ALEXANDROVITCH, after meeting Vronsky on his own steps, drove, as he had intended, to the Italian opera. He sat through two acts there, and saw every one he had wanted to see. On returning home, he carefully scrutinized the hat-stand, and noticing that there was not a military overcoat there, he went as usual, to his own room. But, contrary to his usual habits, he did not go to bed, he walked up and down his study till three o'clock in the morning. The feeling of furious anger with his wife, who would not observe the proprieties and keep to the one stipulation he had laid on her, not to receive her lover in her own home, gave him no peace. She had not complied with his request, and he was bound to punish her and carry out his threat—obtain a divorce and take away his son. He knew all the difficulties connected with this course, but he had said he would do it, and now he must carry out his threat. Countess Lidia Ivanovna had hinted that this was the best way out of his position, and of late the obtaining of divorces had been brought to such perfection that Alexey Alexandrovitch saw a possibility of overcoming the formal difficulties. Misfortunes never come singly, and the affairs of the reorganization of the native tribes, and of the irrigation of the lands of the Zaraisky province, had brought such official worries upon Alexey Alexandrovitch that he had been of late in a continual condition of extreme irritability.

He did not sleep the whole night, and his fury growing in a sort of vast, arithmetical progression, reached its highest limits in the morning. He dressed in haste, and as though carrying his cup full of wrath, and fearing to spill any over, fearing to lose with his wrath the energy necessary for the interview with his wife, he went into her room directly he heard she was up.

Anna, who had thought she knew her husband so well, was amazed at his appearance when he went in to her. His brow was lowering, and his eyes stared darkly before him, avoiding her eyes; his mouth was tightly and contemptuously shut. In his walk, in his gestures, in the sound of his voice there was a determination and firmness such as his wife had never seen in him. He went into her room, and without greeting her, walked straight up to her writing-table, and taking her keys, opened a drawer.

"What do you want?" she cried.

"Your lover's letters," he said.

"They're not here," she said, shutting the drawer; but from that action he saw he had guessed right, and roughly pushing away her hand, he quickly snatched a portfolio in which he knew she used to put her most important papers. She tried to pull the portfolio away, but he pushed her back.

"Sit down! I have to speak to you," he said, putting the portfolio under his arm, and squeezing it so tightly with his elbow that his shoulder stood up. Amazed and intimidated, she gazed at him in silence.

"I told you that I would not allow you to receive your lover in this house."

"I had to see him to . . ."

She stopped, not finding a reason.

"I do not enter into the details of why a woman wants to see her lover."

"I meant, I only . . ." she said, flushing hotly. This coarseness of his angered her, and gave her courage. "Surely you must feel how easy it is for you to insult me?" she said.

"An honest man and an honest woman may be insulted, but to tell a thief he's a thief is simply *la constatation d'un fait.*"

"This cruelty is something new I did not know in you."

"You call it cruelty for a husband to give his wife liberty, giving her the honorable protection of his name, simply on the condition of observing the proprieties: is that cruelty?"

"It's worse than cruel—it's base, if you want to know!" Anna cried, in a rush of hatred, and getting up, she was going away.

"No!" he shrieked in his shrill voice, which pitched a note higher than usual even, and his big hands clutching her by the arm so violently that red marks were left from the bracelet he was squeezing, he forcibly sat her down in her place.

"Base! If you care to use that word, what is base is to forsake husband and child for a lover, while you eat your husband's bread!"

She bowed her head. She did not

437

say what she had said the evening before to her lover, that *he* was her husband, and her husband was superfluous; she did not even think that. She felt all the justice of his words, and only said softly:

"You cannot describe my position as worse than I feel it to be myself; but what are you saying all this for?"

"What am I saying it for? what for?" he went on, as angrily. "That you may know that since you have not carried out my wishes in regard to observing outward decorum, I will take measures to put an end to this state of things."

"Soon, very soon, it will end, anyway," she said; and again, at the thought of death near at hand and now desired, tears came into her eyes.

"It will end sooner than you and your lover have planned! If you must have the satisfaction of animal passion . . ."

"Alexey Alexandrovitch! I won't say it's not generous, but it's not like a gentleman to strike any one who's down."

"Yes, you only think of yourself! But the sufferings of a man who was your husband have no interest for you. You don't care that his whole life is ruined, that he is thuff . . . thuff . . ."

Alexey Alexandrovitch was speaking so quickly that he stammered, and was utterly unable to articulate the word "suffering." In the end he pronounced it "thuffering." She wanted to laugh, and was immediately ashamed that anything could amuse her at such a moment. And for the first time, for an instant, she felt for him, put herself in his place, and was sorry for him. But what could she say or do? Her head sank, and she sat silent. He too was silent for some time, and then began speaking in a frigid, less shrill voice, emphasizing random words that had no significance.

"I came to tell you . . ." he said.

She glanced at him. "No, it was my fancy," she thought, recalling the expression of his face when he stumbled over the word "suffering." "No; can a man with those dull eyes, with that self-satisfied complacency, feel anything?"

"I cannot change anything," she whispered.

"I have come to tell you that I am going to-morrow to Moscow, and shall not return again to this house, and you will receive notice of what I decide through the lawyer into whose hands I

shall intrust the task of getting a divorce. My son is going to my sister's," said Alexey Alexandrovitch, with an effort recalling what he had meant to say about his son.

"You take Seryozha to hurt me," she said, looking at him from under her brows. "You do not love him. . . . Leave me Seryozha!"

"Yes, I have lost even my affection for my son, because he is associated with the repulsion I feel for you. But still I shall take him. Good-bye!"

And he was going away, but now she detained him.

"Alexey Alexandrovitch, leave me Seryozha!" she whispered once more. "I have nothing else to say. Leave Seryozha till my . . . I shall soon be confined; leave him!"

Alexey Alexandrovitch flew into a rage, and, snatching his hand from her, he went out of the room without a word.

CHAPTER V

THE waiting-room of the celebrated Petersburg lawyer was full when Alexey Alexandrovitch entered it. Three ladies—an old lady, a young lady, and a merchant's wife—and three gentlemen—one a German banker with a ring on his finger, the second a merchant with a beard, and the third a wrathful-looking government clerk in official uniform, with a cross on his neck—had obviously been waiting a long while already. Two clerks were writing at tables with scratching pens. The appurtenances of the writing-tables, about which Alexey Alexandrovitch was himself very fastidious, were exceptionally good. He could not help observing this. One of the clerks, without getting up, turned wrathfully to Alexey Alexandrovitch, half closing his eyes.

"What are you wanting?"

He replied that he had to see the lawyer on some business.

"He is engaged," the clerk responded severely, and he pointed with his pen at the persons waiting, and went on writing.

"Can't he spare time to see me?" said Alexey Alexandrovitch.

"He has not time free; he is always busy. Kindly wait your turn."

"Then I must trouble you to give him my card," Alexey Alexandrovitch said with dignity, seeing the impossibility of preserving his incognito.

The clerk took the card and, obviously not approving of what he read on it, went to the door.

Alexey Alexandrovitch was in principle in favor of the publicity of legal proceedings, though for some higher official considerations he disliked the application of the principle in Russia, and disapproved of it, as far as he could disapprove of anything instituted by authority of the Emperor. His whole life had been spent in administrative work, and consequently, when he did not approve of anything, his disapproval was softened by the recognition of the inevitability of mistakes and the possibility of reform in every department. In the new public law-courts he disliked the restrictions laid on the lawyers conducting cases. But till then he had had nothing to do with the law-courts, and so had disapproved of their publicity simply in theory; now his disapprobation was strengthened by the unpleasant impression made on him in the lawyer's waiting-room.

"Coming immediately," said the clerk; and two minutes later there did actually appear in the doorway the large figure of an old solicitor who had been consulting with the lawyer himself.

The lawyer was a little, squat, bald man, with a dark, reddish beard, light-colored long eyebrows, and an overhanging brow. He was attired as though for a wedding, from his cravat to his double watch-chain and varnished boots. His face was clever and manly, but his dress was dandified and in bad taste.

"Pray walk in," said the lawyer, addressing Alexey Alexandrovitch; and, gloomily ushering Karenin in before him, he closed the door.

"Won't you sit down?" He indicated an armchair at a writing-table covered with papers. He sat down himself, and, rubbing his little hands with short fingers covered with white hairs, he bent his head on one side. But as soon as he was settled in this position a moth flew over the table. The lawyer, with a swiftness that could never have been expected of him, opened his hands, caught the moth, and resumed his former attitude.

"Before beginning to speak of my business," said Alexey Alexandrovitch, following the lawyer's movements with wondering eyes, "I ought to observe that the business about which I have to speak to you is to be strictly private."

The lawyer's overhanging reddish mustaches were parted in a scarcely perceptible smile.

"I should not be a lawyer if I could not keep the secrets confided to me. But if you would like proof . . ."

Alexey Alexandrovitch glanced at his face, and saw that the shrewd, gray eyes were laughing, and seemed to know all about it already.

"You know my name?" Alexey Alexandrovitch resumed.

"I know you and the good"—again he caught a moth—"work you are doing, like every Russian," said the lawyer, bowing.

Alexey Alexandrovitch sighed, plucking up his courage. But having once made up his mind he went on in his shrill voice, without timidity or hesitation, accentuating here and there a word.

"I have the misfortune," Alexey Alexandrovitch began, "to have been deceived in my married life, and I desire to break off all relations with my wife by legal means—that is, to be divorced, but to do this so that my son may not remain with his mother."

The lawyer's gray eyes tried

not to laugh, but they were dancing with irrepressible glee, and Alexey Alexandrovitch saw that it was not simply the delight of a man who has just got a profitable job: there was triumph and joy, there was a gleam like the malignant gleam he saw in his wife's eyes.

"You desire my assistance in securing a divorce?"

"Yes, precisely so; but I ought to warn you that I may be wasting your time and attention. I have come simply to consult you as a preliminary step. I want a divorce, but the form in which it is possible is of great consequence to me. It is very possible that if that form does not correspond with my requirements I may give up a legal divorce."

"Oh, that's always the case," said the lawyer, "and that's always for you to decide."

He let his eyes rest on Alexey Alexandrovitch's feet, feeling that he might offend his client by the sight of his irrepressible amusement. He looked at a moth that flew before his nose, and moved his hands, but did not catch it from regard for Alexey Alexandrovitch's position.

"Though in their general features our laws on this subject are known to me," pursued Alexey Alexandrovitch, "I should be glad to have an idea of the forms in which such things are done in practice."

"You would be glad," the lawyer, without lifting his eyes, responded, adopting, with a certain satisfaction, the tone of his client's remarks, "for me to lay before you all the methods by which you could secure what you desire?"

And on receiving an assuring nod from Alexey Alexandrovitch, he went on, stealing a glance now and then at Alexey Alexandrovitch's face, which was growing red in patches.

"Divorce by our laws," he said, with a slight shade of disapprobation of our laws, "is possible, as you are aware, in the following cases . . . Wait a little!" he called to a clerk who put his head in at the door, but he got up all the same, said a few words to him, and sat down again. ". . . In the following cases: physical defect in the married parties, desertion without communication for five years," he said, crooking a short finger covered with hair, "adultery" (this word he pronounced with obvious satisfaction), "subdivided as follows" (he continued to crook his fat fingers, though the three cases and their subdivisions could obviously not be classified together): "physical defect of the husband or of the wife, adultery of the husband or of the wife." As by now all his fingers were used up, he uncrooked all his fingers and went on: "This is the theoretical view; but I imagine you have done me the honor to apply to me in order to learn its application in practice. And therefore, guided by precedents, I must inform you that in practice cases of divorce may all be reduced to the following—there's no physical defect, I may assume, nor desertion? . . ."

Alexey Alexandrovitch bowed his head in assent.

"—May be reduced to the following: adultery of one of the married parties, and the detection in the fact of the guilty party by mutual agreement, and failing such agreement, accidental detection. It must be admitted that the latter case is rarely met with in practice," said the lawyer, and stealing a glance at Alexey Alexandrovitch he paused, as a man selling pistols, after enlarging on the advantages of each weapon, might await his customer's choice. But Alexey Alexandrovitch said nothing, and therefore the lawyer went on: "The most usual and simple, the sensible course, I consider, is adultery by mutual consent. I should not permit myself to express it so, speaking with a man of no education," he said, "but I imagine that to you this is comprehensible."

Alexey Alexandrovitch was, however, so perturbed that he did not immediately comprehend all the good sense of adultery by mutual consent, and his eyes expressed this uncertainty; but the lawyer promptly came to his assistance.

"People cannot go on living together—here you have a fact. And if both are agreed about it, the details and formalities become a matter of no importance. And at the same time this is the simplest and most certain method."

Alexey Alexandrovitch fully understood now. But he had religious scruples, which hindered the execution of such a plan.

"That is out of the question in the present case," he said. "Only one alternative is possible: undesigned detection, supported by letters which I have."

At the mention of letters the lawyer pursed up his lips, and gave utterance to a thin little compassionate and contemptuous sound.

"Kindly consider," he began, "cases of that kind are, as you are aware, under ecclesiastical jurisdiction; the reverend fathers are fond of going into the minutest details in cases of that kind," he said with a smile, which betrayed his sympathy with the reverend fathers' taste. "Letters may, of course, be a partial confirmation; but detection in the fact there must be of the most direct kind, that is, by eye-witnesses. In fact, if you do me the honor to intrust your confidence to me, you will do well to leave me the choice of the measures to be employed. If one wants the result, one must admit the means."

"If it is so . . ." Alexey Alexandrovitch began, suddenly turning white; but at that moment the lawyer rose and again went to the door to speak to the intruding clerk.

"Tell her we don't haggle over fees!" he said, and returned to Alexey Alexandrovitch.

On his way back he caught unobserved another moth. "Nice state my rep curtains will be in by the summer!" he thought, frowning.

"And so you were saying? . . ." he said.

"I will communicate my decision to you by letter," said Alexey Alexandrovitch, getting up, and he clutched at the table. After standing a moment in silence, he said: "From your words I may consequently conclude that a divorce may be obtained? I would ask you to let me know what are your terms."

"It may be obtained if you give me complete liberty of action," said the lawyer, not answering his question. "When can I reckon on receiving information from you?" he asked, moving towards the door, his eyes and his varnished boots shining.

"In a week's time. Your answer as to whether you will undertake to conduct the case, and on what terms, you will be so good as to communicate to me."

"Very good."

The lawyer bowed respectfully, let his client out of the door, and, left alone, gave himself up to his sense of amusement. He felt so mirthful that, contrary to his rules, he made a reduction in his terms to the haggling lady, and gave up catching moths, finally deciding that next winter he must have the furniture covered with velvet, like Sigonin's.

ALEXEY ALEXANDROVITCH had gained a brilliant victory at the sitting of the Commission of the 17th of August, but in the sequel this victory cut the ground from under his feet. The new commission for the inquiry into the condition of the native tribes in all its branches had been formed and despatched to its destination with an unusual speed and energy inspired by Alexey Alexandrovitch. Within three months a report was presented. The condition of the native tribes was investigated in its political, administrative, economic, ethnographic, material, and religious aspects. To all these questions there were answers admirably stated, and answers admitting no shade of doubt, since they were not a product of human thought, always liable to error, but were all the product of official activity. The answers were all based on official data furnished by governors and heads of churches, and founded on the reports of district magistrates and ecclesiastical superintendents, founded in their turn on the reports of parochial overseers and parish priests; and so all of these answers were unhesitating and certain. All such questions as, for instance, of the cause of failure of crops, of the adherence of certain tribes to their ancient beliefs, etc.—questions which, but for the convenient intervention of the official machine, are not, and cannot be solved for ages—received full, unhesitating solution. And this solution was in favor of Alexey Alexandrovitch's contention. But Stremov, who had felt stung to the quick at the last sitting, had, on the reception of the commission's report, resorted to tactics which Alexey Alexandrovitch had not anticipated. Stremov, carrying with him several members, went over to Alexey Alexandrovitch's side, and not contenting himself with warmly defending the measure proposed by Karenin, proposed other more extreme measures in the same direction. These measures, still further exaggerated in opposition to what was Alexey Alexandrovitch's fundamental idea, were passed by the commission, and then the aim of Stremov's tactics became apparent. Carried to an extreme, the measures seemed at once to be so absurd that the highest authorities, and public opinion, and intellectual ladies, and the newspapers, all at the same time fell foul of them, expressing their indignation both with the measures and their nominal father, Alexey Alexandrovitch. Stremov drew back, affecting to have blindly followed Karenin, and to be astounded and distressed at what had been done. This meant the defeat of Alexey Alexandrovitch. But in spite of failing health, in spite of his domestic griefs, he did not give in. There was a split in the commission. Some members, with Stremov at their head, justified their mistake on the ground that they had put faith in the commission of revision, instituted by Alexey Alexandrovitch, and maintained that the report of the commission was rubbish, and simply so much waste paper. Alexey Alexandrovitch, with a following of those who saw the danger of so revolutionary an attitude to official documents, persisted in upholding the statements obtained by the revising commission. In consequence of this, in the higher spheres, and even in society, all was chaos, and although every one was interested, no one could tell whether the native tribes really were becoming impoverished and ruined, or whether they were in a flourishing condition. The position of Alexey Alexandrovitch, owing to this, and partly owing to the contempt lavished on him for his wife's infidelity, became very precarious. And in this position he took an important resolution. To the astonishment of the commission, he announced that he should ask permission to go himself to investigate the question on the spot. And having obtained permission, Alexey Alexandrovitch prepared to set off to these remote provinces.

Alexey Alexandrovitch's departure made a great sensation, the more so as just before he started he officially returned the posting-fares allowed him for twelve horses, to drive to his destination.

"I think it very noble," Betsy said about this to the Princess Myakaya. "Why take money for posting-horses when every one knows that there are railways everywhere now?"

But Princess Myakaya did not agree, and the Princess Tverskaya's opinion annoyed her indeed.

"It's all very well for you to talk," said she, "when you have I don't know how many millions; but I am very glad when my husband goes on a revising tour in the summer. It's very good

for him and pleasant traveling about, and it's a settled arrangement for me to keep a carriage and coachman on the money."

On his way to the remote provinces Alexey Alexandrovitch
stopped for three days at Moscow.

The day after his arrival he was driving back from calling on
the governor-general. At the cross-roads by Gazetny Place, where
there are always crowds of carriages and sledges, Alexey Alexandrovitch suddenly heard his name called out in such a loud
and cheerful voice that he could not help looking round. At the
corner of the pavement, in a short, stylish overcoat and a low-
crowned fashionable hat, jauntily askew, with a smile that
showed a gleam of white teeth and red lips, stood Stepan Arkadyevitch, radiant, young, and beaming. He called him vigorously
and urgently, and insisted on his stopping. He had one arm
on the window of a carriage that was stopping at the corner, and
out of the window were thrust the heads of a lady in a velvet hat,
and two children. Stepan Arkadyevitch was smiling and beckoning to his brother-in-law. The lady smiled a kindly smile too,
and she too waved her hand to Alexey Alexandrovitch. It was
Dolly with her children.

Alexey Alexandrovitch did not want to see any one in Moscow, and least of all his wife's brother. He raised his hat and
would have driven on, but Stepan Arkadyevitch told his coachman to stop, and ran across the snow to him.

"Well, what a shame not to have let us know! Been here long?
I was at Dussot's yesterday and saw 'Karenin' on the visitors'
list, but it never entered my head that it was you," said Stepan
Arkadyevitch, sticking his head in at the window of the carriage,
"or I should have looked you up. I am glad to see you!" he said,
knocking one foot against the other to shake the snow off. "What
a shame of you not to let us know!" he repeated.

"I had no time; I am very busy," Alexey Alexandrovitch responded dryly.

"Come to my wife, she does so want to see you."

Alexey Alexandrovitch unfolded the rug in which his frozen
feet were wrapped, and getting out of his carriage made his way
over the snow to Darya Alexandrovna.

"Why, Alexey Alexandrovitch, what are you cutting us like
this for?" said Dolly, smiling.

"I was very busy. Delighted to see you!" he said in a tone clearly indicating that he was annoyed by it. "How are you?"

"Tell me, how is my darling Anna?"

Alexey Alexandrovitch mumbled something and would have gone on. But Stepan Arkadyevitch stopped him.

"I tell you what we'll do to-morrow. Dolly, ask him to dinner. We'll ask Koznishev and Pestsov, so as to entertain him with our Moscow celebrities."

"Yes, please, do come," said Dolly; "we will expect you at five, or six o'clock, if you like. How is my darling Anna? How long . . ."

"She is quite well," Alexey Alexandrovitch mumbled, frowning. "Delighted!" and he moved away towards his carriage.

"You will come?" Dolly called after him.

Alexey Alexandrovitch said something which Dolly could not catch in the noise of the moving carriages.

"I shall come round to-morrow!" Stepan Arkadyevitch shouted to him.

Alexey Alexandrovitch got into his carriage, and buried himself in it so as neither to see nor be seen.

"Queer fish!" said Stepan Arkadyevitch to his wife, and glancing at his watch, he made a motion of his hand before his face, indicating a caress to his wife and children, and walked jauntily along the pavement.

"Stiva! Stiva!" Dolly called, reddening.

He turned round.

"I must get coats, you know, for Grisha and Tanya. Give me the money."

"Never mind; you tell them I'll pay the bill!" and he vanished, nodding genially to an acquaintance who drove by.

CHAPTER VII

THE next day was Sunday. Stepan Arkadyevitch went to the Grand Theater to a rehearsal of the ballet, and gave Masha Tchibisova, a pretty dancing-girl whom he had just taken under his protection, the coral necklace he had promised her the evening before, and behind the scenes in the dim daylight of the

448

theater, managed to kiss her pretty little face, radiant over her present. Besides the gift of the necklace he wanted to arrange with her about meeting after the ballet. After explaining that he could not come at the beginning of the ballet, he promised he would come for the last act and take her to supper. From the theater Stepan Arkadyevitch drove to Ohotny Row, selected himself the fish and asparagus for dinner, and by twelve o'clock was at Dussot's, where he had to see three people, luckily all staying at the same hotel: Levin, who had recently come back from abroad and was staying there; the new head of his department, who had just been promoted to that position, and had come on a tour of revision to Moscow; and his brother-in-law, Karenin, whom he must see, so as to be sure of bringing him to dinner.

Stepan Arkadyevitch liked dining, but still better he liked to give a dinner, small, but very choice, both as regards the food and drink and as regards the selection of guests. He particularly liked the program of that day's dinner. There would be fresh perch, asparagus, and *la pièce de résistance*—first-rate, but quite plain, roast beef, and wines to suit: so much for the eating and drinking. Kitty and Levin would be of the party, and that this might not be obtrusively evident, there would be a girl cousin too, and young Shtcherbatsky, and *la pièce de résistance* among the guests—Sergey Koznishev and Alexey Alexandrovitch. Sergey Ivanovitch was a Moscow man, and a philosopher; Alexey Alexandrovitch a Petersburger, and a practical politician. He was asking, too, the well-known eccentric enthusiast, Pestsov, a liberal, a great talker, a musician, an historian, and the most delightfully youthful person of fifty, who would be a sauce or garnish for Koznishev and Karenin. He would provoke them and set them off.

The second installment for the forest had been received from the merchant and was not yet exhausted; Dolly had been very amiable and good-humored of late, and the idea of the dinner pleased Stepan Arkadyevitch from every point of view. He was in the most light-hearted mood. There were two circumstances a little unpleasant, but these two circumstances were drowned in the sea of good-humored gaiety which flooded the soul of Stepan Arkadyevitch. These two circumstances were: first, that on meeting Alexey Alexandrovitch the day before in the street he had noticed that he was cold and reserved with him, and putting the expression of Alexey Alexandrovitch's face and the fact that he had not come to see them or let them know of his arrival with the rumors he had heard about Anna and Vronsky, Stepan Arkadyevitch guessed that something was wrong between the husband and wife.

That was one disagreeable thing. The other slightly disagreeable fact was that the new head of his department, like all new heads, had the reputation already of a terrible person, who got up at six o'clock in the morning, worked like a horse, and insisted on his subordinates working in the same way. Moreover, this new head had the further reputation of being a bear in his manners, and was, according to all reports, a man of a class in all respects the opposite of that to which his predecessor had belonged, and to which Stepan Arkadyevitch had hitherto belonged himself. On the previous day Stepan Arkadyevitch had appeared at the office in a uniform, and the new chief had been very affable and had talked to him as to an acquaintance. Consequently Stepan Arkadyevitch deemed it his duty to call upon him in his non-official dress. The thought that the new chief might not tender him a warm reception was the other unpleasant thing. But Stepan Arkadyevitch instinctively felt that everything would *come round* all right.

"They're all people, all men, like us poor sinners; why be nasty and quarrelsome?" he thought as he went into the hotel.

"Good-day, Vassily," he said, walking into the corridor with his hat cocked on one side, and addressing a footman he knew; "why, you've let your whiskers grow! Levin, number seven, eh?

Take me up, please. And find out whether Count Anitchkin"
(this was the new head) "is receiving."

"Yes, sir," Vassily responded, smiling. "You've not been to
see us for a long while."

"I was here yesterday, but at the other entrance. Is this number seven?"

Levin was standing with a peasant from Tver in the middle of
the room, measuring a fresh bearskin, when Stepan Arkadyevitch went in.

"What! you killed him?" cried Stepan Arkadyevitch. "Well
done! A she-bear? How are you, Arhip!"

He shook hands with the peasant and sat down on the edge of
a chair, without taking off his coat and hat.

"Come, take off your coat and stay a little," said Levin, taking
his hat.

"No, I haven't time; I've only looked in for a tiny second,"
answered Stepan Arkadyevitch. He threw open his coat, but
afterwards did take it off, and sat on for a whole hour, talking
to Levin about hunting and the most intimate subjects.

"Come, tell me, please, what you did abroad? Where have
you been?" said Stepan Arkadyevitch, when the peasant had
gone.

"Oh, I stayed in Germany, in Prussia, in France, and in England—not in the capitals, but in the manufacturing towns, and
saw a great deal that was new to me. And I'm glad I went."

"Yes, I knew your idea of the solution of the labor question."

"Not a bit: in Russia there can be no labor question. In Russia the question is that of the relation of the working people to
the land; though the question exists there too—but there it's a
matter of repairing what's been ruined, while with us . . ."

Stepan Arkadyevitch listened attentively to Levin.

"Yes, yes!" he said, "it's very possible you're right. But I'm
glad you're in good spirits, and are hunting bears, and working,
and interested. Shtcherbatsky told me another story—he met
you—that you were in such a depressed state, talking of nothing
but death. . . ."

"Well, what of it? I've not given up thinking of death," said
Levin. "It's true that it's high time I was dead; and that all this
is nonsense. It's the truth I'm telling you. I do value my idea

and my work awfully; but in reality only consider this: all this world of ours is nothing but a speck of mildew, which has grown up on a tiny planet. And for us to suppose we can have something great—ideas, work—it's all dust and ashes."

"But all that's as old as the hills, my boy!"

"It is old; but do you know, when you grasp this fully, then somehow everything becomes of no consequence. When you understand that you will die to-morrow, if not to-day, and nothing will be left, then everything is so unimportant! And I consider my idea very important, but it turns out really to be as unimportant too, even if it were carried out, as doing for that bear. So one goes on living, amusing oneself with hunting, with work —anything so as not to think of death!"

Stepan Arkadyevitch smiled a subtle affectionate smile as he listened to Levin.

"Well, of course! Here you've come round to my point. Do you remember you attacked me for seeking enjoyment in life? Don't be so severe, O moralist!"

"No; all the same, what's fine in life is . . ." Levin hesitated —"oh, I don't know. All I know is that we shall soon be dead."

"Why so soon?"

"And do you know, there's less charm in life, when one thinks of death, but there's more peace."

"On the contrary, the finish is always the best. But I must be going," said Stepan Arkadyevitch, getting up for the tenth time.

"Oh, no, stay a bit!" said Levin, keeping him. "Now, when shall we see each other again? I'm going to-morrow."

"I'm a nice person! Why, that's just what I came for! You simply must come to dinner with us to-day. Your brother's coming, and Karenin, my brother-in-law."

"You don't mean to say he's here?" said Levin, and he wanted to inquire about Kitty. He had heard at the beginning of the winter that she was at Petersburg with her sister, the wife of the diplomat, and he did not know whether she had come back or not; but he changed his mind and did not ask. "Whether she's coming or not, I don't care," he said to himself.

"So you'll come?"

"Of course."

"At five o'clock, then, and not evening dress."

And Stepan Arkadyevitch got up and went down below to the new head of his department. Instinct had not misled Stepan Arkadyevitch. The terrible new head turned out to be an extremely amenable person, and Stepan Arkadyevitch lunched with him and stayed on, so that it was four o'clock before he got to Alexey Alexandrovitch.

CHAPTER VIII

ALEXEY ALEXANDROVITCH, on coming back from church service, had spent the whole morning indoors. He had two pieces of business before him that morning; first, to receive and send on a deputation from the native tribes which was on its way to Petersburg, and now at Moscow; secondly, to write the promised letter to the lawyer. The deputation, though it had been summoned at Alexey Alexandrovitch's instigation, was not without its discomforting and even dangerous aspect, and he was glad he had found it in Moscow. The members of this deputation had not the slightest conception of their duty and the part they were to play. They naïvely believed that it was their business to lay before the commission their needs and the actual condition of things, and to ask assistance of the government, and utterly failed to grasp that some of their statements and requests supported the contention of the enemy's side, and so spoiled the whole business. Alexey Alexandrovitch was busily engaged with them for a long while, drew up a program for them from which they were not to depart, and on dismissing them wrote a letter to Petersburg for the guidance of the deputation. He had his chief support in this affair in the Countess Lidia Ivanovna. She was a specialist in the matter of deputations, and no one knew better than she how to manage them, and put them in the way they should go. Having completed this task, Alexey Alexandrovitch wrote the letter to the lawyer. Without the slightest hesitation he gave him permission to act as he might judge best. In the letter he enclosed three of Vronsky's notes to Anna, which were in the portfolio he had taken away.

Since Alexey Alexandrovitch had left home with the intention of not returning to his family again, and since he had been at the lawyer's and had spoken, though only to one man, of his intention, since especially he had translated the matter from the world of real life to the world of ink and paper, he had grown more and more used to his own intention, and by now distinctly perceived the feasibility of its execution.

He was sealing the envelope to the lawyer, when he heard the loud tones of Stepan Arkadyevitch's voice. Stepan Arkadyevitch was disputing with Alexey Alexandrovitch's servant, and insisting on being announced.

"No matter," thought Alexey Alexandrovitch, "so much the better. I will inform him at once of my position in regard to his sister, and explain why it is I can't dine with him."

"Come in!" he said aloud, collecting his papers, and putting them in the blotting-paper.

"There, you see, you're talking nonsense, and he's at home!" responded Stepan Arkadyevitch's voice, addressing the servant, who had refused to let him in, and taking off his coat as he went, Oblonsky walked into the room. "Well, I'm awfully glad I've found you! So I hope . . ." Stepan Arkadyevitch began cheerfully.

"I cannot come," Alexey Alexandrovitch said coldly, standing and not asking his visitor to sit down.

Alexey Alexandrovitch had thought to pass at once into those frigid relations in which he ought to stand with the brother of a wife against whom he was beginning a suit for divorce. But he had not taken into account the ocean of kindliness brimming over in the heart of Stepan Arkadyevitch.

Stepan Arkadyevitch opened wide his clear, shining eyes.

"Why can't you? What do you mean?" he asked in perplexity, speaking in French. "Oh, but it's a promise. And we're all counting on you."

"I want to tell you that I can't dine at your house, because the terms of relationship which have existed between us must cease."

"How? How do you mean? What for?" said Stepan Arkadyevitch with a smile.

"Because I am beginning an action for divorce against your sister, my wife. I ought to have . . ."

But, before Alexey Alexandrovitch had time to finish his sentence, Stepan Arkadyevitch was behaving not at all as he had expected. He groaned and sank into an armchair.

"No, Alexey Alexandrovitch! What are you saying?" cried Oblonsky, and his suffering was apparent in his face.

"It is so."

"Excuse me, I can't, I can't believe it!"

Alexey Alexandrovitch sat down, feeling that his words had not had the effect he anticipated, and that it would be unavoidable for him to explain his position, and that, whatever explanations he might make, his relations with his brother-in-law would remain unchanged.

"Yes, I am brought to the painful necessity of seeking a divorce," he said.

"I will say one thing, Alexey Alexandrovitch. I know you for an excellent, upright man; I know Anna—excuse me, I can't change my opinion of her—for a good, an excellent woman; and so, excuse me, I cannot believe it. There is some misunderstanding," said he.

"Oh, if it were merely a misunderstanding! . . ."

"Pardon, I understand," interposed Stepan Arkadyevitch. "But of course . . . One thing: you must not act in haste. You must not, you must not act in haste!"

"I am not acting in haste," Alexey Alexandrovitch said coldly, "but one cannot ask advice of any one in such a matter. I have quite made up my mind."

"This is awful!" said Stepan Arkadyevitch. "I would do one thing, Alexey Alexandrovitch. I beseech you, do it!" he said. "No action has yet been taken, if I understand rightly. Before you take advice, see my wife, talk to her. She loves Anna like a sister, she loves you, and she's a wonderful woman. For God's sake, talk to her! Do me that favor, I beseech you!"

Alexey Alexandrovitch pondered, and Stepan Arkadyevitch looked at him sympathetically, without interrupting his silence.

"You will go to see her?"

"I don't know. That was just why I have not been to see you. I imagine our relations must change."

"Why so? I don't see that. Allow me to believe that apart from our connection you have for me, at least in part, the same friendly feeling I have always had for you . . . and sincere esteem," said Stepan Arkadyevitch, pressing his hand. "Even if your worst suppositions were correct, I don't—and never would —take on myself to judge either side, and I see no reason why our relations should be affected. But now, do this, come and see my wife."

"Well, we look at the matter differently," said Alexey Alexandrovitch coldly. "However, we won't discuss it."

"No; why shouldn't you come to-day to dine, anyway? My wife's expecting you. Please, do come. And, above all, talk it over with her. She's a wonderful woman. For God's sake, on my knees, I implore you!"

"If you so much wish it, I will come," said Alexey Alexandrovitch, sighing.

And, anxious to change the conversation, he inquired about what interested them both—the new head of Stepan Arkadyevitch's department, a man not yet old, who had suddenly been promoted to so high a position.

Alexey Alexandrovitch had previously felt no liking for Count Anitchkin, and had always differed from him in his opinions. But now, from a feeling readily comprehensible to officials —that hatred felt by one who has suffered a defeat in the service for one who has received a promotion, he could not endure him.

"Well, have you seen him?" said Alexey Alexandrovitch with a malignant smile.

"Of course; he was at our sitting yesterday. He seems to know his work capitally, and to be very energetic."

"Yes, but what is his energy directed to?" said Alexey Alexandrovitch. "Is he aiming at doing anything, or simply undoing what's been done? It's the great misfortune of our government— this paper administration, of which he's a worthy representative."

"Really, I don't know what fault one could find with him. His policy I don't know, but one thing—he's a very nice fellow," answered Stepan Arkadyevitch. "I've just been seeing him, and he's really a capital fellow. We lunched together, and I taught him how to make, you know that drink, wine and oranges. It's so cooling. And it's a wonder he didn't know it. He liked it awfully. No, really he's a capital fellow."

Stepan Arkadyevitch glanced at his watch.

"Why, good heavens, it's four already, and I've still to go to Dolgovushin's! So please come round to dinner. You can't imagine how you will grieve my wife and me."

The way in which Alexey Alexandrovitch saw his brother-in-law out was very different from the manner in which he had met him.

"I've promised, and I'll come," he answered wearily.

"Believe me, I appreciate it, and I hope you won't regret it," answered Stepan Arkadyevitch, smiling.

And, putting on his coat as he went, he patted the footman on the head, chuckled, and went out.

"At five o'clock, and not evening dress, please," he shouted once more, turning at the door.

CHAPTER IX

It was past five, and several guests had already arrived, before the host himself got home. He went in together with Sergey Ivanovitch Koznishev and Pestsov, who had reached the street door at the same moment. These were the two leading representatives of the Moscow intellectuals, as Oblonsky had called them. Both were men respected for their character and their intelligence. They respected each other, but were in complete and hopeless disagreement upon almost every subject, not because they belonged to opposite parties, but precisely because they were of the same party (their enemies refused to see any distinction between their views); but, in that party, each had his own special shade of opinion. And since no difference is less easily overcome than the difference of opinion about semi-abstract questions, they never agreed in any opinion, and had long, indeed, been accustomed to jeer without anger, each at the other's incorrigible aberrations.

They were just going in at the door, talking of the weather, when Stepan Arkadyevitch overtook them. In the drawing-room there were already sitting Prince Alexander Dmitrievitch Shtcherbatsky, young Shtcherbatsky, Turovtsin, Kitty, and Karenin.

Stepan Arkadyevitch saw immediately that things were not

going well in the drawing-room without him. Darya Alexandrovna, in her best gray silk gown, obviously worried about the children, who were to have their dinner by themselves in the nursery, and by her husband's absence, was not equal to the task of making the party mix without him. All were sitting like so many priests' wives on a visit (so the old prince expressed it), obviously wondering why they were there, and pumping up remarks simply to avoid being silent. Turovtsin—good, simple man—felt unmistakably a fish out of water, and the smile with which his thick lips greeted Stepan Arkadyevitch said, as plainly as words: "Well, old boy, you have popped me down in a learned set! A drinking-party now, or the Château des Fleurs, would be more in my line!" The old prince sat in silence, his bright little eyes watching Karenin from one side, and Stepan Arkadyevitch saw that he had already formed a phrase to sum up that politician of whom guests were invited to partake as though he were a sturgeon. Kitty was looking at the door, calling up all her energies to keep her from blushing at the entrance of Konstantin Levin. Young Shtcherbatsky, who had not been introduced to Karenin, was trying to look as though he were not in the least conscious of it. Karenin himself had followed the Petersburg fashion for a dinner with ladies and was wearing evening dress and a white tie. Stepan Arkadyevitch saw by his face that he had come simply to keep his promise, and was performing a disagreeable duty in being present at this gathering. He was indeed the person chiefly responsible for the chill benumbing all the guests before Stepan Arkadyevitch came in.

On entering the drawing-room Stepan Arkadyevitch apologized, explaining that he had been detained by that prince, who was always the scapegoat for all his absences and unpunctualities, and in one moment he had made all the guests acquainted with each other, and, bringing together Alexey Alexandrovitch and Sergey Koznishev, started them on a discussion of the Russification of Poland, into which they immediately plunged with Pestsov. Slapping Turovtsin on the shoulder, he whispered something comic in his ear, and set him down by his wife and the old prince. Then he told Kitty she was looking very pretty that evening, and presented Shtcherbatsky to Karenin. In a moment he had so kneaded together the social dough that the drawing-room became very lively, and there was a merry buzz of voices. Konstantin Levin was the only person who had not arrived. But this was so much the better, as going into the dining-room, Stepan Arkadyevitch found to his horror that the port and sherry had been procured from Depré, and not from Levy, and, directing that the coachman should be sent off as speedily as possible to Levy's, he was going back to the drawing-room.

In the dining-room he was met by Konstantin Levin.

"I'm not late?"

"You can never help being late!" said Stepan Arkadyevitch, taking his arm.

"Have you a lot of people? Who's here?" asked Levin, unable to help blushing, as he knocked the snow off his cap with his glove.

"All our own set. Kitty's here. Come along, I'll introduce you to Karenin."

Stepan Arkadyevitch, for all his liberal views, was well aware that to meet Karenin was sure to be felt a flattering distinction, and so treated his best friends to this honor. But at that instant Konstantin Levin was not in a condition to feel all the gratification of making such an acquaintance. He had not seen Kitty since that memorable evening when he met Vronsky, not counting, that is, the moment when he had had a glimpse of her on the highroad. He had known at the bottom of his heart that he would see her here to-day. But to keep his thoughts free, he had tried to persuade himself that he did not know it. Now when he heard that she was here, he was suddenly conscious of such delight, and at the same time of such dread, that his breath failed him and he could not utter what he wanted to say.

"What is she like, what is she like? Like what she used to be, or like what she was in the carriage? What if Darya Alexandrovna told the truth? Why shouldn't it be the truth?" he thought.

"Oh, please, introduce me to Karenin," he brought out with an effort, and with a desperately determined step he walked into the drawing-room and beheld her.

She was not the same as she used to be, nor was she as she had been in the carriage; she was quite different.

She was scared, shy, shame-faced, and still more charming

from it. She saw him the very instant he walked into the room. She had been expecting him. She was delighted, and so confused at her own delight that there was a moment, the moment when he went up to her sister and glanced again at her, when she, and he, and Dolly, who saw it all, thought she would break down and would begin to cry. She crimsoned, turned white, crimsoned again, and grew faint, waiting with quivering lips for him to come to her. He went up to her, bowed, and held out his hand without speaking. Except for the slight quiver of her lips and the moisture in her eyes that made them brighter, her smile was almost calm as she said:

"How long it is since we've seen each other!" and with desperate determination she pressed his hand with her cold hand.

"You've not seen me, but I've seen you," said Levin, with a radiant smile of happiness. "I saw you when you were driving from the railway station to Ergushovo."

"When?" she asked, wondering.

"You were driving to Ergushovo," said Levin, feeling as if he would sob with the rapture that was flooding his heart. "And how dared I associate a thought of anything not innocent with this touching creature? And, yes, I do believe it's true what Darya Alexandrovna told me," he thought.

Stepan Arkadyevitch took him by the arm and led him away to Karenin.

"Let me introduce you." He mentioned their names.

"Very glad to meet you again," said Alexey Alexandrovitch coldly, shaking hands with Levin.

"You are acquainted?" Stepan Arkadyevitch asked in surprise.

"We spent three hours together in the train," said Levin smiling, "but got out, just as in a masquerade, quite mystified—at least I was."

"Nonsense! Come along, please," said Stepan Arkadyevitch, pointing in the direction of the dining-room.

The men went into the dining-room and went up to a table, laid with six sorts of spirits and as many kinds of cheese, some with little silver spades and some without, caviar herrings, preserves of various kinds, and plates with slices of French bread.

The men stood round the strong-smelling spirits and salt

delicacies, and the discussion of the Russification of Poland between Koznishev, Karenin, and Pestsov died down in anticipation of dinner.

Sergey Ivanovitch was unequaled in his skill in winding up the most heated and serious argument by some unexpected pinch of Attic salt that changed the disposition of his opponent. He did this now.

Alexey Alexandrovitch had been maintaining that the Russification of Poland could only be accomplished as a result of larger measures which ought to be introduced by the Russian government.

Pestsov insisted that one country can only absorb another when it is the more densely populated.

Koznishev admitted both points, but with limitations. As they were going out of the drawing-room to conclude the argument, Koznishev said, smiling:

"So, then, for the Russification of our foreign populations there is but one method—to bring up as many children as one can. My brother and I are terribly in fault, I see. You married men, especially you, Stepan Arkadyevitch, are the real patriots: what number have you reached?" he said, smiling genially at their host and holding out a tiny wine-glass to him.

Every one laughed, and Stepan Arkadyevitch with particular good-humor.

"Oh, yes, that's the best method!" he said, munching cheese and filling the wine-glass with a special sort of spirit. The conversation dropped at the jest.

"This cheese is not bad. Shall I give you some?" said the master of the house. "Why, have you been going in for gymnastics again?" he asked Levin, pinching his muscle with his left hand. Levin smiled, bent his arm, and under Stepan Arkadyevitch's fingers the muscles swelled up like a sound cheese, hard as a knob of iron, through the fine cloth of the coat.

"What biceps! A perfect Samson!"

"I imagine great strength is needed for hunting bears," observed Alexey Alexandrovitch, who had the mistiest notions about the chase. He cut off and spread with cheese a wafer of bread fine as a spider-web.

Levin smiled.

"Not at all. Quite the contrary; a child can kill a bear," he said, with a slight bow moving aside for the ladies, who were approaching the table.

"You have killed a bear, I've been told!" said Kitty, trying assiduously to catch with her fork a perverse mushroom that would slip away, and setting the lace quivering over her white arm. "Are there bears on your place?" she added, turning her charming little head to him and smiling.

There was apparently nothing extraordinary in what she said, but what unutterable meaning there was for him in every sound, in every turn of her lips, her eyes, her hand as she said it! There was entreaty for forgiveness, and trust in him, and tenderness—soft, timid tenderness—and promise and hope and love for him, which he could not but believe in and which choked him with happiness.

"No, we've been hunting in the Tver province. It was coming back from there that I met your *beau-frère* in the train, or your

beau-frère's brother-in-law," he said with a smile. "It was an amusing meeting."

And he began telling with droll good-humor how, after not sleeping all night, he had, wearing an old fur-lined, full-skirted coat, got into Alexey Alexandrovitch's compartment.

"The conductor, forgetting the proverb, would have chucked me out on account of my attire; but thereupon I began expressing my feelings in elevated language, and . . . you, too," he

462

said, addressing Karenin and forgetting his name, "at first would have ejected me on the ground of the old coat, but afterwards you took my part, for which I am extremely grateful."

"The rights of passengers generally to choose their seats are too ill-defined," said Alexey Alexandrovitch, rubbing the tips of his fingers on his handkerchief.

"I saw you were in uncertainty about me," said Levin, smiling good-naturedly, "but I made haste to plunge into intellectual conversation to smooth over the defects of my attire."

Sergey Ivanovitch, while he kept up a conversation with their hostess, had one ear for his brother, and he glanced askance at him. "What is the matter with him to-day? Why such a conquering hero?" he thought. He did not know that Levin was feeling as though he had grown wings. Levin knew she was listening to his words and that she was glad to listen to him. And this was the only thing that interested him. Not in that room only, but in the whole world, there existed for him only himself, with enormously increased importance and dignity in his own eyes, and she. He felt himself on a pinnacle that made him giddy, and far away down below were all those nice excellent Karenins, Oblonskys, and all the world.

Quite without attracting notice, without glancing at them, as though there were no other places left, Stepan Arkadyevitch put Levin and Kitty side by side.

"Oh, you may as well sit there," he said to Levin.

The dinner was as choice as the china, in which Stepan Arkadyevitch was a connoisseur. The *soupe Marie-Louise* was a splendid success; the tiny pies eaten with it melted in the mouth and were irreproachable. The two footmen and Matvey, in white cravats, did their duty with the dishes and wines unobtrusively, quietly, and swiftly. On the material side the dinner was a success; it was no less so on the immaterial. The conversation, at times general and at times between individuals, never paused, and towards the end the company was so lively that the men rose from the table, without stopping speaking, and even Alexey Alexandrovitch thawed.

PESTSOV liked thrashing an argument out to the end, and was not satisfied with Sergey Ivanovitch's words, especially as he felt the injustice of his view.

"I did not mean," he said over the soup, addressing Alexey Alexandrovitch, "mere density of population alone, but in conjunction with fundamental ideas, and not by means of principles."

"It seems to me," Alexey Alexandrovitch said languidly, and with no haste, "that that's the same thing. In my opinion, influence over another people is only possible to the people which has the higher development, which . . ."

"But that's just the question," Pestsov broke in in his bass.

He was always in a hurry to speak, and seemed always to put his whole soul into what he was saying. "In what are we to make higher development consist? The English, the French, the Germans, which is at the highest stage of development? Which of them will nationalize the other? We see the Rhine provinces have been turned French, but the Germans are not at a lower stage!" he shouted. "There is another law at work there."

"I fancy that the greater influence is always on the side of true civilization," said Alexey Alexandrovitch, slightly lifting his eyebrows.

"But what are we to lay down as the outward signs of true civilization?" said Pestsov.

"I imagine such signs are generally very well known," said Alexey Alexandrovitch.

"But are they fully known?" Sergey Ivanovitch put in with a subtle smile. "It is the accepted view now that real culture must be purely classical; but we see most intense disputes on each side of the question, and there is no denying that the opposite camp has strong points in its favor."

"You are for classics, Sergey Ivanovitch. Will you take red wine?" said Stepan Arkadyevitch.

"I am not expressing my own opinion of either form of culture," Sergey Ivanovitch said, holding out his glass with a smile of condescension, as to a child. "I only say that both sides have strong arguments to support them," he went on, addressing

Alexey Alexandrovitch. "My sympathies are classical from education, but in this discussion I am personally unable to arrive at a conclusion. I see no distinct grounds for classical studies being given a preëminence over scientific studies."

"The natural sciences have just as great an educational value," put in Pestsov. "Take astronomy, take botany, or zoology with its system of general principles."

"I cannot quite agree with that," responded Alexey Alexandrovitch. "It seems to me that one must admit that the very process of studying the forms of language has a peculiarly favorable influence on intellectual development. Moreover, it cannot be denied that the influence of the classical authors is in the highest degree moral, while, unfortunately, with the study of the natural sciences are associated the false and noxious doctrines which are the curse of our day."

Sergey Ivanovitch would have said something, but Pestsov interrupted him in his rich bass. He began warmly contesting the justice of this view. Sergey Ivanovitch waited serenely to speak, obviously with a convincing reply ready.

"But," said Sergey Ivanovitch, smiling subtly, and addressing Karenin, "one must allow that to weigh all the advantages and disadvantages of classical and scientific studies is a difficult task, and the question which form of education was to be preferred would not have been so quickly and conclusively decided if there had not been in favor of classical education, as you expressed it just now, its moral—*disons le mot*—anti-nihilist influence."

"Undoubtedly."

"If it had not been for the distinctive property of anti-nihilistic influence on the side of classical studies, we should have considered the subject more, have weighed the arguments on both sides," said Sergey Ivanovitch with a subtle smile, "we should have given elbow-room to both tendencies. But now we know that these little pills of classical learning possess the medicinal property of anti-nihilism, and we boldly prescribe them to our patients. . . . But what if they had no such medicinal property?" he wound up humorously.

At Sergey Ivanovitch's little pills, every one laughed; Turovtsin in especial roared loudly and jovially, glad at last to have found something to laugh at, all he ever looked for in listening to conversation.

Stepan Arkadyevitch had not made a mistake in inviting Pestsov. With Pestsov intellectual conversation never flagged for an instant. Directly Sergey Ivanovitch had concluded the conversation with his jest, Pestsov promptly started a new one.

"I can't agree even," said he, "that the government had that aim. The government obviously is guided by abstract considerations, and remains indifferent to the influence its measures may exercise. The education of women, for instance, would naturally be regarded as likely to be harmful, but the government opens schools and universities for women."

And the conversation at once passed to the new subject of the education of women.

Alexey Alexandrovitch expressed the idea that the education of women is apt to be confounded with the emancipation of women, and that it is only so that it can be considered dangerous.

"I consider, on the contrary, that the two questions are inseparably connected together," said Pestsov; "it is a vicious circle. Woman is deprived of rights from lack of education, and the lack of education results from the absence of rights. We must not forget that the subjection of women is so complete, and dates from such ages back that we are often unwilling to recognize the gulf that separates them from us," said he.

"You said rights," said Sergey Ivanovitch, waiting till Pestsov had finished, "meaning the right of sitting on juries, of voting, of presiding at official meetings, the right of entering the civil service, of sitting in parliament . . ."

"Undoubtedly."

"But if women, as a rare exception, can occupy such positions, it seems to me you are wrong in using the expression 'rights.' It would be more correct to say duties. Every man will agree that in doing the duty of a juryman, a witness, a telegraph clerk, we feel we are performing duties. And therefore it would be correct to say that women are seeking duties, and quite legitimately. And one can but sympathize with this desire to assist in the general labor of man."

"Quite so," Alexey Alexandrovitch assented. "The question, I imagine, is simply whether they are fitted for such duties."

"They will most likely be perfectly fitted," said Stepan Arkadyevitch, "when education has become general among them. We see this . . ."

"How about the proverb?" said the prince, who had a long while been intent on the conversation, his little comical eyes twinkling. "I can say it before my daughter: her hair is long, because her wit is . . ."

"Just what they thought of the negroes before their emancipation!" said Pestsov angrily.

"What seems strange to me is that women should seek fresh duties," said Sergey Ivanovitch, "while we see, unhappily, that men usually try to avoid them."

"Duties are bound up with rights—power, money, honor; those are what women are seeking," said Pestsov.

"Just as though I should seek the right to be a wet-nurse and feel injured because women are paid for the work, while no one will take me," said the old prince.

Turovtsin exploded in a loud roar of laughter and Sergey Ivanovitch regretted that he had not made this comparison. Even Alexey Alexandrovitch smiled.

"Yes, but a man can't nurse a baby," said Pestsov, "while a woman . . ."

"No, there was an Englishman who did suckle his baby on board ship," said the old prince, feeling this freedom in conversation permissible before his own daughters.

"There are as many such Englishmen as there would be women officials," said Sergey Ivanovitch.

"Yes, but what is a girl to do who has no family?" put in Stepan Arkadyevitch, thinking of Masha Tchibisova, whom he had had in his mind all along, in sympathizing with Pestsov and supporting him.

"If the story of such a girl were thoroughly sifted, you would find she had abandoned a family—her own or a sister's, where she might have found a woman's duties," Darya Alexandrovna broke in unexpectedly in a tone of exasperation, probably suspecting what sort of girl Stepan Arkadyevitch was thinking of.

"But we take our stand on principle as the ideal," replied Pestsov in his mellow bass. "Woman desires to have rights, to be independent, educated. She is oppressed, humiliated by the consciousness of her disabilities."

"And I'm oppressed and humiliated that they won't engage me at the Foundling," the old prince said again, to the huge delight of Turovtsin, who in his mirth dropped his asparagus with the thick end in the sauce.

CHAPTER XI

EVERY one took part in the conversation except Kitty and Levin. At first, when they were talking of the influence that one people has on another, there rose to Levin's mind what he had to say on the subject. But these ideas, once of such importance in his eyes, seemed to come into his brain as in a dream, and had now not the slightest interest for him. It even struck him as strange that they should be so eager to talk of what was of no use to any one. Kitty, too, should, one would have supposed, have been interested in what they were saying of the rights and education of women. How often she had mused on the subject, thinking of her friend abroad, Varenka, of her painful state of dependence, how often she had wondered about herself what would become of her if she did not marry, and how often she had argued with her sister about it! But it did not interest her at all. She and Levin had a conversation of their own, yet not a conversation, but some sort of mysterious communication, which brought them every moment nearer, and stirred in both a sense of glad terror before the unknown into which they were entering.

At first Levin, in answer to Kitty's question how he could have seen her last year in the carriage, told her how he had been coming home from the mowing along the highroad and had met her.

"It was very, very early in the morning. You were probably only just awake. Your mother was asleep in the corner. It was an exquisite morning. I was walking along wondering who it could be in a four-in-hand. It was a splendid set of four horses with bells, and in a second you flashed by, and I saw you at the window—you were sitting like this, holding the strings of your cap in both hands, and thinking awfully deeply about something," he said, smiling. "How I should like to know what you were thinking about then! Something important?"

"Wasn't I dreadfully untidy?" she wondered, but seeing the

smile of ecstasy these reminiscences called up, she felt that the impression she had made had been very good. She blushed and laughed with delight: "Really I don't remember."

"How nicely Turovtsin laughs!" said Levin, admiring his moist eyes and shaking chest.

"Have you known him long?" asked Kitty.

"Oh, every one knows him!"

"And I see you think he's a horrid man?"

"Not horrid, but nothing in him."

"Oh, you're wrong! And you must give up thinking so directly!" said Kitty. "I used to have a very poor opinion of him too, but he, he's an awfully nice and wonderfully good-hearted man. He has a heart of gold."

"How could you find out what sort of heart he has?"

"We are great friends. I know him very well. Last winter, soon after . . . you came to see us," she said, with a guilty and at the same time confiding smile, "all Dolly's children had scarlet fever, and he happened to come and see her. And only fancy," she said in a whisper, "he felt so sorry for her that he stayed and began to help her look after the children. Yes, and for three weeks he stopped with them, and looked after the children like a nurse."

"I am telling Konstantin Dmitrievitch about Turovtsin in the scarlet fever," she said, bending over to her sister.

"Yes, it was wonderful, noble!" said Dolly, glancing towards Turovtsin, who had become aware they were talking of him, and smiling gently to him. Levin glanced once more at Turovtsin, and wondered how it was he had not realized all this man's goodness before.

"I'm sorry, I'm sorry, and I'll never think ill of people again!" he said gaily, genuinely expressing what he felt at the moment.

CHAPTER XII

CONNECTED with the conversation that had sprung up on the rights of women there were certain questions as to the inequality of rights in marriage improper to discuss before the ladies. Pestsov had several times during dinner touched upon these questions, but Sergey Ivanovitch and Stepan Arkadyevitch carefully drew him off them.

When they rose from the table and the ladies had gone out, Pestsov did not follow them, but addressing Alexey Alexandrovitch, began to expound the chief ground of inequality. The inequality in marriage, in his opinion, lay in the fact that the infidelity of the wife and infidelity of the husband are punished unequally, both by the law and by public opinion. Stepan Arkadyevitch went hurriedly up to Alexey Alexandrovitch and offered him a cigar.

"No, I don't smoke," Alexey Alexandrovitch answered calmly, and as though purposely wishing to show that he was not afraid of the subject, he turned to Pestsov with a chilly smile.

"I imagine that such a view has a foundation in the very nature of things," he said, and would have gone on to the drawing-room. But at this point Turovtsin broke suddenly and unexpectedly into the conversation, addressing Alexey Alexandrovitch.

"You heard, perhaps, about Pryatchnikov?" said Turovtsin, warmed up by the champagne he had drunk, and long waiting for an opportunity to break the silence that had weighed on him. "Vasya Pryatchnikov," he said, with a good-natured smile on his damp, red lips, addressing himself principally to the most important guest, Alexey Alexandrovitch, "they told me to-day he fought a duel with Kvitsky at Tver, and has killed him."

Just as it always seems that one bruises oneself on a sore place, so Stepan Arkadyevitch felt now that the conversation would by ill luck fall every moment on Alexey Alexandrovitch's sore spot. He would again have got his brother-in-law away, but Alexey Alexandrovitch himself inquired, with curiosity:

"What did Pryatchnikov fight about?"

"His wife. Acted like a man, he did! Called him out and shot him!"

"Ah!" said Alexey Alexandrovitch indifferently, and lifting his eyebrows, he went into the drawing-room.

"How glad I am you have come," Dolly said with a frightened smile, meeting him in the outer drawing-room. "I must talk to you. Let's sit here."

Alexey Alexandrovitch, with the same expression of indifference, given him by his lifted eyebrows, sat down beside Darya Alexandrovna, and smiled affectedly.

"It's fortunate," said he, "especially as I was meaning to ask you to excuse me, and to be taking leave. I have to start to-morrow."

Darya Alexandrovna was firmly convinced of Anna's innocence, and she felt herself growing pale and her lips quivering with anger at this frigid, unfeeling man, who was so calmly intending to ruin her innocent friend.

"Alexey Alexandrovitch," she said, with desperate resolution looking him in the face, "I asked you about Anna; you made me no answer. How is she?"

"She is, I believe, quite well, Darya Alexandrovna," replied Alexey Alexandrovitch, not looking at her.

"Alexey Alexandrovitch, forgive me, I have no right . . . but I love Anna as a sister, and esteem her; I beg, I beseech you to tell me what is wrong between you? what fault do you find with her?"

Alexey Alexandrovitch frowned, and almost closing his eyes, dropped his head.

"I presume that your husband has told you the grounds on which I consider it necessary to change my attitude to Anna Arkadyevna?" he said, not looking her in the face, but eyeing with displeasure Shtcherbatsky, who was walking across the drawing-room.

"I don't believe it, I don't believe it, I can't believe it!" Dolly said, clasping her bony hands before her with a vigorous gesture. She rose quickly, and laid her hand on Alexey Alexandrovitch's sleeve. "We shall be disturbed here. Come this way, please."

Dolly's agitation had an effect on Alexey Alexandrovitch. He got up and submissively followed her to the schoolroom. They sat down to a table covered with an oilcloth cut in slits by penknives.

"I don't, I don't believe it!" Dolly said, trying to catch his glance that avoided her.

"One cannot disbelieve facts, Darya Alexandrovna," said he, with an emphasis on the word "facts."

"But what has she done?" said Darya Alexandrovna. "What precisely has she done?"

"She has forsaken her duty, and deceived her husband. That's what she has done," said he.

"No, no, it can't be! No, for God's sake, you are mistaken," said Dolly, putting her hands to her temples and closing her eyes.

Alexey Alexandrovitch smiled coldly, with his lips alone, meaning to signify to her and himself the firmness of his conviction; but this warm defense, though it could not shake him, reopened his wound. He began to speak with greater heat.

"It is extremely difficult to be mistaken when a wife herself informs her husband of the fact—informs him that eight years of her life, and a son, all that's a mistake, and that she wants to begin life again," he said angrily, with a snort.

"Anna and sin—I cannot connect them, I cannot believe it!"

"Darya Alexandrovna," he said, now looking straight into Dolly's kindly, troubled face, and feeling that his tongue was being loosened in spite of himself, "I would give a great deal for doubt to be still possible. When I doubted, I was miserable, but it was better than now. When I doubted, I had hope; but now there is no hope, and still I doubt of everything. I am in such doubt of everything that I even hate my son, and sometimes do not believe he is my son. I am very unhappy."

He had no need to say that. Darya Alexandrovna had seen that as soon as he glanced into her face; and she felt sorry for him, and her faith in the innocence of her friend began to totter.

"Oh, this is awful, awful! But can it be true that you are resolved on a divorce?"

"I am resolved on extreme measures. There is nothing else for me to do."

"Nothing else to do, nothing else to do . . ." she replied, with tears in her eyes. "Oh no, don't say nothing else to do!" she said.

"What is horrible in a trouble of this kind is that one cannot, as in any other—in loss, in death—bear one's trouble in peace, but that one must act," said he, as though guessing her thought. "One must get out of the humiliating position in which one is placed; one can't live *à trois.*"

"I understand, I quite understand that," said Dolly, and her head sank. She was silent for a little, thinking of herself, of her own grief in her family, and all at once, with an impulsive movement, she raised her head and clasped her hands with an imploring gesture. "But wait a little! You are a Christian. Think of her! What will become of her, if you cast her off?"

"I have thought, Darya Alexandrovna, I have thought a great deal," said Alexey Alexandrovitch. His face turned red in patches, and his dim eyes looked straight before him. Darya Alexandrovna at that moment pitied him with all her heart. "That was what I did indeed when she herself made known to me my humiliation; I left everything as of old. I gave her a chance to reform, I tried to save her. And with what result? She would not regard the slightest request—that she should observe decorum," he said, getting heated. "One may save any one who does not want to be ruined; but if the whole nature is so corrupt, so depraved, that ruin itself seems to her salvation, what's to be done?"

"Anything, only not divorce!" answered Darya Alexandrovna.

"But what is anything?"

"No, it is awful! She will be no one's wife; she will be lost!"

"What can I do?" said Alexey Alexandrovitch, raising his shoulders and his eyebrows. The recollection of his wife's last act had so incensed him that he had become frigid, as at the beginning of the conversation. "I am very grateful for your sympathy, but I must be going," he said, getting up.

"No, wait a minute. You must not ruin her. Wait a little; I will tell you about myself. I was married, and my husband deceived me; in anger and jealousy, I would have thrown up everything, I would myself . . . But I came to myself again; and who did it? Anna saved me. And here I am living on. The children are growing up, my husband has come back to his family, and feels his fault, is growing purer, better, and I live on. . . . I have forgiven it, and you ought to forgive!"

Alexey Alexandrovitch heard her, but her words had no effect on him now. All the hatred of that day when he had resolved on a divorce had sprung up again in his soul. He shook himself, and said in a shrill, loud voice:

"Forgive I cannot, and do not wish to, and I regard it as wrong. I have done everything for this woman, and she has trodden it all in the mud to which she is akin. I am not a spiteful man, I have never hated any one, but I hate her with my whole soul, and I cannot even forgive her, because I hate her too much for all the wrong she has done me!" he said, with tones of hatred in his voice.

"Love those that hate you. . . ." Darya Alexandrovna whispered timorously.

Alexey Alexandrovitch smiled contemptuously. That he knew long ago, but it could not be applied to his case.

"Love those that hate you, but to love those one hates is impossible. Forgive me for having troubled you. Every one has enough to bear in his own grief!" And regaining his self-possession, Alexey Alexandrovitch quietly took leave and went away.

CHAPTER XIII

WHEN they rose from table, Levin would have liked to follow Kitty into the drawing-room; but he was afraid she might dislike this, as too obviously paying her attention. He remained in the little ring of men, taking part in the general conversation, and without looking at Kitty, he was aware of her movements, her looks, and the place where she was in the drawing-room.

He did at once, and without the smallest effort, keep the promise he had made her—always to think well of all men, and to like every one always. The conversation fell on the village commune, in which Pestsov saw a sort of special principle, called by him the choral principle. Levin did not agree with Pestsov, nor with his brother, who had a special attitude of his own, both admitting and not admitting the significance of the Russian commune. But he talked to them, simply trying to reconcile and soften their differences. He was not in the least interested in what he said himself, and even less so in what they said; all he wanted was that they and every one should be happy and contented. He knew now the one thing of importance; and that one thing was at first there, in the drawing-room, and then began moving across and came to a standstill at the door. Without turning round he felt the eyes fixed on him, and the smile, and he could not help turning round. She was standing in the doorway with Shtcherbatsky, looking at him.

"I thought you were going towards the piano," said he, going up to her. "That's something I miss in the country—music."

"No; we only came to fetch you and thank you," she said, rewarding him with a smile that was like a gift, "for coming. What do they want to argue for? No one ever convinces any one, you know."

"Yes; that's true," said Levin; "it generally happens that one argues warmly simply because one can't make out what one's opponent wants to prove."

Levin had often noticed in discussions between the most intelligent people that after enormous efforts, and an enormous expenditure of logical subtleties and words, the disputants finally arrived at being aware that what they had so long been struggling to prove to one another had long ago, from the beginning of the argument, been known to both, but that they liked different things, and would not define what they liked for fear of its being attacked. He had often had the experience of suddenly in a discussion grasping what it was his opponent liked and at once liking it too, and immediately he found himself agreeing, and then all arguments fell away as useless. Sometimes, too, he had experienced the opposite, expressing at last what he liked himself, which he was devising arguments to defend, and, chancing to express it well and genuinely, he had found his opponent at once agreeing and ceasing to dispute his position. He tried to say this.

She knitted her brow, trying to understand. But directly he began to illustrate his meaning, she understood at once.

"I know: one must find out what he is arguing for, what is precious to him, then one can . . ."

She had completely guessed and expressed his badly expressed idea. Levin smiled joyfully; he was struck by this transition from the confused, verbose discussion with Pestsov and his brother to this laconic, clear, almost wordless communication of the most complex ideas.

Shtcherbatsky moved away from them, and Kitty, going up to a card-table, sat down, and, taking up the chalk, began drawing diverging circles over the new green cloth.

They began again on the subject that had been started at dinner—the liberty and occupations of women. Levin was of the opinion of Darya Alexandrovna that a girl who did not marry should find a woman's duties in a family. He supported this view by the fact that no family can get on without women to help; that in every family, poor or rich, there are and must be nurses, either relations or hired.

"No," said Kitty, blushing, but looking at him all the more boldly with her truthful eyes; "a girl may be so circumstanced that she cannot live in the family without humiliation, while she herself . . ."

At the hint he understood her.

"Oh, yes," he said. "Yes, yes, yes—you're right; you're right!"

And he saw all that Pestsov had been maintaining at dinner of the liberty of woman, simply from getting a glimpse of the terror of an old maid's existence and its humiliation in Kitty's heart; and loving her, he felt that terror and humiliation, and at once gave up his arguments.

A silence followed. She was still drawing with the chalk on the table. Her eyes were shining with a soft light. Under the influence of her mood he felt in all his being a continually growing tension of happiness.

"Ah! I've scribbled all over the table!" she said, and laying down the chalk, she made a movement as though to get up.

"What! shall I be left alone—without her?" he thought with horror, and he took the chalk. "Wait a minute," he said, sitting down to the table. "I've long wanted to ask you one thing."

He looked straight into her caressing, though frightened eyes.

"Please, ask it."

"Here," he said; and he wrote the initial letters, *w, y, t, m, i, c, n, b, d, t, m, n, o, t.* These letters meant, "When you told me it could never be, did that mean never, or then?" There seemed no likelihood that she could make out this complicated sentence; but he looked at her as though his life depended on her understanding the words. She glanced at him seriously, then leaned her puckered brow on her hands and began to read. Once or twice she stole a look at him, as though asking him, "Is it what I think?"

"I understand," she said, flushing a little.

"What is this word?" he said, pointing to the *n* that stood for *never.*

"It means *never*," she said; "but that's not true!"

He quickly rubbed out what he had written, gave her the chalk, and stood up. She wrote, *t, i, c, n, a, d.*

Dolly was completely comforted in the depression caused by her conversation with Alexey Alexandrovitch when she caught sight of the two figures: Kitty with the chalk in her hand, with a shy and happy smile looking upwards at Levin, and his handsome figure bending over the table with glowing eyes fastened one minute on the table and the next on her. He was suddenly radiant: he had understood. It meant, "Then I could not answer differently."

He glanced at her questioningly, timidly.

"Only then?"

"Yes," her smile answered.

"And n . . . and now?" he asked.

"Well, read this. I'll tell you what I should like—should like so much!" She wrote the initial letters, *i, y, c, f, a, f, w, h.* This meant, "If you could forget and forgive what happened."

He snatched the chalk with nervous, trembling fingers, and breaking it, wrote the initial letters of the following phrase, "I have nothing to forget and to forgive; I have never ceased to love you."

She glanced at him with a smile that did not waver.

"I understand," she said in a whisper.

He sat down and wrote a long phrase. She understood it all, and without asking him, "Is it this?" took the chalk and at once answered.

For a long while he could not understand what she had written, and often looked into her eyes. He was stupefied with happiness. He could not supply the word she had meant; but in her charming eyes, beaming with happiness, he saw all he needed to know. And he wrote three letters. But he had hardly finished writing when she read them over her arm, and herself finished and wrote the answer, "Yes."

"You're playing secretaire?" said the old prince. "But we must really be getting along if you want to be in time at the theater."

Levin got up and escorted Kitty to the door.

In their conversation everything had been said; it had been said that she loved him, and that she would tell her father and mother that he would come to-morrow morning.

CHAPTER XIV

WHEN Kitty had gone and Levin was left alone, he felt such uneasiness without her and such an impatient longing to get as quickly, as quickly as possible, to to-morrow morning, when he would see her again and be plighted to her forever, that he felt afraid, as though of death, of those fourteen hours that he had to get through without her. It was essential for him to be with some one to talk to, so as not to be left alone, to kill time. Stepan Arkadyevitch would have been the companion most congenial to him, but he was going out, he said, to a soirée, in reality to the ballet. Levin only had time to tell him he was happy, and that he loved him, and would never, never forget what he had done for him. The eyes and the smile of Stepan Arkadyevitch showed Levin that he comprehended that feeling fittingly.

"Oh, so it's not time to die yet?" said Stepan Arkadyevitch, pressing Levin's hand with emotion.

"N-n-no!" said Levin.

Darya Alexandrovna too, as she said good-bye to him, gave him a sort of congratulation, saying, "How glad I am you have met Kitty again! One must value old friends." Levin did not like these words of Darya Alexandrovna's. She could not understand how lofty and beyond her it all was, and she ought not to have dared to allude to it. Levin said good-bye to them, but, not to be left alone, he attached himself to his brother.

"Where are you going?"

"I'm going to a meeting."

"Well, I'll come with you. Can I?"

"What for? Yes, come along," said Sergey Ivanovitch, smiling. "What is the matter with you to-day?"

"With me? Happiness is the matter with me!" said Levin, letting down the window of the carriage they were driving in. "You don't mind?—it's so stifling. It's happiness is the matter with me! Why is it you have never married?"

Sergey Ivanovitch smiled.

"I am very glad, she seems a nice gi . . ." Sergey Ivanovitch was beginning.

"Don't say it! don't say it!" shouted Levin, clutching at the collar of his fur coat with both hands, and muffling him up in it. "She's a nice girl" were such simple, humble words, so out of harmony with his feeling.

Sergey Ivanovitch laughed outright a merry laugh, which was rare with him.

"Well, anyway, I may say that I'm very glad of it."

"That you may do to-morrow, to-morrow and nothing more! Nothing, nothing, silence," said Levin, and muffling him once more in his fur coat, he added: "I do like you so! Well, is it possible for me to be present at the meeting?"

"Of course it is."

"What is your discussion about to-day?" asked Levin, never ceasing smiling.

They arrived at the meeting. Levin heard the secretary hesitatingly read the minutes which he obviously did not himself understand; but Levin saw from this secretary's face what a good, nice, kind-hearted person he was. This was evident from his confusion and embarrassment in reading the minutes. Then the discussion began. They were disputing about the misappropriation of certain sums and the laying of certain pipes, and Sergey Ivanovitch was very cutting to two members, and said something at great length with an air of triumph; and another member, scribbling something on a bit of paper, began timidly at first, but afterwards answered him very viciously and delightfully. And then Sviazhsky (he was there too) said something too, very handsomely and nobly. Levin listened to them, and saw clearly that these missing sums and these pipes were not anything real, and that they were not at all angry, but were all the nicest, kindest people, and everything was as happy and charming as possible among them. They did no harm to any one, and were all enjoying it. What struck Levin was that he could see through them all to-day, and from little, almost imperceptible signs knew the soul of each, and saw distinctly that they were all good at heart. And Levin himself in particular they were all extremely fond of that day. That was evident from the way they spoke to him, from the friendly, affectionate way even those he did not know looked at him.

"Well, did you like it?" Sergey Ivanovitch asked him.

"Very much. I never supposed it was so interesting! Capital! Splendid!"

Sviazhsky went up to Levin and invited him to come round to tea with him. Levin was utterly at a loss to comprehend or recall what it was he had disliked in Sviazhsky, what he had failed to find in him. He was a clever and wonderfully good-hearted man.

"Most delighted," he said, and asked after his wife and sister-in-law. And from a queer association of ideas, because in his imagination the idea of Sviazhsky's sister-in-law was connected with marriage, it occurred to him that there was no one to whom he could more suitably speak of his happiness, and he was very glad to go and see them.

Sviazhsky questioned him about his improvements on his estate, presupposing, as he always did, that there was no possibility of doing anything not done already in Europe, and now this did not in the least annoy Levin. On the contrary, he felt that Sviazhsky was right, that the whole business was of little value, and he saw the wonderful softness and consideration with which Sviazhsky avoided fully expressing his correct view. The ladies of the Sviazhsky household were particularly delightful. It seemed to Levin that they knew all about it already and sympathized with him, saying nothing merely from delicacy. He stayed with them one hour, two, three, talking of all sorts of subjects but the one thing that filled his heart, and did not observe that he was boring them dreadfully, and that it was long past their bedtime.

Sviazhsky went with him into the hall, yawning and wondering at the strange humor his friend was in. It was past one o'clock. Levin went back to his hotel, and was dismayed at the thought that all alone now with his impatience he had ten hours still left to get through. The servant, whose turn it was to be up all night, lighted his candles, and would have gone away, but Levin stopped him. This servant, Yegor, whom Levin had noticed before, struck him as a very intelligent, excellent, and, above all, good-hearted man.

"Well, Yegor, it's hard work not sleeping, isn't it?"

"One's got to put up with it! It's part of our work, you see. In a gentleman's house it's easier; but then here one makes more."

It appeared that Yegor had a family, three boys and a daughter, a sempstress, whom he wanted to marry to a cashier in a saddler's shop.

Levin, on hearing this, informed Yegor that, in his opinion, in marriage the great thing was love, and that with love one would always be happy, for happiness rests only on oneself.

Yegor listened attentively, and obviously quite took in Levin's idea, but by way of assent to it he enunciated, greatly to Levin's surprise, the observation that when he had lived with good masters he had always been satisfied with his masters, and now was perfectly satisfied with his employer, though he was a Frenchman.

"Wonderfully good-hearted fellow!" thought Levin.

"Well, but you yourself, Yegor, when you got married, did you love your wife?"

"Ay! and why not?" responded Yegor.

And Levin saw that Yegor too was in an excited state and intending to express all his most heartfelt emotions.

"My life, too, has been a wonderful one. From a child up . . ." he was beginning with flashing eyes, apparently catching Levin's enthusiasm, just as people catch yawning.

But at that moment a ring was heard. Yegor departed, and Levin was left alone. He had eaten scarcely anything at dinner, had refused tea and supper at Sviazhsky's, but he was incapable of thinking of supper. He had not slept the previous night, but was incapable of thinking of sleep either. His room was cold, but he was oppressed by heat. He opened both the movable panes in his window and sat down to the table opposite the open panes. Over the snow-covered roofs could be seen a decorated cross with chains, and above it the rising triangle of Charles's Wain with the yellowish light of Capella. He gazed at the cross, then at the stars, drank in the fresh freezing air that flowed evenly into the room, and followed as though in a dream the images and memories that rose in his imagination. At four o'clock he heard steps in the passage and peeped out at the door. It was the gambler Myaskin, whom he knew, coming from the club. He walked gloomily, frowning and coughing. "Poor, unlucky fellow!" thought Levin, and tears came into his eyes from love and pity for this man. He would have talked with him, and tried to comfort him, but remembering that he had nothing but his shirt on, he changed his mind and sat down again at the open pane to bathe in the cold air and gaze at the exquisite lines of the cross, silent, but full of meaning for him, and the mounting lurid yellow star. At seven o'clock there was a noise of people polishing the floors, and bells ringing in some servants' department, and Levin felt that he was beginning to get frozen. He closed the pane, washed, dressed, and went out into the street.

CHAPTER XV

THE streets were still empty. Levin went to the house of the Shtcherbatskys. The visitors' doors were closed and everything was asleep. He walked back, went into his room again, and asked for coffee. The day servant, not Yegor this time, brought it to him. Levin would have entered into conversation with him, but a bell rang for the servant, and he went out. Levin tried to drink coffee and put some roll in his mouth, but his mouth was quite at a loss what to do with the roll. Levin, rejecting the roll, put on his coat and went out again for a walk. It was nine o'clock when he reached the Shtcherbatskys' steps the second time. In the house they were only just up, and the cook came out to go marketing. He had to get through at least two hours more.

All that night and morning Levin lived perfectly unconsciously, and felt perfectly lifted out of the conditions of material life. He had eaten nothing for a whole day, he had not slept for two nights, had spent several hours undressed in the frozen air, and felt not simply fresher and stronger than ever, but felt utterly independent of his body; he moved without muscular effort, and felt as if he could do anything. He was convinced he could fly upwards or lift the corner of the house, if need be. He spent the remainder of the time in the street, incessantly looking at his watch and gazing about him.

And what he saw then, he never saw again after. The children, especially, going to school, the bluish doves flying down from the roofs to the pavement, and the little loaves covered with flour, thrust out by an unseen hand, touched him. Those loaves, those doves, and those two boys were not earthly creatures. It all happened at the same time: a boy ran towards a dove and glanced smiling at Levin; the dove, with a whir of her wings, darted away, flashing in the sun, amid grains of snow that quivered in the air, while from a little window there came a smell of fresh-baked bread, and the loaves were put out. All of this together was so extraordinarily nice that Levin laughed and cried with delight. Going a long way round by Gazetny Place and Kislovka, he went back again to the hotel, and putting his watch before him, he sat down to wait for twelve o'clock. In the next room they were talking about some sort of machines, and swindling, and coughing their morning coughs. They did not realize that the hand was near twelve. The hand reached it. Levin went out onto the steps. The sledge-drivers clearly knew all about it. They crowded round Levin with happy faces, quarreling among themselves, and offering their services. Trying not to offend the other sledge-drivers, and promising to drive with them too, Levin took one and told him to drive to the Shtcherbatskys'. The sledge-driver was splendid in a white shirt-collar sticking out over his overcoat and into his strong, full-blooded red neck. The sledge was high and comfortable, and altogether such a one as Levin never drove in after, and the horse was a good one, and tried to gallop but didn't seem to move. The driver knew the Shtcherbatskys' house, and drew up at the entrance with a curve of his arm and a "Wo!" especially indicative of respect for his fare. The Shtcherbatskys' hall-porter certainly knew all about it. This was evident from the smile in his eyes and the way he said:

"Well, it's a long while since you've been to see us, Konstantin Dmitrievitch!"

Not only he knew all about it, but he was unmistakably delighted and making efforts to conceal his joy. Looking into his kindly old eyes, Levin realized even something new in his happiness.

"Are they up?"

"Pray walk in! Leave it here," said he, smiling, as Levin would have come back to take his hat. That meant something.

"To whom shall I announce your honor?" asked the footman.

The footman, though a young man, and one of the new school of footmen, a dandy, was a very kind-hearted, good fellow, and he too knew all about it.

"The princess . . . the prince . . . the young princess . . ." said Levin.

The first person he saw was Mademoiselle Linon. She walked across the room, and her ringlets and her face were beaming. He had only just spoken to her, when suddenly he heard the rustle of a skirt at the door, and Mademoiselle Linon vanished from Levin's eyes, and a joyful terror came over him at the nearness of his happiness. Mademoiselle Linon was in great haste, and leaving him, went out at the other door. Directly she had gone out, swift, swift light steps sounded on the parquet, and his bliss, his life, himself—what was best in himself, what he had so long sought and longed for—was quickly, so quickly approaching him. She did not walk, but seemed, by some unseen force, to float to him. He saw nothing but her clear, truthful eyes, frightened by the same bliss of love that flooded his heart. Those eyes were shining nearer and nearer, blinding him with their light of love. She stopped still close to him, touching him. Her hands rose and dropped onto his shoulders.

She had done all she could—she had run up to him and given herself up entirely, shy and happy. He put his arms round her and pressed his lips to her mouth that sought his kiss.

She too had not slept all night, and had been expecting him all the morning.

Her mother and father had consented without demur, and were happy in her happiness. She had been waiting for him. She wanted to be the first to tell him her happiness and his. She had got ready to see him alone, and had been delighted at the idea, and had been shy and ashamed, and did not know herself what she was doing. She had heard his steps and voice, and had waited at the door for Mademoiselle Linon to go. Mademoiselle Linon had gone away. Without thinking, without asking herself how and what, she had gone up to him, and did as she was doing.

"Let us go to mamma!" she said, taking him by the hand. For a long while he could say nothing, not so much because he was afraid of desecrating the loftiness of his emotion by a word, as that every time he tried to say something, instead of words he felt that tears of happiness were welling up. He took her hand and kissed it.

"Can it be true?" he said at last in a choked voice. "I can't believe you love me, dear!"

She smiled at that "dear," and at the timidity with which he glanced at her.

"Yes!" she said significantly, deliberately. "I am so happy!"

Not letting go his hands, she went into the drawing-room. The princess, seeing them, breathed quickly, and immediately began to cry and then immediately began to laugh and with a vigorous step Levin had not expected, ran up to him, and hugging his head, kissed him, wetting his cheeks with her tears.

"So it is all settled! I am glad. Love her. I am glad. . . . Kitty!"

"You've not been long settling things," said the old prince, trying to seem unmoved; but Levin noticed that his eyes were wet when he turned to him.

"I've long, always wished for this!" said the prince, taking Levin by the arm and drawing him towards himself. "Even when this little feather-head fancied . . ."

"Papa!" shrieked Kitty, and shut his mouth with her hands.

"Well, I won't!" he said. "I'm very, very . . . plea . . . Oh, what a fool I am . . ."

He embraced Kitty, kissed her face, her hand, her face again and made the sign of the cross over her.

And there came over Levin a new feeling of love for this man, till then so little known to him, when he saw how slowly and tenderly Kitty kissed his muscular hand.

<h2 style="text-align:center">CHAPTER XVI</h2>

THE princess sat in her armchair, silent and smiling; the prince sat down beside her. Kitty stood by her father's chair, still holding his hand. All were silent.

The princess was the first to put everything into words, and to translate all thoughts and feelings into practical questions. And all equally felt this strange and painful for the first minute.

"When is it to be? We must have the benediction and announcement. And when's the wedding to be? What do you think, Alexander?"

"Here he is," said the old prince, pointing to Levin—"he's the principal person in the matter."

"When?" said Levin blushing. "To-morrow. If you ask me, I should say, the benediction to-day and the wedding to-morrow."

"Come, *mon cher,* that's nonsense!"

"Well, in a week."

"He's quite mad."

"No, why so?"

"Well, upon my word!" said the mother, smiling, delighted at this haste. "How about the trousseau?"

"Will there really be a trousseau and all that?" Levin thought with horror. "But can the trousseau and the benediction and all that—can it spoil my happiness? Nothing can spoil it!" He glanced at Kitty, and noticed that she was not in the least, not in the very least, disturbed by the idea of the trousseau. "Then it must be all right," he thought.

"Oh, I know nothing about it; I only said what I should like," he said apologetically.

"We'll talk it over, then. The benediction and announcement can take place now. That's very well."

The princess went up to her husband, kissed him, and would have gone away, but he kept her, embraced her, and tenderly as a young lover, kissed her several times, smiling. The old people were obviously muddled for a moment, and did not quite know whether it was they who were in love again or their daughter. When the prince and the princess had gone, Levin went up to his betrothed and took her hand. He was self-possessed now and could speak, and he had a great deal he wanted to tell her. But he said not at all what he had to say.

"How I knew it would be so! I never hoped for it; and yet in my heart I was always sure," he said. "I believe that it was ordained."

"And I!" she said. "Even when . . ." She stopped and went on again, looking at him resolutely with her truthful eyes, "Even when I thrust from me my happiness. I always loved you alone, but I was carried away. I ought to tell you . . . Can you forgive that?"

"Perhaps it was for the best. You will have to forgive me so much. I ought to tell you . . ."

This was one of the things he had meant to speak about. He had resolved from the first to tell her two things—that he was not chaste as she was, and that he was not a believer. It was agonizing, but he considered he ought to tell her both these facts.

"No, not now, later!" he said.

"Very well, later, but you must certainly tell me. I'm not afraid of anything. I want to know everything. Now it is settled."

He added: "Settled that you'll take me whatever I may be— you won't give me up? Yes?"

"Yes, yes."

Their conversation was interrupted by Mademoiselle Linon, who with an affected but tender smile came to congratulate her favorite pupil. Before she had gone, the servants came in with their congratulations. Then relations arrived, and there began that state of blissful absurdity from which Levin did not emerge till the day after his wedding. Levin was in a continual state of awkwardness and discomfort, but the intensity of his happiness went on all the while increasing. He felt continually that a great deal was being expected of him—what, he did not know; and he did everything he was told, and it all gave him happiness. He had thought his engagement would have nothing about it like others, that the ordinary conditions of engaged couples would spoil his special happiness; but it ended in his doing exactly as other people did, and his happiness being only increased thereby and becoming more and more special, more and more unlike anything that had ever happened.

"Now we shall have sweetmeats to eat," said Mademoiselle Linon—and Levin drove off to buy sweetmeats.

"Well, I'm very glad," said Sviazhsky. "I advise you to get the bouquets from Fomin's."

"Oh, are they wanted?" And he drove to Fomin's.

His brother offered to lend him money, as he would have so many expenses, presents to give. . . .

"Oh, are presents wanted?" And he galloped to Foulde's.

And at the confectioner's, and at Fomin's, and at Foulde's he saw that he was expected; that they were pleased to see him, and prided themselves on his happiness, just as every one whom he had to do with during those days. What was extraordinary was that every one not only liked him, but even people previously unsympathetic, cold, and callous, were enthusiastic over him, gave way to him in everything, treated his feeling with tenderness and delicacy, and shared his conviction that he was the happiest man in the world because his betrothed was beyond perfection. Kitty too felt the same thing. When Countess Nordston ventured to hint that she had hoped for something better, Kitty was so angry and proved so conclusively that nothing in the world could be better than Levin, that Countess Nordston had to admit it, and in Kitty's presence never met Levin without a smile of ecstatic admiration.

The confession he had promised was the one painful incident of this time. He consulted the old prince, and with his sanction gave Kitty his diary, in which there was written the confession that tortured him. He had written this diary at the time with a view to his future wife. Two things caused him anguish: his lack of purity and his lack of faith. His confession of unbelief passed unnoticed. She was religious, had never doubted the truths of religion, but his external unbelief did not affect her in the least. Through love she knew all his soul, and in his soul she saw what she wanted, and that such a state of soul should be called unbelieving was to her a matter of no account. The other confession set her weeping bitterly.

Levin, not without an inner struggle, handed her his diary. He knew that between him and her there could not be, and should not be, secrets, and so he had decided that so it must be. But he had not realized what an effect it would have on her, he had not put himself in her place. It was only when the same evening he came to their house before the theater, went into her room and saw her tear-stained, pitiful, sweet face, miserable with suffering he had caused and nothing could undo, he felt the abyss that separated his shameful past from her dovelike purity, and was appalled at what he had done.

"Take them, take these dreadful books!" she said, pushing away the note-books lying before her on the table. "Why did you give them me? No, it was better anyway," she added, touched by his despairing face. "But it's awful, awful!"

His head sank, and he was silent. He could say nothing.

"You can't forgive me," he whispered.

"Yes, I forgive you; but it's terrible!"

But his happiness was so immense that this confession did not shatter it, it only added another shade to it. She forgave him; but from that time more than ever he considered himself unworthy of her, morally bowed down lower than ever before her, and prized more highly than ever his undeserved happiness.

CHAPTER XVII

UNCONSCIOUSLY going over in his memory the conversations that had taken place during and after dinner, Alexey Alexandrovitch returned to his solitary room. Darya Alexandrovna's words about forgiveness had aroused in him nothing but annoyance. The applicability or non-applicability of the Christian precept to his own case was too difficult a question to be discussed lightly, and this question had long ago been answered by Alexey Alexandrovitch in the negative. Of all that had been said, what stuck most in his memory was the phrase of stupid, good-natured Turovtsin—*"Acted like a man, he did! Called him out and shot him!"* Every one had apparently shared this feeling, though from politeness they had not expressed it.

"But the matter is settled, it's useless thinking about it," Alexey Alexandrovitch told himself. And thinking of nothing but the journey before him, and the revision work he had to do, he went into his room and asked the porter who escorted him where his man was. The porter said that the man had only just gone out. Alexey Alexandrovitch ordered tea to be sent him, sat down to the table, and taking the guide-book, began considering the route of his journey.

"Two telegrams," said his manservant, coming into the room. "I beg your pardon, your excellency; I'd only just that minute gone out."

Alexey Alexandrovitch took the telegrams and opened them. The first telegram was the announcement of Stremov's appointment to the very post Karenin had coveted. Alexey Alexandrovitch flung the telegram down, and flushing a little, got up and began to pace up and down the room. *"Quos vult perdere dementat,"* he said, meaning by *quos* the persons responsible for this appointment. He was not so much annoyed that he had not received the post, that he had been conspicuously passed over; but it was incomprehensible, amazing to him that they did not see that the wordy phrase-monger Stremov was the last man fit for it. How could they fail to see how they were ruining themselves, lowering their *prestige* by this appointment?

"Something else in the same line," he said to himself bitterly, opening the second telegram. The telegram was from his wife. Her name, written in blue pencil, *"Anna,"* was the first thing that caught his eye. "I am dying; I beg, I implore you to come. I shall die easier with your forgiveness," he read. He smiled contemptuously, and flung down the telegram. That this was a trick and a fraud, of that, he thought for the first minute, there could be no doubt.

"There is no deceit she would stick at. She was near her confinement. Perhaps it is the confinement. But what can be their aim? To legitimize the child, to compromise me, and prevent a divorce," he thought. "But something was said in it: I am dying . . ." He read the telegram again, and suddenly the plain meaning of what was said in it struck him.

"And if it is true?" he said to himself. "If it is true that in the moment of agony and nearness to death she is genuinely penitent, and I, taking it for a trick, refuse to go? That would not only be cruel, and every one would blame me, but it would be stupid on my part."

"Piotr, call a coach; I am going to Petersburg," he said to his servant.

Alexey Alexandrovitch decided that he would go to Petersburg and see his wife. If her illness was a trick, he would say nothing and go away again. If she was really in danger, and wished to see him before her death, he would forgive her if he found her alive, and pay her the last duties if he came too late.

All the way he thought no more of what he ought to do.

With a sense of weariness and uncleanness from the night spent in the train, in the early fog of Petersburg Alexey Alexandrovitch drove through the deserted Nevsky and stared straight before him, not thinking of what was awaiting him. He could not think about it, because in picturing what would happen, he could not drive away the reflection that her death would at once remove all the difficulty of his position. Bakers, closed shops, night-cabmen, porters sweeping the pavements flashed past his eyes, and he watched it all, trying to smother the thought of what was awaiting him, and what he dared not hope for, and yet was hoping for. He drove up to the steps. A sledge and a carriage with the coachman asleep stood at the entrance. As he went into the entry, Alexey Alexandrovitch, as it were, got out his resolution from the remotest corner of his brain, and mastered it thoroughly. Its meaning ran: "If it's a trick, then calm contempt and departure. If truth, do what is proper."

The porter opened the door before Alexey Alexandrovitch rang. The porter, Kapitonitch, looked queer in an old coat, without a tie, and in slippers.

"How is your mistress?"

"A successful confinement yesterday."

Alexey Alexandrovitch stopped short and turned white. He felt distinctly now how intensely he had longed for her death.

"And how is she?"

Korney in his morning apron ran down-stairs.

"Very ill," he answered. "There was a consultation yesterday, and the doctor's here now."

"Take my things," said Alexey Alexandrovitch, and feeling

some relief at the news that there was still hope of her death, he went into the hall.

On the hat-stand there was a military overcoat. Alexey Alexandrovitch noticed it and asked:

"Who is here?"

"The doctor, the midwife and Count Vronsky."

Alexey Alexandrovitch went into the inner rooms.

In the drawing-room there was no one; at the sound of his steps there came out of her boudoir the midwife in a cap with lilac ribbons.

She went up to Alexey Alexandrovitch, and with the familiarity given by the approach of death took him by the arm and drew him towards the bedroom.

"Thank God you've come! She keeps on about you and nothing but you," she said.

"Make haste with the ice!" the doctor's peremptory voice said from the bedroom.

Alexey Alexandrovitch went into her boudoir.

At the table, sitting side-ways in a low chair, was Vronsky, his face hidden in his hands, weeping. He jumped up at the doctor's voice, took his hands from his face, and saw Alexey Alexandrovitch. Seeing the husband, he was so overwhelmed that he sat down again, drawing his head down to his shoulders, as if he wanted to disappear; but he made an effort over himself, got up and said:

"She is dying. The doctors say there is no hope. I am entirely in your power, only let me be here . . . though I am at your disposal. I . . ."

Alexey Alexandrovitch, seeing Vronsky's tears, felt a rush of that nervous emotion always produced in him by the sight of other people's suffering, and turning away his face, he moved hurriedly to the door, without hearing the rest of his words. From the bedroom came the sound of Anna's voice saying something. Her voice was lively, eager, with exceedingly distinct intonations. Alexey Alexandrovitch went into the bedroom, and went up to the bed. She was lying turned with her face towards him. Her cheeks were flushed crimson, her eyes glittered, her little white hands thrust out from the sleeves of her dressing-gown were playing with the quilt, twisting it about. It seemed

as though she were not only well and blooming, but in the happiest frame of mind. She was talking rapidly, musically, and with exceptionally correct articulation and expressive intonation.

"For Alexey—I am speaking of Alexey Alexandrovitch (what a strange and awful thing that both are Alexey, isn't it?)—Alexey would not refuse me. I should forget, he would forgive. . . . But why doesn't he come? He's so good he doesn't know himself how good he is. Ah, my God, what agony! Give me some water, quick! Oh, that will be bad for her, my little girl! Oh, very well then, give her to a nurse. Yes, I agree, it's better in fact. He'll be coming; it will hurt him to see her. Give her to the nurse."

"Anna Arkadyevna, he has come. Here he is!" said the midwife, trying to attract her attention to Alexey Alexandrovitch.

"Oh, what nonsense!" Anna went on, not seeing her husband. "No, give her to me; give me my little one! He has not come yet. You say he won't forgive me, because you don't know him. No one knows him. I'm the only one, and it was hard for me even. His eyes I ought to know—Seryozha has just the same eyes—and I can't bear to see them because of it. Has Seryozha had his dinner? I know every one will forget him. He would not forget. Seryozha must be moved into the corner room, and Mariette must be asked to sleep with him."

All of a sudden she shrank back, was silent; and in terror, as though expecting a blow, as though to defend herself, she raised her hands to her face. She had seen her husband.

"No, no!" she began. "I am not afraid of him; I am afraid of death. Alexey, come here. I am in a hurry, because I've no time, I've not long left to live; the fever will begin directly and I shall understand nothing more. Now I understand, I understand it all, I see it all!"

Alexey Alexandrovitch's wrinkled face wore an expression of agony; he took her by the hand and tried to say something, but he could not utter it; his lower lip quivered, but he still went on struggling with his emotion, and only now and then glanced at her. And each time he glanced at her, he saw her eyes gazing at him with such passionate and triumphant tenderness as he had never seen in them.

"Wait a minute, you don't know . . . stay a little, stay!

493

. . ." She stopped, as though collecting her ideas. "Yes," she began; "yes, yes, yes. This is what I wanted to say. Don't be surprised at me. I'm still the same . . . But there is another woman in me, I'm afraid of her: she loved that man, and I tried to hate you, and could not forget about her that used to be. I'm not that woman. Now I'm my real self, all myself. I'm dying now, I know I shall die, ask him. Even now I feel—see here, the weights on my feet, on my hands, on my fingers. My fingers— see how huge they are! But this will soon all be over. . . . Only one thing I want: forgive me, forgive me quite. I'm terrible, but my nurse used to tell me; the holy martyr—what was her name? She was worse. And I'll go to Rome; there's a wilderness, and there I shall be no trouble to any one, only I'll take Seryozha and the little one. . . . No, you can't forgive me! I know, it can't be forgiven! No, no, go away, you're too good!" She held his hand in one burning hand, while she pushed him away with the other.

The nervous agitation of Alexey Alexandrovitch kept increasing, and had by now reached such a point that he ceased to struggle with it. He suddenly felt that what he had regarded as nervous agitation was on the contrary a blissful spiritual condition that gave him all at once a new happiness he had never known. He did not think that the Christian law that he had been all his life trying to follow, enjoined on him to forgive and love his enemies; but a glad feeling of love and forgiveness for his enemies filled his heart. He knelt down, and laying his head in the curve of her arm, which burned him as with fire through the sleeve, he sobbed like a little child. She put her arm around his head, moved towards him, and with defiant pride lifted up her eyes.

"That is he. I knew him! Now, forgive me, every one, forgive me! . . . They've come again; why don't they go away? . . . Oh, take these cloaks off me!"

The doctor unloosed her hands, carefully laying her on the pillow, and covered her up to the shoulders. She lay back submissively, and looked before her with beaming eyes.

"Remember one thing, that I needed nothing but forgiveness, and I want nothing more. . . . Why doesn't *he* come?" she said, turning to the door towards Vronsky. "Do come, do come! Give him your hand."

Vronsky came to the side of the bed, and seeing Anna, again hid his face in his hands.

"Uncover your face—look at him! He's a saint," she said. "Oh! uncover your face, do uncover it!" she said angrily. "Alexey Alexandrovitch, do uncover his face! I want to see him."

Alexey Alexandrovitch took Vronsky's hands and drew them away from his face, which was awful with the expression of agony and shame upon it.

"Give him your hand. Forgive him."

Alexey Alexandrovitch gave him his hand, not attempting to restrain the tears that streamed from his eyes.

"Thank God, thank God!" she said, "now everything is ready. Only to stretch my legs a little. There, that's capital. How badly these flowers are done—not a bit like a violet," she said, pointing to the hangings. "My God, my God! when will it end? Give me some morphine. Doctor, give me some morphine! Oh, my God, my God!"

And she tossed about on the bed.

The doctors said that it was puerperal fever, and that it was ninety-nine chances in a hundred it would end in death. The whole day long there was fever, delirium, and unconsciousness. At midnight the patient lay without consciousness, and almost without pulse.

The end was expected every minute.

Vronsky had gone home, but in the morning he came to inquire, and Alexey Alexandrovitch meeting him in the hall, said: "Better stay, she might ask for you," and himself led him to his wife's boudoir. Towards morning, there was a return again of excitement, rapid thought and talk, and again it ended in unconsciousness. On the third day it was the same thing, and the doctors said there was hope. That day Alexey Alexandrovitch went into the boudoir where Vronsky was sitting, and closing the door sat down opposite him.

"Alexey Alexandrovitch," said Vronsky, feeling that a statement of the position was coming, "I can't speak, I can't understand. Spare me! However hard it is for you, believe me, it is more terrible for me."

He would have risen; but Alexey Alexandrovitch took him by the hand and said:

"I beg you to hear me out; it is necessary. I must explain my feelings, the feelings that have guided me and will guide me, so that you may not be in error regarding me. You know I had resolved on a divorce, and had even begun to take proceedings. I won't conceal from you that in beginning this I was in uncertainty, I was in misery; I will confess that I was pursued by a desire to revenge myself on you and on her. When I got the telegram, I came here with the same feelings; I will say more, I longed for her death. But . . ." He paused, pondering whether to disclose or not to disclose his feeling to him. "But I saw her and forgave her. And the happiness of forgiveness has revealed to me my duty. I forgive completely. I would offer the other cheek, I would give my cloak if my coat be taken. I pray to God only not to take from me the bliss of forgiveness!"

Tears stood in his eyes, and the luminous, serene look in them impressed Vronsky.

"This is my position: you can trample me in the mud, make me the laughing-stock of the world, I will not abandon her, and I will never utter a word of reproach to you," Alexey Alexandrovitch went on. "My duty is clearly marked for me; I ought to be with her, and I will be. If she wishes to see you, I will let you know, but now I suppose it would be better for you to go away."

He got up, and sobs cut short his words. Vronsky too was getting up, and in a stooping, not yet erect posture, looked up at him from under his brows. He did not understand Alexey Alexandrovitch's feeling, but he felt that it was something higher and even unattainable for him with his view of life.

CHAPTER XVIII

AFTER the conversation with Alexey Alexandrovitch, Vronsky went out onto the steps of the Karenins' house and stood still, with difficulty remembering where he was, and where he ought to walk or drive. He felt disgraced, humiliated, guilty, and deprived of all possibility of washing away his humiliation. He felt thrust out of the beaten track along which he had so proudly and lightly walked till then. All the habits and rules of his life that had seemed so firm, had turned out suddenly false and inapplicable. The betrayed husband, who had figured till that time as a pitiful creature, an incidental and somewhat ludicrous obstacle to his happiness, had suddenly been summoned by her herself, elevated to an awe-inspiring pinnacle, and on the pinnacle that husband had shown himself, not malignant, not false, not ludicrous, but kind and straightforward and large. Vronsky could not but feel this, and the parts were suddenly reversed. Vronsky felt his elevation and his own abasement, his truth and his own falsehood. He felt that the husband was magnanimous even in his sorrow, while he had been base and petty in his deceit. But this sense of his own humiliation before the man he had unjustly despised made up only a small part of his misery. He felt unutterably wretched now, for his passion for Anna, which had seemed to him of late to be growing cooler, now that he knew he had lost her forever, was stronger than ever it had been. He had seen all of her in her illness, had come to know her very soul, and it seemed to him that he had never loved her till then. And now when he had learned to know her, to love her as she should be loved, he had been humiliated before her, and had lost her forever, leaving with her nothing of himself but a shameful memory. Most terrible of all had been his ludicrous, shameful position when Alexey Alexandrovitch had pulled his hands away from his humiliated face. He stood on the steps of the Karenins' house like one distraught, and did not know what to do.

"A sledge, sir?" asked the porter.

"Yes, a sledge."

On getting home, after three sleepless nights, Vronsky, without undressing, lay down flat on the sofa, clasping his hands and laying his head on them. His head was heavy. Images, memories, and ideas of the strangest description followed one another with extraordinary rapidity and vividness. First it was the medicine he had poured out for the patient and spilt over the spoon, then the midwife's white hands, then the queer posture of Alexey Alexandrovitch on the floor beside the bed.

"To sleep! To forget!" he said to himself with the serene confidence of a healthy man that if he is tired and sleepy, he will go to sleep at once. And the same instant his head did begin to feel drowsy and he began to drop off into forgetfulness. The waves of the sea of unconsciousness had begun to meet over his head, when all at once—it was as though a violent shock of electricity had passed over him. He started so that he leaped up on the springs of the sofa, and leaning on his arms got in a panic onto his knees. His eyes were wide open as though he had never been asleep. The heaviness in his head and the weariness in his limbs that he had felt a minute before had suddenly gone.

"You may trample me in the mud," he heard Alexey Alexandrovitch's words and saw him standing before him, and saw Anna's face with its burning flush and glittering eyes, gazing with love and tenderness not at him but at Alexey Alexandrovitch; he saw his own, as he fancied, foolish and ludicrous figure when Alexey Alexandrovitch took his hands away from his face. He stretched out his legs again and flung himself on the sofa in the same position and shut his eyes.

"To sleep! To forget!" he repeated to himself. But with his eyes shut he saw more distinctly than ever Anna's face as it had been on the memorable evening before the races.

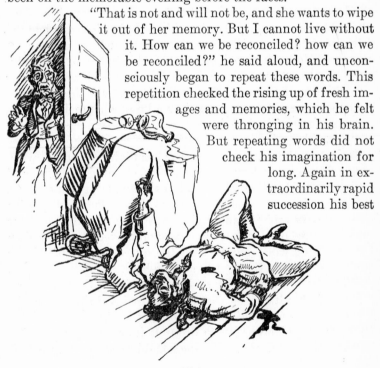

"That is not and will not be, and she wants to wipe it out of her memory. But I cannot live without it. How can we be reconciled? how can we be reconciled?" he said aloud, and unconsciously began to repeat these words. This repetition checked the rising up of fresh images and memories, which he felt were thronging in his brain. But repeating words did not check his imagination for long. Again in extraordinarily rapid succession his best moments rose before his mind, and then his recent humiliation. "Take away his hands," Anna's voice says. He takes away his hands and feels the shamestruck and idiotic expression of his face.

He still lay down, trying to sleep, though he felt there was not the smallest hope of it, and kept repeating stray words from some chain of thought, trying by this to check the rising flood of fresh images. He listened, and heard in a strange, mad whisper words repeated: "I did not appreciate it, did not make enough of it. I did not appreciate it, did not make enough of it."

"What's this? Am I going out of my mind?" he said to himself. "Perhaps. What makes men go out of their minds; what makes men shoot themselves?" he answered himself, and opening his eyes, he saw with wonder an embroidered cushion beside him, worked by Varya, his brother's wife. He touched the tassel of the cushion, and tried to think of Varya, of when he had seen her last. But to think of anything extraneous was an agonizing effort. "No, I must sleep!" He moved the cushion up, and pressed his head into it, but he had to make an effort to keep his eyes shut. He jumped up and sat down. "That's all over for me," he said to himself. "I must think what to do. What is left?" His mind rapidly ran through his life apart from his love of Anna.

"Ambition? Serpuhovskoy? Society? The court?" He could not come to a pause anywhere. All of it had had meaning before, but now there was no reality in it. He got up from the sofa, took off his coat, undid his belt, and uncovering his hairy chest to breathe more freely, walked up and down the room. "This is how people go mad," he repeated, "and how they shoot themselves . . . to escape humiliation," he added slowly.

He went to the door and closed it, then with fixed eyes and clenched teeth he went up to the table, took a revolver, looked round him, turned it to a loaded barrel, and sank into thought. For two minutes, his head bent forward with an expression of an intense effort of thought, he stood with the revolver in his hand, motionless, thinking.

"Of course," he said to himself, as though a logical, continuous, and clear chain of reasoning had brought him to an indubitable conclusion. In reality this "of course," that seemed convincing to him, was simply the result of exactly the same circle of memories and images through which he had passed ten times already during the last hour—memories of happiness lost forever. There was the same conception of the senselessness of everything to come in life, the same consciousness of humiliation. Even the sequence of these images and emotions was the same.

"Of course," he repeated, when for the third time his thought passed again round the same spellbound circle of memories and images, and pulling the revolver to the left side of his chest, and clutching it vigorously with his whole hand, as it were, squeezing it in his fist, he pulled the trigger. He did not hear the sound of the shot, but a violent blow on his chest sent him reeling. He tried to clutch at the edge of the table, dropped the revolver, staggered, and sat down on the ground, looking about him in astonishment. He did not recognize his room, looking up from the ground, at the bent legs of the table, at the wastepaper-basket, and the tiger-skin rug. The hurried, creaking steps of his servant coming through the drawing-room brought him to his senses. He made an effort at thought, and was aware that he was on the floor; and seeing blood on the tiger-skin rug and on his arm, he knew he had shot himself.

"Idiotic! Missed!" he said, fumbling after the revolver. The revolver was close beside him—he sought further off. Still feeling for it, he stretched out to the other side, and not being strong enough to keep his balance, fell over, streaming with blood.

The elegant, whiskered manservant, who used to be continually complaining to his acquaintances of the delicacy of his nerves, was so panic-stricken on seeing his master lying on the floor, that he left him losing blood while he ran for assistance. An hour later Varya, his brother's wife, had arrived, and with the assistance of three doctors, whom she had sent for in all directions, and who all appeared at the same moment, she got the wounded man to bed, and remained to nurse him.

CHAPTER XIX

THE mistake made by Alexey Alexandrovitch in that, when
preparing for seeing his wife, he had overlooked the possibility
that her repentance might be sincere, and he might forgive her,
and she might not die—this mistake was two months after his
return from Moscow brought home to him in all its significance.
But the mistake made by him had arisen not simply from his
having overlooked that contingency, but also from the fact that
until that day of his interview with his dying wife, he had not
known his own heart. At his sick wife's bedside he had for the
first time in his life given way to that feeling of sympathetic
suffering always roused in him by the sufferings of others, and
hitherto looked on by him with shame as a harmful weakness.
And pity for her, and remorse for having desired her death, and
most of all, the joy of forgiveness, made him at once conscious,
not simply of the relief of his own sufferings, but of a spiritual
peace he had never experienced before. He suddenly felt that the
very thing that was the source of his sufferings had become the
source of his spiritual joy; that what had seemed insoluble while
he was judging, blaming, and hating, had become clear and
simple when he forgave and loved.

He forgave his wife and pitied her for her sufferings and her
remorse. He forgave Vronsky, and pitied him, especially after
reports reached him of his despairing action. He felt more for his
son than before. And he blamed himself now for having taken
too little interest in him. But for the little new-born baby he felt
a quite peculiar sentiment, not of pity, only, but of tenderness.
At first, from a feeling of compassion alone, he had been interested in the delicate little creature, who was not his child, and
who was cast on one side during his mother's illness, and would
certainly have died if he had not troubled about her, and he did
not himself observe how fond he became of her. He would go into
the nursery several times a day, and sit there for a long while, so
that the nurses, who were at first afraid of him, got quite used to
his presence. Sometimes for half an hour at a stretch he would sit
silently gazing at the saffron-red, downy, wrinkled face of the

501

sleeping baby, watching the movements of the frowning brows, and the fat little hands, with clenched fingers, that rubbed the little eyes and nose. At such moments particularly, Alexey Alexandrovitch had a sense of perfect peace and inward harmony, and saw nothing extraordinary in his position, nothing that ought to be changed.

But as time went on, he saw more and more distinctly that however natural the position now seemed to him, he would not long be allowed to remain in it. He felt that besides the blessed spiritual force controlling his soul, there was another, a brutal force, as powerful, or more powerful, which controlled his life, and that this force would not allow him that humble peace he longed for. He felt that every one was looking at him with inquiring wonder, that he was not understood, and that something was expected of him. Above all, he felt the instability and unnaturalness of his relations with his wife.

When the softening effect of the near approach of death had passed away, Alexey Alexandrovitch began to notice that Anna was afraid of him, ill at ease with him, and could not look him straight in the face. She seemed to be wanting, and not daring, to tell him something; and as though foreseeing their present relations could not continue, she seemed to be expecting something from him.

Towards the end of February it happened that Anna's baby daughter, who had been named Anna too, fell ill. Alexey Alexandrovitch was in the nursery in the morning, and leaving orders for the doctor to be sent for, he went to his office. On finishing his work, he returned home at four. Going into the hall he saw a handsome groom, in a braided livery and a bear fur cape, holding a white fur cloak.

"Who is here?" asked Alexey Alexandrovitch.

"Princess Elizaveta Federovna Tverskaya," the groom answered, and it seemed to Alexey Alexandrovitch that he grinned.

During all this difficult time Alexey Alexandrovitch had noticed that his worldly acquaintances, especially women, took a peculiar interest in him and his wife. All these acquaintances he observed with difficulty concealing their mirth at something; the same mirth that he had perceived in the lawyer's eyes, and just now in the eyes of this groom. Every one seemed, somehow, hugely delighted, as though they had just been at a wedding. When they met him, with ill-disguised enjoyment they inquired after his wife's health. The presence of Princess Tverskaya was unpleasant to Alexey Alexandrovitch from the memories associated with her, and also because he disliked her, and he went straight to the nursery. In the day-nursery Seryozha, leaning on the table with his legs on a chair, was drawing and chatting away merrily. The English governess, who had during Anna's illness replaced the French one, was sitting near the boy knitting a shawl. She hurriedly got up, curtseyed, and pulled Seryozha.

Alexey Alexandrovitch stroked his son's hair, answered the governess's inquiries about his wife, and asked what the doctor had said of the baby.

"The doctor said it was nothing serious, and he ordered a bath, sir."

"But she is still in pain," said Alexey Alexandrovitch, listening to the baby's screaming in the next room.

"I think it's the wet-nurse, sir," the Englishwoman said firmly.

"What makes you think so?" he asked, stopping short.

"It's just as it was at Countess Paul's, sir. They gave the baby medicine, and it turned out that the baby was simply hungry: the nurse had no milk, sir."

Alexey Alexandrovitch pondered, and after standing still a few seconds he went in at the other door. The baby was lying with its head thrown back, stiffening itself in the nurse's arms, and would not take the plump breast offered it; and it never ceased screaming in spite of the double hushing of the wet-nurse and the other nurse, who was bending over her.

"Still no better?" said Alexey Alexandrovitch.

"She's very restless," answered the nurse in a whisper.

"Miss Edwarde says that perhaps the wet-nurse has no milk," he said.

"I think so too, Alexey Alexandrovitch."

"Then why didn't you say so?"

"Who's one to say it to? Anna Arkadyevna still ill . . ." said the nurse discontentedly.

The nurse was an old servant of the family. And in her simple words there seemed to Alexey Alexandrovitch an allusion to his position.

The baby screamed louder than ever, struggling and sobbing. The nurse, with a gesture of despair, went to it, took it from the wet-nurse's arms, and began walking up and down, rocking it.

"You must ask the doctor to examine the wet-nurse," said Alexey Alexandrovitch. The smartly dressed and healthy-looking nurse, frightened at the idea of losing her place, muttered something to herself, and covering her bosom, smiled contemptuously at the idea of doubts being cast on her abundance of milk. In that smile, too, Alexey Alexandrovitch saw a sneer at his position.

"Luckless child!" said the nurse, hushing the baby, and still walking up and down with it.

Alexey Alexandrovitch sat down, and with a despondent and suffering face watched the nurse walking to and fro.

When the child at last was still, and had been put in a deep bed, and the nurse, after smoothing the little pillow, had left her, Alexey Alexandrovitch got up, and walking awkwardly on tiptoe, approached the baby. For a minute he was still, and with the same despondent face gazed at the baby; but all at once a smile, that moved his hair and the skin of his forehead, came out on his face, and he went as softly out of the room.

In the dining-room he rang the bell, and told the servant who came in to send again for the doctor. He felt vexed with his wife for not being anxious about this exquisite baby, and in this vexed humor he had no wish to go to her; he had no wish, either, to see Princess Betsy. But his wife might wonder why he did not go to her as usual; and so, overcoming his disinclination, he went towards the bedroom. As he walked over the soft rug towards the door, he could not help overhearing a conversation he did not want to hear.

"If he hadn't been going away, I could have understood your answer and his too. But your husband ought to be above that," Betsy was saying.

"It's not for my husband; for myself I don't wish it. Don't say that!" answered Anna's excited voice.

"Yes, but you must care to say good-bye to a man who has shot himself on your account. . . ."

"That's just why I don't want to."

With a dismayed and guilty expression, Alexey Alexandrovitch stopped and would have gone back unobserved. But reflecting that this would be undignified, he turned back again, and clearing his throat, he went up to the bedroom. The voices were silent, and he went in.

Anna, in a gray dressing-gown, with a crop of short clustering black curls on her round head, was sitting on a settee. The eagerness died out of her face, as it always did, at the sight of her husband; she dropped her head and looked round uneasily at Betsy. Betsy, dressed in the height of the latest fashion, in a hat that towered somewhere over her head like a shade on a lamp, in a blue dress with violet crossway stripes slanting one way on the bodice and the other way on the skirt, was sitting beside Anna, her tall flat figure held erect. Bowing her head, she greeted Alexey Alexandrovitch with an ironical smile.

"Ah!" she said, as though surprised. "I'm very glad you're at home. You never put in an appearance anywhere, and I haven't seen you ever since Anna has been ill. I have heard all about it— your anxiety. Yes, you're a wonderful husband!" she said, with a meaning and affable air, as though she were bestowing an order of magnanimity on him for his conduct to his wife.

Alexey Alexandrovitch bowed frigidly, and kissing his wife's hand, asked how she was.

"Better, I think," she said, avoiding his eyes.

"But you've rather a feverish-looking color," he said, laying stress on the word "feverish."

"We've been talking too much," said Betsy. "I feel it's selfishness on my part, and I am going away."

She got up, but Anna, suddenly flushing, quickly caught at her hand.

"No, wait a minute, please. I must tell you . . . no, you." She turned to Alexey Alexandrovitch, and her neck and brow were suffused with crimson. "I won't and can't keep anything secret from you," she said.

Alexey Alexandrovitch cracked his fingers and bowed his head.

"Betsy's been telling me that Count Vronsky wants to come here to say good-bye before his departure for Tashkend." She did not look at her husband, and was evidently in haste to have everything out, however hard it might be for her. "I told her I could not receive him."

"You said, my dear, that it would depend on Alexey Alexandrovitch," Betsy corrected her.

"Oh, no, I can't receive him; and what object would there . . ." She stopped suddenly, and glanced inquiringly at her husband (he did not look at her). "In short, I don't wish it. . . ."

Alexey Alexandrovitch advanced and would have taken her hand.

Her first impulse was to jerk back her hand from the damp hand with big swollen veins that sought hers, but with an obvious effort to control herself she pressed his hand.

"I am very grateful to you for your confidence, but . . ." he said, feeling with confusion and annoyance that what he could decide easily and clearly by himself, he could not discuss before Princess Tverskaya, who to him stood for the incarnation of that brute force which would inevitably control him in the life he led in the eyes of the world, and hinder him from giving way to his feeling of love and forgiveness. He stopped short, looking at Princess Tverskaya.

"Well, good-bye, my darling," said Betsy, getting up. She kissed Anna, and went out. Alexey Alexandrovitch escorted her out.

"Alexey Alexandrovitch! I know you are a truly magnanimous man," said Betsy, stopping in the little drawing-room, and with special warmth shaking hands with him once more. "I am an outsider, but I so love her and respect you that I venture to advise. Receive him. Alexey Vronsky is the soul of honor, and he is going away to Tashkend."

"Thank you, princess, for your sympathy and advice. But the question of whether my wife can or cannot see any one she must decide herself."

He said this from habit, lifting his brows with dignity, and reflected immediately that whatever his words might be, there could be no dignity in his position. And he saw this by the suppressed, malicious, and ironical smile with which Betsy glanced at him after this phrase.

CHAPTER XX

ALEXEY ALEXANDROVITCH took leave of Betsy in the drawing-room, and went to his wife. She was lying down, but hearing his steps she sat up hastily in her former attitude, and looked in a scared way at him. He saw she had been crying.

"I am very grateful for your confidence in me." He repeated gently in Russian the phrase he had said in Betsy's presence in French, and sat down beside her. When he spoke to her in Russian, using the Russian "thou" of intimacy and affection, it was insufferably irritating to Anna. "And I am very grateful for your decision. I, too, imagine that since he is going away, there is no sort of necessity for Count Vronsky to come here. However, if . . ."

"But I've said so already, so why repeat it?" Anna suddenly interrupted him with an irritation she could not succeed in repressing. "No sort of necessity," she thought, "for a man to come and say good-bye to the woman he loves, for whom he was ready to ruin himself, and has ruined himself, and who cannot live without him. No sort of necessity!" She compressed her lips, and dropped her burning eyes to his hands with their swollen veins. They were rubbing each other.

"Let us never speak of it," she added more calmly.

"I have left this question to you to decide, and I am very glad to see . . ." Alexey Alexandrovitch was beginning.

"That my wish coincides with your own," she finished quickly, exasperated at his talking so slowly while she knew beforehand all he would say.

"Yes," he assented; "and Princess Tverskaya's interference in the most difficult private affairs is utterly uncalled for. She especially . . ."

"I don't believe a word of what's said about her," said Anna quickly. "I know she really cares for me."

Alexey Alexandrovitch sighed and said nothing. She played nervously with the tassel of her dressing-gown, glancing at him with that torturing sensation of physical repulsion for which she blamed herself, though she could not control it. Her only desire now was to be rid of his oppressive presence.

"I have just sent for the doctor," said Alexey Alexandrovitch.

"I am very well; what do I want the doctor for?"

"No, the little one cries, and they say the nurse hasn't enough milk."

"Why didn't you let me nurse her, when I begged to? Anyway" (Alexey Alexandrovitch knew what was meant by that "anyway"), "she's a baby, and they're killing her." She rang the bell and ordered the baby to be brought her. "I begged to nurse her, I wasn't allowed to, and now I'm blamed for it."

"I don't blame . . ."

"Yes, you do blame me! My God! why didn't I die!" And she broke into sobs. "Forgive me, I'm nervous, I'm unjust," she said, controlling herself, "but do go away . . ."

"No, it can't go on like this," Alexey Alexandrovitch said to himself decidedly as he left his wife's room.

Never had the impossibility of his position in the world's eyes, and his wife's hatred of him, and altogether the might of that mysterious brutal force that guided his life against his spiritual inclinations, and exacted conformity with its decrees and change in his attitude to his wife, been presented to him with such distinctness as that day. He saw clearly that all the world and his wife expected of him something, but what exactly, he could not make out. He felt that this was rousing in his soul a feeling of anger destructive of his peace of mind and of all the good of his achievement. He believed that for Anna herself it would be better to break off all relations with Vronsky; but if they all thought this out of the question, he was even ready to allow these relations to be renewed, so long as the children were not disgraced, and he was not deprived of them nor forced to change his position. Bad as this might be, it was anyway better than a rupture, which would put her in a hopeless and shameful position, and deprive him of everything he cared for. But he felt helpless; he knew beforehand that every one was against him, and that he would not be allowed to do what seemed to him now so natural and right, but would be forced to do what was wrong, though it seemed the proper thing to them.

CHAPTER XXI

BEFORE Betsy had time to walk out of the drawing-room, she was met in the doorway by Stepan Arkadyevitch, who had just come from Yeliseev's, where a consignment of fresh oysters had been received.

"Ah! princess! what a delightful meeting!" he began. "I've been to see you."

"A meeting for one minute, for I'm going," said Betsy, smiling and putting on her glove.

"Don't put on your glove yet, princess; let me kiss your hand. There's nothing I'm so thankful to the revival of the old fashions for as the kissing the hand." He kissed Betsy's hand. "When shall we see each other?"

"You don't deserve it," answered Betsy, smiling.

"Oh, yes, I deserve a great deal, for I've become a most serious person. I don't only manage my own affairs, but other people's too," he said with a significant expression.

"Oh, I'm so glad!" answered Betsy, at once understanding that he was speaking of Anna. And going back into the drawing-room, they stood in a corner. "He's killing her," said Betsy in a whisper full of meaning. "It's impossible, impossible . . ."

"I'm so glad you think so," said Stepan Arkadyevitch, shaking his head with a serious and sympathetically distressed expression, "that's what I've come to Petersburg for."

"The whole town's talking of it," she said. "It's an impossible position. She pines and pines away. He doesn't understand that she's one of those women who can't trifle with their feelings. One of two things: either let him take her away, act with energy, or give her a divorce. This is stifling her."

"Yes, yes . . . just so . . ." Oblonsky said, sighing. "That's what I've come for. At least not solely for that . . . I've been made a *Kammerherr;* of course, one has to say thank you. But the chief thing was having to settle this."

"Well, God help you!" said Betsy.

After accompanying Betsy to the outside hall, once more kissing her hand above the glove, at the point where the pulse beats, and murmuring to her such unseemly nonsense that she did not know whether to laugh or be angry, Stepan Arkadyevitch went to his sister. He found her in tears.

Although he happened to be bubbling over with good spirits, Stepan Arkadyevitch immediately and quite naturally fell into the sympathetic, poetically emotional tone which harmonized with her mood. He asked her how she was, and how she had spent the morning.

"Very, very miserably. To-day and this morning and all past days and days to come," she said.

"I think you're giving way to pessimism. You must rouse yourself, you must look life in the face. I know it's hard, but . . ."

"I have heard it said that women love men even for their vices," Anna began suddenly, "but I hate him for his virtues. I can't live with him. Do you understand? the sight of him has a physical effect on me, it makes me beside myself. I can't, I can't live with him. What am I to do? I have been unhappy, and used to think one couldn't be more unhappy, but the awful state of things I am going through now, I could never have conceived. Would you believe it, that knowing he's a good man, a splendid man, that I'm not worth his little finger, still I hate him. I hate him for his generosity. And there's nothing left for me but . . ."

She would have said death, but Stepan Arkadyevitch would not let her finish.

"You are ill and overwrought," he said; "believe me, you're exaggerating dreadfully. There's nothing so terrible in it."

And Stepan Arkadyevitch smiled. No one else in Stepan Arkadyevitch's place, having to do with such despair, would have ventured to smile (the smile would have seemed brutal); but in his smile there was so much of sweetness and almost feminine tenderness that his smile did not wound, but softened and soothed. His gentle, soothing words and smiles were as soothing and softening as almond oil. And Anna soon felt this.

"No, Stiva," she said, "I'm lost, lost! worse than lost! I can't say yet that all is over; on the contrary, I feel that it's not over. I'm an overstrained string that must snap. But it's not ended yet . . . and it will have a fearful end."

"No matter, we must let the string be loosened, little by little. There's no position from which there is no way of escape."

"I have thought, and thought. Only one . . ."

Again he knew from her terrified eyes that this one way of escape in her thought was death, and he would not let her say it.

"Not at all," he said. "Listen to me. You can't see your own position as I can. Let me tell you candidly my opinion." Again he smiled discreetly his almond-oil smile. "I'll begin from the beginning. You married a man twenty years older than yourself. You married him without love and not knowing what love was. It was a mistake, let's admit."

"A fearful mistake!" said Anna.

"But I repeat, it's an accomplished fact. Then you had, let us say, the misfortune to love a man not your husband. That was a misfortune; but that, too, is an accomplished fact. And your husband knew it and forgave it." He stopped at each sentence, waiting for her to object, but she made no answer. "That's so. Now the question is: can you go on living with your husband? Do you wish it? Does he wish it?"

"I know nothing, nothing."

"But you said yourself that you can't endure him."

"No, I didn't say so. I deny it. I can't tell, I don't know anything about it."

"Yes, but let . . ."

"You can't understand. I feel I'm lying head downwards in a sort of pit, but I ought not to save myself. And I can't . . ."

"Never mind, we'll slip something under and pull you out. I understand you: I understand that you can't take it on yourself to express your wishes, your feelings."

"There's nothing, nothing I wish . . . except for it to be all over."

"But he sees this and knows it. And do you suppose it weighs on him any less than on you? You're wretched, he's wretched, and what good can come of it? while divorce would solve the difficulty completely." With some effort Stepan Arkadyevitch brought out his central idea, and looked significantly at her.

She said nothing, and shook her cropped head in dissent. But from the look in her face, that suddenly brightened into its old beauty, he saw that if she did not desire this, it was simply because it seemed to her unattainable happiness.

"I'm awfully sorry for you! And how happy I should be if I could arrange things!" said Stepan Arkadyevitch, smiling more boldly. "Don't speak, don't say a word! God grant only that I may speak as I feel. I'm going to him."

Anna looked at him with dreamy, shining eyes, and said nothing.

C H A P T E R   X X I I

STEPAN ARKADYEVITCH, with the same somewhat solemn expression with which he used to take his presidential chair at his board, walked into Alexey Alexandrovitch's room. Alexey Alexandrovitch was walking about his room with his hands behind his back, thinking of just what Stepan Arkadyevitch had been discussing with his wife.

"I'm not interrupting you?" said Stepan Arkadyevitch, on the sight of his brother-in-law becoming suddenly aware of a sense of embarrassment unusual with him. To conceal this embarrassment he took out a cigarette-case he had just bought that opened in a new way, and sniffing the leather, took a cigarette out of it.

"No. Do you want anything?" Alexey Alexandrovitch asked without eagerness.

"Yes, I wished . . . I wanted . . . yes, I wanted to talk to you," said Stepan Arkadyevitch, with surprise aware of an unaccustomed timidity.

This feeling was so unexpected and so strange that he did not believe it was the voice of conscience telling him that what he was meaning to do was wrong.

Stepan Arkadyevitch made an effort and struggled with the timidity that had come over him.

"I hope you believe in my love for my sister and my sincere affection and respect for you," he said, reddening.

Alexey Alexandrovitch stood still and said nothing, but his face struck Stepan Arkadyevitch by its expression of an unresisting sacrifice.

"I intended . . . I wanted to have a little talk with you about my sister and your mutual position," he said, still struggling with an unaccustomed constraint.

Alexey Alexandrovitch smiled mournfully, looked at his brother-in-law, and without answering went up to the table, took from it an unfinished letter, and handed it to his brother-in-law.

"I think unceasingly of the same thing. And here is what I had begun writing, thinking I could say it better by letter, and that my presence irritates her," he said, as he gave him the letter.

Stepan Arkadyevitch took the letter, looked with incredulous surprise at the lusterless eyes fixed so immovably on him, and began to read.

"I see that my presence is irksome to you. Painful as it is to me to believe it, I see that it is so, and cannot be otherwise. I don't blame you, and God is my witness that on seeing you at the time of your illness I resolved with my whole heart to forget all that had passed between us and to begin a new life. I do not regret, and shall never regret, what I have done; but I have desired one thing—your good, the good of your soul—and now I see I have not attained that. Tell me yourself what will give you true happiness and peace to your soul. I put myself entirely in your hands, and trust to your feeling of what's right."

Stepan Arkadyevitch handed back the letter, and with the same surprise continued looking at his brother-in-law, not knowing what to say. This silence was so awkward for both of them that Stepan Arkadyevitch's lips began twitching nervously, while he still gazed without speaking at Karenin's face.

"That's what I wanted to say to her," said Alexey Alexandrovitch, turning away.

"Yes, yes . . ." said Stepan Arkadyevitch, not able to answer for the tears that were choking him.

"Yes, yes, I understand you," he brought out at last.

"I want to know what she would like," said Alexey Alexandrovitch.

"I am afraid she does not understand her own position. She is not a judge," said Stepan Arkadyevitch, recovering himself. "She is crushed, simply crushed by your generosity. If she were to read this letter, she would be incapable of saying anything, she would only hang her head lower than ever."

"Yes, but what's to be done in that case? how explain, how find out her wishes?"

"If you will allow me to give my opinion, I think that it lies with you to point out directly the steps you consider necessary to end the position."

"So you consider it must be ended?" Alexey Alexandrovitch interrupted him. "But how?" he added, with a gesture of his hands before his eyes not usual with him. "I see no possible way out of it."

"There is some way of getting out of every position," said Stepan Arkadyevitch, standing up and becoming more cheerful. "There was a time when you thought of breaking off. . . . If you are convinced now that you cannot make each other happy . . ."

"Happiness may be variously understood. But suppose that I agree to everything, that I want nothing: what way is there of getting out of our position?"

"If you care to know my opinion," said Stepan Arkadyevitch with the same smile of softening, almond-oil tenderness with which he had been talking to Anna. His kindly smile was so winning that Alexey Alexandrovitch, feeling his own weakness and unconsciously swayed by it, was ready to believe what Stepan Arkadyevitch was saying.

"She will never speak out about it. But one thing is possible, one thing she might desire," he went on: "that is the cessation of your relations and all memories associated with them. To my thinking, in your position what's essential is the formation of a new attitude to one another. And that can only rest on a basis of freedom on both sides."

"Divorce," Alexey Alexandrovitch interrupted, in a tone of aversion.

"Yes, I imagine that divorce—yes, divorce," Stepan Arkadyevitch repeated, reddening. "That is from every point of view the most rational course for married people who find themselves in the position you are in. What can be done if married people find that life is impossible for them together? That may always happen."

Alexey Alexandrovitch sighed heavily and closed his eyes.

"There's only one point to be considered: is either of the

parties desirous of forming new ties? If not, it is very simple," said Stepan Arkadyevitch, feeling more and more free from constraint.

Alexey Alexandrovitch, scowling with emotion, muttered something to himself, and made no answer. All that seemed so simple to Stepan Arkadyevitch, Alexey Alexandrovitch had thought over thousands of times. And, so far from being simple, it all seemed to him utterly impossible. Divorce, the details of which he knew by this time, seemed to him now out of the question, because the sense of his own dignity and respect for religion forbade his taking upon himself a fictitious charge of adultery, and still more suffering his wife, pardoned and beloved by him, to be caught in the fact and put to public shame. Divorce appeared to him impossible also on other still more weighty grounds.

What would become of his son in case of a divorce? To leave him with his mother was out of the question. The divorced mother would have her own illegitimate family, in which his position as a stepson and his education would not be good. Keep him with him? He knew that would be an act of vengeance on his part, and that he did not want. But apart from this, what more than all made divorce seem impossible to Alexey Alexandrovitch was, that by consenting to a divorce he would be completely ruining Anna. The saying of Darya Alexandrovna at Moscow, that in deciding on a divorce he was thinking of himself, and not considering that by this he would be ruining her irrevocably, had sunk into his heart. And connecting this saying with his forgiveness of her, with his devotion to the children, he understood it now in his own way. To consent to a divorce, to give her her freedom, meant in his thoughts to take from himself the last tie that bound him to life—the children whom he loved; and to take from her the last prop that stayed her on the path of right, to thrust her down to her ruin. If she were divorced, he knew she would join her life to Vronsky's, and their tie would be an illegitimate and criminal one, since a wife, by the interpretation of the ecclesiastical law, could not marry while her husband was living. "She will join him, and in a year or two he will throw her over, or she will form a new tie," thought Alexey Alexandrovitch. "And I, by agreeing to an unlawful divorce, shall be to blame for her ruin." He had thought it all over hundreds of times, and was convinced that a divorce was not at all simple, as Stepan Arkadyevitch had said, but was utterly impossible. He did not believe a single word Stepan Arkadyevitch said to him; to every word he had a thousand objections to make, but he listened to him, feeling that his words were the expression of that mighty brutal force which controlled his life and to which he would have to submit.

"The only question is on what terms you agree to give her a divorce. She does not want anything, does not dare ask you for anything, she leaves it all to your generosity."

"My God, my God! what for?" thought Alexey Alexandrovitch, remembering the details of divorce proceedings in which the husband took the blame on himself, and with just the same gesture with which Vronsky had done the same, he hid his face for shame in his hands.

"You are distressed, I understand that. But if you think it over . . ."

"Whosoever shall smite thee on thy right cheek, turn to him the other also; and if any man take away thy coat, let him have thy cloak also," thought Alexey Alexandrovitch.

"Yes, yes!" he cried in a shrill voice. "I will take the disgrace on myself, I will give up even my son, but . . . but wouldn't it be better to let it alone? Still you may do as you like . . ."

And turning away so that his brother-in-law could not see him, he sat down on a chair at the window. There was bitterness, there was shame in his heart, but with bitterness and shame he felt joy and emotion at the height of his own meekness.

Stepan Arkadyevitch was touched. He was silent for a space.

"Alexey Alexandrovitch, believe me, she appreciates your generosity," he said. "But it seems it was the will of God," he added, and as he said it felt how foolish a remark it was, and with difficulty repressed a smile at his own foolishness.

Alexey Alexandrovitch would have made some reply, but tears stopped him.

"This is an unhappy fatality, and one must accept it as such. I accept the calamity as an accomplished fact, and am doing my best to help both her and you," said Stepan Arkadyevitch.

When he went out of his brother-in-law's room he was touched,

but that did not prevent him from being glad he had successfully brought the matter to a conclusion, for he felt certain
Alexey Alexandrovitch would not go back on his words. To this
satisfaction was added the fact that an idea had just struck him
for a riddle turning on his successful achievement, that when
the affair was over he would ask his wife and most intimate
friends. He put this riddle into two or three different ways. "But
I'll work it out better than that," he said to himself with a smile.

CHAPTER XXIII

VRONSKY's wound had been a dangerous one, though it did
not touch the heart, and for several days he had lain between
life and death. The first time he was able to speak, Varya, his
brother's wife, was alone in the room.

"Varya," he said, looking sternly at her, "I shot myself by accident. And please never speak of it, and tell every one so. Or
else it's too ridiculous."

Without answering his words, Varya bent over him, and with
a delighted smile gazed into his face. His eyes were clear, not
feverish; but their expression was stern.

"Thank God!" she said. "You're not in pain?"

"A little here." He pointed to his breast.

"Then let me change your bandages."

In silence, stiffening his broad jaws, he looked at her while she
bandaged him up. When she had finished he said:

"I'm not delirious. Please manage that there may be no talk
of my having shot myself on purpose."

"No one does say so. Only I hope you won't shoot yourself by
accident any more," she said, with a questioning smile.

"Of course I won't, but it would have been better . . ."

And he smiled gloomily.

In spite of these words and this smile, which so frightened
Varya, when the inflammation was over and he began to recover,
he felt that he was completely free from one part of his misery.
By his action he had, as it were, washed away the shame and
humiliation he had felt before. He could now think calmly of

Alexey Alexandrovitch. He recognized all his magnanimity, but he did not now feel himself humiliated by it. Besides, he got back again into the beaten track of his life. He saw the possibility of looking men in the face again without shame, and he could live in accordance with his own habits. One thing he could not pluck out of his heart, though he never ceased struggling with it, was the regret, amounting to despair, that he had lost her forever. That now, having expiated his sin against the husband, he was bound to renounce her, and never in future to stand between her with her repentance and her husband, he had firmly decided in his heart; but he could not tear out of his heart his regret at the loss of her love, he could not erase from his memory those moments of happiness that he had so little prized at the time, and that haunted him in all their charm.

Serpuhovskoy had planned his appointment at Tashkend, and Vronsky agreed to the proposition without the slightest hesitation. But the nearer the time of departure came, the bitterer was the sacrifice he was making to what he thought his duty.

His wound had healed, and he was driving about making preparations for his departure for Tashkend.

"To see her once and then to bury myself, to die," he thought, and as he was paying farewell visits, he uttered this thought to Betsy. Charged with this commission, Betsy had gone to Anna, and brought him back a negative reply.

"So much the better," thought Vronsky, when he received the news. "It was a weakness, which would have shattered what strength I have left."

Next day Betsy herself came to him in the morning, and announced that she had heard through Oblonsky as a positive fact that Alexey Alexandrovitch had agreed to a divorce, and that therefore Vronsky could see Anna.

Without even troubling himself to see Betsy out of his flat, forgetting all his resolutions, without asking when he could see her, where her husband was, Vronsky drove straight to the Karenins'. He ran up the stairs seeing no one and nothing, and with a rapid step, almost breaking into a run, he went into her room. And without considering, without noticing whether there was any one in the room or not, he flung his arms round her, and began to cover her face, her hands, her neck with kisses.

Anna had been preparing herself for this meeting, had thought what she would say to him, but she did not succeed in saying anything of it; his passion mastered her. She tried to calm him, to calm herself, but it was too late. His feeling infected her. Her lips trembled so that for a long while she could say nothing.

"Yes, you have conquered me, and I am yours," she said at last, pressing his hands to her bosom.

"So it had to be," he said. "So long as we live, it must be so. I know it now."

"That's true," she said, getting whiter and whiter, and embracing his head. "Still there is something terrible in it after all that has happened."

"It will all pass, it will all pass; we shall be so happy. Our love, if it could be stronger, will be strengthened by there being something terrible in it," he said, lifting his head and parting his strong teeth in a smile.

And she could not but respond with a smile—not to his words, but to the love in his eyes. She took his hand and stroked her chilled cheeks and cropped head with it.

"I don't know you with this short hair. You've grown so pretty. A boy. But how pale you are!"

"Yes, I'm very weak," she said, smiling. And her lips began trembling again.

"We'll go to Italy; you will get strong," he said.

"Can it be possible we could be like husband and wife, alone, your family with you?" she said, looking close into his eyes.

"It only seems strange to me that it can ever have been otherwise."

"Stiva says that *he* has agreed to everything, but I can't accept *his* generosity," she said, looking dreamily past Vronsky's face. "I don't want a divorce; it's all the same to me now. Only I don't know what he will decide about Seryozha."

He could not conceive how at this moment of their meeting she could remember

and think of her son, of divorce. What did it all matter?

"Don't speak of that, don't think of it," he said, turning her hand in his, and trying to draw her attention to him; but still she did not look at him.

"Oh, why didn't I die! it would have been better," she said, and silent tears flowed down both her cheeks; but she tried to smile, so as not to wound him.

To decline the flattering and dangerous appointment at Tashkend would have been, Vronsky had till then considered, disgraceful and impossible. But now, without an instant's consideration, he declined it, and observing dissatisfaction in the most exalted quarters at this step, he immediately retired from the army.

A month later Alexey Alexandrovitch was left alone with his son in his house at Petersburg, while Anna and Vronsky had gone abroad, not having obtained a divorce, but having absolutely declined all idea of one.